William Winwood Reade

Savage Africa

Being the Narrative of a Tour in Equatorial, Southwestern and Northwestern Africa

William Winwood Reade

Savage Africa
Being the Narrative of a Tour in Equatorial, Southwestern and Northwestern Africa

ISBN/EAN: 9783337123468

Printed in Europe, USA, Canada, Australia, Japan

Cover: Foto ©Andreas Hilbeck / pixelio.de

More available books at **www.hansebooks.com**

SAVAGE AFRICA:

BEING

THE NARRATIVE OF A TOUR

IN

EQUATORIAL, SOUTHWESTERN, AND NORTHWESTERN AFRICA;

WITH NOTES ON

THE HABITS OF THE GORILLA;

ON THE EXISTENCE OF UNICORNS AND TAILED MEN;

ON THE SLAVE-TRADE;

ON THE ORIGIN, CHARACTER, AND CAPABILITIES OF THE NEGRO,

AND

ON THE FUTURE CIVILIZATION OF WESTERN AFRICA.

BY

W. WINWOOD READE,

FELLOW OF THE GEOGRAPHICAL AND ANTHROPOLOGICAL SOCIETIES OF LONDON, AND CORRESPONDING
MEMBER OF THE GEOGRAPHICAL SOCIETY OF PARIS.

With Illustrations and a Map.

"Travel, in the younger sort, is a part of education."—*Bacon.*

NEW YORK:

HARPER & BROTHERS, PUBLISHERS,

FRANKLIN SQUARE.

1864.

DEDICATION.

PREFACE.

THE narrative portions of this work have been compiled from letters written home to a friend at monthly intervals. This will account for the familiar and sometimes egotistical tone which I fear that I have not entirely subdued.

Certain grave facts which I plucked in Africa I allowed to ripen in my brain, like fruit laid out in the sun. After mature study and reflection, I have ventured to prepare them into theories, and to offer them to the scientific reader.

I make, of course, no pretensions to the title of Explorer. If I have any merit, it is that of having been the first young man about town to make a *bonâ fide* tour in Western Africa; to travel in that agreeable and salubrious country with no special object, and at his own expense; to *flaner* in the virgin forest; to flirt with pretty savages, and to smoke his cigar among cannibals.

Conservative Club, November, 1863.

CONTENTS.

CHAPTER I.
A LOVELY CHARNEL-HOUSE.

Discovery of Madeira and Legend of Machim.—The Duties of a Tourist.—Madeira.
—Portuguese.—The Convicts of Disease..................................Page 13

CHAPTER II.
A PERISHED PEOPLE.

Peak of Teneriffe.—On Horseback to Laguna.—The Silent City.—Cigars and Brunettes.—Expired Aborigines.. 18

CHAPTER III.
A LANDMARK OF HISTORY.

Sea-torpor.—First Sight of Africa.—The Infanta Henry.—Cape Boiador.—The
Rabbits of Porto Santo.—Portuguese Monopoly and English Smuggling 21

CHAPTER IV.
THE PARADISE OF THE BLACKS.

Sierra Leone: its Description; its Douaniers.—Black Christianity.—Origin of the
White Man.—Nigger Juries.—Ethiopic Character.................................. 25

CHAPTER V.
THE REPUBLIC OF COLORED GENTLEMEN.

Liberia: its Description; its Future and its Resources................................. 34

CHAPTER VI.
THE TITANS OF THE COAST.

Cape Palmas.—The Kru-man.—Engage a Crew.—Book.—Kru Character....... 37

CHAPTER VII.
THE CITY OF GOLD.

The Grave of L. E. L.—Her Death.—Her Husband.—Popular Scandal.—Route to
Coomassi.—Court Reception.—Ashantee Empire: its Constitution.—Decoy Wives.
—Savage Nuptials.. 42

CHAPTER VIII.
LAND OF THE AMAZONS.

Dahomey: its Revenues and Laws.—The Amazons.—Human Sacrifices......... 50

CHAPTER IX.
THE KING OF OILS.

The Mouths of the Niger.—Discovered in the fifteenth Century.—Bonny River.
—Interview with Peppel.—Fernando Po: its Inhabitants.—A Gaboon Legend ....Page 55

CHAPTER X.
COAST SOCIETY.

Unanimous Inebriety.—The Cognac Disease.—Sierra Leone Scandal 63

CHAPTER XI.
THE TRIBE OF COMMERCIAL TRAVELERS.

I enter the Gaboon.—Take a House.—Tornado v. Fever.—Baraka Mission.—My
Steward Mongilomba. — Gaboon Commerce. —The Gorilla Palaver. —Tropical
Rain 66

CHAPTER XII.
THE LAND OF HUNGER.

Coriseo.—The Bapuku Bush.—River Life.—Net-hunting.—Captain taken Prisoner.
—The Muni Country.—Starvation Body and Mind.—Episode of Civilization.—
Turtle-spearing by Moonlight 80

CHAPTER XIII.
THE FALLS OF THE NCOMO.

My Steward Oshupu. — Nengĕ-Nengĕ. — Negro Hospitality. — Description of the
Fans.—Discover the Falls of the Neomo 114

CHAPTER XIV.
THE PHILOSOPHY OF CANNIBALISM.

Cannibalism.—Its Antiquity.—Its Nature in Africa.—Evidence of a Fan.—A Ghoul
Story 135

CHAPTER XV.
DRUGGED ELEPHANTS.

Visit an Elephant Nghâl.—Menagerie in the Forest.—Explanation of the Mystery 140

CHAPTER XVI.
THE CAMMA COUNTRY.

By Sea and Creek.—The Fernand Vaz.—The King of the Rembo. — Arrival at
Ngumbi.—The Princess Ananga.—The Tobacco Question.—Relative Happiness.
—The Cannibal Salute 145

CHAPTER XVII.
THE GORILLA DANCE.

The Gorilla Dance.—On the Track.—Disappointment................................ 164

CHAPTER XVIII.

THE GREAT APE OF EQUATORIAL AFRICA.

Battel, Monboddo, Bowdich, Savage, Wilson, and Du Chaillu.—Examination of their Testimony.—Description of the Ape's Habits.....................................Page 169

CHAPTER XIX.'

DETAINED.

Leave Ngumbi.—Am brought back.—Imprisonment.—The false Ananga.—Great Palaver.—Deputation of Bakĕlĕs.—Set at Liberty.—Dangerous Bar.......... 188

CHAPTER XX.

THE EQUATORIAL SAVAGE.

His Education.—Religion.—Witchcraft.—Government.—Code Moral.......... 204

CHAPTER XXI.

VOLCANIC FLOWER-GARDENS.

Prince's Island.—African Champagne.—Mulatto Politeness.—St. Thomas.—The Dutchman's Church-yard.—Senhor Pereira.—I become a Spy.................. 220

CHAPTER XXII.

AT SEA.

Animal Vegetation.—Short Commons.—Boarded by a Cruiser.................. 230

CHAPTER XXIII.

BLACK IVORY.

The Slave-trade.—Its Results.—Its present State.—Its future Suppression...... 237

CHAPTER XXIV.

THE METROPOLIS OF AFRICA.

San Paolo de Loanda: its Description.—Pecuniary Embarrassment.—Ride in a Palanquin.—Welcomed by Mr. Gabriel.—Portuguese Society.—A Reminiscence... 245

CHAPTER XXV.

BY OX AND HAMMOCK.

Joachim the Swiss.—His best Friend.—En Route for Ambaka.—Bloodthirsty Musquitoes.—The Senhor Mendez.—Routine of Journey.—Mountains à la Suisse.—Arrival at Ambaka.—The War with Cassange.—Governmental Plunder.—The Fashion of secret Poisoning.—The Bœuf-cheval.—The Doorkeeper of Matiamvo.—Joachim is drunk.—Is impertinent.—Loses two front Teeth.—Post-haste.—The Story of Franz.. 252

CHAPTER XXVI.

FEVER AND FLIGHT.

Three Dreams.—Fever.—Mr. Gabriel's Sickness.—His Death.—S. S. Don Pedro.—The White Lady.—The Language of Cigars.................................. 278

CHAPTER XXVII.

THE CONGO EMPIRE.

African Revolutions.—King of Congo.—Benediction of the People.—The Bed-tax. —The royal Harem.—The Pontiff and Priests of Congo.—Religious and Civil Institutions.—An African Napoleon.—The Queen of the Jagas.—Her Valor and Cruelty.—Her bloodthirsty Laws.—Her cannibal Amours.—Her violent Death ....Page 285

CHAPTER XXVIII.

THE ISLANDS OF THE GREEN CAPE.

Santiago.—Trip into the Interior.—A rough Lodging.—Negro Modesty.—San Vincenti.—Character of our Consul.—San Nicholão.—The Town of the Wild Stream. —Quail-shooting.—Boã Vista.—Sal.—Salt-pits.—The Charms of Solitude... 296

CHAPTER XXIX.

UP THE CASEMANCHE.

Return to the Continent.—To the Casemanche in a French Schooner.—Fort Caraban.—The Jolas.—Rice and Palm Wine.—A Shift for a Divorce.—A Scene from the Desert.—A Shot at Antelopes.—Sedhu.—The traveling Marabouts.—The tree Self-Fire.—The Djikijunka.—Journey in Search of it.—Senegambia Scenery.—Mandingo Village.—Native Courtesy.—Edible Earth.—The Trumpet-bird. —Missera.—Description of Djikijunka.—The Feast of Lanterns.—A Christmas Breakfast.—An Evening on the Water 307

CHAPTER XXX.

UP THE GAMBIA.

Colonial Life.—On Board the "Dover."—Ground-nut Diplomacy.—Massacre Christianity.—A day's Shooting.—The nondescript Animal.—African Palavers.—Mr. Rooke, the Apostle.—Missionary Labors.—The dog-faced Baboons.—Strange Story of Sergeant Bonvin.—The Falls of Barraconda.—An angry Hippopotamus 323

CHAPTER XXXI.

THE THREE DOCTORS OF MACARTHY'S ISLAND.

Description of the Island.—The Harmattan.—The Rainy Season.—Deaths of Staff Assistant Surgeons Beale and Trestrail.—Appearance of Beale to Campbell.— Death of Campbell.—The Sentry and the Apparition.—The haunted House.— The Sounds in the Piazza and the Centre Room.—The Man in White.—The Footsteps on the Floor.—The Science of the Spirit-world and its Study........ 337

CHAPTER XXXII.

UP THE SENEGAL.

Calomel and Jaundice.—The Senegal.—Cumar the Pilgrim.—The Moors of the Desert.—Up to Podor.—Mohammedan Negro.—Return from the Campaign.— On the Var.—Farewell 342

CHAPTER XXXIII.

MONSTERS AND FABULOUS ANIMALS.

Origin of Fables.—The Sloth in Africa.—The Roc.—The Unicorn.—Described by the Ancients.—Account of Barthema.—Account of Tellez.—Tailed Men of the Eastern Archipelago.—Tailed Men of Africa.—Tailed Men of Kent.......... 369

CHAPTER XXXIV.
FEATURES OF AFRICA.

The Mother and her Children.—Central Plateau after Buffon, Lacépède, and Ritter.
—Description of the Western Wall.—The Lowlands of Western Africa...Page 383

CHAPTER XXXV.
MALARIA.

Rains, Dew, and Winds malarious.—Human Infection.—Nature of Malaria.—Natural History of Fever.—Siestas and Stimulants...................................... 388

CHAPTER XXXVI.
THE NEGRO.

The true Negro.—African Types.—Degeneration of Animals in Africa.—Aborigines of Africa.—African Languages.—Religion, Manners, and Customs.—The Negress.—African Character.. 397

CHAPTER XXXVII.
THE REDEMPTION OF AFRICA.

Exploration.—Commerce.—Military Protection.—Christian Missions.—Mohammedan Civilization.—Future of Africa.. 431

LIST OF ILLUSTRATIONS.

	PAGE
FUNCHAL, FROM THE BAY	13
FREE-TOWN, SIERRA LEONE	26
MONROVIA, THE CAPITAL OF LIBERIA	35
KRU TOWN, NEAR CAPE PALMAS	38
KRU HOUSES	39
CAPE COAST CASTLE	43
STREET IN COOMASSI	45
CLARENCE, FERNANDO PO	60
HOUSE AT GABOON—RESIDENCE OF THE AMERICAN MISSIONARY	67
MPONGWE GIRL	72
YOUNG GORILLA (after Du Chaillu)	76
AN AFRICAN TORNADO	92
RECEPTION BY THE FANS (after Du Chaillu)	123
FAN DRUM AND HANDJA	127
THE RAPIDS (after Du Chaillu)	132
KILLING ELEPHANTS IN A NGHAL	141
RIVER NAVIGATION IN EQUATORIAL AFRICA (after Du Chaillu)	152
CAMMA MAN AND WOMAN (after Du Chaillu)	156
THE GORILLA DANCE	166
KILLING A GORILLA (after Du Chaillu)	178
GORILLA AND NEST	186
DETAINED	192
THE ORDEAL	215
BY OX AND HAMMOCK	270
THE QUEEN OF THE CANNIBALS	293
THE DJIKIJUNKA (OREAS DERBIANUS)	316
CHRISTMAS EVE IN THE CASEMANCHE	319
A FLOOD IN SENEGAMBIA	365

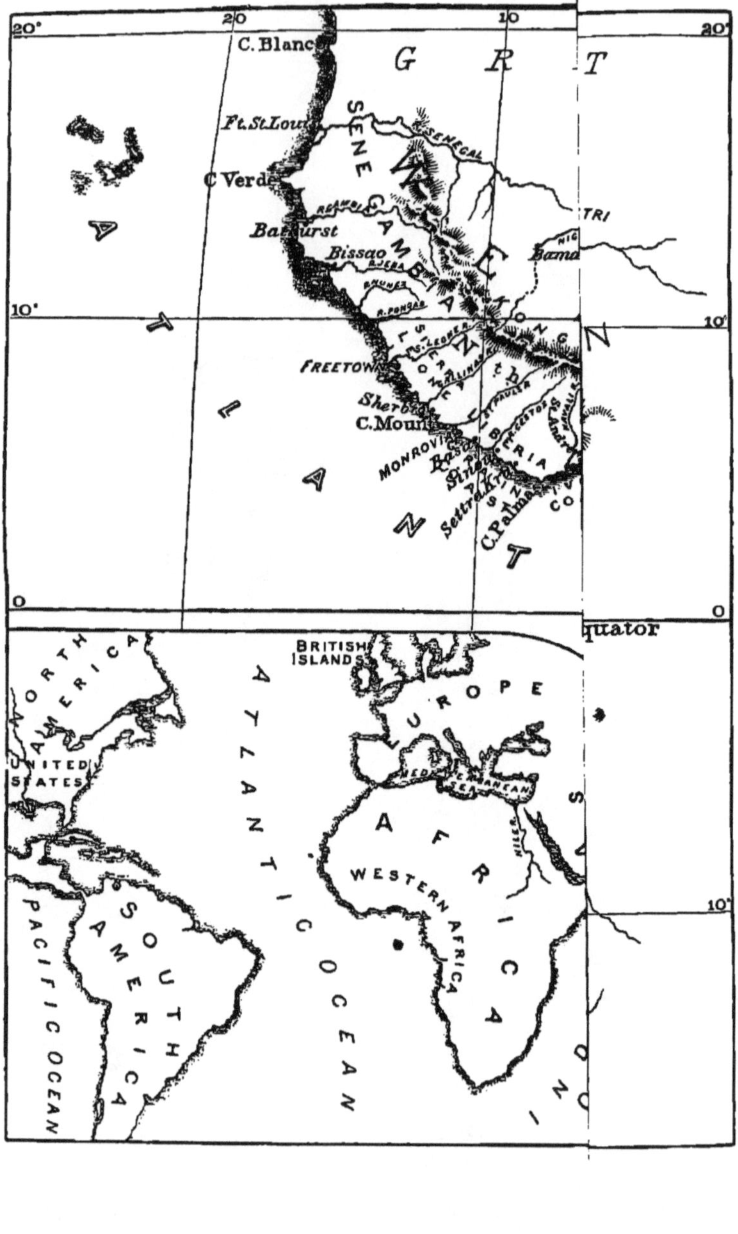
20°
20
10
20°
C. Blanc
G R T
SENE GAMBIA
Ft. St. Lou
SENEGAL
C Verde
Bathurst
Bissao
Bama
10°
10°
FREETOWN
SIERRA LEONE
Sherbro
C. Moun
MONROVIA
LIBERIA
Settra
C. Palma
ATLANT
0
0
quator
BRITISH ISLANDS
EUROPE
NORTH AMERICA
UNITED STATES
ATLANTIC OCEAN
MEDITERRANEAN SEA
AFRICA
WESTERN AFRICA
SOUTH AMERICA
PACIFIC OCEAN
10°

SAVAGE AFRICA.

FUNCHAL, FROM THE BAY.

CHAPTER I.

A LOVELY CHARNEL-HOUSE.

Discovery of Madeira and Legend of Machim.—The Duties of a Tourist.—Madeira.
—Portuguese.—The Convicts of Disease.

Two gentlemen of the court of Lisbon, sailing in the Sea of
Darkness, saw a black cloud. In spite of the prayers and curses
of the common seamen, they resolutely steered toward it. It
was not a demon, as they had supposed, but the loom of an island
completely covered with trees.

When they went ashore they found that they were not its discoverers. They saw a large cedar cross, and near it a grave-stone, on which were engraved the names of Robert and Anna, and the following romantic and highly moral history:

Robert à Machim (this was in the fourteenth century) fell in love with Anna d'Arfet, a young lady of good family. Her father sent him to prison, and married his daughter to a peer. He took her to his castle, near Bristol, which he was suddenly obliged to leave in order to join the king's army. Machim, who had been released, persuaded Anna to elope with him to France. On their voyage a storm drove them out to sea, and finally they found an anchorage off Madeira. Anna, who, like Don Juan, had been torn by the alternate throes of love and sea-sickness, wished to go ashore. The gale returned; the ship broke from her moorings; and, with a few companions, they were left upon the island.

Anna died "of thought," Machim of despair. The sailors prepared the cross, the grave-stone, and the inscription, which Machim had written before his death, and to which he added the request that those who first came to their grave would raise a chapel above their remains.

This was done. The chapel was dedicated to Jesus; its choir paved with the bones of the unfortunate lovers. And to this day they will show you a piece of the original cedar cross in the Chapel of Machico or Machim; to this day in Madeira mothers seat their children on their knees, and tell them of the English lady who came there across the seas.

This story has been told often enough, and, indeed, Madeira has been scribbled threadbare; reams of raptures have been written on its scenery, volumes on its very atmosphere. And yet printed words had not prepared me for the delicious sight which greeted me that morning. Giddy from a week's sickness and confinement in a berth, I almost believed that I was looking at a picture. Madeira has all the appearance of a work of art. It is a landscape which has symmetry, but no grandeur; which is beautiful, but which is not sublime.

As we see it from the harbor, it is a mountain. Its brow is ridged in fantastic forms, and is tinted by the rays of the rising sun. Its green bosom is relieved by white houses, by rosy gardens, and by dark ravines; below lies Funchal, bathing its feet in the waters, and reflecting toward us the first smiles of morning. Yes, it is a pretty picture; and its colors are so fresh and vivid that it seems as if it had just been placed in its dark blue frame of sea and sky.

A boat shot forth from the beach, the Portuguese flag waving in her stern. She came alongside; a bundle of blue papers were handed down and examined; and she left us with her flag still unfurled, a signal that we had obtained our pratique. Some gaudily-painted boats, which had been hovering at a little distance, now swooped down on us like birds of prey; some had cushioned seats for passengers, others were laden with fruit, flowers, and ingenious baskets.

I went ashore, hired a gray nag, and rode up the pebbled mountain road, a ragged guide hanging to my horse's tail with one hand and lashing the flies off him with the other. I stopped at a cabaret half way up, and drank a tumbler of villainous negrinho. Then I visited the Mount Church, the English cemetery, and the nunnery. At the first I bought a picture of the Virgin, at the second an embroidered collar, at the third some artificial flowers made of feathers—an art imported from the New World. Having discharged these solemn duties of the tourist, I played at billiards till the hour of vespers.

The Portuguese gentlemen dress always in black, a fashion which one would think had been invented by the Inquisition. But the ladies wear those handsome black silks which suit all figures and complexions. The peasant women both in costume and appearance resemble our female gipsies, in whom, for my part, I could never see any thing very prepossessing. But the men have one peculiarity in their dress. It is a cloth cap shaped like a small wine-funnel, and is perched on the top of their heads in a most extraordinary manner. As for the men themselves, they lead a life of sloth and starvation: some of them, basking like lizards on the steps of the Mount Church, whine to Mi-lor Inglese for alms, and swear at him roundly when refused. Others prowl about the markets, and pick up a fragmentary existence on fruit and fish.

The inland population must be more industrious, for there is considerable cultivation on this little island. When first discovered it was one dense mass of trees, which the early settlers set on fire so completely that they themselves were nearly sacrificed with the vegetation. The ashes with which the ground was clothed nurtured the sugar-cane which was planted in large quantities, and Madeira became as famous for its sugar as afterward for its wine. But it happened that the sugar-canes were ravaged by a peculiar kind of worm; their culture was abandoned, and John the Second introduced vines from Crete. That these produced one of the finest wines in the world every body knows; but some years ago they were killed by a disease, and, though experiments have been made with every kind of vine, none have flourished since; and the sugar-cane has returned to the soil where once it was grown as a rare and almost unknown plant.

This scourge of the vine resembles the potato disease in its character, giving the leaves a smoke-dried appearance. It seems to have come from the East, and to be conquering turn by turn the vineyards of the West. First it destroyed those of the Cape de Verd Islands, next the Canaries, and afterward Madeira. The orchards of the Azores have suffered from its ravages, and we, a nation of port drinkers, know to our cost that it has touched Oporto. Its sure and gradual progress makes one fear that even port will become a traditionary wine, and, indeed, that some day we shall have no wine at all.

The roads of Funchal and its environs are very neatly pebbled. This admits of the bullock-sledge, a carriage without wheels, in which the native aristocracy travel. This was my first day abroad, and I must give you a foreign scene. I am standing at the porch of an ancient church. The bell is tolling for vespers, and mingles with the song of the fruit-girls in the street. The organ begins to play. I hear a strange rattling on the stones. Two bullocks, models of symmetry, with sleek fawn-colored skins, gallop to my side. A little red curtain is drawn, and a graceful lady descends adjusting her mantilla. She gives me one flash of her black eyes, and a little smile, half meditative, half triumphant, in return to the homage which I am paying her with mine.

I must own to you that it was this little incident alone which assured me that I was really out of England. Like Boulogne, Funchal has an Anglo-stamp upon it: it is ethnologically mongrel—a stepping-stone between home and abroad.

This English aspect is owing to the presence of those poor convicts of disease whom the doctors transport here for death. You may see them there in the garb of health, with roses on their cheeks, and the appetites of healthy men. But those roses are the rouge of disease; that appetite is the gnawing of the canker-worm within.

It is but a lovely charnel-house, this island of Madeira. It is a boudoir and it is a hospital—a paradise and a tomb. Here comes Death, with mock laughter and in tinseled robes. A garland of roses hides the cypress on his brow. He leads his victim to the tomb to the music of the spheres, and then all changes suddenly, like a horrible dream, and some weeping family, whose dear one is gone from them, fly from the scene of a bitter woe. For them Madeira is no longer beautiful; for them the sun is darkness, the flowers are ashes, the warm, soft air is heavy with disease.

B

CHAPTER II.

A PERISHED PEOPLE.

Peak of Teneriffe.—On Horseback to Laguna.—The Silent City.—Cigars and Brunettes.—Expired Aborigines.

THE Peak of Teneriffe! I had expected to see a mountain rising in majestic solitude from the sea. But I saw a high, square-
built mass of hill, which jutted rather than tapered into an apex,
and on which there was sufficient snow to suggest the sublime
idea of a cotton night-cap.

In Santa Cruz I found it more difficult to obtain a horse than
in Funchal. At last I was conducted down a back lane into a
small and very dirty house. Four women were sewing in a parlor, and did not raise their heads when I went in. The walls
were decorated with those old-fashioned colored prints which you
still find in cottages in the country; deformed angels, bloated
Cupids, and stalwart shepherdesses leading lambs which look like
lions. I was taken thence through the chamber (almost filled
with a four-poster, which might have rivaled the great bed of
Ware) into a stable-yard. I was offered my choice of two very
rough ponies, and the object of my preference, having been accou-
tred with a rusty bit, a bridle patched up with string, and a ragged, one-stirruped saddle, was led with a loud clattering through
the bedroom into the parlor, and from the parlor into the street.
I was presented with a guide who did not understand a word of
English, and we started on the road to St. Christoval de la Laguna.

The scenery was wild and barren. The road, which bears the
marks of an ancient pavement, was bordered with cactus-fields.
It was the cochineal harvest, and women were at work collecting
the insect in small pots, with an instrument like a putty-knife.

The cochineal was first imported from Mexico by an enterprising man. The educated people looked upon him as a fool, and
laughed at him; the uneducated, as something worse, and burned
his cacti. But as soon as the pest fell upon the vines* there was

* The vines were imported into these islands from the Rhine, as well as from

a cochineal furore, which is yielding to tobacco since the discovery of *dianthine*. So now, instead of devouring this disease-born insect in our strawberry ices, we take them colored with an agreeable extract from coal-tar.

A ride of five miles brought me to Laguna, which deserves to be called the Silent City. "Their houses were like tombs, and you might write their epitaphs above their doors." There were no pretty girls in the balconies, no tinkling of guitars from within; the houses were moss-covered, the streets grass-grown; animal life rare, saving mildew, which was excessive. I went to an inn, as desolate as a mausoleum, and ate voraciously, feeling like a ghoul. The intense stillness alarmed me: I rushed to the kitchen. There, at all events, I hoped to find something natural and human. But no, it was empty; the fire which had been lighted for my omelette was almost out, and the cinders were dropping with a dismal sound into the grate below.

Laguna is the residence of many political exiles, who feel no desire to see the inhabitants of a world which is forever closed against them. I will not take upon me to assert that fleas fatten on persons of a melancholy temperament, but it is certain that the fleas of Laguna stand unrivaled in size and activity. They are the heroes of many songs of the peasantry, and Peter Pindar, who once dwelt in this cheerful neighborhood, wrote verses in their honor.

I returned to Santa Cruz, which presents a much gayer appearance. La Plaza de la Constitution is the fashionable evening promenade. I sat at the door of the French café, smoking the long, flat cigar of Teneriffe, and stared at brunettes to my heart's content. Then I examined the monument of the four Guanche kings which sit sculptured in the market-place, each holding his thigh-bone in his hand. These Guanches were the aborigines of the island. Large numbers perished from the arms of the Spaniards, and by a famine (the familiar of war) which afterward came upon the island. The rest gradually perished away, under that mysterious agency which the mere presence of white men appears to employ against a weaker race.

Some ethnologists have supposed that these Guanches were a

Crete. "This island produces three sorts of excellent wines," writes Nichols in his description. "Canary, Malmsey (or rather Malvasia), and Verdona, which may all go under the denomination of Sack." But now there are, I believe, neither Canary wine nor Canary birds in the Canaries.

detached race of people, unlike any now existing on the earth.
We have, however, ample evidence, from the writings of the Spanish historians and the English merchant-adventurers of the day,
to show that the Guanches were of Libyan origin, though it is not
possible to identify them with any particular tribe.

The Guanches were a tawny-skinned, black-eyed, flat-nosed people, speaking a dialect analogous with that of the Berbers, and
dwelling in caves. They believed in a Supreme Being, an Evil
Genius, and a future state; they also worshiped two tutelar deities, one of whom protected men, the other women. They had an
order of white-robed priests and priestesses, who preserved their
purity by intermarriage, and the art of embalming; which last,
when they became extinct, died with them. They had lords or
chieftains, under whose command they fought with wooden jave-
lins hardened in the fire. They tilled the ground with bullock's
horns, and lived on a food called gosio, which resembles the cous-
cous of the Senegambia. They fattened their girls for marriage,
believing that fat women were the most fruitful, and on them their
lords exercised the *droit-de-cuisse*. Finally, when they died, the
priests dried them in the sun, embalmed them, and buried them
in caves sacred to the art of sepulture.

CHAPTER III.

A LANDMARK OF HISTORY.

Sea-torpor.—First Sight of Africa.—The Infanta Henry.—Cape Boiador.—The Rabbits of Porto Santo.—Portuguese Monopoly and English Smuggling.

WE continued our voyage with a fair wind and a warm sea. Sometimes we received visits from flying-fish, which fell upon the deck, and even upon the awning above. This little creature skims along the surface of the water, with gauzy wings of the same material as those of the dragon-fly, so like a bird that one might have very good sport taking them on the wing with dust shot. These petty incidents are angel visits at sea, that monotonous and overrated element. Viewed from the shore as it comes dashing upon the black rocks, shivers into a thousand foaming fragments, and runs hissing toward one along the sand, it is certainly a grand sight. But "blue water" itself is, in repose, a flat-faced simpleton, without beauty or expression, except that which it borrows from the sky above it; and, in commotion, a spoiled child whose ships are toys, and who sometimes breaks them open to see what they are made of.

One has so much leisure at sea that one can seldom do any work. The most intellectual travelers must confess that dinner is the great event of the nautical day.

On board ship one lives only when eating or drinking; at other periods one exists. At half past eight we used to sit down to a breakfast of edible cinders. Our cook was a confirmed culprit, who overdid every thing, and who was daily wished back with him from whom cooks are proverbially supposed to come. We had tea and coffee; but as the tea was usually made in yesterday's coffee-boiler, and *vice versâ*, choice became a mere matter of form. Our cinders were handed us on plates which represented an angel receiving fruits from a negress, with the motto underneath, *Spero meliora*. The angel representing the West African Company, the motto, a humane wish for higher profits.

At twelve we spoiled our dinners with cheese and biscuits, and at four o'clock the cook spoiled it again. At ten all the lights

were put out, and each man retired to his oven. This was the
life of a tortoise in the sand, or of a bear in a hollow tree; and I
was glad enough when I heard the cry of "Land ho!" from the
mast-head. In a short time I was looking at the continent of Africa. There was not much to see, it was true. A white surf on
a barren shore. A cluster of trees. Two round hills, the Paps
of the Cape de Verd; and as suggestive of a feminine bust as the
Cape itself of a verdant promontory. But it was Africa, that
land of adventure and romance; and I stood there for two hours,
unable to draw my eyes away.

That miserable group of trees is a grand landmark in the history of navigation. In days when Western Africa was believed
to be one great desert of sand, it gave promise of a rich and fruitful continent, and of the still wealthier India beyond.

In the fifteenth century, when the Crescent began to grow dim
in the West, and Fez and Bagdad no longer remained the capitals
of the world, the Portuguese under Alfonso I. drove the Moors
from Portugal, pursued them into their own country, and, assisted by a band of merchant-adventurers from England, took the
town of Ceuta by storm. During this engagement, Henry, the
third son of the king, then a youth, displayed remarkable valor
and address. When the war was over, he determined not to rest
till he had solved that grand problem of the ancients—the cir-
cumnavigation of Africa. Having had long conversations with
the Moors who had been taken captive, he took up his residence
at the Cape de Sagres, in the southernmost province of Portugal.
There the sight of the sea constantly sustained his passion, and he
could easily communicate with the traveled Moors, who went
trading to the borders of negro-land. He also examined all sailors who came from distant seas; and having sent for *Jacques* from
the island of Majorca (a man celebrated for his knowledge of
navigation, and his skill in the making of charts and instruments),
he placed him at the head of an academy which he founded for
the study of these sciences.

One morning, after he had passed the night in study and reflection, he suddenly ordered two vessels to sail for the Libyan coast,
and these were followed by others which happened to be ready
for sea. The explorers passed Cape Nun, the *ne plus ultra* of the
Spanish voyagers, but were so alarmed at the appearance of Cape
Boiador that they returned. Prince Henry sent two gentlemen
of the court—Juan Gonsalez and Tristan Vaz—who discovered

Porto Santo, one of the Azores, by being shipwrecked upon it. This small success increased Henry's enthusiasm. An emigrant ship sailed to Porto Santo with cattle and agricultural implements, but also with a doe rabbit in a delicate situation. Her progeny, liberated on shore, increased so rapidly that in two years they had eaten up all that was eatable on the island, and the colonists returned. In the mean time the same two gentlemen had discovered Madeira, and Henry endeavored to keep up the national enthusiasm with its products. But these enterprises were not popular. The Portuguese would not believe that it was possible to sail round Africa, and there were several who said that Africa had been allotted to the wild beasts as their proper sphere, and that the impiety of struggling against God's will had already been proved by the rabbits in Porto Santo.

Incredulity and false piety are the most vulgar of all errors, and the most difficult to contest. But Henry persevered, and in 1432, when Gillianez rounded Cape Boiador, they were effectually silenced. The vessels brought back some slaves and gold dust, and these few ounces of precious dirt were more eloquent than the voice of science by induction. The Pope gave to the Portuguese all countries that they might discover to the south of Cape Boiador, and (as Mohammed promised Paradise to all who died under his banner) he granted full absolution to those who might perish in future voyages. Private ventures were now started, and the first regular trade on the West Coast of Africa was that of sealskins.

But now discovery followed discovery, and in an incredibly short space of time the whole coast was laid open to trade. Missionaries were sent out to Senegal, Elmina, Congo, and Benin. Those who wished to trade on the coast had now to pay for licenses, and many Portuguese, whose descendants remain there to this present day, settled in Guinea, and pushed their trade into the far interior. Ivory and gold dust, but principally slaves, became the established articles of commerce.

The Infanta did not die till he had seen Portuguese discovery extended to Sierra Leone; and, tedious as I have already been upon this subject, I can not refrain from eulogizing this wonderful man—of whom you may read with pride, since his mother was an Englishwoman—who, though a prince, was chaste as a templar and studious as a monk; who was the greatest mathematician and the best-read scholar of his day. During forty years he endured the sneers of the Spaniards, who regarded him as a visionary, and the reproaches of his own countrymen, who accused him of wasting ships and men upon chimeras. During forty years he suffered the fate of all men who think in advance of their age; but, more fortunate than most, he reaped present as well as posthumous glory.

A hundred years had passed before the English made a voyage to West Africa. We have, therefore, been reproached with want of enterprise; but the real cause of this apparent apathy was the great power of the Portuguese, and their protection by the Pope. I find that, as early as the reign of Edward the Fourth, the Duke of Medina Sidonia engaged two Englishmen to conduct a trading venture to the West Coast of Africa; and the King of Portugal, hearing of this in time, sent an embassy to England to obtain the prohibition of this enterprise, which accordingly fell to the ground. Many English sailors, however, served in the Portuguese caravels, the fastest vessels of their day, and made voyages to Africa, and afterward to the Indies. In the reign of Elizabeth, vessels were equipped for Africa: another embassy was sent to England. "Our virtuous queen" issued proclamations forbidding, under severe penalties, any infringement of the rights of the Portuguese; and at the same time granted letters patent to several of her subjects to trade on the forbidden coast, where, in 1595, the Dutch began also to settle.

Then commenced a war for the possession of settlements which their victors were forced to abandon soon after they were won.

Africa, like a great Ant-eater, threw gold dust in their eyes. They struggled together in blind avarice that they might fall the more surely into her snares.

CHAPTER IV.

THE PARADISE OF THE BLACKS.

Sierra Leone: its Description; its Douaniers.—Black Christianity.—Origin of the White Man.—Nigger Juries.—Ethiopic Character.

HAVING touched at Gambia, which I shall describe hereafter, we entered the harbor of Sierra Leone; so named by Piedro de Cintra, its discoverer, not from its lions, for none are found in the neighborhood, but from the roaring of thunder which he then heard among its mountains. Sierra Leone is our principal colony upon the coast, and is as beautiful as it is malarious—*anguis in herbâ, pulcherrima.*

Free-town is rudely built, its very rudeness picturesque, and is encircled by mountains embosomed in vegetation. The streets are wide, and are sown with Bermuda grass, for here the climate induces civilization in its babyhood to imitate the effete in its decline.

On the side of the hill which rises behind the town is a charming scene, which I will attempt to describe. You have seen a rural hamlet where each cottage is half concealed by its own garden. Now convert your linden into the graceful palm, your apples into oranges, your gooseberry bushes into bananas, your thrush which sings in its wicker cage into a gray parrot whistling on a rail, your rosy-cheeked peasant lass suckling her child into a black girl combing out her little brother's wool; sprinkle this with strange and powerful perfumes; place in the west a sun flaming among golden clouds in a Prussian-blue sea dotted with white sails; imagine those mysterious and unknown sounds, those breathings of the Earth-soul, with which the warm night of Africa rises into life, and then you will realize one of those moments of poetry which reward poor travelers for long days and nights of naked solitude.

If pleasure is one's object in traveling, every purpose is answered by reading a volume of adventures, drinking a cup of strong tea, and allowing one's imagination to wander. Thus one

can make charming discoveries; and the custom is common
enough; but to shackle the ethereal explorer with a vile body
which savages can detain, and malaria enfeeble, is one of those
vulgar errors which only young or foolish men fall victims to.

FREE-TOWN, SIERRA LEONE.

Sierra Leone was colonized in 1787 by emigrants from England, consisting of four hundred negroes and sixty women of the

town. The original stock was dying out, when the slave-trade was abolished, and the colony was fed with liberated slaves—a practice which is continued to this day. When a slaver is taken, the prize is sent to Sierra Leone (or, in certain latitudes, to St. Helena), and the rubbish is shot into a place called "The Queen's Yard." Here the *ci-devant* slaves, who firmly believe that they are going to be eaten, are offered their choice of temporary bondage in two forms—apprenticeship or enlistment. The latter is often preferred, it being considered more honorable to be called "Queen-man" than "Free-man."

By this means a very mongrel population is introduced, and not a very virtuous one; for a large proportion of all slaves are sold out of their own country for their crimes. But then the first inhabitants of Rome were a mob of thieves, fugitive slaves, and miserable exiles, all of different countries and of different tongues. It is encouraging to find in Sierra Leone the same elements of future glory.

The inhabitants of the colony may be divided into four classes:

1st. The street-vendors, who cry cassada cakes, palm-oil, pepper, pieces of beef under such names as *agedee, aballa, akalaray,* and which are therefore as unintelligible as the street cries of London. This is the costermonger type.

2dly. The small market-people, who live in frame houses, sell nails, fish-hooks, tape, thread, ribbons, etc., and who work at handicrafts in a small way.

3dly. The shop-keepers who inhabit frame houses on stone foundations, and within which one may see a sprinkling of mahogany, a small library of religious books, and an almost English atmosphere of comfort.

Lastly, the liberated Africans of the highest grade, who occupy two-story stone houses inclosed all round by spacious piazzas, the rooms furnished with gaudy richness, and the whole their own property, being built from the proceeds of their theft or thrift.

As a commercial race the liberated Africans will always prosper. But it remains to be seen if they are yet civilized.

On our arrival the "Armenian" was soon surrounded by boatfuls of negroes who called themselves Englishmen, but who resembled baboons. The mail-boat was returning from the land, and a man standing in the bows was clearing a passage to the ladder with a boat-hook. In one shore-boat a boy grasping the rope refused to "move on." The sailor offered to strike him, taking care not to do so, that being a matter of law.

"God damn you!" cried a negro in the same boat; "you hit that boy, that all!"

A little violent in his language, thought I; but this proves what I have often heard (was it in Exeter Hall? I think it must have been), that the negro is full of love and sympathy for his brethren.

But it so happened that the boy's defender, growing angry with him for some reason, ordered him out of his boat. He tried to get into another, where he was no better received. Having a foot on each gunwale, and the boats gradually receding from one another, as boats always do in such cases, he fell into the water. There his struggles were viewed with supreme indifference, although the bay is full of sharks; and one of these must soon have had an oily repast, had not the same sailor hauled him out with his boat-hook, which this time was not found so offensive.

But I would not judge of the liberated Africans by the mob, which in all countries is tolerably brutal. I preferred to follow the maxim of Voltaire, " *Qu'il faut plutôt juger d'une puissante nation par ceux qui sont à la tête que par la populace.*" Accordingly, I went ashore with two French traders, one of whom carried a very heavy and suspicious-looking carpet bag, the other an open box of cigars. On the quay we were confronted by two custom-house officers (colored).

One of these made a movement toward the carpet bag, which was intercepted by the gentleman with the cigars.

"I assure you," he said, politely, "that I have brought them ashore simply for my own smoking."

A negro's attention, like a child's, is riveted by the least thing which is held "up before it." The two officials immediately closed upon the cigars; the carpet bag progressed rapidly toward the town.

"You see," continued the Frenchman, speaking with great deliberation, "that there is only one pound here. They are a hundred and ten to the pound. Would you like to count them, gentlemen?"

The carpet bag turned a corner.

"I buy them," continued the French trader, keeping his eyes fixed upon the huge orbits of the negro's, "from a gentleman with whom I am personally acquainted, and—"

"But where is de oder gentleman wid de—"

"And I can assure you that they are really excellent."

"But wher'm oder—"

"As I told you before, gentlemen, I am not at liberty to sell them, but I shall be most happy to present you each with one. Will you give yourself the trouble to take one, sir?"

He crammed one into each of their hands, and having favored them with a few more urbane speeches and with a quantity of bows, left them to the enjoyment of their small gratuity, and me to the suspicion that they were little better than Continental *douaniers*.

The next day was Sunday, and in the morning I had a valise carried up to the house to which I had been invited. When I offered the man sixpence, the ordinary fee, he demanded an extra sixpence "for breaking the Sabbath." I gave it readily, and was pleased to find that the labors of our missionaries had not been in vain.

But, unhappily, as I was on my way to church, I met a negress accompanied by a very beautiful child. I asked the woman if that was her daughter.

"Yes, sar, that my proper daughter."

Wondering what sort of person her improper daughter might be, I remarked that she was very pretty.

"Ah! you think him fine?"

"Yes," said I.

"Fine too much—eh?"

Presuming that the adverb was here used merely in a superlative sense, I nodded my head.

The old woman came up to me mysteriously, and put her paw on my wrist.

"You like to buy him?"

"*What!*" cried I.

"You like buy him, pay me plenty dash;* then you take him what place you like; s'pose you no sit down here, take him other coast; s'pose you want leff (leave) him, leff him, he come back here; s'pose you no want leff'm, no leff'm."

Ah! thought I, here is a poor benighted creature who has never heard the voice of instruction, who has never received—

"*Hei-gh!*" she cried, "you no hear bell stop? Me go now.

---

* Dash, from the Portuguese *das-me*, give me: in the same manner, palaver comes from *palabra*; picaninny from *picania*; custom from *costume*, etc.

After church we palaver. Gib me plenty dash; den we drink rum; den you take him—palaver said!"

I went down rather disgusted to my friend the French merchant at the hotel. He was in the act of buying a remarkably ugly young woman, whom he told me was to be housemaid in his Rio Grande factory. He signed the bill of sale as I entered; and having given the father a glass of rum, and promised him his cloth and muskets on the morrow, they exchanged the *Palaver said!* without which no bargain can be ratified, and then the virtuous parent left the room.

The Frenchman, observing my surprise, informed me that this was the regular mode of procuring servants at Sierra Leone. When he had explained the system, I saw that it was virtually the same as that of English "hiring fairs," where shepherds, carters, grooms, and milkmaids pledge themselves to farmers for a year or so, and can be sent to prison if they run away. But he also added that fathers and mothers were equally willing to let out their daughters to residents for the vilest purposes, and concluded with some remarks upon Sierra Leone and the negro, which my respect for the philanthropists of Exeter Hall prevent me from repeating.

Three or four residents having afterward dropped in, we established a conversazione, refreshing ourselves with pale brandy and the limonade gazeuse of Marseilles.

I soon discovered that Sierra Leone is a true paradise of the blacks. Here the negro is triumphant, and the white man holds him in awe—the reason being that liberated Africans are admitted to all the privileges of English citizens, and numbers have outmastered intellect—a product, moreover, which is not copious in the Anglo-African formation.

The negro imitates the white man as the ape imitates the negro. The result in both cases is a caricature. The rich negro of Sierra Leone is dressed as if he had taken a bath in a rainbow; and his manners are so strained and pompous that a close imitation of them, even in the broadest farce, would be looked upon as a rough overacting of character. But most comical of all is the manner in which negroes identify themselves with the parent country. To hear them talk, you would think that their ancestors had come over with William the Conqueror; and that they even take to themselves all the glories of our history, the following anecdote will prove. The French consular agent having some time ago overstepped the limits of the land, a warrant was taken out against him. Holding the sable powers in great contempt, he armed himself with a pair of pistols, and defied them with the air of a brigand at the Victoria. "Ah!" cried the two constables, rapidly retreating, "we no care for you, one dam Frenchman. I tink you forget *we win Waterloo*—eh?"

It is one of the chief peculiarities of the Sierra Leone negro that he hates, with an intense and bitter hatred, this white man to whom he owes every thing. This Christian feeling is propagated even by the native preachers, for one is said to have explained our origin from the pulpit in the following manner:

"My breddren, you see white man bad too much, ugly too much, no good. You want-sabby how man like dat come to lib in the world? Well, I tell you. Adam and Eve dey colored people, very hansum; lib in one beautiful garden. Dere dey hab all things dat be good. Plantains, yams, sweet potatoes, foo-foo *palm wine*—he-igh, too much! Den dey hab two childrum, Cain and Abel. Cain no like Abel's palaver; one day he kill'm. Den God angry, and he say, *Cain!* Cain go hide himself; he tink him berry claber. Heigh-heigh! God say again, Cain, you tink I no see you, you bush-nigger—eh? Den Cain come out, and he say, 'Yes, massa, I lib here—what de matter, massa?' Den God say in one big voice like de tunder in de sky, 'Where'm broder Abel?' Den Cain turn white all ober with fear—dat de first white man, breddren."

This is very profane; but profanity is only dangerous in the pulpit, and when it is spoken in earnest. This absurd anecdote will make you laugh, and that is all; but you must remember that the effect upon that man's congregation would be very different, and would certainly not tend to promote an amiable feeling toward the white population.

This hatred of the white man becomes really dangerous in a court of justice, when cases of black *v.* white come before black juries. These men do not want for intelligence; but they form no idea of the sacredness of their calling, and give verdicts at will where their private feelings are concerned. This explains how it is that trial by jury has only been adopted by refined nations. In a savage or semi-civilized state, the heads of the people alone are qualified to judge.

It is a common story here that if you call a black man a nigger you are liable to a fine of five pounds for defamation of character. I do not know if this is really the case, but any thing broader than mere insult is perilous in the extreme.   A gentleman who had discharged his servant was annoyed by the man entering his private yard.   He ordered him out; the negro was insolent, and refused to go.   The white man then did what most Englishmen would have done: he took him by the scruff of the neck and kicked him out.   The case was brought before a black jury, who fined him £50.

I had anecdotes of negro jury injustice from so many respectable informants that I could do no less than believe it to be common. I was a little staggered, certainly, when I read in the Rev. J. Leighton Wilson's work on West Africa the following paragraph :

"But perhaps the most interesting point of view in which the liberated Africans are to be seen, and which will render their moral condition most intelligible to those at a distance, is when they sit at the Quarter Sessions as petty, grand, and special jurors."

But the following evidence from *Sierra Leone*, a work written by Mr. Shreeve, who had resided many years in that colony, will prove, I think, that Mr. Wilson's remark must be intended for irony.   Nothing can render their "moral condition more intelligible" than these extracts; though whether it is an "interesting point of view" to those white men whose liberties or fortunes may be at stake, I will leave the reader to judge.

After observing that the negro's system of physiognomy tends to represent all men bad who happen to be white, and that the white man can not obtain justice in Sierra Leone; after quoting an instance in which a man who had killed another (probably a white victim) was found Not Guilty in spite of all evidence, " a decision at which even the culprit himself appeared astonished, and a virtuous indignation from many ran through the hall," Mr. Shreeve observes :

"Another reprehensible practice, or rather vice, in which many jurors indulge, is ardent spirits, from which may be traced their frequent, hasty, vociferous, and unjust decisions: this baneful indulgence is evident to all in court; and upon a late trial, at which I was present, a juror was so disorderly that the judge was obliged to impose a fine of £5, and lock the Bacchanalian up till it was paid.   Another matter of serious importance, and often fatal to the course of justice, is the common practice of private communication of interested parties with jurors upon their retiring to find a verdict; and again, that of parties being permitted, through the absence or favoritism of the bailiffs, to eavesdrop at the door of the jury-room, and not only to overhear their deliberations, but actually communicate in the native language with those upon whose impartiality at the moment perhaps a life depends."

Finally he adds, " Here Justice should be painted like Le Brun's Revenge, with a bowl and dagger, not with the balance and the sword."

You will perhaps suppose that this dislike for us has proceeded from acts of cruelty and oppression. But no, they have less to complain of in that way than our laboring classes at home. We are their liberators, their shelterers, their protectors—but we are really their masters. They acknowledge our supremacy, but they detest us for it; they do not love the hand which showers gold upon them from above: they prefer the baser metals, which they can grub up from beneath their feet. Paramount in their own paradise, they find themselves pigmies when they stir abroad; the politest words which they receive are tinged with a condescension which goes through them like a sword. Sensitive and vain, they hanker for dominion; possessed of neither patience nor persistence, they can never obtain it save in their own small spheres.

I do not wish to detract an item of true worth from Sierra Leone. The town itself is a useful mart to which native merchants of all kinds find their way. It is a good school for the wretched savage disembarked from the slaver. There are negroes in the colony who are skilled in the usual handicrafts, and more still (for trade is always preferred to work) have settled as sub-colonists in various parts of the coast. This diffuses English language and English habits in a mutilated state, if it does no more.

A certain skill in mechanics, without the genius of invention; a great fluency of language, without energy in ideas; a correct ear for music, without a capacity for composition—in a word, a display of imitative faculties, with an utter barrenness of creative power—there is your negro at the very best.

Even these are rare, almost exceptional cases; and to show such trained animals as fair samples of the negro is to make an exhibition of black lies. One might almost as well assert, after the sights which one sees at a country fair, that all pigs are learned; that the hare plays on a drum in its native state; and that it is the nature of piebald horses to rotate in a circle to the sound of a brass band.

C

CHAPTER V.

THE REPUBLIC OF COLORED GENTLEMEN.

Liberia: its Description; its Future and its Resources.

WE are now passing along the coast of Liberia, and a word or two on this country will make so good an appendix to my last, that I shall pass over Cape Palmas for the present.

I have shown you a colony in which a white bishop and a white governor possess the nominal dominion over soul and body, but where the real power belongs to the black. Now what think you of a state in which no white man is allowed to have land at all?

Liberia is a republic of American negroes. They have a black president, black senators, black merchants, and a black populace. Every thing is done in small mimicry of their step-mother.

Their metropolis (and only town) is called Monrovia. It is built on the peninsula of Cape Mesurada, is three quarters of a mile long, and half that distance in breadth. The houses are framed dwellings of a story and a half high, raised on a stone or brick foundation of six feet. There are four churches; below the high bluff on which the town stands are six or seven substantial warehouses. There is also a tavern (there are only four in West Africa altogether), which is kept by a preacher and a temperance man, and where ale, porter, wine, and cherry brandy may be obtained. The landlord probably compounds with his outer conscience—by which I mean that which speaks with the brazen trumpet of scandal, and not with the still, small voice, which one can more easily shut one's ears to—as a Mr. Cooper did who kept a hotel before him. This worthy man set forth that nothing was more repugnant to his feelings than to sell ardent spirits; but that, if gentlemen *would* have them, the following was his price— which he made very high, probably for the purpose of deterring them from sin.

The trade of this country is palm-oil, camwood, and ivory. The settlers grow the usual African products, including a fine kind of coffee, and have established sugar-mills. The merchants have also trading craft built by themselves, and ranging from ten to fifty tons.

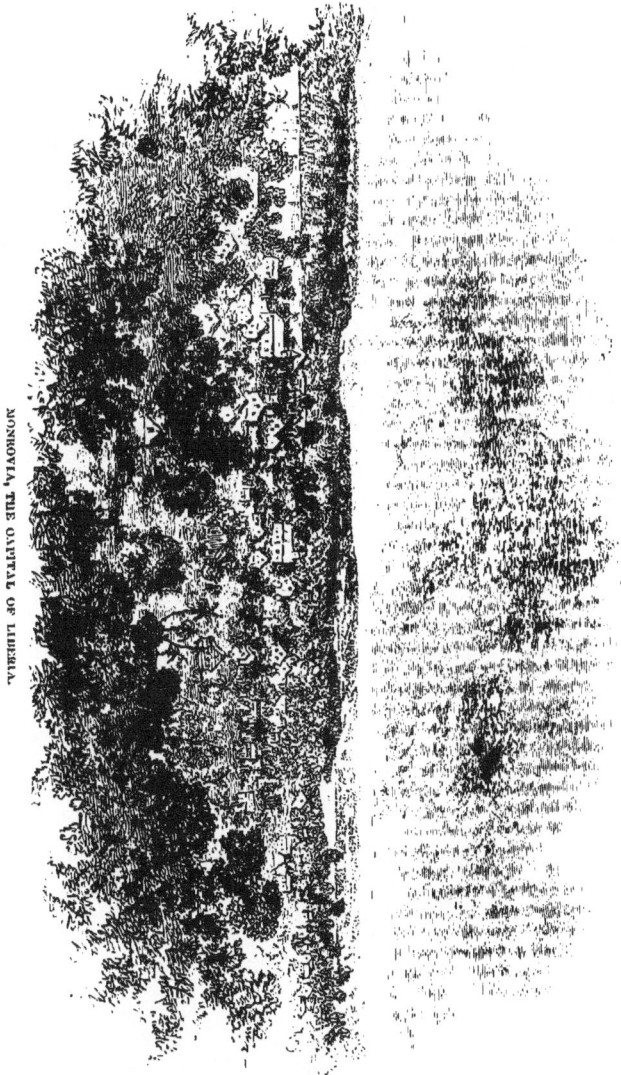

MONROVIA, THE CAPITAL OF LIBERIA.

The negroes are sent out by a society, which supports each in-dividual during the first six months. This fresh-blood supply is indispensable to the welfare of Liberia, which consequently suffers from the troubles of the Disunited States. But, in spite of all drawbacks, the indolence of many emigrants, and the itch for preaching, which seems to torment Ethiopic humanity as it does most low orders of men, one must allow that the progressive effort is a creditable one. We must not expect wonders, and we must reject the poetical balderdash sometimes served up in this Land of the Free, where so many are only free to starve. But the fact is, that any country, even fever-stricken Liberia, is better for the free man of color than America. It was said of Sparta in old days that none were so free there as those that were free, nor so enslaved as those who were slaves. In America, the model land of liberty, the black man is happier as a cotton slave in the South than as a social slave in the North. In the first instance, he is not more wretched than an English farm-laborer or a Manchester operative. In the latter case he is a Paria, a man without caste, a reptile which every hand avoids, and upon whom every white foot tramples. But if Liberia is to be great, it must become a kingdom.

In West Africa there are but two powerful states (Ashantee and Dahomey), and despots rule them both. There is now but one great republic in the two worlds, and that is divided by a civil war. The Jews, the Romans, the Italians, the Dutch, the French tried republics, and have returned to monarchy. The earth should be a reflection of heaven, and heaven is an empire.

CHAPTER VI.

THE TITANS OF THE COAST.

Cape Palmas.—The Kru-man.—Engage a Crew.—Book.—Kru Character.

WE anchored off Cape Palmas, a bold headland upon which are built the houses of an American mission, and at a little distance a Christian village. One can see a forest interior, with small hills jungle-crowned; a narrow river, which is guarded by a furious surf, and said to flow from the head-waters of the Nun.

The steamer came here for the exclusive purpose of taking Kru-men. These men are the Titans of the coast, and are indispensable to active commerce in Africa. A vessel has seldom been long in harbor before half her crew have been so weakened by sickness as to be unable to man the yards. After lying the usual term of months in an oil river, so many of the hands have died that it is frequently impossible to sail her home without assistance.

The Kru-men are natives of the Grain Coast, and appear to have taken but lately to maritime pursuits, for I meet with no mention of them in the old writers.

They are men of a Herculean type, a contrast to most savage tribes, who are slim, muscleless, and soft-handed. Strength is the result of regime. Savages are less muscular, as it has been proved, than we are. But that is owing rather to their indolent life than to an inferior physical organization. We have no grounds for supposing that these Kru-men were originally a finer race of men than the other tribes of the coast. They are now the most athletic race in the world. They are Goliaths of strength, as well as of stature. Regular work and a regulated diet can work marvels upon the framework of the savage, and can modify not only an individual, but a race.

Every trader takes a number of these for the term of his voyage, which usually lasts two years; and they are also employed in the factories. They are paid from three to five dollars a month, the first month paid in advance, and an agreement made to send them back to their own country free of expense as soon as their time is out.　Their rations are usually a pint and a half of rice per diem, with meat or fish on Sundays.　Sometimes they have a daily allowance of trade-rum as well.

KRU TOWN, NEAR CAPE PALMAS.

The men-of-war are supplied from a Kru colony at Sierra Leone with these men, who receive the pay and rations of common seamen.　South of the Congo their place is taken by the

Cabinda tribe, who are neither so able nor so willing as the Kru.

They are such rank pilferers that they will upset your boat in a surf, save your life with one hand, and pick your pocket with the other; for they are as much at home in water as on land, and may be classed among the amphibious animals.

They are gluttons and drunkards, but also faithful, hard-working, and well-behaved when not too kindly treated. Then the low nature displays itself, and insolence ensues. The old maxim, slightly altered—

> A *Kru-man*, a dog, and a walnut-tree,
> The more you beat them, the better they be—

applies well enough when the punishment is really deserved.

It has always been an understood thing among slavers that Kru-men and Cabindas are not to be carried away. In some cases faith has been broken, and in every case the Kru-men have pined away and died, or, as the slavers express it, "sulked them-

KRU HOUSES.

selves to death." They have a tender affection for their mothers, and an *amor patriæ*, which is rarely found among negroes. Indeed, it is not strange that they should love their beautiful country, with its groves, its flowers, and its sea, which has no sharks. They are likewise subject to a yearning for dog's flesh, which, perhaps, they prefer to scenery, and which they find difficult to obtain abroad.

When the Kru-man becomes rich he buys a few wives, retires from business, and lives like a private gentleman on his own estate, which is cultivated by his spouses. But, even when the term of his labors is over, he has many dangers to undergo. If he is set on shore at any distance from his native place, he is sure to be plundered by the intermediate tribes. And when he has regained his own home, he finds his relatives but little more merciful. He is treated to his face as if he were a rich man suddenly become defunct. Guns are fired; women dance joyously and sing his praises; a council of the next of kin is held for the division of his property, over which they quarrel bitterly; and full display is made of those emotions, which in England are felt, but concealed, at the reading of a will. The amount of property which the man is allowed to retain depends entirely on the number of his cousins. Yet such is the vanity and sensitiveness of the negro that he would rather give up all than run the risk of being called a stingy fellow.

As soon as the anchor was dropped a crowd of canoes skimmed through the surf, and were soon at the ship's side. These canoes are more diminutive than you can well conceive. The Kru-man squats in it on his knees, and bales the water out with one of his feet. Sometimes he paddles with his hands; sometimes, thrusting a leg in the water, he spins the canoe round when at full speed like a skater on the outer edge. If it should capsize, as the laws of equilibrium sometimes demand, he turns it over, bales it out with a calabash, swimming all the while, and glides in again, his skin shining like a seal's.

When the Kru-men were admitted on the main deck, the palm-oil traders examined them as a Yorkshireman would a horse, or a Georgian planter a slave at an auction. The very big men were put aside as being of a lazy temperament. Those who had a raw were carefully rejected. Clean-limbed men at five foot nine, or so, were at a premium. Having gained a wrinkle or two from the ship's surgeon, who had spent his lifetime on the Coast, I picked out five to serve me as a boat's crew. All of them wore

bracelets of ivory, a sign that they had been to the Cameroons or
the Gaboon.

They demanded first where I was going to take them: on hearing their destination, they replied that plenty shark lib at Lagos;
plenty sick at Bonny; but that Gaboon was a fine place.

I then told them that they would be paid five dollars a month.
They desired to be given the usual advance and a "book." This
thirst for literature astounded me; but the doctor, coming to my
aid, informed me that "book" was a generic term for all things
written, and that they wanted an agreement.

An old man now presented himself. His forehead was smeared
with white earth, which he told me was great fetich. It was
great fetich indeed. These chiefs keep their fathers' skull when
half decomposed in a dark room, placing the earth below. A
liquid matter oozing from the skull falls upon the earth, which
on great occasions is used as I have described.

He told me that his name was King George, and that he had
come to make palaver for these boys. This meant, it seems, that
he was to receive their agreement, and first month's wages.

Every one has heard the story of the actor, who, having pledged
every thing else of value, finally pawned himself, and sent the
duplicate to the manager. In the same way my boys had borrowed money from King George, pawning their bodies as security.
I was the manager who paid book and part of their debts in order to obtain their services.

As native names, however melodious, are difficult to remember,
traders christen these converts to commerce with the most absurd
appellations. The names of my five men were Smoke-Jack, Dry-
Toast, Cockroach, Pot o' Beer, and Florence Nightingale. I made
the usual arrangements with the purser for their board and passage. They were to receive a pint and a half of rice daily;
which, as they starve, like most savages, in their own country,
they regarded in the light of high living. I gave each of them a
red cap like a bargee's, and a blue flannel shirt. They used to
come to me every day, ask me what my name was, inquire after
the health of my near relatives—as negroes always do—and beg
a little tobacco. They elected a head man to rule over them;
his duties, as they told me, consisted in receiving their rations,
and in portioning them out to each; in being the bearer of my
orders or their complaints; and in thrashing any one of the
"gang" who misbehaved himself.

CHAPTER VII.

THE CITY OF GOLD.

The Grave of L. E. L.—Her Death.—Her Husband.—Popular Scandal.—Route to Coomassi.—Court Reception.—Ashantee Empire: its Constitution.—Decoy Wives. —Savage Nuptials.

THERE is only one thing to be seen at Cape Coast Castle. I was loitering in the court-yard of the fort when I asked a companion where it was. He answered by pointing to my feet, and I found that I was standing on the grave of L. E. L.

Once, as I was crossing the cold and desolate moors of Shetland, I found a golden-crested wren lying dead upon the ground. Such matters do not often touch us when we are very young. But I remember that I looked at the corpse of this, the smallest and most delicate bird of Europe, with emotion. It seemed so strange and so sad to find it in a land where no trees grow, where no skylarks sing, and where it had been killed by the cold winds and the bitter sea-spray which blast the flowers before they have time to bloom.

And sadder and stranger it seemed to find the grave of a poetess in this jail and pest-house of nature—this plague-spot of the universe. Her sepulchre a stone-yard, with grim cannon and piled pyramids of balls. Her requiem, the dull tread of the sentinel; the gay song from the mess-room; the ceaseless washing of the waves against the rocks below.

This was her tomb before she died. She was alone from morning till night. Her husband's ill health increased her anxieties, redoubled her ennui. The climate began to rob her of her only occupation. Her ideas did not flow so readily; she could no longer concentrate her thoughts; her brain, which had once flashed fire, grew cold and dull. A ship was about to sail to England. She wrote letters to all her friends, and a few hours afterward she was found a corpse.

The World, if it sometimes kills its victims, will always embalm them with its tears. None had been attacked so ferociously as Byron and Miss Landon—none more bitterly lamented. In the latter instance its grief took the selfish form of revenge.   A disgraceful and groundless charge was made against Governor Maclean.

CAPE COAST CASTLE.

The death of Mrs. Maclean is one of those mysteries of Africa which must forever remain unrevealed.   I will not revive those calumnies against her husband, of whom all in Africa speak with

affection, and who now lies buried by her side.   Their enemies
are silent now.

Her glory and her sorrows are passing away with the generation among whom she shone.   Her poetry is now but little read;
the letters on her grave are being trodden out by careless feet like
mine.   And yet the story of L. E. L. will ever remain the sweetest and most touching tradition of the Poets.

Near Cape Coast Castle lies the kingdom of Ashantee, whose
monarch slew Sir Charles Macarthy at the head of his troops, and
conquered the English on the brink of the sea.

In the centre of his kingdom is Coomàssi, the City of Gold.

If you were going to that city you would obtain a hammock
and a number of bearers.   Having had a row with them all about
the distribution of your luggage, you would start in a very bad
temper, and proceed about two miles through a shrubby country;
forest-trees would gradually spring up around you, and you would
enter a valley profusely covered with pines, aloes, and lilies; you
would walk on a soil of red clay, with a coating of sand, and
quartz fragments on the path.   You would find few inhabitants,
and poor cultivation in the country, and your heart would be rejoiced by the cries of parrots, toucans, and crown birds.   You
would sleep at *krooms* or villages, to which the *caboceer*, or chef de
village, would welcome you; and would be offered a very bad
bed in a hovel made of hurdles attached to a framework of long
poles, and the interstices filled up with red clay.

A second stage of your journey would be through the dark forest, your attendants yelling horribly to drive away the evil spirits.   You would have the pleasure of seeing around you silk-cot-
ton, wild orange, tamarind, ganian, and wild cedar-trees, with pine-
apples peeping forth at the edges of the path.   Sometimes you
would pass over pieces of swampy ground covered with rank
grass and flags.   Sometimes the tinkling of an iron castanet would
be heard, and a party of men would pass you armed with muskets and knives, bearing loads of ivory, and followed respectfully
by their wives or daughters.   Having crossed the River Praa,
you would pass through a country of a forest character, and on approaching Coomassi you would send on a messenger with a present; you would probably receive an escort in return, with an assurance from the king that he is having the streets cleaned in
your honor.

Finally you would reach Coomassi, and would enter the city by
a broad and pleasant street choked with people, who would give
you a tumultuous welcome with their cries and the clapping of

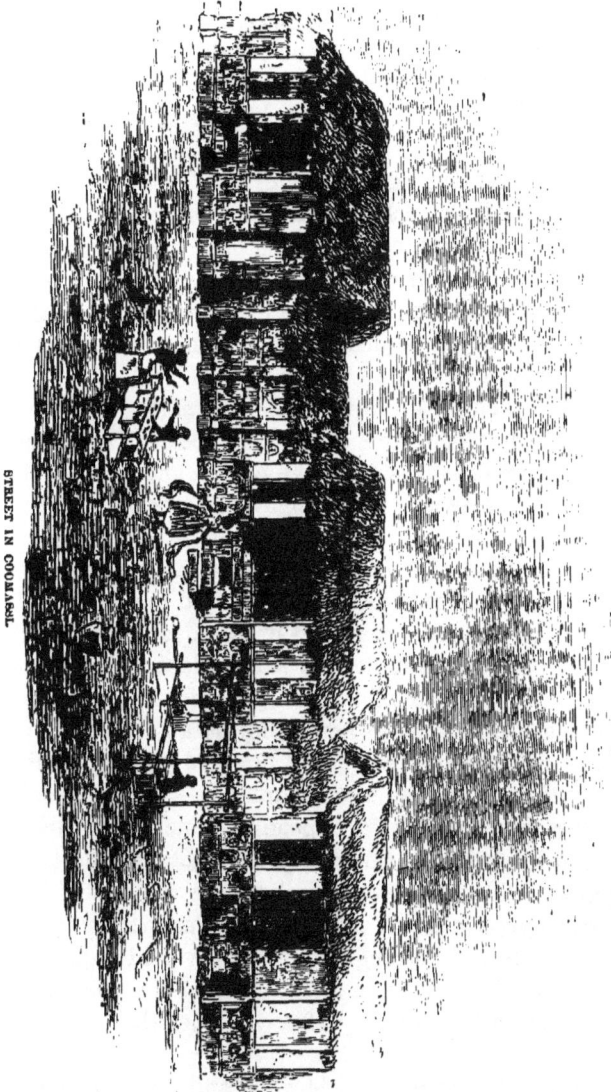

STREET IN COOMASSI.

their hands.   You would be saluted, according to the African
fashion, with constant discharges of musketry; while horns, drums,

flutes, and rattles would modestly contribute toward deafening you completely.

Passing from the vulgar, you would enter an avenue of caboceers, seated on stools, with gaudy-hued umbrellas raised above their heads; these men would be surrounded by their household suites, like the feudal lords of ancient days; their garments of costly foreign silks unraveled and weaved anew into elaborate patterns, and thrown over the shoulder like the Roman toga, leaving the right arm bare; a silk fillet encircling the temples; Moorish charms, inclosed in small cases of gold and silver, suspended on their breasts, with necklaces made of aggry beads, a peculiar stone found in the country, and resembling the glein-ndyr of the Ancient Britons; lumps of rock-gold hanging from their wrists, which would be so heavily laden as to be supported on the heads of their favorite boys; while handsome girls would stand behind, holding silver basins in their hands.

You would then pass into the Moslem quarter, and you would see these traveling merchants dressed in robes of Turkish-cut silk, with trowsers and turbans of native cotton, and small body-vests braided with silk twist. You might also see an inferior class wearing the Arabic *kus-sabi,* the common dress of the Atlas mountaineers—a simple tunic without sleeves, and falling to the knee.

And finally you would pass into the royal presence. The sun glistening upon the gold ornaments of the royal guards might perhaps remind you of the diamonds which blaze at drawing-rooms. You would see a throne of rude but ingenious workmanship, its arms and legs carved into grotesque forms, and embossed with ornaments of gold. The king would not give you his hand to kiss, but he would give you the usual salutation—"He thanks the gods that he sees you and all your people," which, as you have not come without a present, is probably sincere. Having told him a few agreeable falsehoods, and his boys having brandished their swords over your head in a threatening manner, singing all the while his praises and "strong names," you would be shown into a house, and would receive in the course of the evening a little palm wine, and a kind inquiry after your health. ˙

It is the general tradition of Moslem and Pagan that the tribes of Ashantee, Gaman, Dinkira, and Akim were driven by the believers in the early age of Islam from their original inheritances in Ghobagho, Ghofan, and Tonouma to the forests of Wangara, where, finding themselves in a land of gold, they defended themselves, and purchased their independence with their blood. Of these petty kingdoms Ashantee and Dinkira were the most prominent, and a long rivalry existed between them. The King of Dinkira having seduced one of the King of Ashantee's wives, sent to his court as an embassadress, war was proclaimed, and Dinkira was destroyed. This was in the year 1132 (A.D. 1719), as preserved in the Moslem records. From that moment Ashantee from a monarchy became an empire, which extended to the very border of the sea, the coast-tribe (Fanti) being his vassals. Thus, unlike other inland nations, the Ashantees have free communication with the white men, and that ruinous system of middle-men which prevails almost every where else is here unknown.

The King of Ashantee is apparently an utter despot. There are, however, certain restraints upon his power, in the shape of a House of Lords, consisting of four nobles, and a House of Commons, called the Assembly of the Captains. In state affairs the king receives their opinions privately, that his infallibility may not be doubted by the vulgar.

The most remarkable of the customs of Ashantee, though not peculiar to that kingdom, being almost universal in Africa, is the hereditary succession, which does not descend from father to son, but from the king to his brother, to his nephew, and so on. This is a legal illustration of the proverb, "It is a wise child that knows its own father." When a daughter of the royal house bears a son, it is certain that he has the blood royal; but they reason that even queens may be frail, and that the offspring of the king's wife may be possibly the begotten of a slave.

The sisters of the king may negotiate with whom and with as many as they please, for the contribution of royal heirs, provided always that the man is strong, good-looking, and of a decent position in life: conditions which these ladies can not, I am sure, find very harsh.

The king is forbidden by law to have more than three thousand three hundred and thirty-three wives. It is not known whether he is compelled to maintain that moderate number; but the fact is that almost all of these are plantation slaves: the connubial institution is very different here from in England, and a wife is chosen rather for the strength of her limbs than for the softness of her features.

And when one's wife is found to possess the art of pleasing, and is skilled in the science of seduction, how do you think she is employed in this virtuous land? The punishment in crim. con. cases is death or slavery, redeemable by a heavy fine; it is even forbidden, as it was by Lycurgus, to praise the beauty of another man's wife, that being adultery by implication. Well, these charming women are taken from the plow-tail, or rather from their spade-handles, and are elevated to the rank of Delilahs. They insnare foolish youths with their smiles, intoxicate them with their caresses, and are surprised by the husband at an appropriate moment. This is a perfect trade over many parts of Africa, and the King of Ashantee is not ashamed, they say, to set his subjects the example. Go and read *La Sirène*, by Count Xavier de Montépin, and tell me whether truth is not stranger, ay, and sadder than fiction. There the siren has one moment of compunction ere she yields her victim to the assassins: as for these women—but it is not the women, it is the men whom we must blame. A woman rarely commits a wicked action to which she has not been inveigled or driven by a man.

I will describe to you a lady's social progress in this country. As a little girl she goes decently naked, a custom which Columbus observed to be common to most primitive races. When Nature announces her womanhood, she is clothed: often before this period she has been purchased and betrothed; and no very long time is allowed to elapse before she is claimed by her husband.

The young bride is painted with chalk, giving her the appearance of wearing a lace jacket on a black velvet body; a silk robe descends from the waist to the ankle, fitting over a bustle; on her arms and ankles are massive bracelets, and her head is covered with ornaments of gold.

A crowd of young companions parade her in the streets, singing a song in honor of her virginity. Then the spouses retire; the crowd remain without; for the spirit of jealous curiosity, so powerful in the negro, demands a proof of the lady's purity. If the husband is satisfied, he "gives her chalk," as their saying is, and she comes out sprinkled with chalk-powder. If not, the dowry is returned to the husband, though sometimes it becomes a matter of litigation, the law being the same as that prescribed in Deuteronomy.

When conception becomes apparent, the girl goes through a ceremony of abuse, and is pelted down to the sea, where she is cleansed. She is then set aside; charms are bound on her wrists, spells are muttered over her, and, by a wise sanitary regulation, her husband is not allowed to cohabit with her from that time until she has finished nursing her child.

A woman in labor is placed on a stool, as in most of the countries of the East, and it is considered disgraceful in her to utter a cry. The mother is convalescent a few hours afterward, and hides from mankind, being held impure for seven days. On the eighth day the child is baptized by the father, who squirts a mouthful of rum into its face, and calls it by the name of some relative or intimate friend. The mother carries it on her bustle, exposed to all weathers, in consequence of which a very large proportion die: she suckles it for two years or more; and as long as the child is under her care she is exempt from labor, and is treated with great respect.

"And what becomes of her when she is an old woman?" you will ask.

Now with us old age feminine has its pains and its regrets, but it also has little pleasures and privileges of its own : the old woman in the alms-house, with her composed features and her placid cup of tea, or the ancient duchess who receives the homage of young lords with an appalling dignity, are happy enough in their own way, though the one must sometimes think of Jem the Carter, with whom she romped in hay-fields and kept company on Sunday "arternoons," and though the other must sometimes remember the proud days of her beauty, and must now and then look at her shriveled skin with something like a sigh.

But it is difficult and it is distressing to conceive that this young girl, with her merry black eyes, and her gleaming smiles, and all her sweet and enticing ways, will some day become a hag, with pendent breasts, and bleared eyes, and hideous yellow teeth, and features falling to the ape's—a wretch who works like a slave, and who is beaten by the man whose savage passions have drained her of her youth and her beauty before her time.

D

CHAPTER VIII.

LAND OF THE AMAZONS.

Dahomey: its Revenues and Laws.—The Amazons.—Human Sacrifices.

I HAVE said nothing of the religious and political economy of Ashantee, because it differs in no important respects from that of its rival power.

Two hundred and fifty years ago, Tacudona, chief of the Foys, laid siege to the city of Abomey. Meeting with a vigorous resistance, he made a vow that, should he conquer, he would sacrifice its prince Da to the gods. When he had taken the town he began to build a large palace to celebrate his victory. He killed Da on its foundations by ripping open his belly, and called the building *Da-omi*, which signifieth Da's belly, from which time he took the title of King of Dahomey.

The neighboring tribes, anxious to preserve the balance of power, attacked the growing state, which proved triumphant over all, extending its dominion to the very foot of the Atlas, and obtaining a port for foreign trade by the subjugation of Whydah.

It is supposed that taxes are the scourge of civilization, but in this barbarous land there is a fixed system of taxation, which falls heavily upon all classes. Tax-gatherers are stationed at all the markets, and receive cowries on all the articles exposed for sale, in proportion to their quantity. Palm-oil, for instance, pays one gallon in eighteen.

The income-tax is paid under a polite disguise. At the annual *Customs*, a grand religious festival, each man brings a present to the king in proportion to his rank. A tax is levied on slaves; there are duties on foreign trade; if a cock crows it is forfeited, and as it is the nature of cocks to crow, they are ingeniously muzzled; there are even turnpikes in this unfortunate land; and, to crown all, the King of Dahomey, like the King of Ashantee, is heir-at-law to every body in his kingdom.

Thus the real wealth of the realm is vested in the hands of royalty, which keeps a large standing army, keeps up the public roads, receives strangers — Christian, Moslem, or Pagan — with much grandeur, and regales the populace with a spectacle of human sacrifices, as Nero fed the Romans with contests of wild beasts and gladiators.

The criminal law is brief and severe. Treason, cowardice, adultery, and murder are punished with death. The caboceer of a village or district can proclaim a court by prostrating and kissing the ground; the culprit can be tried by an assembly of caboocceers: if condemned to death, he is handed over to the Milgan, or chief executioner, who is the highest person in the state; if to slavery, to the Mayo, or grand vizier, who has the second power; but in all cases the verdict must receive confirmation from the throne, and the sentence must be executed at the capital, and notice given of it by the public crier in the market. Civil suits in both these kingdoms are almost as complicated as in Westminster Hall, and are as often artificially prolonged. There is no need of lawyers here. Every negro appears to be as subtle as an attorney in sharp practice, and as eloquent as a Q. C. What do you think of this, for example? A man has a fowl killed by another man's dog. After three years have elapsed he enters his indictment, suing not only for the fowl itself, but for the eggs which it would have laid, and for the chickens which it would have hatched in those three years.

Fetich is a generic term for the physical machinery of religion: the relics of the Catholic Church, the surplices of the Anglican, and the spiritual ebullitions of camp-meetings, would come under that denomination. The religion of Dahomey is essentially of a fetich character. They have their rites of circumcision and baptism; they venerate snakes, to whom they erect temples, where a harmless species is maintained; they have their priests and priestesses, but they have also the unknown, unseen God, whose name they seldom dare to mention, and of whose great attributes they speak not without fear and trembling. The worship of God in the absurd symbol of the lower animals I do not wish to defend, but it is all that these poor savages can do; and is not that less impious than to speak of the Deity with blasphemous familiarity as our illiterate preachers often do?

Dahomey is a despot, but, as with Ashantee, there are wheels within wheels, which direct his power, and chains, unseen but strong, which restrain. The people lick dirt before the nobles, and the nobles at a court levée, having cast off all their finery,

enter the king's presence on all-fours. There they wallow in
palatial dust, and only speak when they are spoken to. This,
done at public audiences, imposes upon visitors, and is devised
with a salutary purpose. The mob, seeing the men whom they
honor thus submissive before the sovereign, feel it little disgrace
to be slaves, and do not think of sedition. They have no demo-
cratic organs or pot-house Ciceros there to make them discontented without bettering their condition. In private, the nobility,
from slaves, become councilors; and it is in private that the real
business of the state is done.

Drunkenness is bad taste in England, but in Dahomey it is a
sin; and the late king kept a drunkard on rum, after the Spartan
principle, that his beastly appearance might deter the people from
this vice.

In republican Africa and in polished Europe adultery is a
venial offense, a simple matter of bullocks and sheep, or pounds,
shillings, and pence. Under this barbarous despot it is a crime,
which can only be expiated by life-long slavery or by sudden
death. In Ashantee the law is milder, and the vicious results I
have described.

Those whom we call "social evils" are here recognized as social
necessities. To counteract the only evil of polygamy (as far as
Africa is concerned), viz., the inability of the poorer people to
purchase wives, the government organizes a body of women, who
"ply their nefarious trade" on fixed days at a regulated price,
and who add to the royal revenue by paying a tax. This constitution is certainly indelicate; but indecorum, of all vices the
most censured in England, is among these miserable people no
vice at all, since it happens to be conducive to connubial virtue.

The River Volta alone separates the two great empires of
Africa, and which is the greater of the two? That has always
been a matter of argument.

I accede to Ashantee superior wealth and population, but I
think it stands to reason that Dahomey must prove victorious in
pitched battles. Both derive their power from the European
trade. The wealth of Ashantee lies in her gold mines, of Dahomey in her slaves. The Ashantees dig for their luxuries, the
Dahomans fight for them. The latter nation is in fact a miscellaneous banditti, for there are few pure Dahomans. Agriculture
and the arts are discouraged: the nation is an army, war is their
trade, men are their spoil. The constitution of Amazons does

not appear to me an extraordinary one. In Africa the sphere of
woman is slavery. Among the agricultural tribes she is made to
till the ground; among the pastoral, to tend the herds; in golden
Ashantee, to work at the mines; in fighting Dahomey, to join the
army.

She is also employed in diplomatic missions and in commercial enterprise. She is shepherd, agriculturist, warrior, trader,
embassadress, and sometimes queen. In this practical country
one meets with admirable illustrations of the axiom of Plato, in
the fifth book of his Republic, that, "So far as her nature is concerned, the woman is admissible to all pursuits as well as the
man."

Dahomey has become celebrated not only by its army of
Amazons, but by its *Siquiahi*, the watering-of-the-graves-of-the-
ancestors: the translation is Hibernian; for the graves are watered with blood, which is not water, although on such occasions
it flows as if it were.

A huge platform is erected in the centre of the market-place,
and is encircled by a parapet breast-high. On this platform are
tents, gorgeous umbrellas, banners, cloths, and all the insignia of
native wealth and power. There are heaps of cowries, and tobacco, and kegs of rum to distribute to the mob; the king's
wives, present at the ceremony, are as composed as Spanish ladies
at a bull-fight, as also are the victims themselves, with whose blood
the graves of the king's ancestors are to be watered.

Below there is a savage and naked mob.

When the presents with which the king indirectly pays his
warriors have been flung down and scrambled for, the victims,
with white caps on their heads and lashed down in small canoes,
are borne to the edge of the parapet, and the mob cry, "Feed us,
king! feed us, king, for we are hungry." They are then thrown
over, and are dispatched by the men beneath.

Descriptions of this revolting custom, as it is popularly called,
have from time to time reached England, and have excited a
strong feeling upon the subject. Missions have been dispatched
to this monarch in the hope of inducing him to abolish these barbarities. They have failed, and must always and inevitably fail,
as those who understand African constitutions will admit.

Human sacrifices are perpetrated by all the pagan nations of
Africa; the more powerful the nation, the grander the sacrifice.
It enters into the African religion as it entered into all the relig-

ions of antiquity. The Druids, the Egyptian priests, our great masters of the ancient world, tolerated human sacrifices. Even in the days of Themistocles three Grecian youths were sacrificed.

The Africans have sometimes their enlightened kings, as the old barbarians had their sages and their priests. But it is seldom in the power of the heads of a people to alter those customs which have been held sacred from time immemorial. The despots of Africa are ruled by laws more stern and ruthless than themselves. They are not allowed to eat or to drink in public; in some cases they may not even be seen, and therefore consent to the petitions of their subjects by protruding one of their feet from beneath a curtain. Were they to rebel they would be dethroned. Vox populi, vox diaboli. The mob of Dahomey are *man-eaters:* they have cannibal minds; they have been accustomed to feed on murder; were the king, whom we supplicate, to attempt compliance with our requests, the graves of his ancestors would be watered with his own blood.

CHAPTER IX.

THE KING OF OILS.

The Mouths of the Niger.—Discovered in the fifteenth Century.—Bonny River.—
Interview with Peppel.—Fernando Po: its Inhabitants.—A Gaboon Legend.

WHEN we left Lagos harbor we left behind us all signs and symptoms of civilization. I found that my fellow-passengers consisted entirely of men of a seafaring appearance, with bronzed faces, large freckled hands, a lust for Cognac, and large powers of conversation—on oil.

Day after day the same flat, unwholesome-looking shore; river after river opening before us as we passed—the many mouths by which the fatal Niger pours its dark waters into the sea.

Brown waves rolled round us, and with the land-breeze a fetid stench was blown toward us—the miasma of this Great Dismal Swamp. The tainted air, the gloomy view, the brutal company, disposed my mind to those reflections which the sight of those rivers alone might have awakened.

Africa has its martyrology. Here, indeed, our flags do but seem to wave over sepulchres. Here the history of the white man is an elegy.

The mouth of the Niger is now no longer a mystery of Africa; but it was one in which scores of brave men had been entombed before it was unriddled. Their graveless epitaphs are moss-grown now. Lander was buried in Fernando Po, but no one could show me where. Great travelers are creatures of the day, and can reap but little posthumous renown. Their light, though dazzling, is not creative. It is the reflection of a curiosity which must pass away. They bring new toys from Nature to us, the children of civilization. We worship them, play with them, yawn over them, break them, and forget them always.

It is a singular, and to me a very melancholy truth, that many lives were thrown away in this search for the Niger's mouth, from a lack of careful theoretical inquiry, or from that spirit of ignorant skepticism which is so stubbornly developed among the theorists of science.

It is well known that the Jesuits discovered and described the sources of the Blue Nile before Bruce was born; but most of my readers will, I think, be surprised to learn that the Portuguese settlers navigated the Niger in the sixteenth century by its mouth. I happened to meet with this passage in Villault de Bellefond: " We went up the Niger as far as Benin;" and found additional particulars in Des Marchais, which proved that the Bight of Benin, according to the testimony of the natives, received this eccentric river. Yet so little regard can have been paid to their testimony, that, when Reichard first broached that theory, it was unanimously ridiculed, till closer inquiries had proved its probability, and actual enterprise its truth.

On the 26th of January we entered Bonny, the wealthiest of these rivers of corruption. Here the traders do not dare to live ashore, but inhabit the large hulks of ancient merchantmen. A thatched roof above, with the lower deck arranged into chambers and store-rooms, convert them into floating houses, which often from houses become hospitals.

West Africa is essentially a land of oils; this is its real wealth; and the exports of ivory and gold are small in comparison. The commissions are large, in order to tempt these factors to brave a climate whose dangers they assist with their intemperance, and still more with their inanity.

The trade is active enough, but from its nature is attended with much delay. The Bonny natives go to market in the interior. The oil is brought to them little by little in calabashes. This they pour off into barrels. It is then brought on board one of the hulks, and is purchased with goods of European manufacture.

These black traders are now almost too much for the white ones in those matters of low cunning which enter so largely into commerce of a petty nature. The days have gone by when charcoaled powder and coraline could be passed off upon the simple natives with impunity. A little can still be done with false weights and measures, but the good old days are gone forever, and the natives have learned to turn the dirty tables upon those who could once cheat them as they chose. On the Gold Coast gold is adulterated with copper; on the Ivory Coast teeth are plugged with lead and heavy clay; here oil is so ingeniously mixed with sand that every drop must be boiled down before the factors dare send it home to their employers. None are so bitter as sharpers when they happen to be taken in, and none complain

so loudly of these "thieves and swindlers" as those who make
their living by them.

The owners, who are of course men of a very different stamp,
have formed an association for the mutual preservation of all
their interests, but the factors lose no opportunity of evading these
laws and cheating one another when they can.

Among the whites there is no real unity: nobody trusts his
neighbor. This gives the blacks a great advantage. Savages as
they may be, rivals as they are, they can at least combine with
that honesty which is always the best policy. If a negro, for instance, cheats a white man, the latter puts up with it. His brother members of the association would freely promise to refuse to
deal with the negro, but he knows very well that a canoe loaded
with palm-oil could not be resisted by one of them. On the other hand, if a white man flagrantly offends, the native traders
unite and "shut the trade" to him. A case of this kind happened not long ago in the Benin. They found that a certain trader
used a smaller cowrie-tub than the others: they also found that
while other salt-tubs had one stave across it, to make the salt fall
light and take up more space, his had two. A council was held:
the trade was shut; not a canoe came near him; and he was
forced to leave the river.

I went ashore with the doctor on a visit to Peppel, the famous
King of Bonny. The town itself is built on black mud, and the
broadest street was far more filthy than the filthiest slum in Westminster. The palace is composed of two or three hovels encircled
by a mud wall. In one of these was seated the monarch, and the
scene was well adapted to the muse of his poet-laureate. The
Africans have a taste for crockery-ware much resembling that of
the last generation for old china, and a predilection for dog-flesh,
which is bred expressly for the table, and exposed for sale in the
public markets. And there sat Peppel, who had lived so long in
England; behind him a pile of willow-pattern crockery, before
him a calabash of dog stew and palaver sauce. It is always thus
with these savages. The instincts inherited from their forefathers
will ever triumph over a sprinkling of foreign reason. Their intellects have a *rete mucosum* as well as their skins. As soon as
they return to their own country they take off all their civilization and their clothes, and let body and mind go naked.

Like most negroes of rank, Peppel has a yellow complexion as
light as that of a mulatto. His features express intelligence, but

of a low and cunning kind. In every word and look he exhibited that habit of suspicion which one finds in half-civilized natures.

The doctor, who was apparently an old friend, told him that I had just come out to Africa. Peppel asked eagerly if I was going to settle in Bonny. On my answering in the negative, he showed plainly enough that he was disappointed in not getting his *shake-hand dash*, as the propitiatory present of a new trader is called.

I then asked him whether he liked England or Bonny best. He gave me the Irishman's answer by asking which of the two I preferred. I replied enthusiastically, Bonny. But he only laughed incredulously, and remarked, wisely enough, that every man liked his own country best.

Here the doctor, who was a Glasgow man, and had not been bred a courtier, exclaimed,

" Why, Peppel, ye're grown just as fat as an old sow!"

The king pleaded deafness.

" Eh, mon!" repeated the doctor, earnestly, " ye're no deef; but ye're just as fat as a pig."

As Peppel still assured him that he could not hear a word, he did not repeat the compliment, but said that I had come out to shoot beasts. This was a little too strong for the polite Peppel. Nothing is more difficult for a negro to understand than the mania for slaying quadrupeds, which, from being periodical, becomes chronic in some European constitutions; and he became so taciturn and sulky that we found ourselves obliged to go.

Owing to some skillful representations which Peppel made while in England, and to the ignorance which prevails upon matters African, a farmer and a lady's maid, and some other misguided individuals, came out with the king in his yacht. The farmer soon found that it was not easy to cultivate black mud, upon which one could not walk without sinking up to the waist; the lady's maid made a plant upon Peppel, which provoked the jealousy of the queen, who is, moreover, so nearly related to him that she might cry like Juno, " Incedo regina, Jovisque et soror et conjux."

As for the people who were to receive royal salaries and apartments in the palace, they were presented each with a couple of yams, Peppel declaring that the state of his exchequer would admit of no larger disbursements.

Some people say that his income is more than £15,000 a year: it is at least certain that more wealth is possessed and less displayed by Bonny than by any other African power. At present Peppel is a merely nominal king; the real majesty lies in the hands of four regents. Under this temporary truce between king and nobles a fire is smouldering, say the traders, and that some day there will be fierce massacres in Bonny town. Peppel had formerly been dethroned because he had shot with his own hand one of his wives who had displeased him; he had murdered a chief named Manilla Peppel; and Dáppa, the king, had died so suddenly that it was thought he had been poisoned: there was then a civil war; three hundred of Peppel's men had blown themselves up with gunpowder, and these were the Curtii who had closed the gulf.

The "Armenian" lay in the river to load with the red palm-oil. A little steamer called the "Retriever" carried us on to Fernando Po.

The Peak of Fernando Po is 10,000 feet high, and is a more perfect cone than that of Teneriffe. It is wooded to the summit with fine timber, and renders Clarence Bay the most beautiful spot on the West Coast of Africa. This island is one of the state prisons of Spain; and a large guard-ship is at once the residence of the governor, who fears land, and of the prisoners, who covet it.

Fernando Po is inhabited by a very peculiar tribe, named properly the *Adiya*, but who are called by the English *Bubis*, from their mode of address—*Bubi* in their language meaning friend. These people are gentle, but have a marvelous hatred of civilization. The town of Clarence is composed entirely of Sierra Leone colonists, Kru-men, etc. The aborigines live in little huts in the forest.

I went to see one of their towns, called *Bannebar*, about three miles distant. There was a mission house there of Spanish Jesuits, who had apparently succeeded in making the natives wear something in the shape of clothing, for in the remoter parts of the island they leave nothing whatever to the imagination. With that exception they could scarcely have seemed more barbarous than they were. It was the first time that I had seen savages, and the spectacle was not encouraging. I did not see a woman who was not laboring under some disgusting disease of the skin. I am told that there is an ulcer here, of a phagedænic nature, which appears almost incurable, and which the bite of an insect or the abrasion of a cuticle is sufficient to cause. One gentleman on the island, who was bit by a musquito on the leg, had to suffer amputation! and yet there are medical men who have spoken of

CLARENCE, FERNANDO PO.

Fernando Po as a sanatorium, which it can only be when the mountain has been cleared and colonized.

The natives sometimes wear on the head a covering which is made like an osier basket, and is secured to their hair by skewers made of the small bone of the monkey's leg. The hair itself is adorned with ochre, which they form into small lumps, giving their heads the appearance of being covered with yellow pills. Round the left upper arm is bound a piece of string, in which the men carry a knife and the women a pipe. These women are hideous and chaste. When an infidelity is committed the male offender has his left hand cut off, and the stump plunged in burning oil; for the second offense he loses his right hand; for the third he suffers death. It is not known if the women are punished; but among savages generally (they know no better) it is the seducer who suffers, not the victim, as with us.

These Aníya present the same type as the mountaineers of the neighboring parts of the continent. I afterward heard a legend at the Gaboon which pretends to explain their migration and their nakedness.

The first man called all people to one place. His name was *Raychow.* "Hear this, my people," said he. "I am king in this river. I am going to give a name to every place." One day he came with his people to the Hole of Wonga-Wonga, which is a deep pit in the ground from which fire comes out at night. Men spoke to them from the Hole, but they could not see their forms. *Raychow* made his son descend into the Hole. The son of the King of the Hole appeared to him, and defied him to a contest of skill in throwing the spear. If he lost he would be killed. If he gained he would be restored in safety. He won. Then the son of the King of the Hole said, "You are fortunate in having conquered me, for I am a spirit. Ask for whatever you wish." The king's son demanded a remedy for every disease that he should name. The spirit gave him the medicines, and said when he had finished, "There is one sickness which you have forgotten. It is *kra-kra.* Of that you will die."

A tribe called *Ndiva*, which was then strong and numerous, but of whom four men alone remain, gave him a canoe and forty men to take him back to his father's town. When he saw his father he did not say a word. His father said, "My son, if you are hungry, eat." He did not answer. His father said, "Do you wish me to kill you a goat?" There was no reply. At last he said, "Do you want me to build you a fetich-house?" Then he answered "Yes." When the house was built, he stored up his

medicines there.   Then he said, "I go to make the Moondah enter the Orongo (Gaboon).   So he went and dug a canal, and by
the time that it was finished all his men had died.   Then he said
he would go and kill river-horses in the Benito.   He had killed
four, and as he was killing the fourth the people descended from
the mountains against him.   So he made his fetich on his great
war-spear, and he sang,

> My spear, go kill these people,
> Or these people me will kill.

The spear slew the army, and the remainder of the tribe migrated in terror to Fernando Po.   Then said their king, "None of
my people may wear cloth till we have conquered the Mpongwe."
And to this day the Búbis go stark naked, and entertain a savage
hatred against the natives of the Gaboon.

CHAPTER X.

COAST SOCIETY.

Unanimous Inebriety.—The Cognac Disease.—Sierra Leone Scandal.

Such are the scenes of the colonial coast through which I rapidly passed, and have as rapidly described. But, ere I introduce you to the savages of Equatorial Africa, I must give you some idea of Anglo-African existence.

In England inebriety no longer remains a fashion. The interval between the disappearance of the ladies and the announcement of coffee is becoming more and more brief as the age progresses. It is not impossible that we may see this barbarous custom pass away with rectors of the old school, and with port wines of '24.

Debauch was already diluted in England when in India it reigned triumphant. Our officers used to spend their leisure hours in smoking Manillas, sipping brandy-pawnee, and scratching their musquito-bites. But Bass and Allsopp, those benefactors of the human race, created a revolution in the history of drink. The vicious maddening brandy gave way to the genial bitter beer. Field-sports took the place of the saltatory exhibitions of the nautch girls. Healthy vigor succeeded drunken inanition.

There is still one corner of the globe where the "good old fashions" prevail, and where it is considered in bad taste to be temperate. During the first day which I spent in Africa I saw something in the way of deglutition which made me open my English eyes. I was introduced into a great many different houses, and in each a black servant, apparently without orders, but as a simple matter of course, brought us something to drink. In one house it would be Champagne, in another it would be Hollands out of a stone bottle, in a third it would be old Jamaica rum. A day divided into sips would be wound up with an evening which made me agree with a late Governor of the Gambia, "That Africa must be the healthiest place in the world, for that men could nowhere else drink in such a manner."

The first sight which had attracted my attention when I landed at Bathurst was the number of black policemen who strutted about, their staves in their hands, with airs of inexpressible pomposity. As they never told any one to move on, and as cooks in Africa are masculine, I was at a loss to understand for what purpose they had been organized. But it was explained to me. When officers are drunk they ride home on the backs of constables. How touching are these provisions of Nature! In winter a moss grows on the rocks of Lapland for the sustenance of the reindeer. In the dreary depths of the Sahara the traveler finds green oases and sparkling springs. So in this barbarous land, where there are neither cabs nor wheelbarrows, Providence has furnished policemen.

Drink is an institution of Anglo-Western Africa, cold brandy and water the national beverage. A man is estimated by the proportion of water which he mingles with his spirit. Moderate men are milk-sops; abstinent ones are pariahs; for here, without drink there can be no union.

When one sits down to table with Anglo-Africans, one observes now and then their faces twitch spasmodically as if they had received an electric shock. These facial contortions are the relics of intermittent fever. At the same time you become aware that a grosser disease is present among your companions. One of them will attempt to catch a spectral fly which day and night is flitting before him; another directs your attention to a swarm of bees in a corner of the ceiling; and a third whistles to a black dog which no one can see except himself.

That which would be very amusing were it not so sad, is the assurance with which some cadaverous ensign informs fresh-comers that it is impossible to live in that climate without brandy and water. His bloodshot eyes, his trembling hand, his deadened appetite, bely his words; but still he drinks on. He must follow the general example. Here all prostrate themselves before the shrine of Bacchus; not the young laughing god, with garlands on his rosy brow and smiling nymphs upon his knee, but a naked, solitary, wasted wretch, without beauty and without disguise; with filmy eyes, and hollow cheeks, and fetid breath; a ghost of health, intellect, refinement, departed never to return.

Brandy and water is certainly the most prevalent and fatal cause of disease on the West Coast of Africa. "Died of brandy and water" is a common phrase. It is the inevitable consequence of a life deprived of the influence of ladies, of books, and of athletic sports. Drunkenness is the ulcer of inanition.

That which astonished me very much at first was the absence of all mental culture in these colonies. Nobody speaks of new books, or of any thing higher than local gossip or routine. Sometimes one meets with vestiges of intellect worn and wasted away in this atmosphere of the vitiated and the gross. Happily I know exceptions to this rule as to all others; but there are few residents who can resist the influences of climate and company, which not only enervate the body, but degrade the mind.

At Sierra Leone there once existed, it is true, some semblance of society, as we understand the word in Europe. There were occasionally balls, to which women went to talk scandal and men to drink Champagne.

There were also tea-parties, at which the ladies assembled to play at loo, and where large sums of money were lost and never paid, from which many enmities resulted. There were also prayer-meetings, where they criticised each other's consciences. In fact, scandal, gambling, and false devotion—the three cardinal passions of ladies of a certain age—were carried to such extremes, that the whole coterie dissolved; and, as far as I could learn when I was there, no visits at all were interchanged.

E

CHAPTER XI.

THE TRIBE OF COMMERCIAL TRAVELERS.

I enter the Gaboon.—Take a House.—Tornado v. Fever.—Baraka Mission.—My Steward Mongilomba. —Gaboon Commerce. —The Gorilla Palaver. —Tropical Rain.

I WAS disappointed of an interview with Richard Burton, who was up the Cameroons, a volcanic mountain as high as the Peak of Teneriffe. However, during the few days which I spent at Fernando Po, I was located at his house, and had at my disposal a library of which the profound and varied nature was an index to that great mind.

I obtained a passage on board the "Minerva," a vessel bound for the Gaboon. On the morning of my departure I felt a slight pain in my forehead; I had no appetite for breakfast; I was gid-dy and languid. These were the incipient symptoms of malari-ous fever, which I had contracted somewhere on the coast, and which had been incubating in my system. I got on board the "Minerva," and laid myself under many blankets. But perspira-tion would not come, though my hands felt as if I were holding them before a furnace. Then I took some warm drink, and im-mediately dissolved. I was very weak after this, and could not touch meat for some days; but a mild cathartic, followed by grad-ual doses of quinine, restored me to perfect health, and I saw that the ordinary fever-fit is little worse than an English cold—a stu-pefying nuisance, that is all.

The "Minerva" touched at the Malimba River, a little to the south of the Cameroons, and at Botanga. The latter is the lar-gest ivory mart of Equatorial Africa. Its little river falls into the sea, a large and noisy cataract, and the Elephant Mountain, which Burton has since ascended and described, rears its huge back at no great distance from the sea.

On the fourteenth day of our voyage the sea-breeze bore us up a river which, with its strong salt tides and sluggish stream, re-sembled an arm of the sea. This was the Gaboon.

On the right-hand bank I soon discovered the fort and comp-

toirs of the French ; a little farther up a village of English factories; and behind these, perched on a green hill, the houses, school,
and church of an American mission.

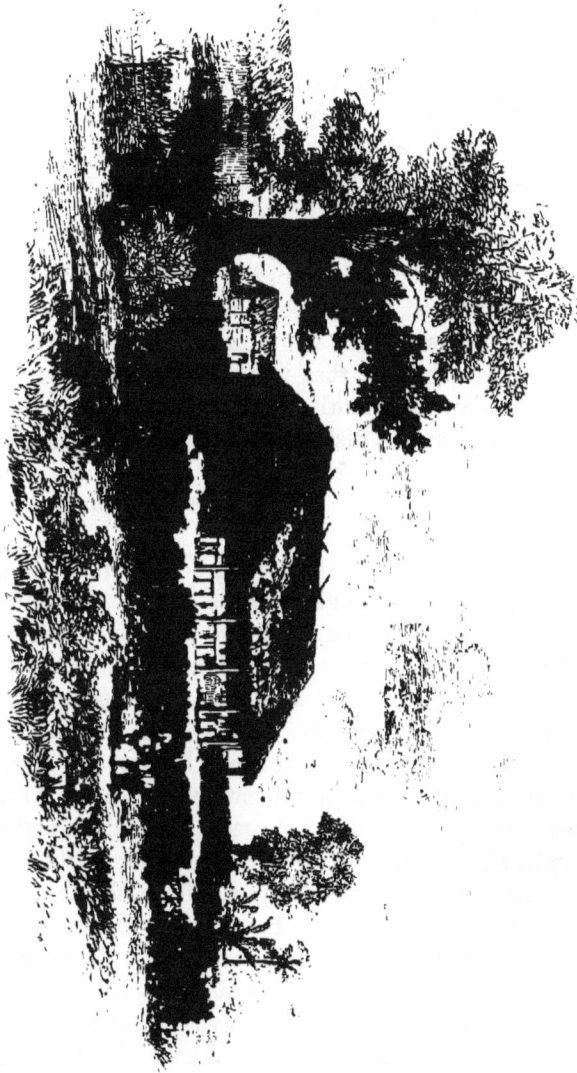

HOUSE AT GABOON—RESIDENCE OF THE AMERICAN MISSIONARY.

On the left bank, concealed within a creek, lies the town of
King William, or Roi Denis, the bamboo metropolis of Gaboon.
As soon as I had landed I made inquiries about a house, and

the next day I was shown one. It was built upon piles—a con-sideration of some importance where the soil exhales disease. It possessed three rooms, all of which had a "deck" or planked floor, and throughout which a sofa, a chest of drawers, a table, and two chairs were tastefully distributed.

In the smallest room of the three I found the black proprietor, shivering under fever, and surrounded by his wives. He offered me a hot hand, and his house at a price which was hotter still. He wanted for that barbarous dwelling forty dollars a month. I tendered six, and quitted him, to all appearance an insulted man.

I was receiving temporary board and lodging in one of the En-glish factories. Two or three days after the gentleman appeared and made me an elaborate apology. When I had called on him he had fever; he had talked foolishness; he did not know what he had said. I was a great white man; he was only a poor ne-, gro; I wanted his house; that was enough; he must give it me —at twelve dollars the month.

This proposal was not disinterested, but it was reasonable; his first had been absurd. *In febre veritas.* It would seem that fever, like drunkenness, exposes a man's vices, caricatures his foibles, and extinguishes his virtues.

The next morning, as I was writing before breakfast, the lines began suddenly to intermingle, and the opposite wall made me a profound salutation. At the same time my head felt as if it were a clock being violently wound up. This was a return of the fe-ver which had attacked me at Fernando Po. I conquered a great inclination to lie down, and moved my baggage into the house, which occupied me till the afternoon. During the whole time I had been compelled to watch my property like an Argus. Be-sides Smoke-jack, Dry Toast, Cockroach, Pot o' Beer, and Florence Nightingale, all of whom were tolerably accomplished thieves, I received visits from several villagers, who broke the tenth com-mandment every time that they looked at their neighbor's goods. Against these the manners of the country forbade me to shut my doors; but at that moment I looked back on "The Swan," in Swan Street, Shoreditch, and other tavern haunts of thievery, as temples of honesty in comparison. When all was brought into one room and piled round me, I laid down on the sofa. Some graceful young men entered playing on musical instruments. My landlord's head wife, when she saw that I had fever, brought me a cup of tea.

Night came at last; my cork bed was spread on the floor; upon it a rug and the sofa pillow; a lantern and a cup of water by the side. My Kru-man bade me good-night and left me.

I was dropping off to sleep, when I heard a low, sighing sound, which gradually swelled into a roar, mingled with the shouts of the villagers as they ran to their houses. It was a tornado. The sea dashed fiercely against the rocks under my window. Presently I felt rain upon my face, and, looking up, saw that some of the thatch had been blown away. In a short time I became an islet in a small lake of rain-water. I took up my bed and ran, looking for a dry plank, which I at length discovered in one of the other rooms.

When I awoke in the morning I found that the fever had made its exit, as often happens when the system receives a shock. The Lincolnshire fenners, when seized with ague, jump immediately into the water. Here it was the water which had descended upon me.

While I was at breakfast I was informed that Captain Walker, of Barrack, wished to see me. I wondered who this military visitor could be, and found that it was the Rev. Mr. Walker, of Baraka. Captain, it seems, is a title which Kru-men bestow upon all white men of position.

Mr. Walker came to renew an invitation, which I had already declined, that I should take up my abode with him.

"You are not very comfortable here," he said, smiling.

I was about to assure him that I was extremely comfortable there, when I happened to look round me, and saw myself enthroned in a chaos of saddles, gun-cases, carpenter's tools, cooking utensils, tents, and the fragments of a cast-iron stove. I understood, for the first time, the blessings of those who have nothing. Anxiety is one's property-tax in the wilderness. I said I was afraid that I should inconvenience him—one always does say these things.

"On the contrary," he answered; "as you have not been in a hot country before, you will be sure to have a bad fever, and it will be more convenient for me to attend you in my own house than here."

Who could refuse a favor offered in so simple and delicate a manner? From that day my house was doomed to hold lumber, and I was shown by Mr. Walker into a chamber from which I could see twenty miles of blue river, and trees shadowy in the dis-

tance. There was a little table covered with a white cover for
my books, a chest of drawers for my clothes, and a bed draped
with musquito curtains of snowy gauze.

Here I led a pure and frugal life, of which the memory remains,
though the reality is not likely to return. To those at Baraka
and Corisco who gave me their experiences and their examples, I
owe my health, and not improbably my life; for if one wishes to
preserve these in Africa, one must give Epicurus the cold shoulder
and enter the school of the Stoics.

I was in search of an interpreter, when one day a very plain
negro accosted me. His name was Mongilomba. A short conversation proved to me that he was intelligent, and I engaged
him as my steward, or head man. In the afternoon he came to
me, and said that his "brother" wished me to write him out an
agreement. I did so. The next morning he returned, and said
that his "brother" wished me to insert the date. At the same
time this individual presented himself. He was a young man of
stern appearance, and who scanned the paper, when dated, with a
legal eye. In fact, as I afterward found out, he was no relative
of Mongilomba, but, having had documentary experiences, had
acted as family solicitor in the affair.

Mongilomba was fat and youthful. His skin was bronze-color,
pleasantly mottled with black spots; for the coloring matter is
sometimes laid on by Nature with eccentricity. Like many men
of talent, he was indolent, but a good story-teller, an able orni-
thologist, and a superb politician. It was said of Pericles that
even when thrown in the arena he would yet argue so cunningly
as to persuade his conqueror that he himself had been victorious.
So, when Mongilomba lost my best scalpel, he proved to me that
it had slipped from his hand in such a manner that no one in his
place could possibly have observed the loss. Again, when once
I had directed him to dry a pair of stockings by the fire, and he
had brought me them back in a state of ashes, he demonstrated
that fire is a fickle and devouring element, whose ravages the
wisest men are unable at all times to anticipate.

When, enraged by some negligence of this Ethiopian philosopher, I assailed him with words, his face would remain imperturb-
able, and he would return me those soft answers which do not
turn away wrath. If, on the other hand, he saw that I was not
quite sure of my ground, he would indulge in majestic soliloquies
in Mpongwe, and treat my insinuations with supreme contempt.

For that matter, he was always a little haughty, and only shook hands with me in the morning when he woke in a good humor.

Under Mongilomba's patronage, I mingled with the Mpongwes of Gaboon, observing their manners, and sometimes making them tell me their traditions.

They are the most refined tribe of Equatorial Africa, their languages possessing the softness and melody of Tuscan. Their women are graceful and good-looking. These are perfect coquettes in the arrangement of their hair and person. They paint themselves with a rouge obtained from the root of the camwood-tree, and with white chalk, which contrasts with their black skin to advantage. They go almost naked; but the color removes all idea of indecency, except, perhaps, in prudish and unchaste minds. Their skin, soft and glossy as rich black velvet, is their chief beauty, as it is that of a thorough-bred horse or hound. It is true that the bust, with other women the chief charm, is in them the sole disfigurement, except in very young girls. Even these strive to emulate the pendent beauties of their seniors; for in savage, as well as in civilized countries, the deformities of age or vice can be rendered fashionable.

Their head-dress is their glory; and in shaving their hair, as they do when mourning, they make a greater sacrifice than our English widows, who in such cases merely change their costume from Madame Elise to Mrs. Jay. With regard to the dressing of the hair, there is not much to distinguish between the two; for the belles of the Gaboon ridge their hair over frisettes to make it appear abundant, and, forming it into fantastic shapes—usually that of a Roman casque—plaster it down with palm-oil, the basis of many Bond Street pomades. They also wear artificial hair in rosettes over the ears, and use for hair-powder the scrapings of a fragrant bark. The tout ensemble is completed with a prettily-carved hair-pin of ivory or ebony. Round their necks are strings of different colored beads "tastefully arranged" by themselves; but on their calves and ankles are huge brass rings, made out of those rods which are used for staircases. It is a practice which I can not defend, for it gives them an ungainly gait; and I have heard that if they happen to fall into the water, these encumbrances prevent them from coming up again. The practice, I fancy, must have been invented by a married man who did not wish his wife to go abroad; the origin, they say, of that fashion

which obliged the women of ancient Egypt to walk with bare
feet, and the Chinese with crippled ones.

MPONGWE GIRL.

The Mpongwe masculine are a little touched with dandyism;
they love to walk with an old umbrella-stick, and to hear their
cloth trailing behind them on the ground.   But they are men of
business, and all speak English more or less.   Excepting a few
country dignitaries, their aristocracy is composed of white men's
stewards, agents, and interpreters; for wealth is their touchstone
of nobility.

They are polite, shrewd, close observers of character, indolent
of body, keen of brain, dishonest on a large scale; they disdain to
pilfer, preferring to swindle in a business-like manner; they possess the art of skillful evasion, and "fides quam Punica," a perfidy
more than legal.

I will give the best instance that occurs to me.   Krinji was the
salaried pilot and interpreter of the local government.   He could
speak Dikělě, Shekani, and Panwe or Fanh, the three dialects of
the interior, as well as French, English, Spanish, and Portuguese.
But when a negro is talented, white men suffer.   A new commandant having arrived in the Gaboon, he made the usual com-

MPONGWE MAN.

plimentary visit to King George, a powerful chieftain across the water, one of whose subjects had run away with Krinji's wife. Preparations having been made for a big palaver, the following conversation ensued in full native council.

Commandant. King George, the king of my country has sent me to take care of this river. I have come to bid you good-day. I hope that we shall be friends.

Krinji (interpreting). King George, the commandant says he has heard that one of your people has taken away my wife. He says that you must send her back directly.

King George. Your wife is nothing to me. Tell the commandant I can not trouble myself about a little palaver like that.

Krinji. King says he is very much pleased to see a great white man like you. He would like very much to be your friend.

Commandant. Tell the king I am very much pleased to hear

those words. If he takes care of the French so that they have good trade, I will take care that he does not remain unrewarded. It is only by promoting peace and concord that our mutual interests will be benefited.

King George. What does he say?

Krinji. He says strong words. He says, Are you blind, that you do not see the men he has brought here with guns and swords? If you do not bring my wife very quickly here, he will make all your people dust, and your town ashes.

King George (to his men). Go out and get your guns. If there is trouble, kill Krinji first, but do not hurt the great white man.

Commandant. What are they all running out for?

Krinji. The king has told them to kill a sheep for your dinner. They run quickly because they love you.

Commandant. Oh, tell the king if I stop to dinner I shall lose the tide. I must go now.

Krinji. Well, King George, I ask the white man not to be angry about my palaver. You are my friend, and I do not wish to see you dead. So he says that he will go now, but if you do not send my wife in three days, he will bring a ship with big guns to burn your town.

The commandant, on hearing afterward how he had been tricked, was too much amused to be angry; but matters became more serious when Krinji, piloting a man-of-war, ran her aground, that he might have opportunities of plunder. A warrant was issued against him; he disappeared, and probably victimized the human race in some other quarter of the coast.

The trade of this part of Africa is conducted on very primitive principles. A factory in the Gaboon is not a mammoth building, which vomits endless smoke and resounds with perpetual machinery. It is a ground-floor house built of a kind of palm, vulgarly called bamboo. There is a spacious piazza floored with deal, where the factor and his subordinates take their meals. On the left hand a door leads to the kitchen; on the right hand, to the parlor and a bedroom or two; in the centre is the store. Here you may see bales of Manchester cloth, American tobacco in leaf, barrels of coarse powder, casks of Coast o' Guinea rum, and Birmingham trade-guns, long as the ancient matchlocks, their stocks painted in a bright red.

At six o'clock the storekeeper opens the establishment, and natives throng in to make small purchases in beads, brass rods, crockery-ware, and rum.   The clerk sits down to his accounts; the factor examines the books, or writes letters to his employers, or superintends the stalwart Kru-men as they roll casks up the beach through the surf.

Then canoes come sailing down the river with the land-breeze, bringing their petty cargoes of country produce.   Others are being filled with European goods, and await the changes of wind to carry trade into the interior.

This is done in Gaboon, and in most parts of the coast, upon the celebrated Trust system.   The negroes of the sea-board reserve the monopoly of trade between the Bushmen and the whites. It would be almost as difficult for a native of the interior to sell an article to a European as it would be for an author to bring out a book without the aid of a publisher.

Now, as the Mpongwe are seldom rich enough to buy the goods, and as the terms of the Bushmen are for cash payments only, the traders are compelled to *trust* the Mpongwe with a quantity of cloth, tobacco, rum, and muskets, and to send them into the interior.   The Mpongwe will then take up his residence in a bush-village, the chief of which will provide him with a house, with food, and with a wife.   The Bushmen go into the forest, cut up ebony and redwood into billets, collect bees'-wax, and, bleeding a vine of the *ficus* order, dry the milk into cakes of an inferior caoutchouc.   The natives of other villages are sometimes allowed to bring their contributions; while elephants' tusks, which have descended from the interior, bought and rebought from hand to hand, come at length into the possession of the Mpongwe.

When he has bartered away all his goods, he loads his canoe, returns to his factory, and receives a large commission, which is also paid in goods; for specie is not current in Africa-on-the-Line.

Careful and pinching traders as these Mpongwe are, they soon squander away the treasures they have earned.   Every man is besieged on his return by a crowd of hostile friends, who only leave him when his wealth has been dissolved in rum.   There are many excellent business men, who in private life are weak, vain, extravagant, and who seem to leave their brains behind them in their offices.   Such are the Mpongwe, or tribe of commercial travelers—men who prey upon ignorance in the bush, and are devoured by flattery in the town.

Sometimes these rum-revels precede the trade, and all the trust

is spent before a stick of ebony is bought. Then the white man
loses. Bad debts, Mr. Snip, extend beyond the limits of great
cities.

As the interior of Africa becomes better colonized, a direct
trade will be established, and this middle-man, broker-system destroyed. It is not without art that it has been so long preserved.

The Mpongwe used to carry fabulous accounts of the white
man among the Bush tribes. He was said to be a creature of un-
tamable ferocity, from whom their lives were always in danger;
and who was, moreover, an eater of men, buying slaves to cook
them beyond the seas.

The Bush tribes of the Gaboon have by this time seen enough
of white men to know such tales to be false; and occasionally an
enterprising man attempts to defraud the customs. I will give an
instance.

One day Mongilomba came and told me that there was a fresh-
killed gorilla for sale. I went down to the beach, and saw it lying in a small canoe which it almost filled. It was a male, and a
very large one. The preserved specimen can give you no idea
of what this animal really is, with its skin yet unshriveled and
the blood scarce dry upon its wounds. The hideousness of its
face, the grand breadth of its breast, its massive arms, and, above
all, its hands, like those of a human giant, impressed me with emotions which I had not expected to feel. But nothing is perfect.

YOUNG GORILLA (after Du Chaillu).

The huge trunk dwindled into a pair of legs, thin, bent, shriveled,
and decrepit as those of an old man.

My admiration was so transparent that the proprietor demand- ed ten dollars—a small price for the *Troglodytes prodigiosus* accord- ing to English views; a large one according to those of the She- kani.   Having paid him in cloth, tobacco, and powder according to his liking, I took possession of the ape, which I intrusted to the custody of Mongilomba.

A few hours afterward I saw three old men leaving the mission house; as soon as I saw Mr. Walker, he informed me that there was a palaver about my *njina*, and advised me to go down and see about it.   A negro argument is vocally equal to an Irish fair. When, on approaching the spot, I heard a hubbub which nothing short of fair fighting would have raised in Tipperary, I ran there as quickly as I could.

The gorilla was hanging from the branch of a tree, half skin- ned.   Mongilomba was being pulled by one party away from the tree, and being pushed by another party toward it.   Public opin- ion is never unanimous.   At last, one man pulling him or push- ing him a little too hard, he hit out in a style which was really creditable in a negro—above all, the gentle Mongilomba.   I re- covered from my surprise sufficiently to knock up a bit of a ring. My man was already "peeled."   Not even his hair was in his way.   Having just lost a brother, he had shaved his head (a pro- ceeding very unjust toward an innocent population), and had re- tired into dark mourning—*costume de paradis*.

They went at it, and Mongilomba had planted one facer with great success, when less chivalrous by-standers interfered.   Two slaves who had no concern in the matter drew knives upon each other; and I, walking up to the three old men, clearly the insti- gators of the row, requested to know what it was all about.   They replied that the man from whom I had bought the *njina* was a Shekani, and that he had no right to sell it to me, the same being an infringement of laws and customs immemorial.   I explained to them in return that, though their laws forbade the Shekani to sell, the laws of the white man allowed me to buy, and that if in a very few minutes the crowd was not dispersed, I should have to walk them, the three patriarchs, up to the French commandant's. This had the desired effect, and peace was restored; but I am fearful that the Shekani was not allowed to take all his goods back to his own village.

After I had spent a few days in Glass Town, I resolved to make a trial-trip into the interior, to learn if gorillas were plentiful in the region of the Gaboon; to obtain information respecting their habits from the true ape-hunters, who inhabit the bush villages only; and to find out what preparations I should require to make for a longer incursion.

I returned in six days, having spent that period among the Shekanis, about fifty miles S.E. from Baraka, by river and creek navigation. I had slept among savages; I had felt the silence of the virgin forest; I had seen the tracks of gorillas; and I had culled good material. On the other hand, all my dreams of shoot-ing were dispelled; I had discovered that it was not a game country.*

I now made preparations for a visit to Corisco, and announced, this project to my Kru-men. During my little trip they had been models of obedience, for in the bush I was their only friend; they were completely in my power, and, so far from wishing to desert me, they were in constant fear lest I should be offended and leave them among the natives, who would promptly have made them slaves.

But they detested this life, for them so monotonous, and in which they were obliged to suffer privations. Kru-men will work like oxen and under a burning sun; but they must have their regular meals, plenty of companions, and, after their day's work is done, their own dirty hovel, where they can sing the songs of their country in a strange land.

Now they were on civilized *terra-firma*, so the next morning Smoke-jack, Dry Toast, Cockroach, Pot-o'-Beer, and Florence Nightingale presented themselves before me in grave procession.

"What is the matter, Smoke-jack?" said I; for Smoke-jack was the representative of his people.

Smoke-jack picked up a piece of wood with his toes, looked at it with a perplexed air, and threw it away. I repeated the ques-tion.

"Mass'r! we go for bush with you. Paddle plenty. Musquito bite we too much. We no catch good chops (get good living) there. S'pose Kru-man no chop fine, he no fit work fine."

"Well?"

---

* I had forgotten to say that a Mr. Leveson, known in the sporting world as the Old Shekarry, offered me his company shortly before I left England, and came with me as far as the Gaboon. On my arrival I preferred to travel alone (as a man should always do when he means hard work), and he having at this same time made an incursion of eight days without seeing gorillas, returned to North Guinea, and afterward to England.

Smoke-jack (gathering courage). "Now you won't catch Corisco! (With scorn), Corisco no place at all! No factory lib there.
No Kru-boy lib there. Bush nigger lib, that all. Gaboon fine
place. I like to sit down here long time, for true; but Corisco
no place at all."

I went to Corisco without them, and paid them wages for doing nothing. This was a fatal error. They became idle and discontented; insinuated that I had no more worldly substance than
a missionary man; and demanded that I should send them back
to "we country" forthwith. This I naturally felt disinclined to
do; so paid them their dues, and procured them a better master.

Argal, ye who take Kru-men, treat them with severe kindness;
see that they be well fed; if ye have no work for them, set them
to rub the rust off your cables; and, above all, be careful to preserve that distance which Providence has been pleased to place
between you.

The *middle-dry*, as is called that changeable season between the
heavy rains of November and March, had passed; and I remember well my first genuine equatorial shower—for tornadoes are
exceptional phenomena.

There was a monstrous spider in my room the night before.
At 10 A.M. every thing became dark, and the wind whistled coldly through the trees. First it pattered, then it poured straight as
a line, and with the violence of a Malvern douche. The native
girls shrugged their bare shoulders as they put out their buckets
and tubs. As for me, looking at the dingy clouds, the drenched
landscape, and the rain-drops dancing in their own puddles, a hollow tooth beginning to ache, and a chill running down my back
like an iced snake, I almost believed that I was once more in dear
old England.

CHAPTER XII.

THE LAND OF HUNGER.

Corisco.—The Bapuku Bush.—River Life.—Net-hunting.—Captain taken Prisoner.
—The Muni Country.—Starvation Body and Mind.—Episode of Civilization.—
Turtle-spearing by Moonlight.

EVEN in this luxuriant land Corisco is distinguished by its
beauty. It is a little world in miniature, with its miniature forests, miniature prairies, miniature mountains, miniature rivers,
miniature lakes, and miniature precipices on the sea-shore.

Its sandy beach would afford the conchologist a good harvest
of sea-shells; and a dredge, having never yet been used, might
bring up treasures from the sea for science. There are seven species of land-shells on this island, which is not volcanic, and which
bears evidence of having been immersed beneath the sea. Its
formation is sandstone; and of islands which have springs of fresh
water, it is said to be the nearest to a continent—a distance of
ten miles. From its soil spring no less than fifteen varieties of
the banana. Its flora is varied and abundant; and the *Elais Guine-
ensis* is plentiful enough to supply the natives with all the palm-
oil they require for their food and their toilette.

This little island abounds with birds, many of which migrate at
certain seasons to the main land. The parrots, for example, are
found there only in the dry season—there are other birds which
frequent it only in the rains. In the string of ponds or small
lakes in the centre of the island is a species of alligator which bur-
rows in the dry season, and may then be dug out of the ground
in a torpid state. Tortoises and snails hibernate in a similar manner. The snail during this period covers the mouth of his shell
with a kind of filament, as may be proved by keeping one in a
drawer for any length of time. It has also the power of mending
its own shell when broken; for I have seen a shell which had been
cracked, and by some means glued together, probably by that secretion from the loose skin or "mantle" which forms the shell
itself.

Corisco Bay possesses a hundred species of fish which the natives are in the habit of taking, and to which they have given names. In the ponds, too, is a small black fish, which is, I believe, unknown to ichthyologists. It is caught in the dry season (June, July, and August), and the natives take care that it is not rendered extinct by "preserving" half the water.

I passed a week in this beautiful place, where I met not only with pleasing scenes, but with very kind friends. Had I come to Africa for pleasure I should have staid there longer. But the continent looked me every day in the face, and a self-imposed duty drove the *Heautontirumenos* away.

An English barque was lying off Bapuku, a little river about thirty miles north of the Muni. Her carpenter had been sent to Corisco for provisions, and offered me a passage, which I was very glad to accept.

It was the object of my voyage to remain a month or so among the Bapuku tribe, who were savages of a low order, that I might study man in a debased state, and also to find whether the gorilla was found so far north.

We started on the 18th of March at midday, when the wind begins, or ought to begin to blow. On this occasion it was behind its time, and we laid, as I have laid many a time, in that terrible bay, a white-hot unclouded sun above, a calm, implacable sea below.

Sometimes there is no sea-breeze, and this day had all the appearance of a dead calm. The Kru-men were ordered to the oars, and languidly dipped them into the sullen deep. Others stood up, shading their eyes, and trying to see the first ripple on the brink of the horizon. Presently one of them turned the wetted palm of his hand seaward. *Wind come!* he cried. In a moment the oars were shipped and the sail set, which, at first flapping dubiously against the mast, then coyly expanding, received the breeze in its white swelling bosom, and bore us along to the music of the waters bubbling from the bow.

The Kru-men began to make straw hats and to mend their shirts, which they held between their toes, while they worked away with plantain-fibre and perforated fish-bone for needle and thread.

Butterflies were flying about in the middle of the bay—alighting on the water, they would spread out their wings, and lie there for a moment kissing the sea.

Sometimes their fragile corpses floating by showed that this

F

was not always done with impunity; and one of these insects perching exhausted upon the shoulder of a Benga, he shook it off in a great fright, declaring that it was bad fetich.

Many of our butterflies are to be seen in West Africa, especially the common cabbage, the saffron, and the blue heath species. But their ways are not as the ways of butterflies in England. I have seen swarms of butterflies flying over the tops of the highest trees, and the flight, which must have been a migration, lasting a considerable time. I have seen them perched upon snake-dung by half-dozens, possibly engaged in extracting those medicinal virtues which Dr. John Hastings asserts to be contained in the excrements of serpents. But most remarkable of all is the fact, that in the heart of the virgin forest, where flowers are never found, where the song of a bird is seldom heard, where a single sun-ray can scarcely penetrate, I have repeatedly observed a large blue butterfly, the most beautiful which I have seen in Africa, and which I never met with in a purer atmosphere.

The breeze was continuous, but not fresh enough for the ship's long-boat, which had been built for heavy seas. At sunset no ship was visible, and the carpenter became alarmed. The barque, he told me, was lying close under the shore in a small bay, so that the trees shut out the light from her. There was no moon, and he feared that we should miss her. "The second mate had passed her one black night a matter of five miles, and was never the same man a'terward. Dead? yes, *he* was dead, and most on 'em there as wasn't dead was dying."

The sun set red and angrily. The clouds began to rise heavily overland. One of them took the shape of a hand, black, sinister, and gigantic as that of a demon, the thumb and fingers perfectly formed, and pointing upward. The men showed it to one another, but did not speak.

With the shades of descending night the carpenter grew gloomier still. When the last red beam vanished, and the western sky changed rapidly to lurid yellow, and from yellow to the dull ashy gray of early night, he looked upon himself as a doomed man. The second mate, he told me, in utter oblivion of his first version, had gone one stormy night ten miles beyond the ship, and had died the next morning as soon as he came on board.

As the spring rains were now at their height, and as a proportion of $\frac{5}{7}$ falls by night, I was disgusted, but not surprised, to see a flash of lightning over the trees. The carpenter put on an old-fashioned oil-skin and I a pocket mackintosh, weight 12 oz. The former, however, best resisted the onslaught of the skies, which can be no more compared with an English shower than the falls of Niagara with a Scotch cascade.

The rain was as thick as a mist, and, as it turned out, the captain had hoisted no mast-head light. Without the lightning we certainly should not have found the ship that night, especially as the carpenter was so afraid of our passing her that at first he would not let us approach her at all.

But when a happy gleam showed us the naked masts in the distance, the men gave a cry of delight, and pulled together with a will. Soon we glided under the dark sides; the ladder fell clattering; and a lantern, held by a sailor, poured its yellow light upon us.

The carpenter took me down into the cabin, and introduced me to a man who was lying in his shirt and trowsers on the after-lockers, which probably he found cooler than his cot. A Malay steward, with a villainous expression of countenance, placed before me a piece of salt junk, some ship's bread, and a bottle of beer. Having made a good supper, I was shown into a comfortable bunk.

The next morning I examined the barque with curiosity, for a Coast trader has her singularities. The decks fore and aft were covered with awnings, from which were hung pumpkins, bunches of plantains, specimens of a bladder-fish, and other curiosities. Cages ingeniously made of rope, or of old soap-boxes, with rusty bars of hoop-iron, were filled with gray parrots, which, screaming incessantly, reminded me of the Pantheon bazar. A small dove-cote was nailed against the main-mast, from which the pigeons made short and timorous flights. A tame rabbit was running about on the poop, licking the planks, and sometimes visiting the steward's pantry below in quest of more substantial nourishment. In the hold there was a poor show of ebony billets, and the ship was high out of water—a sign that she had taken in but little cargo.

On the forecastle head were four sickly wretches, two of them playing at draughts with men made out of a shark's back-bone; one of them fondling a green monkey; the last sitting with head on his yellow hand, and his eyes fixed on that sea which afterward became his grave.

I rented that day a house in the village, and having staid there

two days, hired a canoe, and, attended by Mongilomba and two
Bapuku guides, ascended the river.

During the whole of the first day the banks were screened by
the mangroves which sprang from beds of soft black mud—res-
ervoirs of disease—exhaling by day a fetid stench, by night a fatal vapor.

But the mangrove foliage has a beauty even in its sameness,
and possesses more life than the forest, always desolate and dark.
Kingfishers of a fabulous brilliance, which dies with the bird,
may be seen perched among the maze of branches, from whose
green recesses comes many a sweet sound. And beneath us,
from the water-depths, arose the insect-like hum of the musical
fish.

The quantity of tannin which mangrove bark contains, and its
stubborn resistance of decay, when cut, will yet give it commercial importance; and some day it may supersede palm-oil, as palm-
oil in Upper Guinea has superseded slaves.

When we had passed the salt tides, the mangroves gradually disappeared; the banks became high and steep, with a red clay soil;
the caoutchouc vine, virgin from the knife, arched itself across the
river; and huge trees protruded their roots through the banks,
like the bones of an extinct mammoth.

I had now entered the dominions of the Balengi, a bush tribe
of the Muni and Bapuku countries.

It was long after dark when we arrived before the village, our
destined lodging for the night. The guides bawled to the inhabitants to bring out lights. But this happened to be a common
strategy in native warfare. The citizens, feeling no desire to ex-
hibit themselves as illuminated targets, replied with shouts of an
interrogative and distrustful nature. My guides answered, "Our
names are Toko and Okota. We bring white man."

These words, *We bring white man*, had the magical effect of an
"open sesame." It was to say, "We bring you a strange monster of the sea, who seldom wanders so far inland; and never
without cloth, tobacco, or other marine productions which black
men love."

Two women came down to the bank holding torches, and two
men stood by them leaning on their guns. Having landed, I was
escorted through a cluster of houses, the Leith of this *mighty* Ed-
inburgh.

The path was rough and tortuous. Trunks of trees were here

and there stretched across it, and upon them were placed lumps of blazing country light, in honor of their first white visitor.

This "country light," as it is called in the Coast patois, is a gum which exudes from the large tree of which they build their canoes; it is bound round with leaves into the shape of a torch, and yields, when burning, a faint but pungent perfume.

When I arrived in the town the king came to greet me, dressed in his regal robes, an old pea-jacket and a pair of duck trowsers. After we had exchanged a few polite falsehoods, after the manner of well-bred people, he ushered me into the palace, which was a bamboo hut, containing very little besides dirt and smoke.

I had shot a monkey that day, and having had no dinner, I resolved to take it under the name of supper. I summoned my courage and Mongilomba, who assured me that the *simiæ* were remarkably fine eating. We then debated upon the subject; for the art of roasting on crossed sticks, which seems the first principle of rudimentary cooking, is utterly unknown in Equatorial Africa, where every thing is boiled in clay pots. At last I left it entirely in the hands of Mongilomba, who said that he would cook it with odika.

This odika is a rich, dark vegetable gravy, obtained from the kernel of a wild mango, which, when pounded, moulded into the shape of a pyramid, and smoked, is not unlike in appearance to the cakes of greaves with which dogs are fed, and will keep as long.

The king having expressed a desire to join my repast, and having contributed a bunch of plantains thereto, we dined in great state. The table was covered with a red cloth. There was a dingy salt-cellar, from which we helped ourselves to dingier salt. The dish which contained the monkey *à l'odika*, having been fractured, had to be supported by a leaf doubled underneath, and oscillated upon it like the tortured Sybarite. The plantains were served in a wash-hand basin, and Mongilomba, opening my chest, in which he allowed me to keep a few of my own clothes, put on a clean shirt (publicly) with a dignity becoming the occasion.

My tongue received the first morsel of monkey with a doubt, which leaped into gusto. In that superb *bonne-bouche*, the delicacy of a pullet and the rich savor of a hen pheasant palpitated on my palate turn by turn. When the meal was ended, and sweet digestion crept within my frame, I sank into a voluptuous reverie, which intensified itself into sleep. The triumph of mind min-

gled with the languor of matter and made me dream. The discovery of a new dish, says Brillat-Savarin, does more for mankind
·than the discovery of a new star. I had not only discovered a
vegetable gravy, I had discovered that monkey had a game flavor. I saw *monkey à l'odika* in all the cartes of the London res-
taurants. I saw myself invested with the freedom of the city by
a grateful corporation.

Awaking, I saw before me a man who was eating voraciously.
The stomach is a region of sympathy (Van Helmont). I watched
him at first with good-natured sympathy; secondly, with curiosity; thirdly, with envy. What was it he was eating? A grayish-
colored mess piled in a calabash. Into this he dipped his wooden
spoon with movements so rapid that they would have excited my
admiration had not they aroused my fear.

In a few moments it would all be gone.

I had seen nothing like that before. Perhaps it was the wondrous haschisch which Monte Christo gave to his guest in the palace cave. It would at least be something far better than monkey
or odika, this dish which the man continued to eat with yawning
mouth and glaring eyes.

I demanded a little, and took a huge glutinous mouthful. Success in experiment had made me rash. Scarcely had it entered
my mouth than it flew out, accompanied with oaths. "Bring me
some water, Mongilomba," I spluttered. "It's soap and red pepper!"

"He no soap, sir; he grow for bush. What time you see soap
grow for bush?"

Mongilomba was right. It was a kind of fruit which tastes exactly like yellow soap, and which the natives eat boiled and sea-
soned with pepper—a fact which may be interesting to botanists,
but which destroyed my digestion.

As has always been my habit when traveling in the interior, I
had the village hunters called in, and conversed with them, *via*
Mongilomba, upon the habits of wild beasts. Among others, I
was shown the great elephant hunter of the river. He had killed
four during his lifetime, which was thought extraordinary. It is
indeed extraordinary that they should be able to kill a single elephant with such guns and powder as they obtain from traders.
They load these seven-and-sixpenny guns in a most absurd manner: some powder is poured in from a calabash, and some dry
grass is rammed on top of that; then some bullets or bits of old

iron, and more grass for wadding; then *more powder* and grass; and iron and grass again to finish with.

When the gun does go off (it often flashes in the pan), it makes a noise like a small field-piece, and they never hold it to their shoulders for fear of the recoil, which they avoid by springing on one side. The guns burst frequently enough, and this very man had lost three in that manner—with the last one his left hand as well.

An elephant hunt is an important affair, which is undertaken only after ceremonies of fetich. The charm of the first class is an aerolite covered with the ashes of a certain plant, the hand and gun-barrel smeared therewith. The hunter's apparel on these occasions is confined to a few stripes of paint.

It was arranged that the next morning we should go net-hunting, and, having spent the night as usual between my cork bed and rug, I awoke at daybreak, and crept out into brief twilight.

The first thing that met my eyes was Mongilomba with a looking-glass and a calabash of hot water, engaged in some mysterious operation. I approached him closely enough to see that he had been boring his ears. Through the holes he was passing two little wooden pegs smeared with palm-oil. The wood distended the apertures; the oil alleviated the pain.

Having accomplished this with many grimaces, which served to illustrate the proverb, " Il faut souffrir pour être beau," he took a piece of stick, one end of which was chewed into a pulp, dabbed it into a powder which was made from the cuttle-fish, and rubbed his teeth fiercely. He then took up a small looking-glass, and looked at his extremely ugly face with a simple earnestness comical to behold. A gradual grin stole over his features, and he laid the mirror down with a guffaw of perfect self-complacency.

I thought that this would be the right moment to remind him that he had a master, who took his breakfast early. He seemed displeased at this ill-bred interruption, and imperiously ordered the king's women to clean a pot and get a fire ready. A white cock was offered for sale, and bought, after much haggling, for a head of tobacco. As these fowls can only be caught by hand at roosting-time, I had to put a rifle-ball through him, upon which they cried, " Heigh! this be devil-man! He use no flint; and he kill with one ball in him gun."

I now went to superintend the cooking of the fowl; for Mongilomba, who was subject to fits of abstraction, had once forgotten to remove that which we relish only in woodcock and snipe.

The women, in a shed which was roofed but left open at the sides, began to prepare their fire. Four half-burnt logs were placed with their charred extremities radiating toward a common point; at this point the hollow space was filled with live ashes, dry leaves, and sticks. A woman's lips served as bellows, and soon kindled a brisk flame.

A clay pot was then produced, the bottom lined with plantain leaves, which saved the trouble of cleansing it. It was filled with water, and a fowl was plucked, drawn, quartered, and thrown in. Meantime another royal lady was pounding the kernels of a nut into a paste, using as her mortar a thick slab of hard wood, and for her pestle a round hard fruit about twice the size of an orange. The paste was thrown in and stirred, and half a dozen red peppers added. When the fowl was ready, I placed two sea-biscuits in the wash-hand basin, poured the hot mess upon them, and so manufactured the best compound that can be made with such poor materials.

A cup of tea having concluded my repast, I inquired if my companions were ready. But they had been so intently watching my breakfast that they had forgotten their own. It was natural that they should be astonished when they saw me boiling water in a canteen kettle; throwing in a handful of black leaves —this, by-the-by, is the best way of making tea, as the leaves discharge more virtue than when water is poured upon them—letting it stand, as they thought, to get cool; adding what they supposed to be lumps of white salt; and, finally, pouring forth into an enameled iron cup a mixture resembling the stagnant water which they saw every day in the swamps, drink it with apparent relish.

When they had eaten some boiled plantains and cassada, their staple diet, they made a start with seven nets, made of vegetable fibres, and two dogs. In a quarter of an hour we had left behind us all signs of man, and, walking upon the ancient tracks, we plunged into the depths of the dark and silent forest.

On arriving at a suitable place, the nets were set. This was done much upon the same principle as in rabbit-warrens; they were raised to the height of three feet, and formed a line extending for about a quarter of a mile. The hunters filed off quietly to some distance behind these nets, and then approached in a semicircle, making all the noise they could. The two dogs had wooden rattles round their necks, and worked very well, but I often wished that the beaters had an English gamekeeper behind them; for they avoided the thick places, where game was most likely to be found. The whole job was done in a slovenly manner, and game was scarce. In fact, this method of hunting was well calculated to expose the nakedness of the land. There were a few deer, which laid about in the wood singly like hares, and, like hares, preferred to steal back when you wished to drive them forward. After several·blanks, a bush - deer (Cephalolophus sylvicultrix) was caught. As I had given orders that no animal should be killed till I had seen it, I was called to the spot, and found a reddish-colored doe struggling in the net, sometimes giving a sharp bark, and snapping with her teeth like a dog. Feeling no inclination to have the taming of such a shrew, I gave the death-signal, and a clumsy *coup-de-grace* was given with an axe. Her head was tucked through her hind legs, and these tied to her fore legs. Thus made a bundle of, she was crammed into a basket, and strapped on to the back of a young woman who was emblematically covered with red paint, and who had accompanied us in case of such a contingency; for it is astonishing how these black lords of creation detest that kind of work. Once at Bapuku a man refused to guide me through the forest to a plantation, a distance of two or three miles, for fear that I should kill some game on the road and compel him to carry it—indolence refined to foresight.

It was to one of these plantations that I determined to go immediately on my return, which took place next day, as the hunters refused to go out while there was meat in the town. I had been told that the elephants came every night to eat the plantains and to root out the cassada, and that thereby the villages were reduced almost to starvation.

An African plantation is formed on the principle of a backwood "clearing," but in a very incomplete manner; and this is perhaps the only part of the world where a man goes up a tree to cut it down. Passing a vine-hoop round the tree and his waist (as the natives of Senegambia do when they ascend the palm-tree for its wine), the woodman mounts about twelve feet, where the trunk has, of course, a much smaller circumference, hacks it into two with his rude axe, and jumps down nimbly at the right moment. The trees are suffered to lie where they happen to fall. All that is done is to burn the branches off. The women then scrape holes in the ground, plant plantain and cassada, and Nature does the rest. Batatas are sometimes grown, but not often, as that involves the labor of ridging the soil, from which, on the following year, a thick shrubby vegetation invariably springs.

There are usually two or three huts on a plantation where the women sleep in the hole-scraping season. Having arrived at the Bapuku plantation with Abauhi, a Corisco man and a Bapuk native, we took possession of a small hovel, much to the disgust of two venerable hags therein dwelling. However, I gave them tobacco, and Abauhi polite words. The ogresses, appeased, went off to another hut. Night approached, and I took my dinner—a handful of parched ground-nuts and a cup of fragrant tea.

I had previously walked round the plantation, and had found but one elephant's track—that a week old. I was clearly a victim of African exaggeration; but this had already happened so often that I was now inured to it. I could also console myself with the reflection that I should enjoy a better night's rest where I was than in the town; even at that distance I could faintly hear the sound of the eternal drum.

Whether negroes sleep at all (except on rainy days) is a matter which requires serious investigation. They certainly at night do not, and it would be easier to get to sleep at 1 A.M. in a bedroom looking out on the Haymarket in London than it is in an African village—so noisy are these children of Ham.

At first, owing to the strength of my tea, or the extreme lightness of my repast, I felt no inclination for my cork couch, and, seating myself on the trunk of a fallen tree, I listened to the tiger-cat's melancholy cry, and to those birds of the forest, which, day or night, seem never to be silent.

Presently these sounds were hushed; the sea-breeze, which had rustled the leaves of the forest, died away: all nature held her breath.

Above the trees, which stood black against the sky, rose a red and sullen moon.

The atmosphere seemed in flames; I breathed with difficulty; and a sense of loneliness began to creep upon me.

At such moments as these it is a terrible thing to be far away from all civilized beings. There are some who say that there is no solitude so sad as the solitude of the city. It is because they have never been in the desert. In the city there are varied sights and sounds which prevent one from looking inward too long. In monotonous Africa the eye can seldom relieve the mind; self-communion becomes eternal. Reflection from a blessing broods

itself into a woe. It leaves the intellect to rankle in the heart.
In this detestable land, as the body grows enfeebled, the mind,
joined to it by subtle links, becomes diseased as well. Our sweetest memories are hideously distorted and deformed. In the love,
the friendship, the fidelity which we have enjoyed, we detect a
deep-laid deceit, a sordid scheme. Deriving no consolation from
the past, we can have no hope for the future. We perceive no
possibility of success in our enterprise; we are ridiculed and
ruined; we think of what we might have done, and that is the
saddest of all human thoughts. Crushed in a vice of horror and
despair, we put the revolver to our ear—and why? because a thun-
der-storm happens to be coming on, and the air is rather close.

I went to bed, and was awoke by the rumbling of thunder, and
by the wind howling in the distance. The men opened their
sleepy eyes, rubbed them, and hastily made up the fire. We
could see the lightning through the chinks, and the tornado approached us with a dreadful sound. As it burst on us, there was
a report like a musket-shot close to us.

"Who that?" cried Abauhi, starting up.

He was answered by a loud struggling crash at the very door.
The two men gave a yell, and literally tore their way out through
the fragile hovel wall. No passion is so infectious as fright, and
I made what is called in turf parlance a "good third."

The first moment out of doors nearly deprived me of my breath,
so fiercely fell the rain: the large and violent drops made my
hands and face smart, as if the rain had been hailstones. In two
minutes I was drenched to the skin; in five minutes, to the bone.
Meantime I continued to follow my men through bush and bram-
ble at a tearing pace, till I became anxious to learn the purpose
of our Hegira. When I stopped, Abauhi cried, "Do you love
me? Do you love me? Do not stay there!"

"Why not?" said I, sulkily, for I had just fallen among thorns.

"Look!" he said, with a superb gesture; "you no see that
tree?"

I looked and saw a tree torn in half by the wind; the upper
part falling to the ground, while the lower trunk remained standing, gaunt and bare as a sepulchral stone.

The tree must have been cut half way through by a native, and
the work completed by the wind. This natural explanation did
not occur to me at the time, and the effect, which seemed at defi-
ance with all the natural laws, was startling enough.

And the thunder was terrific. Sometimes it encircled the whole horizon with a long continuous booming sound, as if Jupiter was driving his chariot round the firmament; sometimes it burst into sharp stunning reports, with a sound like the whizzing of shot and shell a few yards above our heads, or as if ten thousand cart-loads of stones had been thrown down in mid air. These awful crashes of the clouds, unlike any thing one hears in England, made me tremble in spite of myself; and the natives, flinging their clench-ed hands toward the sky, cried, "Njambi! Njambi! let us live!"

Abauhi was not the less sedulous of the two in these pagan prayers. In fine weather a good Christian, he returned to hea-thenism when it blew tornadoes.

Corisco obtained its name from the coruscations (*coruscão*) of lightning, which at this season are here so frequent and so vivid. Having escaped from the dangerous neighborhood of the trees (for the plantation had not been properly cleared), we could now watch these celestial fireworks without fear. Sheet lightning in a broad lurid blaze; chain lightning in its most fantastic and beautiful forms; the forked lightning, as it carried living death from sky to earth—all these we saw sometimes in several parts of the heav-ens at once. Abauhi, who feared thunder, looked at the forked lightning with indifference; but his terror on finding blue sparks in his friend's wool defies description.

Tornadoes, like a woman's wrath, are furious, but brief; and we soon returned to our hut. There the men took off their waist-cloths, wrung them out, rubbed themselves, and were as well as ever, while I could only shiver in my wet clothes.

We waited for the dawn. At times a sturdy branch would fall to the ground, yielding only when the foe had passed. Then we heard shouts and reports of guns. This was being done at a neighboring plantation to frighten away the elephants—the plan-tation, by-the-by, which I should have been taken to, had not my guide, preferring a short walk, remained at the nearer one.

I was surprised when I heard that elephants feed on stormy nights by preference, but such I have since found to be undoubt-edly the case, and beasts of prey have the same habit. One might suppose that the latter choose bad weather like other poach-ers, who then anticipate less interruption; the former, as do horses, cows, hares, rabbits, and other vegetarians, like to take their green meat in a shower.

As soon as day broke I went out. An enormous branch had

fallen within three yards of our hut, so that we had had a narrow escape. While I was looking at the tree bereft of its better half, an animal, which I supposed to be a bat, flew from it, and perched upon another tree at twenty yards' distance, giving a peculiar curve on alighting, as the flying-fish does when it enters the sea. To my amazement, it then changed into a creature like a squirrel, which ran up and down the tree with inconceivable rapidity, and disappeared on the other side. I ran there, rifle in hand, but could see no more of it. I was so perplexed thereby that I thought it must have been an optical illusion; for the day was yet dim, and my head was sadly dizzy and confused. But some days after I asked Mongilomba if such an intermediate type existed, and he described this flying lemur, or squirrel, with great preciseness.

When we came near the town, some women washing in a spring, on catching a glimpse of us, rushed off with hideous yells. An English holloa brought them to, and they explained to us, laughing, that they were at war with a clan of the Balengi, and they had taken us for light skirmishers. I must explain to you that the "noble savage" makes war exclusively by ambuscade, and shoots women and children by preference—a practice attended with less risk and equal glory.

We found the very plantains of the village gardens torn up by the roots, and half of the houses flat on the ground. No one would have supposed that those prostrate masses of wood, misshapen and blackened by rain, had once been human dwellings. Nor would one have supposed that those were the owners who were chattering, laughing, and evidently appreciating what was ridiculous in their own misfortunes as keenly as their dearest friends could have done. That which an old writer said of the negro is perfectly true, "in weal and in woe they are always the same, and it is only by their clothing one can tell whether they are mourning or rejoicing." Extremes do really meet, it seems, and these poor wretches possess that indifference to misfortune which is the highest triumph of philosophy.

My house had not been blown down, but the rain had entered through the roof, and caused internal inundation. In Africa the sun is a tyrant; but, like all tyrants, he gives us some blessings. I longed for his warmth and light, but the clouds remained inexorable. I cowered over a few spluttering sticks, and presently fell into a restless slumber. It was more than restless; I went to sleep a man, and I awoke a child. In two hours I had become powerless. The captain of the barque came in as I awoke, and, seeing my white face, invited me aboard. I opened my mouth to answer, but could think of no appropriate words. I had just commenced a sentence, which, as they told me afterward, related exclusively to other matters, when I fainted. One cup of water dashed into my face, and another down my throat, brought me to. I was carried down to the beach in a chair by the four Kru-men. As I was getting into the boat, Mongilomba crept up to me mysteriously.

"Sir, Mr. Reade, if that captain give you medicine, you ask him to drink a little himself first."

These words fell on dull ears at the time, and afterward, when I became capable of thought, they made me laugh, the advice was so purely African. On all parts of the Coast a negro does not offer you a drink without tasting it first, a custom which hints at evil antecedents. What would become of all our doctors, thought I, if they had to take their own prescriptions? But there was more in Mongilomba's warning than I then supposed.

When one takes fever from a sudden cause, as from sol-lunar influence, from a fit of sudden joy or fear, a violent debauch, an imprudent indulgence, or, as in my case, from exposure to bad weather, the disease soon passes, if it does not prove immediately fatal. In a week I was as well as I had ever been.

This week was very monotonous, as you may well suppose. In the morning before breakfast the captain would go ashore, and return with a few billets of ebony in his boat. At eight o'clock a breakfast of salt junk or coffee, after which I would divide time between some books, which I had borrowed from the excellent mission library at Corisco, and a promenade on deck. At one o'clock invariable pea-soup was followed by inevitable fowl, and at six o'clock tea, which had exchanged its own flavor for that of stale hay, owing to long residence on the Coast.

The owners of the barque had not been fortunate in their venture. Victualed for a seven months' voyage, she had already been out of Liverpool a twelvemonth, and had taken in no cargo to speak of. On the other hand, all the cloth and almost all the other goods had been given out on terms extremely advantageous to the captain, had they been fulfilled. But the middle-men, finding that he drove hard and unfair bargains, persuaded their elastic consciences that they were justified in cheating him, which they accomplished easily enough by drinking his rum, smoking his tobacco, and distributing his cloth among their friends.

So the captain found himself in the position of a large creditor —a position which has its pleasures, its privileges, and, above all, its respectability. Unhappily, in the grammar of commerce *will owe* is frequently the future of the verb *to dun*. Redwood was due to him in Corisco, rubber in the Muni, and ebony at Bapuku. The black traders held him in awe, and also (as is natural) a little in abhorrence. They shunned him when they could, and when they could not they became obsequious. This afforded him smiles for his vanity, but tears for his purse.

Now, as he knew very well that these men had run through his trust, and could not now buy the native produce if they wished; as he did not take enough in a week to pay the ship's expenses for a day; as three out of a small crew had already died, and the others were too weak to do a stroke of work, I felt inclined to inquire why he remained any longer on the Coast. When I asked this question of the mate, he looked at the carpenter, the carpenter looked at him, and I received no answer.

The captain was in the habit of speaking against the mate with a pertinacity which I could not understand. He would call me aside at every available moment, and tell me how much trouble he had with him, and what a curse it was to have a drunkard aboard. "You would not think, Mr. Reade, that Mr. Jones had been a master, but he has. Yes, sir, that man's had a ship of his own — a ship of his own. Oh, what a curse is drunkenness! Well might John the Baptist turn all the wine into water at Galilee in Cana—that is a lesson to us all, sir. It was only the other day that I told him if he went on so, I couldn't give him a character to the owners. Then he'd have to go before the mast, as many and many a drunken master has done before him. And I asked him what his wife and his poor children would do then? And he burst out a'crying, and said he would give it up—yes, he *would* give it up—what is the matter, steward?"

Here the Malay showed his master a key, and said that he had found it in Mr. Jones's berth while he was cleaning it out: he thought that it was the key of the locker.

"That can't be, for I have the key of the locker in my pocket. Why, it's a duplicate key! Ah! sir, he's a bad man—a bad man. Steward, see whether there is any beer gone."

The steward opened the locker with the duplicate key, and said

G

that all the beer was gone. The captain turned up the whites of
his eyes at a large pumpkin which was hanging just over his
head. "May the Lord forgive him! three dozen of beer, Mr.
Reade, that man must have drunk. It's a wonder he's alive. But
if his liver ain't jaundiced here, it's because it must frizzle in hell
forever and ever and amen! Oh, sir, is it not indeed awful, the
revenge of the Almighty!"

The mate was a red-faced, bottle-nosed *chien-de-mer*, with a
rough and ready way about him which might have been assumed
(nothing is oftener assumed by artful knaves), but which certainly prepossessed me in his favor. His grog-blossoms had sprung
from a moist soil, no doubt; but I had always seen him sober.
And this was the answer which I invariably made when harassed
with the captain's confidences; to which the latter would reply
that Mr. Jones had now brought his health to such a state that he
could not drink any spirituous liquors.

The skipper himself was a short, pale-faced man, with dull eye,
and his mouth always a little open, like a fish. I knew that he
was Scotch or North Country by his drawling tone and his manner of relieving dorsal irritation. He drank nothing but water,
and had a shaking hand, probably the result of repeated fevers.

He was very frequently ill, and after I had seen his method of
treatment I could only wonder that he remained alive. It was
the most ludicrous and painful sight which I have ever witnessed.
He had given himself a colic with some medicinal poison, and was
lying on the after-lockers with *The Seaman's Medical Guide* or
Companion to the Medicine-chest before him. At first he could not
find colic, which happened in that book to be spelt with an *h*.
But he was not to be balked; he turned to diarrhœa, and treated
himself for that. Soon afterward, while turning over the leaves,
in case any thing might strike his fancy, he fell upon *cholic*, and
immediately had the prescription mixed. Finding no relief within the space of an hour, he adopted the second treatment. This
went on during two days. At short intervals we would hear a
sepulchral voice from below, "Steward, bring me the medicine-
book and my eye-glass." Then it would be, "Steward, I think
I'll take a little so and so;" or, "Steward, I'll try a glass of such
and such a medicine to-day." Sometimes it was castor-oil, sometimes it was quinine, sometimes laudanum, or æther, or tincture
of myrrh, or anti-bilious pills (eight to a dose), and once it was
croton-oil—an experiment which he did not deem requisite to repeat.

I was surprised to see him come on deck again; the mate, how-ever, assured me that the treatment had this time been mild, in a comparative point of view. Unhappily, his patients had not such strong "physical" constitutions.

One evening when we were at sea, a sailor came to him and said that he was teased with a spitting of blood. "I never heard of such a thing," growled the captain, and looked upon the man as a *lusus naturæ.* "Have you got pains any where?" The man replied that he had pains in the head. "Well, if you have pains in the head, that shows it comes from the head; and, turning to me, he explained that the bleeding came down from the head into the mouth by channels. "Ah!" thought I to myself, "there is only one Channel you know much about." What it was he gave the sailor I can not pretend to say, but I know that the poor fel-low soon afterward went over the side in company with a white sheet and a cannon ball.

I do not think that such cases can be called exceptional in the smaller class of trading vessels. Place powerful drugs in ignorant hands, and what can you expect? A sailor kills more people even than a surgeon. I have heard of a half-drowned man being rolled along the deck on a barrel till all signs of life had departed; and of another, in a fit of apoplexy, being carried below head-fore-most, in obedience to the strict injunctions of the officer in com-mand. I have known captains who believed that quinine would cure every thing, from bronchitis to Guinea-worm, as long as it was used on the West Coast of Africa. I have known others who denounced it as "a damned piece of quackery," and who gave calomel (always a poison in cases of malarious fever) to their pa-tients at the period when strong broths and tonics were required to restore their strength.

It does appear a great evil that, in such an age as this, hund-reds of vessels should every year leave England for distant and often unhealthy coasts, having on board no better physician than the master with his medicine-chest, and no better surgeon than the carpenter with his axe. But if it is unjust to the sailor to send him on the seas without medical attendance, it would be more unjust to send young surgeons on long voyages in which they would gain little experience save in ennui and in vice. Things, I fear, must stand as they are; there are limits to human charity.

Having seen as much of the Bapuku country as I wished, I felt anxious to return to Corisco, in order to ascend the Muni. But still the captain remained. The natives, having no " oaks to sport," carefully hid themselves in the suburbs (thick forest) when they saw their dun in the distance. Eventually they tried to starve him off by refusing to sell him provisions. Indeed, they were almost famished themselves. The harvests of these people suffice merely for their necessities. When cloth and beads tempt them to part with their plantains and cassada, they are obliged to pay for their vanity with hunger. During one or two trips which I had made by land along the coast to neighboring villages, I had found the greatest difficulty in purchasing vegetables for my men. I could make a dinner off a toucan, a monkey, or a squirrel, because I had come from a carnivorous land; but these natives would rather " go with hunger" than eat flesh or fish alone, such diet producing dysentery.

From what I heard afterward, I don't doubt that our skipper would have loitered on much longer had it not been for a little incident which effectually disgusted him with Bapuku.

One morning I was coming into the town after a night's lying out after elephants, when I was told that the white captain was a prisoner. I took my rifle out of Abauhi's hands, but, on my appearance, the natives, as if anxious to show that they had no quarrel with *me*, crowded round me more than usual, shaking my hand, and giving me their salutation. On that morning, too, a man lent me his canoe to go off to the ship in—for nothing! the only genuine gift which I ever had made me by a negro, except a finely-woven mat which Mongilomba gave to me and stole from me afterward.

I sent Mongilomba one way and Abauhi the other to collect information. The result was as follows. The captain had invited one of his debtors on board, and had presented an obstacle to his return in the shape of a padlock and chain. This was all well enough, and perfectly in accordance with Coast customs. But when captains seize such hostages for debt, they take care to put neither themselves nor their men in the power of the enemy. This was our hero's first voyage in the trade. He had no small ideas of his own importance, and of the influence which he exercised over aborigines. So he was in the habit of going ashore as usual.

After three days the prisoner said that he did not find solitary confinement very amusing, and that he was now willing to pay his debts. " But," said he, " the Bushmen to whom I gave trust have my wood. They will give it up to none but me. If you keep me, how can I pay you? Let me go, and take my son in my place. In three days all shall be right between us."

This proposal seemed fair enough. The man sent for a slave with orders to personate his son, and was then set at liberty.

This morning, the captain, coming ashore, was met by his debtor on the beach. "Well, have you got any wood for me?" "Yes," answered the man, "I have got ten pieces. Would you like to come and see them?" The captain thought he should like to go and see them. They let him look at the wood; two or three others sauntered up, a rope was thrown over his head, and his hands were tied behind him.

At the intercession of his interpreter, a Benga of Corisco, the injured chieftain agreed to take a Kru-man in the captain's stead. "Black man," moralized Mongilomba, "always listen to other man's palaver; if palaver be good, he take him; but white man have hot head, hot hand, hot tongue, and ears be cold."

I was taken to the king's house, which on such occasions is the state-prison; the king himself happened to be absent, but Nettlerash, the head Kru-man, was there, his feet in the stocks and scowls on his brow.

No lawyer can be more stubborn on the question of precedent than a negro. They are Tories of an old school, happily become extinct, who love customs because they are customs, and hate innovations because they are innovations. Had it been customary in the Kru country to smoke palaver-prisoners with damp leaves and red peppers, as they do in Cameroons and Congo, Jack would not have grumbled; it was not his fate that he repined against, but the stocks. "I no sabee this thing," he said; "this no fashion in we country."

When I had come on board the captain tried to bely his pale face with a valiant tongue. "When the king comes down the river he will soon bring these fellows to reason."

Royalty, however, is not always so complaisant as people may wish, nor here so powerful as they suppose. The term *king*, which I use because it is the term universally used by traders, will perhaps give you an erroneous idea of these constitutions, which, as I will explain hereafter, are less monarchical than republican.

After three days' palaver the two prisoners (slave and Kruman) were exchanged. During this interval the carpenter was *down* with an attack of fever, and declined the captain's offer of physic with a polite firmness which first amused and then astonished me; for when I offered him some quinine, much in the same manner as one offers a cigar to a friend who one knows does not smoke, he accepted it with an *empressement* as marked as that with which he had refused the captain's. And now I remembered that though the mate and carpenter had never spoken to me against the captain, they never addressed him except when duty required. And every evening they would stand by the main shrouds talking together in a low voice, always stopping when I approached them in my walk to and fro upon the poop.

There was some mystery in all this, from which that Malay, with his sinister eyes and his soft, catlike steps, I felt sure could not be absent. But soon these thoughts were driven from my mind. The blue-Peter was hoisted to the fore, and a gentle wind bore us to Corisco. There, the captain having taken in provisions, he crossed the bay and anchored at the mouth of the Muni; while I, entering the bamboo mission house, was welcomed by bright faces, and, eating blackberry jam from the mountains of Pennsylvania, related the small adventures which now, dear reader, I narrate to you.

A Cape Lopez built canoe had drifted up with the strong north current, which sometimes throws cocoa-nuts and uprooted palm-trees upon the Corisco beach. It had been found upon an islet near Corisco, and became the property of those who found it: a law which applies to all godsends of that nature, including strangers.

Abauhi, who was one of the owners, showed me this canoe. It could hold more than a dozen people, had a round bottom, but a square stern, which distinguished it from the canoe proper in Mpongwe.

Twenty dollars made Abauhi and Co. happy men. Five dollars more rigged her out complete, with mast, sail, and sheet, rudder, paddles, and two long poles to punt her with in shallow water. We had a trial trip, and Mr. Mackey pronounced her an admirable bargain. He was a great authority in nautical matters; for when one lives in small islands, a sail becomes one's horse and a boat one's carriage.

As I was busy one morning writing out my pocket-book memoranda preparatory to a start, Mongilomba told me that "a Gaboon boy" wished to see me. Without farther warning he introduced the family solicitor. His face was now more suppliant than stern; he was the type of an attorney who waits on a wealthy client for the first time; a portrait of avarice veiled by humility; a loaded gun with the hammer down on the nipple to hide the cap.

He wished to enter my service as cook, a vacancy in my retinue of which Mongilomba, the temporary substitute, had frequently reminded me. His name was Cabinda, *anglice* Robert—for all civilized negroes have a European cognomen. He had been ship's cook during a voyage to Liverpool and during another to New York. He had seen air-balloons, railways, and snow. He garnished his language with round oaths smelling of the sea, and professed a love of adventure, a contempt of danger, and a great partiality toward myself.

Such a man was irresistible. I engaged him at three dollars a month, on the agreement that I would double his pay if he accompanied me among the cannibals of the Ncomo (which Mongilomba had declined to do), and that he should forfeit the whole of his previous pay if he refused.

On the 29th of April I left Corisco without a wind, and after a long and severe day we reached at sunset the Alobi or Musquito Islands. These must have been originally floating beds of sand, sown with seeds by the land-breeze and the birds. Lying in the mouth of the Muni, they form a good site for a factory.

Little Alobi has been the scene of a tragedy. Not many years ago a Captain Stewart was factor upon that island. He was a violent man, who never treated the natives well, and who, when he was drunk, baited them with bull-terriers. All this was borne without resistance, but not without resentment.

It happened that he had a debtor who had openly said that Stewart should never get a cake of rubber out of him. This was a wound to his pride as well as to his pocket, and since the man took care not to venture within his power, he seized two of his relatives, who were fishing out at sea, chained them hand and foot, and placed them on board one of his owner's vessels landing off Alobi.

Somebody foolishly untied their hands, and they, being probably in fear of their lives, jumped overboard, and tried to swim ashore. Both were drowned; their bodies were washed up on the beach, and marks were found on the back of one of them, which might have been caused by the rocks, but which resembled gunshot wounds.

That day Captain Stewart was tried by a council of Makágas, which was held in presence of all the people. The prisoner was not present, but was as much in their power as if jailers had him under lock and key. The cause was argued as fairly as if he had been arraigned before an English court of justice. There were some, I was told, who pleaded for him, attempting to prove that no willful murder had been committed, and pointing out the risk they ran of losing the white man's trade by an act of violence. But the two corpses lying in their midst, the death-wail of the women ringing in their ears, the bitter memories of past brutality, accused with a voice too stern to be silenced by motives of mere prudence. The verdict was given; the sentence was passed; the execution was prepared.

The moody looks of the people, their whisperings, their grand council, and the consciousness of his own cruelty, made Stewart feel that he was in danger. Before he went to sleep he set a guard of Kru-men at his door.

It was a large room with a glass window. In one corner was the bed: here Mrs. Stewart slept. Her husband, who was a bulky man, used to sleep on a mat in the middle of the floor. A cotton wick, floating in a small bowl of palm-oil, lighted the room sufficiently for that which followed.

Imagine, in the dead of the night, the sound of footsteps stealthily approaching; a whispered threat, and the Kru-men flying from their post; something dark behind the window; a blaze of fire; a crash of shivered glass; a loud report; the room filled with smoke; and a poor woman awaking to see the blood streaming from her husband's breast.

When she found that he still lived, she called the Kru-men, and sent them over to Corisco for Mr. Mackey, who has some knowledge of surgery. She was kneeling by the wounded man, trying to stanch his wound, when the door was burst violently open. A band of naked men poured into the room, their foreheads blackened with the war-paint, and brandishing weapons in their hands.

Mrs. Stewart had flung herself upon her husband's body; two powerful arms tore her from him, and held her struggling as she saw a gun-muzzle placed to his breast. When the deed was done they went away, without mutilating the corpse, without insulting its widow. It was a judicial assassination.

The English consul came over to the island, arrested two of the murderers without resistance, and handed them over to the Spanish authorities at Fernando Po. They were acquitted, and, I think, justly. If white men act like savages, let them be judged by savage laws.

The successor of Captain Stewart lives in the hulk of a large merchantman which had been wrecked off Corisco and vended for a song. Now she was fitted up with a thatched roof, like the hulks of Bonny, and from wreck became dwelling-house.

Here this young man led the life of an industrious hermit, communicating with the outer world once a month, when a schooner belonging to the firm brought him letters with European goods, and took away his letters with native produce. In itself this existence could not have been agreeable; but, remember, he was the Cæsar of Alobi, while, had he been in England, he would have been a slave on a high stool, or a fetch-and-carry machine behind the counter.

I slept there that night, breakfasted on board the barque the next morning, and sailed up the Muni with the sea-breeze at midday.

The Muni possesses the same character as the other rivers of Equatorial Africa. Its banks are of all the most densely wooded, the only gaps in that high green wall being made by the native villages. There are many shallows and sunken rocks; but, as far as I could learn, vessels of fair tonnage could be navigated to the falls, which are seventy miles from the mouth of the river, and which, after the heaviest rains, are said to be worth seeing.

I passed the night at the town of a powerful chief named Mtevo. As it was one of my objects in this trip to hunt the gorilla, which is not found in the Bapuku country, I asked him if they existed in the neighborhood of his town. He said that his natives could show them to me in one minute, which probably would have been a long one had I remained in the Muni till I had succeeded.

I started the next morning at daylight in a small canoe, with Robert and two Balengi guides, leaving Mongilomba and the others behind me. After two hours' paddling we branched off into a tributary stream, which took us by a northeasterly course to the foot of one of the spurs of the Sierra del Crystal, a distance of fifty miles perhaps from the coast.

The Spaniards of the Middle Ages would sometimes dedicate a city to "Our Lady of Mercy" after butchering the inhabitants. Equally appropriate is the name " Crystal Mountains" applied to these forest-covered hills, which are so dark and gloomy, and where a Scotch mist appears the nearest approach to fine weather. But pure streams flow from its black and impure breast, like moral lessons from a libertine author; and one can seldom, in Africa, drink water so cool and sweet as that which bubbled past my canoe that afternoon.

In the evening I arrived at my destination. There I found low filthy huts, abject savages, many of the women wearing fresh-plucked leaves round their loins—a mode of apparel which excited the disgust of the refined Robert. None of them had seen a white man before; but here even curiosity, that arch-passion of lower humanity, had become extinct. Their looks and actions betrayed the indifference of brutes.

I spent some days hunting among them, and always without success. In the recesses of the virgin forest, as in the dark depths of the sea, animal life is rare. All living creatures love light and fresh air, those grand stimulants of existence. The gorilla, it is true, shuns the gay prairies, and seems to love the sombre twilight of the wood; but in this part, where he was to be found more frequently than in any other part of the Muni country, I found his tracks less frequently than I had found them on the southern side of the Gaboon. In none of the villages which I entered could I find a skull or bone of the animal; and I also heard on good authority, that a man who hunted daily in the Muni would see a gorilla only perhaps once or twice in a year.

It rained almost incessantly, and the hardships of hunting were doubled by the eternal moisture and monotony. When "my lodgings were on the cold ground," I would wake up so dizzy that I could scarcely stand. A strong cup of tea would revive my drooping spirits; but the struggle day after day through forest undergrowth, and the utter lifelessness of all around, began to disgust me. Added to this, my boots were turning to black pulp, and my feet, being frequently soaked in putrid water, fell into a state which rendered walking at all a matter of intense difficulty.

When I returned to the village I found little to recompense me for the fatigues and disappointments which body and mind had undergone. There were no songs, nor merry dances to the sound of the drum and the clapping of female hands. I would lie down soon after dark, with a round log of wood for my pillow, and try to sleep away those long, long African nights which never change.

As for subsistence, though it is a fine country for a vegetarian, my meat-trained system could extract small nutriment from plantain, and cassada. Even these were not too abundant; and I remember Robert's face as he came to me one banyan day with a plantain mashed up into a doughy state, not unlike the description I have heard of the *stick-jaw* puddings which are served in Yorkshire schools. "Eat this, sir," said he; "he no good for mouth, but he fill 'm belly."

My life was really supported on tea—which, as is now generally allowed, is capable of forming tissue—and by the wild sugarcane (imphi). This last is a true food, containing not only sugar, but a considerable portion of gluten, and of those animal substances which are present in all our forms of vegetable food. And here I used to eat it in the primitive manner described by Lucan (iii., 237):

"Quique bibunt tenerâ dulces ab arundine succos."

One would not suppose, now, that in a place like this, where it rains nine months in the year (on the mountains I believe that it rains twelve), there would be fetich for rain-making. Yet there is. It is a kind of centipede, which is bound to a herb and plunged into a calabash of water. This is done in time of war, when the villagers dread an attack from the enemy; for when it rains, negroes do not fight, but hibernate in their huts.

This centipede, moreover, is said to have the power of ejecting a liquid, which is not precisely aromatic, into a man's eye, when taken up by hand. I contented myself by pressing one with my foot, and there was certainly a considerable discharge of some secretion.

I spoke to these villagers, who were also Balengi, about the mountain region to the northeast, but obtained almost all my information from one of the guides whom I had brought with me from *Mteros*. He told me that there were some very high mountains three days' journey in that direction, and that the country was inhabited by his own people. I asked him if there was a mountain there "which smoked." He replied that there was, and also described some mountains which were not covered with trees like the Sierra del Crystal, but with rocks which looked like white salt. He said that he knew the country very well, and that the gorilla was found there. He had never heard of a gorilla killing a man. He also told me that the Balengi of those parts frequently made use of a leaf which, on being rubbed between the hands till the man perspired very much, would smoke and burst into a flame.

The statement respecting the white-topped mountains (whether snow or stone) may, I think, be believed, as negroes can only tell lies by exaggeration, or by turning truth inside out; they can not create falsehood. But the volcano statement was in answer to a leading question; and I have repeatedly remarked that they will almost always give those answers which they imagine will be most pleasing—an amiable trait in their character, but one which leads to error.

I returned to Mtevo's town, and after paying the men, and making the king a present, we started at 4 A.M. with the land-breeze, which usually begins to blow at that hour. Both Robert and I had slight fever. He was sick, and after each outpouring drank a pannikin of salt water to supply the vacuum. I had general languor, pains in the head, callousness about personal property, and indifference to all things mundane.

I stopped at the barque where I had left some of my things. The captain was away aboard the hulk on a visit; so, handing over my weather-beaten canister to the steward, I requested him to make me some tea.

When he brought it he told me that there had been "an awful row," and spun a long yarn, which, as he spoke in a low voice for fear of being overheard, and as I, not caring for servant's scandal, did not listen, was thrown away upon me.

The mate came down and said to me, "Have you any trade powder with you, Mr. Reade?" "I have one cask," said I. "Then look after it, sir, whatever you do; for that man has said that he will blow up the ship."

I turned round and looked at the Malay. His thin lips were pinched together.

"There is my report of the matter, carpenter," said the mate to that dignitary, who had just come below. "If you think it'll do, why, I'll copy it into the log-book, now I'm about it."

The carpenter took the slate out of the chief officer's hand, and read it out in an under tone. It was, as nearly as I can remember, as follows:

"*April* 28. The mate having given the steward an order in the absence of the captain, the steward answered that he would see him damned first. When the mate repeated the order and called him a saucy fellow, he ran into his bunk, where he had two guns ready loaded, and aimed one of them at me, but providentially it flashed in the pan. I had him put into irons. At two o'clock

P.M. the master came on board in a state of beastly intoxication, and ordered the steward to be taken out of irons, although he had threatened to shoot me and blow up the ship as soon as he was loose. As they were taking the irons off him, the master, seeing. he was mad-drunk, asked where he had got the liquor from, and when he found the steward had stole some rum which he kept for his private use, he snatched up an axe and would have killed the man on the spot had not the ship's carpenter canted off the blow with his arm."

Having heard all this, I expressed my surprise that the captain should be in a state of "beastly intoxication." He had never drunk any thing stronger than water in my presence, and had repeatedly told me that he could not take a glass of beer, even in England, without its completely upsetting him.

This innocent remark was followed by "startling disclosures." "It appeared" that the captain had been a warrant-officer in the navy, and had commanded several merchantmen; but his vice had always proved his ruin, and he had been long out of employ when this vessel was fitting out for sea. His specious tongue then won him a berth which first-class men do not care to accept; and he was drunk before the vessel was clear of the Mersey.

"The only time as he has been sober, Mr. Reade," continued the mate, "was at Bapuk when you was there, and then he'd got himself into such a horful diseased state as he *couldn't* drink. Ah! what a time we've had! Here's been the crew as sick as sheep, and we lying in that rotten hole (that's what *I* call it leastways), not taking enough in a week to pay a day's expenses. I've talked to him times on times, sir; I've asked him what he'll do when they turn him out of it, as they surely will; I've even wrote it down on the slate and showed it to him. Well, he blubbered like a cow; but what good's that? What goes out of him blubbering, goes in again from the bottle, hot and strong.

"That ain't the wust, or near the wust, Mr. Reade. The second mate as is gone was a plain, free-spoken kind of man, and he made no secret of it that he'd tell the owners a tale or two as soon as he got home—how the captain drunk up a locker of beer and wine as had been shipped in case of sickness—how he sarved out the crew, flogging on 'em; let alone his adulterations with them oily black girls, when he's got a wife of his own at Liverpool and all. Well, sir, the second mate fell ill at Brass—for that's where we went to fust; and a rare, nasty, fever-stricken, God-forgotten place is Brass—the wust river in all that stinking Bight. Well, sir, the second mate was lying on these here lockers ' down' with fever, very bad, and the captain he was below, drunk (or *pretend- .ing to be drunk*, as some on 'em says), and he says to him, ' Cheer up, old fellow,' says he, ' cheer up, and have a drop o' something, and you'll be all right to-morrow. Wait a moment,' he says, ' and I'll give you a composing draught.'

"It *was* a composing draught, for it was a tumbler of brandy and raw laudanum mixed. And the mate he drank it up, and never spoke again."

Mongilomba's warning and the carpenter's persistent refusal of the captain's medicines flashed upon me.

" We're afraid to go to sea with that man," said the mate. "He *dursent* go to Liverpool."

I advised them to write to the Consul of Fernando Po as soon as they arrived at Gaboon, where the captain intended to victual the barque for her voyage home. I then paddled over to the hulk, where the last doubts I might have had regarding the real drunkard were dispelled.

He was lying on a sofa with an empty brandy-bottle by his side and a very red face. He explained to me that he was prevented by some mysterious impediment from rising as politeness suggested, and that there were sensations in his head which he was at a loss to understand. Muttering something about his poor steward, who had been put in irons by his drunken mate, and having asked me if I had shot any gurril—l—las, he dropped off into a swinish sleep.

To finish this character. When the barque arrived at the Gaboon, which was not till a month afterward, the mate and the carpenter went to the Rev. W. Walker, of whom they had heard me speak in high terms, and whose fellow-laborers at Corisco had rendered them many kindnesses, and they told him the story which I have just related.

Mr. Walker visited the captain, informed him that his officers and crew demanded a consular investigation, and advised him to avoid that investigation by making over his command to the chief officer, and leaving the ship.

The captain was guilty and alarmed. Against him were charges of cruel treatment, embezzlement, and willful murder. Only the Malay remained on his side, even supposing that the affair of the axe had not altered that youth's affections.

And so he took a step which is perhaps without parallel: he accepted the advice of one who was a foreigner, who had no kind of authority over him, and whom he detested, as villains detest good men. He gave up the command of a fine vessel, and landed his chest and carcass at a place where he possessed nothing but a bad name.

The last time that I saw him was on board the English vessel which left me at Prince's Island. He told me with his unaltered assurance that he had sent his barque home, and had staid behind to collect his debts, and was now on his way to Fernando Po to obtain the assistance of the consul. I could see that he had hopes of utilizing me, for I had left the Gaboon with the intention of returning to Fernando Po.

He was lodged in the mate's cabin, and, after dinner, that officer came in and said to the skipper, "He won't take any thing, sir; says he's determined to turn over a new leaf."

"But he must take something," said the captain, "if it's only a drop."

"Don't think he will, sir—seems very owdacious over it."

This reminded me of the got-up scene with the steward and the key of the locker. I peeped into the mate's cabin an hour afterward. The mate had turned in. The man was drinking alone.

I walked on deck an hour longer. Then I looked down through the sky-light.

He was raising a bottle to his mouth. His watery eyes fluttered from side to side, till suddenly they became charged with blood. His face from purple became livid; he tried with red and swollen hands to grasp unseen objects, and fell to the floor—dead drunk.

Corisco Bay abounds in white mullet and green turtle. The former are taken in casting-nets ingeniously made of the pine-apple fibre, which has a gloss like silk. When one sees the mullet splashing in the shallows, he runs for his net, steals through the water as silently as he can, raising his feet high, casts his net, and (if not a water-haul) draws it in full of shining struggling things, which drown on shore, and are interred in negro stomachs.

The turtle are caught in seines or speared by moonlight; and as soon as I heard that Abauhi was a skillful turtler, I told him that I wished to see him take one. He said that it was now full moon, and that if it did not rain I might witness the performance that very night.

At sunset I watched the dark mountains across the bay. Not a cloud rose over them. At eight o'clock I went to Abauhi's house. He said that when the moon rose above the plantations we could go.

It was one of those nights during which, say the natives, it is impossible to catch fish, because the sky has too many eyes.

When the moon had risen above the broad green-leaved trees, Abauhi, taking two long spears and followed by two subordinates, led the way down to the beach. He then asked me if I could swim, as sometimes canoes would upset in the struggle between man and reptile. I was obliged to confess that I could not. He appeared surprised at my venturing on the water at all in such a case, and wished me to go home again. Finding that I was not inclined to do this, he placed me in the bottom of the canoe, holding the sides with my hands, and told me not to move after we had once started.

This injunction was quite unnecessary. During the first five minutes my body remained rigid as a pointer's, and my hair was erect in terror. As we wobbled along, it seemed to me that only a succession of miracles kept us from capsizing. But, after a little time, I saw and admired how nicely these men preserved the equilibrium of the canoe with light touches of the paddle and inclinations of their bodies.

Now Abauhi stood up in the prow, a foot on each gunwale, the moon shining on his swelling arms as he bent the stout spear-staff and threw his limbs into attitudes vigorous and graceful as those of an Apollo.

Two mortal hours, and nothing had been seen. Clouds encircled and threatened to obscure the moon. My joints became horribly cramped, and when I looked at the dark water as we passed, I could not believe that it was possible to see a turtle where I could see only the reflections of the stars.

The two men continued to paddle on without saying a word, and Abauhi remained attentive as ever, his eyes lowered and his spear upraised.

Suddenly that spear was hurled into the water. The men uttered a yell. Something large and black dashed through the air. Abauhi seized a paddle, and the canoe seemed to fly. Before us was a cloud of white foam. I holloaed till I was hoarse, and danced about, forgetting that I might upset the canoe, and that I could not swim. Fox-hunting, sir, was a mere shadow of it. Imagine the first whimper, the view-holloa, and the who-hoop! compressed into one sensation!

The foam ahead I believed to be the turtle itself; but it was the staff of the spear. This requires explanation. The point of the spear, which is small and with an almost imperceptible barb, is tied by a string to the butt. When the turtle is struck the barb remains in its flesh, and the staff, separated from it, but retained by the strings, floats on the surface, prevents the turtle from diving, and marks its course.

As soon as he had caught the staff, Abauhi drew the turtle toward the surface, playing him like a salmon. The second spear was thrown; again the turtle sprang; we had another "burst," but a very short one. The reptile was "distressed," and with a yo hee yo! (borrowed from English sailors) was hauled into the canoe, where Abauhi welcomed him by patting him on the head and spitting down his mouth. This, he told me, was "play," and showed me a scar on his arm which some turtle had inflicted in a sportive retribution.

We drew cover for an hour longer without a find, and returned to Corisco. The turtle, lying at the bottom of the boat, uttered the most extraordinary sounds, all of which caricatured humanity. Sometimes it was that kind of wheezing sound peculiar to old women and sheep; sometimes a harsh, dry, consumptive cough; sometimes that deep-drawn, gasping, eructative sigh, with which boozy bachelors relate the romances of their youth.

I really began to pity the poor animal, with its chronic influenza and its symptoms of "decline." It made delicious soup, however, and very different from that of Guildhall. All its meat is superb, and especially the liver, fried. Of this I ate the next evening to repletion, and dreamt that I was alderman-soup in the infernal regions, being lapped up by plethoric green turtles in scarlet robes.

H

CHAPTER XIII.

THE FALLS OF THE NCOMO.

My Steward Oshupu. — Nengĕ-Nengĕ. — Negro Hospitality. — Description of the Fans.—Discover the Falls of the Ncomo.

On Monday, the 5th of May, I left forever this beautiful island, and the friendly hearts which it contained. After two days in my canoe I arrived in the Gaboon ; and, after three more spent in copying out a vocabulary of the Fan dialect lent to me by Mr. Preston, one of the missionaries, I was ready to visit the Cannibals of the Crystal Mountains, and to search for the rapids of the Ncomo.

But, first, I had to get men. Mongilomba had given up a good place rather than go among the Fans, with whom he had previously formed a slight acquaintance as a trader. Almost all the Mpongwe had the same fear of them. But Robert, my new steward, remained faithful to his promise and his interests.

Robert had his enemies, like all men suddenly raised to distinction. As steward to a white man, he was envied by a score of small-souled negroes, who soon contrived that I should learn his antecedents.

"Robert," I said, one day, "I thought that your 'country name' was Cabinda?"

"Yes, sir; my 'country name' Cabinda."

"How is it that every body calls you Oshupu here? I never hear any one call you Cabinda."

(With a puzzled face), "Oshupu, sir!" (brightening), "Oh! yes —Oshupu—that one name of play my friends like to call me. I not know why they no call me Cabinda, because Cabinda my proper name for true."

"Were you ever cook at a white man's factory, Robert?"

"No, sir," said Robert, coldly.

"When a man takes another man's wife for bad things, what do you think of that man, Robert?"

"I think him bad man, sir."

"Very good; and why do you think him a bad man?"

"When white man want wife, sir, he take him: same way, suppose little dog want wife, he go town, he see other little dog; he like him; other little dog say, I like you; they say that with nose, sir. Then palaver said! But we country fashion (here Robert drew himself up) no same as that. S'pose I want wife, I go to man and say, 'I want marry your son—'"

"His son!"

"No, sir—him you call—not him son—when him son be girl—"

"Daughter."

"Yes, sir, him daughter. Well, he say, Gib me plenty dash, my friend, and you can have him. So I pay plenty dash; my wife come; she go work my garden; she go cook my dinner; she go give me son that be girl, and I sell him when he get big for plenty dash too. Black man's wife same as white man's money. S'pose man take wife, he take money; he bad man too much."

"I shall ask you one more question, Robert. Why did you say the other day that Corisco was a bad place, and that you were glad to go away?"

"I can't tell you lie, sir, because you clever too much. Why I no like Corisco, those Benga boys frighten me. They say, 'You Gaboon boy, you steward to white man in we country, some day you have palaver you no like.'"

"Now, *Oshupu*," said I, "you were cook at Walker's factory; you were caught stealing, and he sent you to prison; when you came out, you ran off with a man's wife, and had to hide yourself in Corisco. When you were at Corisco, you had another 'wife palaver,' and it was only by the husband's forgiving you (for one dollar) that you were able to get away at all."

Oshupu was about to commence flat denial, looked at me, saw it was useless, and held his tongue.

"Now," said I, "I don't care how much you thieved before I took you, or whom you plunder after I leave you; but if any thing is stolen from me while you are my steward, or from any of my friends here, I shall take it out of your wages, and if I find that it is you, shall send you to prison as well."

"Yes, sir."

"Also," said I, in the stern voice of a moralist, "it is perfectly immaterial to me how many wife palavers you get into, but don't suppose that I shall get you out of them. If a Bushman catches you, what does he do?"

"Locks me up in house, sir, and puts my feet in wood. Then my friends pay plenty dash."

"What do you call plenty dash?"

"One gun," said Oshupu, in the tone of a man reading out an inventory—"one chest, three pieces satin striped, six brass rods, two mugs, one basin, one half barrel powder."

"Good!" said I, not without admiring this system of fixed damages; "and if your friends don't pay?"

"Then they kill me," said Oshupu, composedly.

"Well," said I, with equal calmness, "you must mind what you are about; for they may kill you first, and grill you afterward, for all I care."

"Yes, sir," said the rascal, grinning.

You will perhaps be surprised that I should take with me in so responsible a position a man whom I knew to be a thief. But, in the first place, I had no choice. It was *aut fur aut nullus*. In the second place, I can believe that there are cooks who are indifferent to policemen, gamekeepers who do not poach, old servants who do not tyrannize, but I can not believe that there are negroes who do not steal. I except the Mohammedans; but the Christians, I regret to say, have the same bias for petty larceny. This is reckoned as no crime among them, but as one of the industrial arts, though the bungler who allows himself to be detected is punished and laughed at.

I could take my precautions against the pilfering propensities of my steward, but his amorous frailties occasioned me much uneasiness. Negroes are always at extremes. Oshupu not only broke the seventh commandment, he smashed it all to bits.

I did not object so much to the presents of my beads which he made to his paramours (though he was always the soul of liberality), as to a palaver among the Fans, which would inevitably crush my projects by robbing me of my interpreter.

Oshupu assured me repeatedly that I might calm my apprehensions upon his account; but I knew that good intentions only spice desire, and that prohibition to impetuous natures presents that kind of obstacle which invites surmounting. I took my own precautions, therefore, and, as long as we remained among the Fans, never allowed him to go out of my sight, and padlocked him every night into my own room.

Oshupu brought me four men from Cape Lopez, where Mpong-we is spoken with a provincial accent. I asked them if they would be afraid to go with me among the cannibals. They replied that they would go with me wherever I chose. Accordingly, I made out an agreement whereby they were to receive a shilling a day (in current goods), but to forfeit the whole of their wages if they refused to enter the Fan country. At the foot of this document I wrote their names, and, after they had signified before witnesses their full comprehension of its contents, I put a pen between each man's fingers, and guided it to form a cross. This being done, each man glared, awe-struck, at the work of his own hands, and went off loudly debating on the mysteries of black and white.

As I felt confident of safety among savages who had never seen a white man, I did not arm myself, taking only a huge single-barreled duck-gun (unloaded), which was to be carried behind me as an emblem of power. I had found that shooting flamingoes and pelicans caused delay, and I wished to make this trip as speedily as possible, that I might have time to visit the Camma country to the south.

I was not very sanguine of being able to discover the falls of the Gaboon. A M. Braouézzec, *lieutenant de vaisseau*, whom I afterward met in the Senegal, and who has drawn some excellent charts of the Gaboon and its tributaries, had made the attempt in vain; and Mr. Preston, who had resided seven months on the borders of the Fan country, and who could speak their language, had not had an opportunity during all that while of ascending the Ncomo to any distance, on account of the petty wars always raging there. I was not favored with the same facilities as these gentlemen; I could only hope to succeed by a stroke of fortune, and I resolved to put the fickle goddess to the proof.

A knowledge of tides and winds is as necessary to the traveler by canoe as a knowledge of omnibuses in London to the Londoner. We started on the 10th of May at nine o'clock A.M., with the ebb, and by midday had reached Konig Island with our paddles. This islet, as its name implies, was anciently a Dutch settlement. I was shown some big guns which had been left there, and which no one has meddled with since.

I climbed almost to the summit of this island, which is a forest mountain, and crawled into a cavern, which they told me was inhabited by a spirit. It was tunnel-shaped, of sandstone formation, the bottom grooved by a streamlet, through which I had to wade, and which soon convinced me that there was more water than spirits there. Crabs, newts, toads, and nasty unknown things ran from under my feet; spiders, stifled by the smoke of my torch, fell upon me from above; and my "country light," blazing furiously, converted the cave into a furnace. I came crawling out, with a face like a frying-pan, my shoulders covered with suffocated spiders, and found my men surprised that I had escaped from the lair of Mbwiri.

By the time that I had eaten my barbarous dinner it was two o'clock. We stepped from the ebb into the sea-breeze, which, having escorted us till eight o'clock, handed us again into the tide.

Now I could see the dim sky becoming black to the northeast, and hoisting rain-signals in the plainest manner. But I did not fear these clouds. Storms never come up against the tide. Over and over again I had observed this at Corisco. I had seen the dark clouds hovering over the main land till the tide changed, and then the storm came up with all the fury of an element which had been kept waiting.

"Now what can be the reason of this?" I exclaimed, looking upward. "Are there tidal currents in the air which coincide with those in the water? Yes, that must be it. Ah! how marvelous it is that the fury of the heavens should be shackled by a law invisible but undeviating, by a—"

Here a large drop of rain fell straight into my upturned eye, causing intense pain. At the same time I saw (with my other one) that my men had taken down the mast. And at the distance of a hundred yards I observed a streak of white water which uttered a hissing noise, and which grew nearer and larger, and was rising to a roar.

"It appears to me," I said, after the drenching shower had passed, "that tornadoes must be considered as exceptions."

It must have been long after midnight when a light gleamed on me through the thick river mist. At first it seemed far, far away, and in another moment we found that it was close beside us—a phenomenon you may have noticed with link-boys in a London fog. This was the mast-head light of a French guard-ship, stationed at the *Thule* of their possessions in Gaboon; for at this point the Gaboon receives a large tributary, which is called the Boqué; and here the main stream loses its native name of

Orongo, and is called the Ncomo.　Nothing is more common than to find in Africa different rivers called by the same name, and the same river by different names, whence much confusion in geography.

At this junction of the Boqué, which Captain Burton had, only a few weeks previously, traced to its source, and of the Ncomo, which, as I said before, was maiden water after a certain distance, is a little island called Nengĕ-Nengĕ (Island-Island.)　It had once been a missionary station, but had been abandoned.　Most of its inhabitants, however, were Christians, and the mission house remained in good repair.　Sadder mementoes of the good men were to be found in three white tombs, which were almost hidden by shrubs and fragrant grass.

Having been obliged to sleep in wet clothes, I got up very shaky in the morning.　A repast, consisting chiefly of strong tea and sulphate of quinine, did me good, and I talked about going on. But a few small obstacles arose.　In the first place, it would be necessary to procure two Bakĕlĕ, who could speak not only their own language, but also Mpongwe and Fan, and who would assist in paddling the canoe against the powerful stream we should have to encounter.

There were some Christian Bakĕlĕ, who said that they would be most happy to escort me on the morrow, but that they did not wish to break "him Sabby day;" for it happened to be Sunday, I must tell you.　Of course I acceded to this most reasonable request; but on explaining to my pious friends that they would have to paddle for some days without remittance, they speedily backed out of the bargain.　Like many other people who are not Bakĕlĕ, however severely they may read the injunction "On the seventh day ye shall rest," they can close their eyes to the first command, "Six days shall ye labor."

Then my four Cape Lopez men came up to me and tendered their resignation.　I asked them the reason.　They had just heard, they replied, that the people of the Ncomo "chopped man;" they did not like that fashion, and they would rather not go.

All this was said as coolly as if I had not told them beforehand that I was going among cannibals, and as if they had not agreed to go with me.　However, I knew that it would be useless to argue the matter.　Hiding my vexation, I told them I had no desire to take them any where against their will, and that they were at liberty to go where they pleased.　Would I take them back?　No,

decidedly not; I was going to visit the Ncomo. Would I give
them chop? No; why should I give chop to men who were not
in my canoe? This discomfited them rather: they had no means
of returning or of getting food. They saw themselves brought to
a stand-still, appetites excepted.

Oshupu was furious, and I could no longer retain my forced indifference when the villains' backs were turned. I was on the
borders of the Fan country, and I could not move a step. Before
me lay the Promised Land of Man-Eaters. I could not cheerfully
return to the wilderness of civilization. Failure now seemed more
than probable, and delay was inevitable. Now to delay is to stagnate; to stagnate in Africa is to sleep in the snow. It is death.

While cogitating thus dismally, I saw a small canoe push off
from the south side of the river. As soon as it touched land, a
young slave sprang up the bank and offered me a letter. And
what do you think it was in that barbarous spot? An invitation
to dinner, written in good English, and signed *John Ragenji*, who
was sub-trader to one of the Gaboon agents, and who had a factory there. I immediately ordered my carriage, that is to say, my
canoe, and was paddled up to Mr. Ragenji's door.

John was seated in his bamboo piazza in company with another small trader. He had a good-natured mouth, a sweet voice,
and sly, small eyes. He welcomed me with a grand show of cordiality, and, following the custom of his tribe (which is that also
of the Spaniards and Portuguese), requested me to look upon his
house and furniture as my own personal property, and upon himself as my devoted slave.

The other man's name was Tibbett. He was an American negro, who had returned to his mother-land, and had gracefully con-
formed to her customs by abandoning Christianity and marrying
fifteen wives. He had the charge of a French factory up the Boqué, and, having spent several years among our neighbors, his face
had acquired that low type which abounds in the refuse of Gallic
sea-ports.

John proved himself at his own table to be almost a gentleman,
though he fell into the somewhat common error of apologizing
for the meagreness of a better dinner than he usually served, and
perhaps took a little too much trouble to impress upon me that if
I had dined with him in his house at Glass Town he would have
given me Champagne.

"Hospitality," writes some pompous fool, "among civilized nations loses its purity from the ostentation which enters into all its actions." Now the hospitality of the African savage is precisely that of an English hotel, viz., accommodation for the night, which you pay for in the morning. The hospitality of the half-civilized negro is bestowed with the *ne plus ultra* of middle-class vulgarity. But Ragenji, I repeat, was a subdued specimen of the class, and did not remind me very often that I was eating a dinner which he had paid for.

After the dinner was cleared away we drank bottled ale till John became quite "laughful," as he expressed it. This I thought a propitious moment to request his advice and assistance in my difficulties.

His advice was not encouraging. It was to return to Gaboon, to discharge my Lopez men, and to take Kru-boys. I therefore followed a custom common enough in this selfish world. I rejected his advice, and declared that I would be "only too happy" to receive his assistance. "If," I said, "you can get me two Bakělě who can manage to talk Mpongwe and Fan between them, I will go on with these two men, and take my chance of enlisting recruits among the Fans themselves."

John sent out a slave to make inquiries and to publish my wishes.

Tibbett had grown as sad over his beer as John had grown merry. "You should not go up the Ncomo," said he; "the Panwe there are very wild. You had much better come up my river."

I laughed at him, and John poured me out some more beer.

"Yes, we are gay now," said Tibbett, gloomily. "I hope we shall all be happy to-morrow."

Here Ragenji blew his nose with his fingers, and passed a cambric handkerchief lightly across his nostrils.

"It grieves me to the heart," continued the specious Tibbett, "to see you going among those people: they will be sure to make you trouble."

What with his forebodings, and Ragenji's genteel manners, I spent a pleasant and amusing evening; in the course of which John whispered to me not to mind Tibbett, "who talk nonsense plenty, because he wish you in his river;" and Tibbett observed to me, in a momentary absence of his host's, that John was a good man, but was not my friend in helping me up the Ncomo.

In the morning the two Bakělě were ready. I summoned my Cape Lopez men, informed them of this circumstance, and solemn-

ly dismissed them—a bold stroke of policy, considering that they
had already left me of their own accord. But you can easily understand that they felt a violent desire to offer me services which
were no longer indispensable. I took them back with an air of
magnanimity, and at midday we started.

After twelve miles of paddling, the first range of hills visible
from Nengĕ-Nengĕ from blue became green, and the current from
the source began to struggle with the tide from the sea. Here a
Fan called to us from the right-hand bank, and said that we must
not pass without trading at his town. The Bakĕlĕ interpreter
replied that we were not come to trade, but to see the river. The
Fan replied that he would examine the boat, and go with us as
far as the next village, to know if what we said was true. This
far-sighted man was soon alongside of us in a rude little wobbling
canoe. When he had seen that we had only merchandise sufficient for current expenses, I told him in English, which was translated into Mpongwe, which was translated into Dikĕlĕ, which was
translated into Fan, that we were going to the end of the river;
that, as he paddled so well, and was such a fine-made young man,
I would give him a brass rod a day if he would join us. On receiving this gilded pill, he opened his mouth with a grin which
showed his villainous filed teeth, and swallowed it like a perch.

He left his canoe at the village of Olenga, where we arrived
after sunset, and where I resolved to pass the night. A large
crowd collected at the landing-place.

The sight of these Fans (Fanli. pl. Ba-fanh) reminded me of the
pictures of Red Indians which I had seen in books. They were
coronets on their heads, adorned with the red tail-feathers of the
common gray parrot. Their figures were slight; their complexion coffee-color; their upper jaws protruding gave them a rabbit-
mouthed appearance. Their hair was longer and thicker than
that of the Coast tribes; on their two-pointed beards were strung
red and white beads. Their only covering was a strip of goatskin,
or sometimes that of a tiger-cat hanging tail downward; more
often still a kind of cloth made from the inner bark of a tree, and
which is by no means a contemptible fabric. On the left upper-
arm a bracelet of fringed skin.

Their physiognomy expressed good-natured stupidity, which,
as far as I had means of judging, was entirely borne out by their
behavior.

I examined these people with the interest of a traveler; they

RECEPTION BY THE FANS (after Du Chaillu).

hailed me with the enthusiasm of a mob. The chief's house, to which I had been conducted, was surrounded by a crowd of cannibals four deep; and the slight modicum of light which native architecture permits to come in by the door was intercepted by heads and parrot feathers. At the same time, every man talked as if he had two voices.

Oshupu obtained me a short respite by explaining to them that it was the habit of the animal to come out to air himself, and to walk to and fro in the one street of the village.

Being already inured to this kind of thing, I went out at sunset and sat before the door. Oshupu squatted beside me, and, playing on a musical instrument, gave this proceeding the appearence of a theatrical entertainment.

And this taught me how often an actor can return the open merriment of the house with sly laughter in his sleeve. One seldom has the fortune to see any thing so ludicrous on the stage as the grotesque grimaces of a laughing audience. But oh, if Hogarth could have seen my cannibals!

Here stood two men, with their hands upon each other's shoulders, staring at me in mute wonder, their eyes like saucers, their mouths like open sepulchres. There an old woman, in a stooping attitude, with her hands on her knees, like a cricketer "fielding out;" a man was dragging up his frightened wife to look at me, and a child cried bitterly with averted eyes.

I then remembered that in my petticoated days a certain domestic negress used to haunt the same localities as my nursemaid. Nothing could have struck me with more horror than the sight of this melanous but innocent-intentioned female. I had art-instincts within me even then. I would have dreams of beautiful angels, in evening dresses, who took me on their laps and kissed me; and sometimes of this horrible woman, with her sooty skin, her crisp hair, her thick, ugly lips, when I would wake up too frightened even to cry, with my small body in a cold sweat. But now the tables were completely turned. I found myself looked upon as a striking likeness of their Evil Spirit, who is said to be white, and to be dressed in unknown garments, as ours is said to be black, and not to be dressed at all. So, when I appeared in a Bush village, the women and children fled from me in tears, and the dogs with dismal howls, not knowing how to bark.

After the Fans had taken the edge off their curiosity, and had dispersed a little, I rose to enjoy my evening promenade. All

stared at me with increasing wonder. That a man should walk
backward and forward with no fixed object is something which
the slothful negro can not understand, and which possibly appears
to him rather the action of a beast than of a human being.

It was not long before they contrived to conquer their timidity.
I observed two or three girls whispering together and looking at
me. Presently I felt an inquisitive finger laid on my coat, and
heard the sound of bare feet running away. I remained in the
same position. Then one bolder than the rest approached me,
and spoke to me smiling. I assumed as amiable an expression as
Nature would permit, and touched my ears to show that I did not
understand. At this they had a great laugh, as if I had said something good; and the two others began to draw near like cats. One
girl took my hand between hers and stroked it timidly; the others, raising toward me their beautiful black eyes, and with smiles
showing teeth which were not filed, and which were as white as
snow, demanded permission to touch this hand, which seemed to
them so strange. And then they all felt my cheeks and my
straight hair, and looked upon me as a tame prodigy sent to them
by the gods. And all the while they chattered, the pretty things,
as if I could understand them.

Now ensued a grand discussion: first my skin was touched,
and then my coat, and the two were carefully compared. At
length one of them happened to pull back my coat, and on seeing
my wrist they gave a cry and clasped their hands unanimously.
They had been arguing whether my coat was of the same material as my skin, and an accident had solved the mystery.

I was soon encircled by women and children, who wished to
touch my hands and to peep under my cuffs—a proceeding which
I endured with exemplary patience. Nor did I ever spend half
an hour in a Fan village before these weaker vessels had forgotten that they had cried with terror when they first saw me ; and
before I also had forgotten that these amiable Yaricos would stew
me in palm-oil, and serve me up before their aged sires, if so ordered, with as little reluctance as an English cook would crimp
her cod, skin her eels alive, or boil her lobsters into red agony.

The full moon began to rise. When she was high in the heav-
ens I had the fortune to witness a religious dance in her honor.
There were two musicians, one of whom beat an instrument called *handja*, constructed on the principle of an harmonicon—a piece
of hard wood being beaten with sticks, and the notes issuing from

calabashes of different sizes fastened below.*   The other was a
drum which stood upon a pedestal, its skin 'made from an elephant's ear.   The dull thud of this drum, beaten with the hands,
and the harsh rattle of the handja, summoned the dancers.

FAN DRUM AND HANDJA.

They came singing in procession from the forest.   Their dance
was uncouth; their song a solemn tuneless chant; they revolved
in a circle, clasping their hands as we do in prayer, with their
eyes fixed always on the moon, and sometimes their arms flung
wildly toward her.

The youth who played the drum assumed a glorious attitude.
As I looked upon him—his head thrown back, his eyes upturned,
his fantastic head-dress, his naked, finely-moulded form—I saw
beauty in the savage for the first time.

The measure changed, and two women, covered with green
leaves and the skins of wild beasts, danced into the midst, where

* This instrument is found every where in Western Africa.   It is called *balonda*
in Senegambia, *marimba* in Angola.   It is also described by Frœbel as being used by
the Indians of Central America, where, which is still more curious, it is known by the
same name—*marimba*.

they executed a *pas-de-deux* which would have made a *première danseuse* despair. They accompanied their intricate steps with miraculous contortions of the body, and obtained small presents of white beads from the spectators.

It has always appeared to me a special ordinance of Nature that women, who are so easily fatigued by the ascent of a flight of stairs or by a walk to church, should be able to dance during any length of time; but never did I see female endurance equal this. Never did I spend a worse night's rest. All night long those dreary deafening sounds drove sleep away; and the next morning these two infatuated women were still to be seen, within a small but select circle of "constant admirers," writhing their sinuous (and now somewhat odorous) forms with unabated ardor.

Before I left the village I engaged another man, which gave me a crew of eight. I also purchased a smooth-skinned sheep, and upon this poor animal, as it lay shackled in our prow, many a hungry eye was cast. When it bleated the whole crew burst into one broad carnivorous grin.

Bushmen can sometimes enjoy a joint of stringy venison, a cut off a smoked elephant, a boiled monkey, or a grilled snake; but a sheep—a real domestic sheep!—an animal which had long been looked upon as the pride of their village, the eyesore of their poorer neighbors—which they had been in the habit of calling "brother," and upon whom they had lavished all the privileges of a fellow-citizen! That fate should have sent the white and wealthy offspring of the sea to place this delicacy within their reach, was something too strong and sudden for their feeble minds. They were unsettled; they could not paddle properly; their souls (which are certainly in their stomachs, wherever ours may be) were restless and quivering toward that sheep, as (I love to invent metaphors) the needle ere it rests upon its star.

When one travels in the company of cannibals it is bad policy to let them become too hungry. At midday I gave orders that the sheep should be killed. There was a yell of triumph, a broad knife steeped in blood, a long struggle; then three fires blazed forth, three clay pots were placed thereon, and filled with the bleeding limbs of the deceased. On an occasion like this, the negro is endowed for a few moments with the energy and promptitude of the European.

Nor could I complain of needless delay in its preparation for the table, which was red clay covered with grass. The mutton, having been lightly warmed, was rapidly devoured.

After this they wished to recline among the fragments of the feast and enjoy a sweet digestive repose. But then the white man arose and exercised that power with which the lower animals are quelled. His look and his tone drove them to their work, though they did not understand his words.

In the evening I arrived at the village of *Itchongué*, and having seen on our way the remains of a raft, which the Fans had used in a migration from the interior, I resolved to collect as much information as I could about the country from which they had come. I accordingly summoned the oldest man of the village, and, giving him a little tobacco, told him that he should have some more if he would answer the questions which I put to him. To these questions he gave me remarkably clear and concise answers, notwithstanding the number of interpreters through which our words were filtered. The negro's faculty for language is of the greatest assistance to the traveler; and it is marvelous with what truth and rapidity a long sentence is passed from a cultured language to a savage dialect.

The result of my conference was as follows: "The people of his town came from a country called Vinja, far away. In that place it was all forest, as upon the Ncomo. The *nji* (gorilla) was there so common that you might hear its cry from the town. He had never heard of a nji killing a man. The leopard killed men, and the elephant sometimes did so when it was wounded. The animals there and on the Ncomo were the same except one, which, as far as I could judge from his description, seemed to be something like a rabbit with a bushy tail. The people of that country wore a piece of goatskin in front and another piece behind. They were cannibals. Goats and fowls were exceedingly plentiful in that country. It was with them that the young men bought their wives. That was the country where the iron came from, and the ivory too. Some of it was obtained, as in the Ncomo, by killing the elephants in a *nghál*, but most of it in this manner: There was a large marsh or lake where, in the rainy season, the elephants came to bathe themselves. They would often sink into the mud, and, being unable to extricate themselves, would die there. In the dry season the natives would collect the teeth, and send them down to the white men of the sea.

"The manner in which they had migrated was on foot through

I

the forest. They prepared large quantities of dried plantains,
cassada, and various kinds of fruits. While they were traveling
the moon became dark eleven times. Their custom was to walk
three days, to remain encamped about two days, and so on.

"In Vinja there was a river about as broad as the Ncomo at Itchongué—i. e., about fifteen yards across. It was called the Wola."

When I left Itchongué the next morning, I was informed that
I might possibly arrive at the rapids in two days, and that I should
see no more towns. Accordingly, I laid in a stock of torches and
provisions, but found that the river-sides became more thickly
populated as we went on, which proved that the Fans were still
streaming toward the west, and that the natives of Itchongué were
consummate liars. When we passed one of these villages the natives rushed to the brink of the bank above our heads and made
creditable efforts to render earth Pandemonium. All entreated
my two Fans to stop; but the voice of the sea-monster sounded behind them, and they still went resolutely on. At last some "spirited proprietors," who did not mind paying for a novelty, offered
a fowl if they would land and let them see the white man. As
fowls are not to be got every day, I gave orders to land accordingly. After I had been exhibited as usual, Oshupu claimed the
fowl. An altercation arose. The natives appeared to be demand-
ing something against which Oshupu and the Bakělě expostulated, sometimes bursting into roars of laughter. Containing my
wrath, I humbly requested an explanation. Oshupu said that it
was only "them dam niggers' nonsense." I reiterated my request,
and he told me, with a little diffidence, that the inhabitants of the
village, especially the ladies, would be "only too happy" to give
me a fowl if I would divest myself of the skin of the sea-animal I
wore, and appear before them in those simple garments which
Njambi had bestowed'upon me with his own hand. The ladies
wished it to be clearly understood that they did not object to a
fragment of goat's skin, a couple of plantain leaves, or any thing
in reason, but they thought it very foolish of me to hide my skin.
Was I ashamed of it because I was not black?

As I had still a little modesty left, and as it looked as if it was
going to rain, I thought it best to decline their offer, and, without
entering into any argument, returned to my canoe. Soon after
passing the village of Fotúm the stream became so strong that,
had not my canoe been well manned, we could have made no
headway against it. Presently we came to a little island where a

THE RAPIDS (after Du Chaillu).

tributary called the Juba joined the Ncomo. Upon this islet, which is called Ncomo-Juba, I discovered the traces of hippopotami, of whose existence in the Gaboon the Mpongwe were ignorant. I was surprised to find them in a torrent only ten yards wide. Close to their huge footmarks were the broken shells of alligators' eggs, which proves the fallacy of an assertion frequently made that these animals will not live together. In the Fan and Vaz, however, the river-horses frequent only the lower, and the alligators the upper river.

Now the scenery began to repay me for the monotonous hours of my little voyage. We glided into the bosom of the mountains, which rose beside us abrupt and vertical like green walls. Through the mass of leaves I could see here and there pale slender branches, or some giant trunk looking down upon us from above. And from the depths of these precipice-forests came all manner of strange bird-cries, like the sawing of wood, the gurgling of water, the scream of a child.

And now the stream came round a bend of the river with such fury that we remained struggling several minutes, sometimes gaining, sometimes losing a yard. At length, with the aid of poles, we weathered the point, and there before us were the rocks rearing their dark heads among the foam. The roaring of the waters, the excited cries of the boatmen, the sight of a higher mountain than I had yet seen, gave me a glimmering of what it is an explorer feels when he achieves a triumph. I could look round and say, "Here have men striven to come, and none have succeeded but myself. For the first time the breath of a white man mingles with this atmosphere; for the first time a leathern sole imprints its pressure on this soil; for the first time a being who has heard Grisi, and who faintly remembers the day when he wore kid gloves, invades this kingdom of the cannibal and the ape."

As for my Lopez men, they had been so firmly imbued with a geographical theory of their own that rivers have no end, that these rapids, though not the end of the river, were sufficient to make them believe that I was a magician. They were, moreover, very proud of having contributed their efforts to this discovery, clapped each other's hands and breasts with boisterous laughter, and sang a song in honor of Reedee and the Ncomo.

Oshupu whispered to me his conviction that he was the greatest Mpongwe that had ever breathed, and claimed a dollar which I had promised to give him in case we arrived at the rapids.

I walked a little way up the mountain's bank to gain a view of the river above the falls. There I found it a swift and savage stream which no boat could stem, and which, still ten yards wide, must probably wind for some distance among the hills.

As my feet were still in a bad state from my exertions in the Muni, I had been obliged to make this invasion in a pair of carpet slippers. I could therefore neither ascend the mountain, which was about two thousand feet high, nor follow the river to its source, both of which I felt a violent inclination to do.

It is true that, had I succeeded in both these grand efforts, no substantial benefits would have resulted for mankind. The measured height of a new mountain, or the discovered sources of an ancient river, are, after all, but the pedantries of enterprise. Yet these have magnets which allure life-efforts, and which interest the mass. And are not these tastes typical of man's great mental conflicts? Do we not love to enthrone ourselves on obstacles because they are difficult and steep, and to trace back all that is great and noble to its humble source?

.

CHAPTER XIV.

THE PHILOSOPHY OF CANNIBALISM.

Cannibalism.—Its Antiquity.—Its Nature in Africa.—Evidence of a Fan.—A Ghoul Story.

Among most savage nations, it is customary to kill the cripple at its birth, and those old persons who can no longer support themselves. Among these enlightened people, the only hospital, the only poor-house, is the grave.

There is a stern wisdom in this mode of legislation which one can not refrain from admiring. The commonwealth is looked upon as a tree from which the withered and useless branches are pruned, and which increases consequently in strength and beauty.

They sometimes go so far as to utilize the waste matter. The admirable Alphonse Karr suggested that, as the world of intellect progressed, the word "refuse" would become obsolete, and that even relatives might be turned to account. His was a bold flight of fancy, that of a man entering a restaurant, and calling for a maiden aunt à la papillote, or for a portion of cold grandmother. Yet I have mingled with a race, the politest which I have met in Africa, who have attained to this height of commercial refinement.

The existence of cannibalism, which some authors have ventured to deny, is supported by a cloud of authors. Herrêra asserts that the Mexicans discussed the human victims whom they sacrificed. Marco Polo relates that in his time the Tartar magicians enjoyed the right of eating the criminals condemned to death. Juvenal, who had traveled among the Egyptians, accused that enlightened people of the crime; and, according to the history of Abd-Allatif, physician of Bagdad, translated by Silvestre de Sacy, man-eating in the thirteenth century pervaded all classes of Egyptian society, and became a fashion of the beau monde. Here are his own words: "When the poor began to eat human flesh, the horror and astonishment caused by reports so dreadful were such that these crimes furnished the never-ceasing subject of every conversation. But at length the people became so accustomed to it, and conceived such a taste for this detestable food, that people of wealth and respectability were found to eat it as their ordinary food, to eat it by way of *regale*, and even to lay in a stock of it.

It is also interesting to learn from a most credible witness that we ourselves are descended from cannibals, or, at all events, that our northern neighbors are. Witness this passage of St. Jerome: "Quid loquar de cæteris nationibus, quum ipse adolescentulus in Galliâ viderim Scotos gentem Brittanicam humanis vesci carnibus, et quum per silvas porcorum greges pecudumque reperiant, tamen pastorum nates et fæminarum papillas solere abscindere, et has solas ciborum delicias arbitrari!"

But Zeno, Diogenes, Chrysippus, and Montaigne defended cannibalism on high moral grounds; and among certain people the custom is viewed in a sentimental light. Osculati, the Italian traveler, when among the Mayorunas, in his descent of the Mapo to the Amazonas, says that a Mayoruna, who had been baptized, when at the point of death was very unhappy; and on being asked why he was so, replied that he was wretched indeed, because, dying as a Christian, instead of furnishing a meal to his relations, he would be eaten up by worms.

It is at least certain that cannibalism, though more disgusting, is less cruel than murder; yet it would not be good taste in the lady who shudders over these pages to snatch up a paper and read with ardor the details of that which would strike a Fan with horror.

In Africa there are two kinds of cannibalism. The one is sacrificial, and is performed by the priests, whose office it is to eat a portion of the victim, whether man, goat, or fowl. This custom, prevalent among many ancient nations, is still extant in many parts of North Guinea, especially in the Delta of the Niger.

The other is simply an action of *gourmandise*. A cannibal is not necessarily ferocious. He eats his fellow-creatures, not because he hates them, but because he likes them. A *craving for meat*, to which the natives of these parts are subject, and for which, in all their dialects, there is a special term, may first have suggested the idea; but I am rather inclined to believe that it is a practical extension of the sacrificial ceremony. Neither the women nor the young men are allowed to touch the dainty: it is reserved by the patriarchs, and the head which is supposed to contain a grand fetich falls to the king.

Although the missionaries had mixed a great deal with the Fans, they told me that they had never got a clear confession of cannibalism from one of them, though they had "no more doubt that the Fans ate men than they had that they ate plantains." It was, however, never denied of the tribe, but only of themselves as individuals. Thus the natives of village *A* would deny stoutly that they were cannibals, but they would accuse the villagers of *B*. The villagers of *B* would disown the soft impeachment, and denounce the natives of *A* as cannibals of the most confirmed order. Similar answers had been returned to me by the Fan slaves whom I had met with among the Bush tribes of the Muni. *They did not eat men, but the other people of their tribe did.*

I resolved to exercise a little finesse in the investigation of this matter, and after I had passed the villages which had been previously visited by white men, I called a veteran cannibal to me, and questioned him about the people beyond the mountains to the east. Did they eat men? Oh yes, they all ate men. *And he ate men himself.* As he volunteered this statement, he burst into a loud roar of laughter, which we all joined very heartily. I asked him if *man* was good. He replied, with a rapturous gesture, that it was "like monkey, all fat."* I then wished to learn the class of persons he had been in the habit of discussing. He said, only prisoners of war; that some of his friends were in the habit of eating witches condemned to death, but that, for his part, he did not think them wholesome. The best of it was, that he thought I was a cannibal too; a belief which is universal among the Bush tribes of Western Africa, and of which the slave-trade has been the cause. I remember that when I was in the Camma country, a Bakéli slave, who had been brought down from the far interior, and who had never seen a white man before, squatted before me a long time, with his great round, prominent eyes on my face, and his mouth wide open. At last he heaved a gasp of wonder, crying, "*And are these the men that eat us?*"

My veteran now asked me why we took the trouble to send such a long way for people to eat. Were the black men nicer

---

* "We had a fugitive Indian from the Guaisia in our canoe who had become sufficiently civilized in a few weeks to be useful to us in placing the instruments necessary for our observations at night. He was no less mild than intelligent, and we had some desire of taking him into our service. What was our regret when, talking to him by means of an interpreter, we learned 'that the flesh of the marimonde monkeys, though blacker, appeared to him to have the taste of human flesh.' He told us that his *relations* (that is, the people of his tribe) preferred the inside of the hands in man, as in bears. This assertion was accompanied with gestures of savage joy."— HUMBOLDT's *Personal Narrative*, iv., 428.

than white men to eat? My answer was dictated by a motive of policy. I said that the flesh of the white man was a deadly poison, and so, not being able to eat one another, we were obliged to send to this country.

I asked him if it was true that the Fans ate their own relatives when they died. Upon this he affected great horror, and said that they could not do such a thing as that. Nevertheless, the evidence of all the neighboring tribes is unanimous upon this point, which, if I can not positively assert, I certainly can not disprove. The same custom is said to prevail in other parts of Africa. Mollien, for instance, iu writing of the cannibals of Maniana, affirmed that they killed invalids, and ate their grandfathers, and when a stranger died among them, put up his corpse to auction. I believe, therefore, that this custom exists, though perhaps only partially, among the Fans; and that it is regarded as a species of vicious cannibalism, which they will not acknowledge to strangers.

I can at least vouch for the truth of a story which appears much more incredible, which was alluded to rather than related by M. Du Chaillu, and met with a great deal of disbelief. I thoroughly investigated the matter, and can in this respect bear out his narrative. The story is as follows: According to a custom common to the most ancient nations, the Mpongwe bury articles of value with their dead. The burying-ground of the tribe is a small prairie on the south side of the river, and at some distance from the mouth. There one may see the stool or jug which marks the grave of a man, or the calabash which marks that of a woman, or the skeletons of the slaves, whose bodies are thrown on the ground without the honor of interment. Now a clan or family of Fans, who were migrating toward the sea, and had settled among the Shekanis, came by night to the burying-ground, opened all the graves, robbed them of their treasures, and had filled two canoefuls ready to carry away, when they found a fresh-buried corpse in one of the graves. This they also took possession of, and, having come to a convenient place, under the shelter of some mangrove-trees, they lighted fires, boiled the body in the pots which they had just disinterred, and ate it on the very spot where I was first told this story.

Nevertheless, I beg to assure any future traveler in Equatorial Africa that the Fans are an extremely courteous and amiable tribe. He will not suffer any danger of death from their being cannibals. I went among them, as I have already said, unarmed. On the other hand, should he chance to die among them from dysentery, brought on by a vegetable diet (which is always probable), he will have the satisfaction of reflecting in his last moments of life that his body will be carefully prepared for the tomb, and that it will be viewed as a sacred legacy by those who give it burial.

CHAPTER XV.

DRUGGED ELEPHANTS.

Visit an Elephant Nghâl.—Menagerie in the Forest.—Explanation of the Mystery.

Two days after I had returned to Glass Town I heard that some elephants had been inclosed in a *nghâl*. It is not every day that one has a chance of seeing wild elephants penned in like sheep, so I started immediately with crew and canoe to view the phenomenon. After fifteen miles of the broad river, we turned off into by-creeks lined with mangroves. It happened to be low water, and we cut off several branches incrusted with oysters, which we picked off *seriatim*, opened with great difficulty, and found them tasteless and flabby, owing to the heavy rains.

Now and then we caught sight of a single man or woman in a small canoe. These always made off with velocity, abandoned their boats in the black mud, and hid themselves in the maze of mangroves. So large a canoe as mine seldom appeared in these out-of-the-way places except for purposes of war, which appears to be chronic among these aborigines.

Grebes and egrets flew about in clouds. Sometimes we saw grave pelicans perched upon trees, where, in spite of their huge goose-like feet, they appeared to be perfectly at home. Land-crabs darted about in the muddy banks, dodging in and out of innumerable holes like rabbits in a warren; and "jumping Johnnies," a curious little animal, something between newt, frog, and fish, hopped away as we shot past with our gay Camma song, and our paddles sprinkling silver water in the air.

We put up for the night at a plantation-village, which, belonging to a great chieftain of Gaboon, was surrounded by farms, and inhabited by agricultural slaves.

The next morning I set out for the *nghâl*, which was about two miles from the village, taking with me some white beads, my price of admission to this menagerie of the bush.

Some Fan hunters, I was told, had found that three elephants frequented this part of the forest. Paying a ground-rent to the

Mpongwe, owners of the soil, they had built their *nghâl* and had succeeded in inclosing the elephants.

I found a few acres of ground inclosed by posts and railings, the stoutest fence which these savages can build. Round it, at intervals, were the huts of the hunters and their families. Very simple dwellings were these—roofs of dry leaves supported by four poles, and bamboo settles within.

KILLING ELEPHANTS IN A NGHAL.

The ground inclosed was one of those comparatively open patches which are sometimes met with in the equatorial forests, covered with a thick shrubby vegetation, and a large tree standing here and there. Under one of these, which was pointed out to me, the elephants were said to be sleeping. I wished to go inside the *nghâl*, and to creep up close to them. This the Fans would not hear of, though I offered them beads *ad libitum*. No, they feared that my white face would frighten the elephants, and that they would break away. "If they do that, sir, Mr. Reade," whispered Oshupu, "these people make you pay plenty for that palaver."

While we were disputing there was a great commotion, and a crowd of young men came running round. The elephants were awake. I was carried with the stream, mounted on the railings, and one of them was pointed out to me. He was a fine old tusker, and was not more than a hundred yards from me. He was swinging himself on three feet, sometimes lazily raising his trunk to the tree above him, and apparently unconscious of the Babel around.

The elephant, we have always been led to believe, is, even in its wild state, one of the most intelligent and most wary of animals: in strength, the mammoth of modern days; in habit, the most averse to human intrusion. It is a reflecting, contemplative animal, with strongly-developed tastes for solitude and peace.

Now imagine this giant of intelligence decoyed into so palpable a trap. Imagine this monster, which can uproot trees, confined within a fence not strong enough to resist a calf. Imagine this philosopher of so high an order surrounded by talking savages. You do not know how a negro talks. What can be the feelings of the elephant, with his retiring nature and his gentle repugnance to man, in such a position? Why, he would be a Timon of Athens "blocked" at Temple Bar.

Unable to imagine this, you will perform an easier mental operation. You will disbelieve it. In the reader's case I should do the same. But here I was with the wretched animal before my eyes, and I was under the painful necessity of believing them.

I asked how the elephants came within the *nghál*, which, rude as it was, must have occupied these savages a considerable time to put up. Were they driven there? No. The elephants were in the neighborhood. The *nghál* was built. A gap was left open, which they showed me; for they had not even taken the trouble to close it: it was just large enough for an elephant to enter.

The medicine-men made fetich for them to come in; they came in. The medicine-men made fetich for them to remain; and they remained. When they were being killed fetich would be made that they might not be angry. In a fortnight's time the new moon would appear, and the elephants would then be killed. Before that time all the shrubs and high grass would be cut down; the fence would be strengthened, and interlaced with boughs. The elephants would be killed with spears, cross-bows, and guns.

At this moment a man came round singing in a melancholy voice, and dabbing the fence with a rag steeped in a dark brown liquid. The chief of the hunters informed me that the fetich was held every day when the sun was at that part of the sky. Its power would be rendered null and void by the presence of a white man. They would be happy to see me at the new moon.

I took this hint, which was accompanied with much broad laughter, but my trip to Camma prevented me from accepting their invitation. The killing of the elephant, however, though the most exciting, is a feature far less remarkable than their presence in the *nghâl*, and their retention there during so long a period.

"There is something still unexplained," writes Sir Emerson Tennent, "in the dread which an elephant always exhibits on approaching a fence. . . . Sportsmen observe that the elephant, even when enraged by a wound, will hesitate to charge its assailant across an intervening hedge, but will hurry along it to seek for an opening."

Might this *nghâl* then be built across the elephant's "road?" and might he, turning aside, enter by the gap the first opening which presented itself? But how account for his calmness, when the Indian elephants, as we know, display the greatest violence on finding themselves entrapped? In Asia an army is required to inclose them, and they are only tamed, as they are attracted, by the aid of female decoys.

I can only surmise that the elephants are attracted into the *nghâl* by means of some plant for which they have the same mania as cats for verbine, and rabbits for oil of rhodium. Such herbal secrets as we know are often possessed by the medicine-men, or priest-doctors, among savage nations. This must have been the "fetich" which made them come in.

Animals have strong antipathies. The dark brown liquid sprinkled on the fence might possibly have been the "fetich" which made them remain; and herbs with stupefying properties scattered on the ground, or poisoned plantains, the "fetich" which prevented them from being angry when they were being killed.

A slave, who belonged to the unvisited kingdom of Maticamoo, and whom I saw some months afterward in Angola, told me that in his country the hunters contrived to drug the elephants by placing poisoned food in their haunts before they attacked them.

One will naturally inquire why the Fans resort to so laborious a method of killing elephants as that of decoying them into an inclosure, and keeping them there till a certain period of the moon. To this I reply that there can be little doubt that elephants were once caught alive in this manner in Africa, as in India. We know that the Africans once possessed the secret of taming elephants, and that it has expired with many sciences and arts. The elephants which performed in the Roman amphitheatres, dancing, and writing on tablets, were African. We see them represented in the ancient medals with the convex forehead, and the huge pendent ears which mark the type. Polybius tells us also that Hannibal had eighty elephants at the battle of Zama; and Sallust relates that Sextius, the Quæstor of the Proconsul Calphurnius, seized thirty elephants at Vacca, part of the royal stud of Jugurtha.

I will finally quote the English translation of Leo Africanus to prove that this method of killing elephants has been practiced in the more northern parts of Africa:

"And although it be a mightie and fierce beast, yet there are great store of them caught by the Ethiopian hunters in manner following: These hunters, being acquainted with the woodes and thickets where they keepe, use to make among the trees a rounde hedge of strong boughes and rafters, leaving a space open on the side thereof, and likewise a doore standing upon the plaine ground, which may be lift up with ropes, whereby they can easily stoppe the said open place or passage. The elephant, therefore, coming to take his rest under the shady boughes, entereth the hedge and inclosure, when the hunters, by drawing the said rope and fastening the door, having imprisoned him, descend downe from the trees and kill him with their arrows, to the end they may get his teeth, and get sale of them. But if the elephant chanceth to break through the hedge, he murthereth as many men as he can find."

CHAPTER XVI.

THE CAMMA COUNTRY.

By Sea and Creek.—The Fernand Vaz.—The King of the Rembo.—Arrival at Ngumbi.—The Princess Ananga.—The Tobacco Question.—Relative Happiness. —The Cannibal Salute.

HAVING made myself tolerably well acquainted with the countries of the Muni and Gaboon, I now desired to visit the Fernand Vaz, a river about two hundred miles south of the latter, and to enter the interior of the Camma country.

I did not find it easy to carry out this project. There was no kind of communication between these two rivers, since the only trader in the Fernand Vaz (a Captain Lawlin) had lately died there. I knew that to go by land would be almost impossible, since a large delta is formed by the Nazareth and Faz rivers, and a huge swamp barrier thereby opposed. And at this time of year the wind blows always from the southwest, and one can not sail a canoe against the wind.

But it happened that a Captain Johnson had been sent out from Boston to take charge of the vacated factory. He was in Gaboon, and about to sail to Camma in a fine surf-boat, sloop-rigged. He was glad to get a companion, I a passage, and we agreed to go together. On the 28th of May we set sail, and stole slowly from the river into the broad and swelling sea.

During five days we enjoyed that romantic freedom of ocean life, of which poets have written so much, and which consists in being hermetically imprisoned in a small conveyance, and in being at the mercy of every wind and current. However, we contrived to enjoy ourselves tolerably well. At sunrise we would breakfast off a piece of salt beef soaked and boiled over night, with a dish of plantains, a pot of coffee, Durham mustard, chutney, and pickled onions—necessities of civilized life, but luxuries here. After meals, we dipped our fingers in the great finger-basin over the boat's side, and dried them with flourishes in the air, like the Normans of ancient days.

During these excursions I took no stimulants but tea, and some-

K

times, but rarely, a pipe of tobacco. Johnson, on the contrary, lived on gin. He had a case of Hollands, upon which he rested his elbow by day, and his head by night. It was a pillow, half an arm-chair, a solace, and an occupation. He had two china mugs, one of which he filled at intervals of fifteen minutes with spirits, the other with water. He emptied the gin mug first, and the water mug afterward. There was a fixed method in his debauchery which I could not but admire. It was a systematic suicide, which he told me was necessary for the preservation of his health; and he died a few months afterward without having for an hour neglected these somewhat perilous precautions.*

In the bows there was a tub half filled with sand wherein blazed a fire, which, like that of the vestals, was never suffered to go out. Round this would be squatting or lying four Kru-men, two Camma men, the boat's cook, and Oshupu.

Sometimes when there was no wind we would run in near the shore and anchor. Then the anchor-watch would sleep like a dormouse, and the captain like a hare. At the first puff of a fair wind this wonderful man would spring into full life, and cry, "Now, then, hurry up, hurry up there! Now, Captain Jack, wake your boys there—give them hell!" And, Captain Jack, the head Kru-man, having waked his boys and given them "hell" in the language of the Grebboes, the anchor would be hauled up with a hoarse rattle, we would dash on through the morning dusk, the spray falling over us, the ruddy glare of the tub-fire on the sail, the water bubbling music beneath us, while the captain, in a nautical ecstasy, would cry, "Go it, Sal! and *I'll* hold your bonnet!"

It was the first week of the dry season, and we did not have a single shower, which, as we had no awning, was just as well. The natives had begun to burn the grass of the little prairies which crowned the hilly shore between Gaboon and Cape Lopez. At night these presented exactly the appearance of burning mountains.

On the fifth day we entered the Delta at the fork of Cape Lopez, that labyrinth of streams which connect the Nazareth and Fernand Vaz rivers. After ten miles we left the mangroves behind us, and passed through a mass of marshy undergrowth, from

---

* In England a drunkard acknowledges that he is ruining his health, and owns (when sober) that he is the victim of an infatuation. In Africa, where debauchery is death, he tells you that you must always keep a bottle of brandy ahead of the fever.

which rose graceful palms, their leaves rustling in the wind. The country seemed to be one vast swamp, in which locomotion on land could only be achieved on stilts. One small pebbled spot there was on the bank, and hither the boat was directed by the men, without orders. On inquiring the reason, we were sternly informed that people who made this voyage always got out there. This was unanswerable; we got out accordingly, and stretched our limbs, which were tolerably cramped by remaining in almost the same position for six days and nights.

Here I was amused by seeing two land-crabs sparring, it was so complete a caricature of a prize-fight. They sidled up to one another, and round and round on their hind claws. Presently one darted in a quick blow; the other avoided it with the "back run" after the most approved method of the P. R. The boxing attitude, though not assumed by the gorilla, is adopted by some of the lower orders in creation. A rat, for instance, when "cornered," squats on its hind legs, with its fore paws hanging down in front.

In the daytime the voyage was far pleasanter than by the process of "beating" out at sea. Our progress was slow but sure; and there was generally something to look at—a monkey, a jumping-Johnny, or an eagle. But with the night came misery upon our heads. Then rose the musquitoes, and swarmed around us. Then from the swamps rose the gray deadly vapor, which, breathing poison, enveloped us like a shroud. In the morning we would wake and look curiously at each other's pale faces. But the salt beef was an excellent restorative, and we would soon recover from the effects of a sleep which in Europe supplies stamina, in Africa frequently disease.

On the afternoon of the seventh day we emerged into a beautiful river, its banks lined with villages and green prairies. Down to the beach poured men and women when our sail was seen, and cried, "Trade come! Lawli's son!! Lawli's son!!!" There had been no trade in the river for several months, and these people had ragged waist-cloths and no tobacco. They welcomed Johnson (whom they supposed to be Lawlin's son—Heaven knows why; but, having seen so few white men, they think that we are all related to each other, and that we represent a small sub-marine family), as poor men "out of work" touch their hats with cordial fingers to the farmer who finds them a job.

We had entered the river about ten miles from the mouth.

Ten miles more and we arrived at Captain Lawlin's factory, which
was in excellent repair, and placed under the charge of Retimbo,
a native king or head man. He came to meet us, and with his
battered beaver hat, a belcher round his neck, and a short stick in
his hand, reminded me of Sam Collins, the comic Irishman. After dinner we went to look at Captain Lawlin's grave.

This man deserves a public epitaph. He was an American,
and had spent much of his life in this river, for which he had done
so much, and in which he died at the age of seventy. His factory
had formerly been on the other side of the river, and he had called it New York. In '57 he had received an island as a gift from
the natives. This island, which he called Brooklyn, was surrounded by a belt of trees, inclosing a prairie in the centre. His first
step was to cut down and uproot the trees on the south side. He
built a large factory of bamboo, floored it with planks sawn from
native timber, and built a wharf or pier adjoining. The bamboo
huts of his Kru-men and Camma laborers made quite a little village, which he built like a college, having a quadrangle of sand in
the midst. In this sand-square was a large bell, upon which were
chimed the sea-bells half-hourly, day and night, while a Kru-man,
always on guard with a musket, chanted the "All's well!" in sentry fashion.

Behind his village was the prairie, in which a herd of antelopes
might be seen feeding every morning, and which he allowed no
one to molest. A herd of river-horses sported round the island,
raising their huge black heads, and spouting jets of foam into the
air; and the social grosbeaks had formed their republic, like a
miniature rookery, in the trees round the house.

This man was so much beloved and honored by the natives
that they made him a *Makaga*—one allowed to speak in council
—a privilege which no white man but himself has ever received.
An African M.P., he soon created revolutions in the Legislature,
a fact which in itself proves what influence he must have exercised. All absurd customs which tended to excite war or ob-
struct trade were abolished, and a warlike aggression was subject
to severe penalties, as my narrative will presently show. The
thief and the adulterer were handed over to the prosecutor, who
could kill, flog, or enslave, the latter being the usual course pursued. Murder was to be punished by hanging; and an execution
was actually carried out while I was in the river. Without this
explanation, the use of the slip-knot in Africa would have puz-

zled me amazingly; and it proves to us that we must be careful in considering the customs of natives who have received white men among them.

When Lawlin died—that is to say, six months previous to my arrival—he was buried in the prairie, at his own request. A Spanish carpenter had made him a wooden tomb, painted to resemble stone, encircled by a railing. A Christian native (so they told me) had painted this below:

SACRED TO THE MEMORY

OF

CAPT^N. RICHARD E. LAWLIN, OF N.Y.

DIED ON THE 6TH OF DECEMBER, 1861.

"One soweth and another reapeth."

JOHN, iv,, 37.

☞ Reapers, behold the sower!!

I sat down by this grave. No one but those who have traveled in a wild, and desert, and sickly land can understand the emotions with which one contemplates the grave of a white man in the wilderness. It diverts one from the ignoble realities of savage life, and fills one's eyes with those tears which the proudest man is not ashamed to shed.

But I was soon recalled to positive existence. On arriving at Brooklyn, I had sent for a man, named Mafuk, whom I wished to take with me as co-interpreter with Oshupu, and who was acquainted with the creeks and windings of the river, the position of its villages, the tastes and prejudices of its inhabitants.

Mafuk now stood before me. He was an extremely small man, with a yellower face, and something more nearly approaching a beard than one usually finds among these people. Small as he was, he was far from wanting in self-sufficiency, and freely indulged in that familiarity which is the parent of contempt. He began in this manner; and I must premise that a negro always makes inquiries concerning the welfare of one's near relatives.

"How do you do, my dear friend?"

"I am very well."

"Oh, you very well? dat good thing! How your father live?"

I answered that he "lived well."

"And your mother—she well too?"

This catechism began to annoy me, and I answered gruffly in the affirmative.

" You got a sister?"

" What's that to you?" cried I, savagely.

Mafuk gave a shrug of his shoulders, as much as to say, " How extremely ill bred these white men are!"

"I only ask you that, my dear friend," he expostulated, in an oily tone.

"Mafuk," I replied, with concentrated rage, "you are not my dear friend at all. But if you like to take four dollars a month, you may be my servant."

" Please, sir, five—"

"Four dollars a month," I repeated; "if you get me a canoe and four men to paddle in two hours' time"—here I looked at the sun, that great time-piece of the desert—"if not, I shall take another steward."

Mafuk vanished, and returned under the time prescribed: the men were hired at a fathom of cloth a day: the canoe belonged to the factory, and was, of course, lent to me by my companion, whose property it became. It was arranged that we should start at daylight on the following morning; and I never had afterward to complain of Mafuk's inquiries about my family, or of his calling me his dear friend.

I laid out that night on the other side of the island for hippopotami; but none came ashore, possibly because the moon was so very bright. However, I afforded excellent sport to a squadron of musquitoes, who lanced me incessantly till they had raised red spots all over me like miniature mole-hills.

Before daylight I commenced to make my preparations for the interior, which, always the same, I will, once for all, describe.

My canoe would be furnished with mast and sail, spare paddles, and long poles for punting, or to moor by in the shallows; a large stone jar or cask filled with water for the men; a smaller one for my own private drinking. My bed was spread in the stern, so that I could lie down if I wished; and my rug folded into a seat in the bow, on which I would sometimes perch myself, gun in hand, when I wished to shoot a specimen to preserve, or for my dinner.

My men's provisions were bunches of plantains, bought at a shilling the bunch, or at least its equivalent in the currency—a fathom of cloth, or two heads of tobacco, or ten strings of beads, or one brass rod, or a red cap such as worn by our " bargees." Then there were bars of iguma, which is the cassada thus prepared.

RIVER NAVIGATION IN EQUATORIAL AFRICA (after Du Chaillu).

The species cultivated in Equatorial Africa being that which is regarded as poisonous in a raw state, the root is soaked eight or ten days in fresh water; though black mud, which some prefer, answers the purpose as well. It then becomes soft and ready to fall to pieces; is pounded into dough, moulded into rolls a foot and a half in length, like Titanic sausages, bound up in leaves, and steamed for an hour or two. The result of all this is, in appearance, not unlike the worst kind of Welsh cheese, but possessing a strong acrid taste, which, fortunately for mankind, is not to be found in any other form of food. However, the cassada, when simply boiled, has actually no taste at all.

This was all that I was actually required to find; but when harder work than usual was required of them I used to buy them dried fish, and give them a little tobacco as well. Besides, we generally managed to pick up something along the river banks— a monkey, a squirrel, a toucan, a parrot, or, if we were fortunate, a guana; which animals, in spite of "their deformitie and lothsomnes," I, with Peter Martyr, "affirm to be of more pleasant taste than eyther our phesaptes or partriches."

One tin box, water-proof, and not too heavy, contained my ammunition, a bottle of chlorodine in case of dysentery, of quinine for fever, one spare shirt, two pairs of stockings, a measuring tape, twine, a pair of scissors, a *couteau de chasse*, some kind of book which required study, a pound of tea, a few ditto of sugar, two or three tins of prepared cocoa, and a bottle of oil, to protect my guns from rust, which in this moist climate forms in a manner exceeding all belief. I carried a double-barreled rifle and fowling-piece, which I had obtained from Mr. John Lang, of Cockspur Street, and, though I had not many opportunities of testing the former on living objects, I had reason to be highly satisfied with both.

Another tin box, similar in size and make, contained my cash, which in this country is very cumbersome, consisting of those articles which I have just mentioned. The cloth is measured, I said, by fathoms. This is done by one's steward, who stretches his arms out straight from the shoulder, which comes to six feet or thereabouts. If the purchaser has longer arms than the steward, he calls it short measure; if he is not well-developed in that respect, he laughs at you in his sleeve. My stewards, however, had never afforded them much gratification in that way. Mongilomba had extremely fat, short arms, and Oshupu had an ingenious method of "palming," which the natives had occasionally discovered, and which I had strictly forbidden. But he continued to do it, although it did him no benefit: he must have been actuated by a pure love for dear deceit—a chivalrous feeling for frâud.

One pays one's men and buys one's goats and sheep with cloth: of all imports, it has the most certain sale; for Manchester dresses Africa. Nothing is considered so low as the beautiful grass cloths which are fabricated here. We know that there are many girls who look better in a plain cotton print than in silk and satin, but who dare not wear them in society. As cotton is to grass cloth in Africa, so is cotton to silk and velvet in England. You see that fashion is every where the same tyrant. In order to carry all this "material" for young ladies' dresses, I was obliged, like a husband traveling with his wife, to reduce my personal necessities to a very small compass. I wore an old volunteer uniform coat, which, being plain drab, was a good shooting color. Trowsers and flannel shirt to match. In my breast pocket a compass, a pocket comb, and a tooth brush, wrapped up in paper. In my tail-pockets my powder-horn and shot-belt, and my memorandum-book, at one end of which I kept my diary, at the other recorded my *impressions de voyage*. A piece of soap wrapped up in a Turkish towel completed my toilet apparatus.

I remember that when I was a little boy I used to regard yellow soap, rough towels, and starched shirts as inventions of the Enemy of Mankind, and observed, with some acuteness, that this curse fell on higher beings. Sometimes, lying in my snug bed, with all the repulsive duties of the toilet to be undergone, I would watch the sparrows as they dipped their heads in a puddle of water on the leads, ruffled their feathers, smoothed them again with a few pert shakes, and fly away in full dress to some *déjeuner* or *matinée musicale*, and I would yearn for the simple wardrobe of a bird with all the ardor of my young soul.

In the bush my wish was completely realized. Every night I was forced to sleep in my clothes, taking off only my cap and my boots. Soap became quite a luxury, for it is not to be met with in these African wilds, and is, perhaps, the only substance which ants will not eat nor negroes steal. One's wash-hand basin is a river or a pool. European wash-hand basins have certainly a large sale, but they are used exclusively for culinary purposes, and in these the dinner of a rich Bushman is served. Upon this point I soon conquered a natural repugnance; but the sight of my dinner in one of those domestic vessels which we do not usually admit into our sitting-rooms was, I own, a little too much for me.

Economical of space as of time, I did not even indulge in Mongilomba's luxury, a looking-glass; but thereby I gained a novelty, a rare acquisition in the nineteenth century.

When I see you again I shall probably not recognize you; while you, having looked at yourself every day (and, I dare say, a great many times every day) in the looking-glass, will scarcely be conscious that you have changed. I find that this kind of life makes one's face turn all kinds of colors, like a live chameleon or a dying dolphin. Sometimes it's yellow or tawny; or pale and ash-colored (which indicates religious despondency); or a faint whitey-brown, with a lovely tinge of black.

When my eyes have an interview with my face after a long separation, their first impression is that they are under an illusion, till a farther scrutiny, with disgust, compels them to acknowledge me as their owner. Thus you see that the privilege of incredulity is not to be reserved by the intelligent British public. The man who travels in Africa can learn to doubt the veracity even of his looking-glass.

Once fairly off, my Camma men played all kinds of antics, singing furiously. Then they slapped the water with the flat part of the paddle, and, holding it above them, the point downward, let a drop of water fall into their mouths. After this they seemed better, and paddled steadily on till the afternoon.

We were passing a large village, when Mafuk stopped the men, and told me that the King of the Rembo (native name for the upper part of the Fernand Vaz) was staying there, and that it would be a breach of etiquette to enter his country without asking his permission.

Accordingly, I went ashore and received an introduction to Quenqueza, the king of the Rembo, a fine old man, with features more after the North American type than that of the negro. After a few courtesies had passed between us, I told him that I purposed visiting Ngumbi, his metropolis; and that, if I was satisfied that he would be my friend, I should set up a factory there. Quenqueza approved of this scheme most warmly, and said that he himself would accompany me there on the morrow or the day after. Now I have never yielded to negro procrastination, nor delayed a moment longer in one place than could be spent to ad-

vantage, and it was only by persevering in this rule that I have
been able to do so much in a few months. Accordingly, I answered that I was pressed for time, and that I could not wait.
But I might as well have talked to him of the integral calculus as
of the value of time—an article which they spend as ladies do
their pin-money, and only know that it is gone when they find
their pockets empty. The old man asked me to stop a day or
two, as you would ask me to stay "a minute" while you filled
your pipe.

GAMMA MAN AND WOMAN (after Du Chaillu).

I would not give in. Quenqueza declared that he could not
go that evening, and that I should not go save in his company.
I declared that I would return to the factory, and go up the Ogo-
bi (Nazareth) the next day. I ordered my men into the canoe,

and, seating myself in the stern, cried *Kabbi!* (paddle) in a stern voice. Quenqueza, seeing that I was in earnest, begged me to listen to him. I could not leave the Camma or lower river without the permission of the King of Camma. He lived close by. A swift messenger should be sent to him. The king would come. I would give him a glass of rum, and he would give me permission to enter the Rembo. I would give him (Quenqueza) also a glass of rum, and he would then take me to his town. I acquiesced in these conditions, which were reasonable enough, bought a fowl, had it cooked, and dined there surrounded by spectators. I had just finished my repast when the King of Camma arrived with his retinue. I shook hands with him and offered him the glass of rum. He appeared to want it, but looked around him uneasily. Somebody handed him my Turkish towel. He hid his face and the glass of rum under this. When it was removed the glass was empty, and his eyes were slightly bloodshot. I inquired what this remarkable ceremony might mean, and was told that it was forbidden by law to see the king drink. I then asked his permission to go up the river, which he gave me in a very husky voice.

The King of the Rembo came into the canoe, and sat beside me on a mat spread out in the bottom of the stern. About midnight we reached Sika, a settlement rich in plantations. Here I saw a phenomenon—a native woman who could speak good English. She had been brought up by the missionaries at Baraka, and had been married by Retimbo, tenant of Brooklyn aforesaid.

Next day the river narrowed, and its fringe of swamp disappeared. The day passed without any incident except that of my washing my head over the side of the canoe. On seeing my hair all white and foamy with soap, Quenqueza remarked that the ways of the white man were wonderful.

The river banks were very high, and many of the villages were perched precipitously above our heads. On the third day the river had become as narrow as the Ncomo at Fotúm. The sun was now sinking behind the trees, and the glare of daylight softening into dusk, when we saw a light twinkling feebly in the distance. This was Ngumbi, the capital of the Rembo, and residence of the King Quenqueza.

When the men saw this light they uttered a murmur of joy, and bent low over their swift paddles. Then Quenqueza rang an iron bell which he carried always at his waist, and, raising his hands, he cried, "Spirit of my father, protect this white man who comes to visit us! Preserve him from sickness while he stays. Make his heart good toward us when he goes away."

My *entrée* to the town was not attended with that prestige which one might have desired. A fine dry path led from the town down the bank to the water-side. To my disgust, the men paddled by this, and stopped before a strip of black mud of an epicene character, being neither land nor water, but forming a barrier between the two. All tripped over it lightly enough, not sinking lower than their ankles; but it was necessary that I should be carried; so a tall man stooped down like a camel, and I sat astride on the back of his neck, his head making an excellent pommel, and atoning for the shortness of the wool bridle. Presently he began to flounder; I instinctively pressed his head between my knees, and his struggles increasing, my shooting boots began to play the devil's own tattoo on his belly. But now I found that from a camel my man had become a horse. He was sinking in the mud, the surface of which I was rapidly approaching. The polite Mafuk uttered a cry of horror, and raised my pendent legs. Another man offered me his back. I climbed on to it with a gymnastic genius developed by despair. Mafuk held up my legs behind me like a lady's train; and so we struggled on to dry land.

I asked why the king had not come by the proper path. They answered that the path had been bewitched, and that if the king passed by there he would die.

I joined the king in the palaver-house, a large building roofed and supported by poles. Here a crowd collected to see the white man. Two of the king's wives brought water in calabashes to wash our feet, according to a custom ancient and hospitable. My boots and stockings sadly puzzled the royal dame; and these Oshupu took off, with many sneers against her ignorance. Then the lady washed the feet of the pilgrim.

Sandals being here unknown, the sole of the foot is of course hard and horny, and it is that part of the foot which requires most cleansing in the negro. The lady, taking hold of my foot at first with extreme fear, as if afraid that it would crumble to pieces between her hands, afterward rubbed the sole in the orthodox manner, upon which I laughed hysterically, and kicked the calabash into her face.

I was obliged to pass myself off as a trader, for this reason. These people have never seen any white men except those who are traders: There has never been a fort here, not even in the grand days of the Portuguese. As is natural enough, the civilized natives of the Fernand Vaz believe that we are a nation of merchants, peaceful, inoffensive—rather helpless men, but endowed by some mysterious dispensation of Njambi with untold wealth. The Bush tribes suppose that we live under the sea; that our clothes are the skins of those strange monsters which dwell in deep waters; and that Manchester cloth is prepared from a marine vegetable.

Now the interests of Mafuk, my Camma steward, were not the interests of Quenqueza. Quenqueza wished me to build my factory at Ngumbi; and no doubt, in his heart, Mafuk would have preferred it near the mouth of the river. I point out to you this little difference of opinion, not only to explain the king's parable, but also an incident which occurred some time afterward.

When our feet had been washed, the king, in the presence of his people, solemnly bade me welcome. After I had "returned thanks in a brief and appropriate speech," the king told me this parable:

"There was a man named Njabi, who had four sons, Eye, Nose, Mouth, and Skin, and he had one daughter, whose name was Heart, who was never at rest, and she made him visit countries far away. Then he went to see his brother *Qua-qua*. There was one man, *Seringila*, a great liar and tale-bearer, and he tried to make these two brothers enemies; but they remained friends, and burnt this liar and tale-bearer, *Seringila*. Then were their two towns joined together; the town of Njabi and the town of Quaqua became one; but Njabi was the chief."

Then the king explained that I was Njabi, and that he was Quaqua, and that if any man made mischief between us, we would burn him. Here he gave a stern look at Mafuk, who trembled violently. Quenqueza seemed pleased when he saw me writing this in my pocket-book, and when I had finished, he asked me to put down, "*The King of the Rembo told me this story.*"

As I was seated in my house, the door opened, and a beautiful girl entered, accompanied by Osh'upu. She was tall and finely-moulded, her hands and feet exquisitely small; her complexion of that deep warm bronze color, which is as different from the animal blackness of the Coast negroes as it is from the sickly yel-

low of the Hindoos. Her eyes were large, and filled with a soft
and melancholy expression. She came gracefully toward me,
and, holding out her hand, murmured in a soft voice, *Mbolo.*

This young lady was an emblem of hospitality. She told me,
through Oshupu, that the king, her father, had ordered her to attend upon me in person (for that is the highest honor that can be
paid to a guest); and, having asked me if I was pleased with the
arrangements of the house, she smiled and went out.

We spent hours every day in each other's company. At first
she was full of timidity, for she had never seen a white man before; but this she disguised, lest she should hurt my feelings, and
I could read it only in her fluttering eyes and in her poor little
heart, which used to throb so loudly when we were alone.

It is impossible to imagine a more delicious study than this
pretty savage afforded me. I found her as chaste, as coquettish,
and as full of innocent mischief as a girl of sixteen would have
been in England. In a little while I found myself becoming fond
of her.

At daybreak every morning she presented me with a cup of
tea, which Oshupu had taught her to make, and with cakes made
of ground-nuts and plantains pounded together. When I came
back from the forest, worn out and dispirited, Ananga was there
to receive me, and to bathe my wearied feet. She would bring
me my dinner, which she had cooked with her own hands, like
the daughters of the ancient Patriarchs. She would stand by
me all the while; for she would let no one wait on me but her;
and, by devouring me with her looks, would anticipate all my
wants.

When I had finished my dinner, we would sit side by side, and
I would look at my face in her eyes—the only mirror which I
possessed. But, though one can exchange gleams of eloquence
with the eyes, it is difficult to sustain a lengthened conversation.
We soon tried to invent some method of conveying tangible
ideas. She would point to something, and pronounce its name in
Mpongwe. I would say it after her; if incorrectly, she would
laugh, and clap her hands, and repeat it with emphasis. If I pronounced it rightly, she would utter a long sonorous Y-o-o, the affirmative of pleasure.

One day Ananga reproached me with being artificial. What
made me wear so many clothes? she asked, with inexpressible
scorn. I replied that it was one of the foolish fashions of my

country. And was it a fashion of my country, she asked, to wear the hair of a wild beast on my head, and to paint my face white? On my replying that Njambi had thought fit to create me with these deformities, she uttered a cry of derision, and, taking hold of my hair, pulled it severely. When it did not come out, her eyes dilated, and she looked at me in stupefaction. Then, wetting her finger, she rubbed my cheek with it, and fled in terror to my interpreters. They laughed at her uproariously, and she came back in a shamefaced manner, and sat beside me without speaking.

One day I put my hands in my pockets. The sudden disappearance of two important members filled her with dismay; but, when I explained the phenomenon, she went into convulsions of delight. Nothing would now content her but diving her hands all day long into these wonderful "holes," as she called them; and she used even to hold *soirées*, to which her numerous sisters were invited. I was made to put my hands in my pockets at least fifty times an evening; and my hands themselves were passed from one to the other, and examined by these young philosophers, as if they were newly-discovered fossils.

One day Ananga came into my house with a pipe in her mouth. I snatched it from her furiously. She called Mafuk, who usually acted as our interpreter, and said gently that she would not smoke if I disliked it; but how was it offensive to me? She had seen her father smoke in my presence without my appearing to be annoyed.

I said that it was proper for men to smoke, but that it was not proper for women to smoke.

She glanced superciliously at my clothes, and asked whether that was another fashion of my country. I replied that it was. She asked me why it was not considered proper for the women to smoke in my country.

I said that there were very good reasons.

"Ah!" she cried, clapping her hands, "I know why. Tobacco is very dear in your country, so you will not give any to your wives!"

I assured her, with some indignation, that she was mistaken. In our country, I said, the women have the same rights as the men.

"Then why do they not smoke tobacco?"

"Because they do not like it," said I, desperately.

L

"Then, if they like tobacco, they can smoke it," continued the inexorable Ananga.

"No," said I; "the men in our country know that tobacco is not good for the women, and that they would not like it, so they make a law that no woman shall smoke it."

Ananga shook her little head.

"If women try it, they like it," she said. "You do not let them try it, because you fear they like it. Dirt is not good to eat: you do not make law that no woman eat dirt. Tobacco is good to smoke, so you make law that woman do not smoke tobacco. I should not like to go to your country. I think the women work very hard there."

"Oh no," said I, brightening up; "a fine lady in my country has no work to do at all. You are the daughter of a king, but you have to beat up food and cook your father's dinner. In my country the servants do all that, and the fine lady has plenty of money, and beautiful clothes, and can have her hair dressed all day long if she likes."

"Eh!" cried Ananga, clapping her hands, "that country of yours is a fine place. If I was fine lady there, I would take my canoe and my slaves, and go where I pleased, and not ask leave of my father."

"No," said I, "our fine ladies can not do that. They must not go out alone."

"Why not?"

I was puzzled again. How could she understand these refinements of decorum? I could only reply that it was a fashion of my country.

"Ah!" said Ananga, curling her lip, "I see the fashion of your country. You keep your women like slaves, for fear they run away to the Bush, and smoke tobacco."

Our evenings were spent in festivity. When the moon, that great silver globe-light, was suspended in the sky, the young people met in the centre of the town to dance and sing. They would range themselves in two lines, the men opposite the women. They would advance and retire like long undulating waves, singing in turn, and clapping their hands in time. These songs were sometimes witty, but almost always impossible to translate—exceeding in grossness all that I have heard among gipsies in the country, thieves in Whitechapel, or costermongers in the New Cut.

But, one evening, I discovered a new and an innocent pleasure —one which you, in your wretched Europe, can never hope to enjoy.

To bestow a kiss upon lips which tremble with love for the first time is certainly an epoch in a man's existence. Then, imagine what it must be to kiss one who has never conceived the possibility of such a thing, who has never dreamt that human lips could be applied to such a purpose!

I will own, however, that the romance was preceded by a touch of the ridiculous. Ananga and I were seated side by side on the threshold of my house. The sun had sunk into an ocean of foliage; the earth, released from its burning rays, exhaled her sweetest scents and songs. The blue river glided softly by, and kissed the palm trees' fringed and drooping leaves. The parrots flew whistling round the town, and perched on the neighboring trees to roost. As it grew darker and darker, fires, one by one, blazed on the earth, stars in the sky, fireflies in the air.

From a distant cottage came the voice of a young girl, and the tinkling of the harp with which her lover accompanied her song.

It was one of those moments in which the heart rises to the lips, and makes them do all kinds of silly things. I kissed Ananga, the daughter of the king.

She gave a shriek, and bounded from the house like a frightened fawn. This mode of salutation is utterly unknown in Western Africa. She knew that the serpent moistens its victim with its lips before it begins its repast. All the tales of white cannibals which she had heard from her infancy had returned to her. The poor child had thought that I was going to dine off her, and she had run for her life.

I will not tell you how Oshupu brought her back, panting and trembling, and her cheeks wet with tears; how I explained to her that this was only a fashion of my country, and how she offered her pouting lips (slightly shuddering) in atonement of her folly. But I do think, and I will always maintain, that, though the negro intellect is not yet in a fit state to grasp the doctrinal mysteries of our Church, yet a mission for the diffusion of this Christian practice among a benighted people would meet with eminent success, and would make innumerable female converts.

CHAPTER XVII.

THE GORILLA HUNT.

The Gorilla Dance.—On the Track.—Disappointment.

In describing one of the many days which I passed in search of the Great Invisible, I shall describe all; for the gorilla country, from the Muni on the north to the Fernand Vaz on the south, presents an agreeable uniformity in its features and productions.

I had been out several times in the Ngumbi forest, where gorillas are certainly more abundant than in any other bush which I have visited, and had begun to despair of success, when, one evening, Etia, the chief hunter of the village, came and told me that he had heard the cry of a *njina* close to one of the neighboring plantations. He said that we should certainly be able to kill him the next day, and that during the night he and his friends would celebrate the gorilla dance.

This Etia was a Mchâgâ slave. His skin, to use Oshupu's comparison, was like that of an old alligator—all horny and wrinkled; his left hand had been crippled by the teeth of a gorilla; his face was absurdly hideous, and yet reminded me of something which I had seen before. After puzzling myself for a long time, I at last remembered that it was the mask which Mr. Ryder wore in the character of Caliban at the Princess's which Etia resembled so closely. That night I could well have imagined him less man than monster. In the house allotted to the slaves, three old men, their faces grotesquely chalked, played the drum, the sounding log, and the one-stringed harp. To them danced Etia, imitating the uncouth movements of the gorilla. Then the iron bell was rung, and Ombuiri, the Evil Spirit, was summoned to attend, and a hoarse rattle mingled with the other sounds. The dancers rushed yelling into the midst, and sprang into the air. There would be a pause, broken only by the faint, slow tinkling of the harp; then the measure grew quicker and quicker, and the drum would be beaten, and the sticks thundered on the log.

In another dance Caliban assumed the various attitudes pecul-

THE GORILLA DANCE.

iar to the ape. Now he would be *seated* on the ground, his legs apart, his hands resting on his knees, his head drooping, and in his face the vacant expression of the brute ; sometimes he folded his arms on his forehead. Suddenly he would raise his head with prone ears and flaming eyes, while a loud shout of applause would prove how natural it was. In the chorus all the dancers assumed such postures as these, while Etia, climbing ape-like up the pole which supported the roof, towered above them all.

In the third dance he imitated the gorilla getting attacked and being killed. The man who played the hunter inimitably acted terror and irresolution before he pulled the trigger of his imaginary gun. Caliban, as Gorilla, charged *upon all-fours*, and fell dead at the man's feet, in the act of attempting to seize him with one hand.

You may be sure that nothing short of seeing a gorilla in its wild state could have afforded me so much interest, or given me so good a clew to the animal's real habits; for here could be no imposture. It was not an entertainment arranged for my benefit, but a religious festival held on the eve of an enterprise.

I staid up all night, for I was too excited to sleep, and the dancing was not discontinued till cock-crow. Etia told me to get myself ready, for that when the cock crowed the third time it would be light. My fire and kettle were prepared, and I took my breakfast in the dark. Etia, who had danced for hours, but who had not perspired, and who wanted no refreshment, also prepared for the chase. A box in the shape of a bandbox, made of the bark of a tree, contained his ammunition ; the locks of his gun were covered by a piece of monkey-skin ; he took off his iron bell, his ornaments—every thing, in short, but his waist-cloth.

Taking with me a Camma man named Tsambo, who could speak a little English, we started in the gray morning dusk. We passed the first plantation after half a mile through shrubby vegetation. Then we descended a steep hill, and entered a valley of black mud, over which logs had been thrown by way of stepping-stones; and upon them, being narrow and slimy, I found it difficult to maintain my equilibrium. Now we were in the forest. Sometimes a little brown squirrel, with black stripes on his back and sides, would run through the bushes; or a black monkey would make off, jumping from tree to tree with a huge crash, and chattering all the while, as if knowing that I had it in my power to have his skin made into a muff for a Regent Street window.

These, with the stridulent chirping of the cicada, which Anacreon could sing, but which I could only curse, were all the sounds I heard.

We came to a plantation at some distance from the town. It filled a valley. Etia and his brother hunter pointed to the hill which rose on the other side, and, skirting the plantation, we kept to the hill and wound our way toward it. When we had reached the other side Etia became black marble. I looked down and saw, as I had often seen it before, the fresh track of a gorilla. They followed it with the instinct of a beast of prey. A particle of earth or rotten wood misplaced, a speck of mud upon a fallen leaf, a bent twig, was enough for them. The track led us into thick undergrowth. Here we crawled on all-fours along the path which the beast had made. Leaves and small branches fresh torn bestrewed the path, and sometimes a sturdier one rent in twain displayed the power of that mighty arm. Etia gave a low cry, like that of a gazelle, and pointed to some dung still smoking. It was now agreed that the two Mchâgâs should reconnoitre, and, if either succeeded in finding him at feed, they should return and guide me to the spot. So they crept off, taking a few paces and then stopping, like an ape crawling through the wood and feeding on his way. After a little while I heard the cry of a forest bird. This was a signal. They returned, Etia with a bunch of plantains. The track had taken us back to the plantation. The gorilla had been feeding, and had just torn this bunch of plantains from a tree. He had smelt Etia and had bolted.

We toiled along for some time, and in the afternoon we came suddenly upon the track again. It happened to be a moist soil, and we were able to follow it up rapidly, and soon we could hear the ape breaking the branches ahead of us. The two non-combatants now remained behind, and Etia and I crawled cautiously till we were very close to the gorilla, which was slowly retreating before us, breaking the branches as it went.

I was trembling all over, and I could feel my eyes dilating as if they would burst from my head. I grasped my gun tightly and clenched my teeth. At length I was to be rewarded for my five months' labors and disappointment.

But I happened to step on a dry branch, which broke (as it seemed to me) with a sound like thunder. The noise ahead of us ceased for a moment. Then there was a mighty rush, followed by infernal silence. *The gorilla had run away!*

CHAPTER XVIII.

THE GREAT APE OF EQUATORIAL AFRICA.

Battel, Monboddo, Bowdich, Savage, Wilson, and Du Chaillu.—Examination of their Testimony.—Description of the Ape's Habits.

ANDREW BATTEL, of Leigh, in Essex, was taken prisoner by some Indians near Rio Janeiro in 1582, and the Portuguese, having detained him a prisoner four months at Rio Janeiro, sent him to St. Paul's de Loanda. He was imprisoned in a fortress on the Coanza, and then sent to the 'Congo in a pinnace, to trade for "elephant's teeth, wheate, and oyle of the palme-tree." From there he was sent on to Longo (Loango), where he bought ivory at three tusks for a yard of cloth, with a large quantity of grass cloth and elephant's tails. After relating his remarkable adventures during the eighteen years which he spent in Angola, he describes the Congo and Angola kingdoms, their natives, and their natural productions. And it is from him that we receive our first account of the gorilla, to which the old Italian and Portuguese writers have but obscurely referred.

In quoting at length this authority and others, I am aware that I only follow in the footsteps of other writers on the subject, especially the author of *Man's Place in Nature*, who has shown himself no less industrious as an antiquarian than illustrious as an anatomist. But, as this question of the gorilla's habits remains one of controversy and of doubt, I think that I had better sum up all the evidence afforded by other travelers before I add to it my own.

In describing the province of Mayumba, which is a few journeys south of the Fernand Vaz, Battel says, " Here is a great river called *Banna;* in the winter it hath no barre, because the generall winds cause a great sea. But when the sunne hath his south declination, then a boat may goe in, for then it is smooth because of the raine. This river is very great, and hath many fine islands, and people dwelling in them. The woods are so covered with baboones, monkies, apes, and parrots, that it will feare any man to

travaile in them alone.   Here are also two kinds of monsters
which are common in these woods and very dangerous.

"The greatest of these two monsters is called *Pongo* in their language, and the lesser is called *Encêgo*.   The *pongo* is in all proportions like a man, but that he is more like a giant in stature than
a man; for he is very tall, and hath a man's face, hollow-eyed,
with long hair upon his browes.   His face and eares are without
haire, and his hands also.   His bodie is full of haire, but not very
thicke, and it is of a dunnish colour.   He differeth not from a
man but in his legs, for they have no calfe.   Hee goeth always
upon his legs, and carrieth his hands clasped on the nape of his
necke when he goeth upon the ground.   They sleep in the trees,
and build shelters for the raine.   They feed upon fruit that they
find in the woods, and upon nuts, for they eate no kind of flesh.
They can not speake, and have no understanding more than a
beast.   The people of the countrie' when they travaile in the
woods make fires where they sleepe in the night, and in the morning, when they are gone, the *pongoes* will come and sit about the
fire till it goeth out, for they have no understanding to lay the
wood together.   They goe many together, and kill many *negroes*
that travaile in the woods.   Many times they fall upon the elephants which come to feed where they be, and so beate them with
their clubbed fists that they will runne roaring away from them.
Those *pongoes* are never taken alive, because they are so strong
that ten men can not hold one of them; but yet they take many
of their young ones with poisoned arrowes.   The young pongo
hangeth on his mother's bellie, with his hands fast clasped about
her, so that when the countrie people kill any of the females they
take the young one, which hangeth fast upon his mother.   When
they die among themselves, they cover the dead with great heapes
of boughs and wood which is commonly found in their forests."

In Purchas's marginal note he adds: "He told me, in conference with him, that one of these *pongoes* tooke a *negro* of his which
lived a month with them.   For they hurt not those which they
surprise at unawares, except they look on them, which he avoyd-
ed.   He said their highth was like a man's, but their bignesse
twice as great.   I saw the *negro* boy.   Their strength.   What the
other monster should be he hath forgotten to relate; and these
papers came to my hand since his death, which, otherwise, in my
often conferences, I might have learned."

This Banna River is probably the Fernand Vaz, the bar of

which is rendered impassable for a large boat by the winds, which blow continuously from the southwest during the winter or dry season. The gorilla, however, is not known by the name of pongo among any of the Camma tribes. It is the name of the country derived from that of its people. The Pongo country extends from the Gaboon to the Fernand Vaz. But the name of the other monster *encêgo* is correct enough. It is the chimpanzee, which is still called *nchigo* throughout Equatorial Africa, afterward corrupted into *Jocko* by Buffon.

The chimpanzee, as far as we know at present, is distributed over a larger area than the gorilla, being common not only in Equatorial Africa, but in the mountains of Sierra Leone. A young chimpanzee was brought from Angola in the earlier half of the 17th century, presented to Frederick Henry, Prince of Orange, anatomized by Tulpius and Tyson, described by Dapper, and borrowed only the other day by Professor Huxley from the Cheltenham Museum.

I was surprised to find in Lord Monboddo's "Origin and Progress of Language" (vol. i., p. 281) a most important passage, which has escaped the notice of critics throughout this long controversy. It is a letter written by a merchant of Bristol, who had been captain of a trader on the West Coast of Africa, and procured for Lord Monboddo by Mr. Bell, who had been governor of Cape Coast Castle. It is very remarkable as mentioning the *three* species of manlike apes in Western Africa.

"Of this animal there are three classes or species: the first and largest is, by the natives of Loango, Malemba, Calenda, and Congo, called or named impungu. This wonderful and frightful production of nature walks upright like man, is from 7 to 9 feet high when at maturity, thick in proportion, and amazingly strong; covered with longish hair, jet black over the body, but longer over the head; the face more like the human than the chimpenza, but the complexion black, and has no tail. When this animal sees a negroe it mostly pursues and catches them; it sometimes kills them, and sometimes takes them by the hand and leads them along with him. Some that have made their escape say that this animal, when it goes to sleep, does not lie down, but leans against a tree. In this position, when the prisoner finds it asleep, he steals away the hand or arm softly from his, and so steals away quietly—sometimes discovered and retaken. It lives on the fruits and roots of the country, at the expense chiefly of the labor of the natives; and when it happened to be where there is no water, there is a tree with a juicy bark, which it strikes with its hand, bruises, and sucks the juice; and some of this tree it often carries with it when it travels, in case it should not find it or water by the way. And, indeed, I have heard them say that it can throw down a palm-tree by its amazing strength to come at the wine.* I never saw this animal; but there was a young one brought down from the inland country to the King of Malemba, which is next to Cabenda, while my son was there. The people that brought it down said it was quiet and composed the several months they had it, eating, and taking its victuals and drink quietly. It was brought down with a yoke about its neck, and its hands tied like the other slaves that came with it, and came down quietly. But when it came to the king's town, such amazing crowds came to see it from all quarters, it grew sullen and sulky; for, being so exposed, it would eat no victuals, and died in four or five days. It was young, about six feet and a half high. I have never seen this animal, nor my son; but he, in his last voyage, saw the hand of one of them, cut off about four inches above the joint of the wrist. It was dried and withered, yet in that state its fingers were as big as three of his, or bigger than his wrist—rather longer than the proportion of ours; and the part, when cut off in that wrinkled state, bigger than the biggest part of his arm; the upper part of the fingers, and all the other parts, covered with black hair; the under part like the hand of a negroe. It is said to be the strongest of all the beasts in the wood; and all are afraid of it. I have not heard of this animal any where but on the coast of Angola.

"The chimpenza, as the natives call it, the third and smallest class of this species, resembles the other in shape, only smaller, and walks oftener on all-fours than upright. We scarce know when this animal comes to a state of maturity, or the common period or length of its life. I am informed the females have their times like women. I had one on board, of the male sex, but it was very young. My son had a she one aboard his ship last voyage. The natives that brought it down said that it was three years old; but there was no appearance of the menses in the time he had it on board, which was three or four months. It is said

---

* The Jagas are the only tribe who cut down the palm-trees in order to tap them. Their usual method is to ascend the tree by means of a hoop, tap it, and hang a calabash for the sap to run into.

of this animal that they associate in communities, and build little towns or villages; that when their houses are finished they immediately leave them, and go to building more, never choosing to sleep but as few nights as possible in one place. They have their games and pastimes like the natives; and it is said that they have a king, who does not work himself, but orders. This animal, when taken young and used to the natives in their dwellings, does not like to stir out of doors after dark; nor can they force it. One, at Serraleon, in my time, when the women used to go out to gather sticks, went with them and gathered its bundle; and when they went for water, carried its pitcher or jar, and brought it home full with the rest. It is covered with a longish hair, jet black, the hair on the head longest, and shaded in the middle to each side; the complexion of the face rather darker than the mulattoe; the face flattish; a large, wide mouth, almost from ear to ear; small flattish nose, longish chin, eyebrows and forehead like ours, and good regular teeth like ours: makes comical grimaces with its face, and in its face is most like to the ugliest mulattoe woman you ever saw, but uglier. Its face can not help exciting laughter; and I have heard the natives say, if they are laughed at and made game of, they certainly took it to heart and died. My answer to him was, if that was the case they must die, for it was impossible to look at them without laughing. This animal I have only seen at Serraleon and the coast of Angola, never on the Gold Coast; the impungu I have never heard of but on the coast of Angola. The chimpenza, at its full growth, is from two to three feet high on all-fours; is very strong—much stronger than man in proportion—as appears by a droll adventure that happened near Cabenda with one of these animals a little before my son was there last. As the women in that country do mostly the work of the field, one of them told her husband that something ate the corn and sugar-canes. He accordingly gets up next morning, loads his gun, and, seeing some of these animals among the corn, fires among them and wounds one, which happened to be a female. The husband, alarmed at its cries and exasperated, pursues the man, who had just time to get into his house and shut the door before the chimpenza came up with him. It soon burst open the door, seized the man, drags him out, and hauls him along. The wife cries out and alarms the neighbors, saying an old man with a white face, which the chimpenza resembled, had run away with her husband. They gathered as many as they could and as soon to rescue the man; but the chimpenza had got him near to where his wife was before they came up, and would not let him go till they had shot him dead. The man used to come to the factories, and goes by the name of Chimpenza, and I suppose will as long as he lives. The animal lives chiefly, or altogether, on the fruits of the country, such as plantains, bananas, palm-nuts, sugar-canes, and ears of corn, which they roast as the natives do. I asked how they made their fire; was told they take a stick out of the black people's fire that are at work in the field, and so make their own. When a he one catches a black woman, it commonly forces and lies with her; if there are several, they all do it, it seems, in their turns.

" The itsena* is a species between the two former, less than the impungu, and larger than the chimpenza—like the chimpenza in every respect, unless in size. They keep to themselves, the chimpenza and they not agreeing. N.B.—All the three species have no tail."

In the year 1819, when Bowdich, who had been "sent on a mission to Ashantee," visited the Gaboon, he heard of a great ape called the "ingena," five feet high, and four across the shoulders, the builder of a rude house, on the outside of which it slept.

It is very remarkable that none of the Gaboon traders or the French officers should have acquainted men of science with the existence of an animal which the natives talk so much about: this is owing, probably, to that spirit of incredulity which has retarded so many discoveries. It was not until 1846 that Mr. Wilson, an American missionary, who has written an excellent work on Western Africa, and who first reduced the Mpongwe language to a grammatical system, met with a skull of this now notorious ape. His evidence is as follows:

" But the most formidable of all animals in the woods of Africa is the famous but recently-discovered Troglodytes Gorilla, called, in the language of the Gaboon, *njina*. The writer was the first to call the attention of naturalists to this animal. Toward the close of 1846 he accidentally came across the skull of one, which he knew at once, from its peculiar shape and outline, to belong to an undescribed species. After some search a second skull was pro-

---

* The itsena must certainly be the ingena, or njina. Is there, then, a species of ape which is larger than the gorilla, as this would seem to imply? Not in the Camma or Gaboon countries certainly. If it exists it must be in the mountains of Loango.

cured, but of smaller size. No other portion of the skeleton could be procured for some time afterward. The natives, however, seemed to be perfectly familiar with the habits and character of the animal, gave minute accounts of its size, its ferocity, and the kind of woods which they frequented; they also gave confident assurances that in due time a perfect skeleton should be produced. . . . . The writer has seen one of these animals after it was killed. It is almost impossible to give a correct idea either of the hideousness of its looks, or the amazing muscular power which it possesses. Its intensely black face not only reveals features greatly exaggerated, but the whole countenance is but one expression of savage ferocity. Large eyeballs, a crest of long hair, which falls over the forehead when it is angry, a mouth of immense capacity, revealing a set of terrible teeth, and large protruding ears, altogether make it one of the most frightful animals in the world. It is not surprising that the natives should be afraid to encounter them, even when armed. The skeleton of one presented to the Natural History Society of Boston is supposed to be five feet and a half high, and, with its flesh, thick skin, and the long, shaggy hair with which it is covered, must have been nearly four feet across the shoulders. The natives say it is ferocious, and invariably gives battle whenever it meets a single person. I have seen a man the calf of whose leg was nearly torn off in an encounter with one of these monsters, and he would probably have been torn to pieces in a very short time if his companions had not come to his rescue. It is said they will wrest a musket from the hands of a man, and crush the barrel between their jaws; and there is nothing, judging from the muscles of their jaws or the size of their teeth, that renders such a thing impossible."

At the same time, Dr. Thomas Savage, who was a member of the same mission as Mr. Wilson, made diligent inquiries among the negroes respecting the habits of the ape, and the results of his researches were published in the "Boston Journal of Natural History," 1847. I give the following extracts:

"The habitat of the engé-ena is the interior of Lower Guinea, while that of the enché-eko is nearer the sea-board. . . . . . The gait is shuffling; the motion of the body, which is never upright as in man, but bent forward, is somewhat rolling, or from side to side. The arms being longer than the chimpanzee, it does not stoop much in walking; like that animal, it makes progression by thrusting its arms forward, resting the hands on the ground, and then giving the body a half-jumping, half-swinging motion between them. In this act it is said not to flex the fingers as does the chimpanzee, resting on its knuckles, but to extend them, making a fulcrum of the hand. When it assumes the walking posture, to which it is said to be much inclined, it balances its huge body by flexing its arms upward.

"They live in bands, but are not so numerous as the chimpanzees; the females generally exceed the other sex in number. My informants all agree in the assertion that but one adult male is seen in a band; that when the young males grow up a contest takes place for the mastery, and the strongest, by killing and driving out the others, establishes himself as the head of the community.

"Their dwellings, if they may be so called, are similar to the chimpanzee, consisting simply of a few sticks and leafy branches supported by the crotches and limbs of trees; these afford no shelter, and are occupied only at night.

"They are exceedingly ferocious, and always offensive in their habits, never running from man as does the chimpanzee. They are objects of terror to the natives, and are never encountered by them except on the defensive. The few that have been captured were killed by elephant-hunters and native traders, as they came suddenly upon them while passing through the forests.

"It is said that when the male is first seen he gives a terrific yell, that resounds far and wide through the forest, something like Kh-ah! Kh-ah! prolonged and shrill. His enormous jaws are widely opened at each expiration, his under lip hangs over the chin, and his hairy ridge and scalp are contracted upon the brow, presenting an aspect of indescribable ferocity.

"The females and young at the first cry quickly disappear. He then approaches the hunter in great fury, pouring out his horrid cries in quick succession. The hunter awaits his approach with his gun extended; if his aim is not sure, he permits the animal to grasp the barrel, and as he carries it to his mouth (which is his habit) he fires. Should the gun fail to go off, the barrel (that of the ordinary gun, which is thin) is crushed between the teeth, and the encounter soon proves fatal to the hunter.

"In the wild state their habits are in general like those of the *Troglodytes Niger*, building their nests loosely in trees, living on similar fruits, and changing their place of resort from force of circumstances."

KILLING A GORILLA (after Du Chaillu).

The next evidence is that of Mr. Ford, also an American missionary of the Gaboon, who contributed a paper on the Gorilla to the Philadelphia Academy of Sciences in 1852. After speaking of the geographical distribution of the gorilla, he says: .

"He always rises to his feet when making an attack, though he approaches his antagonist in a stooping posture.

"Though he never lies in wait, yet when he hears, sees, or scents a man, he immediately utters his characteristic cry, prepares for an attack, and always acts on the offensive. The cry he utters resembles a grunt more than a growl, and is similar to the cry of the chimpanzee when irritated, but vastly louder. It is said to be auidible at a great distance. His preparation consists in attending the females by whom he is usually accompanied to a little distance. He, however, soon returns, with his head erect and projecting forward, his nostrils dilated, and his under lip thrown down; at the same time uttering his characteristic yell, designed, it would seem, to terrify his antagonist. Instantly, unless he is disabled by a well-directed shot, he makes an onset, and, striking his antagonist with the palm of his hands, or seizing him with a grasp from which there is no escape, he dashes him upon the ground, and lacerates him with his tusks.

"He is said to seize a musket, and instantly crush the barrel between his teeth. . . . . . This animal's savage nature is very well shown by the implacable desperation of a young one that was brought here. It was taken very young, and kept four months, and many means were used to tame it; but it was so incorrigible that it bit me an hour before it died."

The next authority upon the gorilla is that of M. P. B. Du Chaillu, who was a trader in the Fernand Vaz River, and to whom science stands indebted for no less than sixteen well-preserved specimens of this ape. As a careful and industrious collector of skins, M. Du Chaillu has achieved labors worthy of an Audubon. His account of the gorilla's habits, which was prepared in New York, does not, however, add any thing of value to the foregoing descriptions. The supposed facts which I have already quoted have been moulded round him into adventures of which he was made the hero. In the history of these exploits, it is stated, in addition, that the gorilla, when enraged, beats its breast with its hand, thus making a noise which can be heard at the distance of three miles, and that he kills his antagonists with a single blow of his paw, ripping open the skull or the belly. After five months' careful investigation, I found that the gorilla neither beats his breast like a drum, nor attacks man in the above manner; that M. Du Chaillu has written much of the gorilla which is true, but which is not new; and a little which is new, but which is very far from being true.

Therefore, in presenting to the reader the evidence of the native hunters which I collected in the gorilla country, and in comparing it with that collected in the same manner by Messrs. Savage, Ford, etc., I am compelled to put aside as worthless the evidence of M. Du Chaillu, who has had better opportunities than any of us of learning the real nature of the animal, but who has, unhappily, been induced to sacrifice truth to effect, and the esteem of scientific men for a short-lived popularity.*

When I was traveling in the interior of the gorilla country, I used to inquire at the village where I passed the night if there was any hunter there who had killed a gorilla. If such a man happened to be there, he would be brought to me, and I would question him, through an interpreter, on the habits of the ape. This plan I pursued among the Balengi of the Muni River; among the Shekani, the Bakĕlĕ, and the Fans of the Gaboon; and among the Commi of the Fernand Vaz, and the slaves whom they employed as hunters, belonging to the Mchaga, Ashira, Apinji, and other tribes of the interior. It was in this last river, where gorillas are most plentiful, that I obtained most information. These notes I compared, and have reserved those facts only which are corroborated by the united testimony of hunters from those three distinct parts of Equatorial Africa—the Muni, the Gaboon, and the Fernand Vaz.

At Bapuku the gorilla is not known to the Coast tribes. The most northerly point where I heard of its existing was on the banks of a small river above Cape St. John's. It is found less frequently in the Muni than it is in the Gaboon, and more frequently in the Fernand Vaz than in the Gaboon. I was credibly informed that it is found in Mayumba (where Battel speaks of its existence), and as far south as Loango; but I am inclined to believe that it is distributed over a much larger area than is at pres-

---

* In a paper which I read before the Zoological Society, and which has been published in their "Proceedings," I stated the evidence upon which I have been led to assert that M. Du Chaillu never killed a gorilla. In other respects his book is a medley of truth and fiction, and of which I can give a minute analysis if required.

ent supposed. The chimpanzee is found as far north as Sierra Leone, and I imagine that the gorilla will always be found in the same regions as the chimpanzee. The latter is found nearer the sea-coast, and in more open localities than the former. This will explain how it is that more is known of the one than of the other. The Fans told me that the *nji* was very common in the country far away to the northeast, from which they had migrated, so much that in that country they could hear its cry close to the town; and at Ngumbi I was told that the gorilla dance came from a country three months' journey in an easterly direction.

While the chimpanzee frequents the neighborhood of small prairies, the gorilla seems to love the sombre twilight of the thick forest. He goes on all-fours, sometimes alone, sometimes accompanied by his female and young one. He tears small branches and leaves from the trees at the height of three or four feet from the ground, and sometimes ascends the trees to eat of the fruit. There is one kind of grass which grows in small tufts, of which he is so fond that it is an almost certain indication of his presence in the neighborhood. At morn and eve he visits the village plantations, and eats the plantains and sugar-cane, uttering a plaintive cry. At night he chooses a large tree to sleep in.

When the female is pregnant the male builds a rude nest, usually about fifteen or twenty feet from the ground. It is a mere layer of dry sticks and young branches, which he tears off the tree with his hands. Here the female is delivered, and the nest is then abandoned. At the rutting season the males fight for their females. A reliable informant had seen two gorillas fighting. One of them was much larger than the other, and the smaller one was killed. From this we may, I think, infer that gorillas are polygamous, like stags, cocks, pheasants, and other animals which battle for wives.

The ordinary cry of the gorilla is of a plaintive character, but in rage it is a sharp, hoarse bark, not unlike the roar of a tiger. Owing to the negro propensity for exaggeration, I at first heard some very remarkable stories about the ferocity of the gorilla; but when I questioned the real hunters, I found them, as far as I could judge, like most courageous men, modest and rather taciturn than garrulous. Their account of the ape's ferocity scarcely bears out those afforded by Drs. Savage and Ford. They deny that the gorilla ever attacks man without provocation. "Leave njina alone," they say, "and njina leave you alone." But when the gorilla, surprised while feeding or asleep, is suddenly brought to bay, he goes round in a kind of half circle, keeping his eyes fixed on the man, and uttering a complaining, uneasy cry.   If the hunter shoots at him, and the gun misses fire, or if the ape is wounded, he will sometimes run away.   Sometimes, however, he will charge, with his fierce look, his lowered lip, his hair falling on his brow.   He does not, however, appear to be very agile, for the hunters frequently escape from him.

His charge is made on all-fours: he seizes the offensive object, and, dragging it into his mouth, bites it.   The story of his crushing a musket-barrel between his teeth is general; and a French officer told me that a gun was exhibited at the French settlements in the Gaboon twisted "*comme une papillote.*"   This, however, is not very wonderful, for the cheap Birmingham guns, with barrels made of "sham dam skelp" iron, which are sold to the natives, might easily be bent and twisted by a strong-jawed animal.

I heard a great deal about men being killed by gorillas, but wherever I went I found that the story retreated to tradition. That a man *might* be killed by a gorilla I do not affect to doubt for a moment, but that a man *has* not been killed by one within the memory of the living I can most firmly assert.   I once saw a man who had been wounded by a gorilla.   It was Etia, the Mchaga hunter, who piloted me in the forests of Ngumbi.   His left hand was completely crippled, and the marks of teeth were visible on the wrist.   I asked him to show me exactly how the gorilla attacked him.   I was to be the hunter, he the gorilla.   He took the attitude depicted in the engraving, page 186.   I pretended to shoot at him.   He rushed toward me on all-fours, and, seizing my wrist with one of his hands, dragged it to his mouth, bit it, and then made off.   So, he said, the njina had done to him.   It is by these simple tests that one can best arrive at truth among the negroes.

The leopard is considered a far more ferocious and formidable animal than the gorilla.   The chimpanzee also attacks man when assailed; so does the orang-outang; so, indeed, do all animals, from elephants to insects.   I can see no reason for supposing that the gorilla is more savage or more inclined to attack man than other animals which, like the gorilla, are wary and timid, and which use their keen faculties of scent and hearing to escape from him.

In my humble character as a mere collector of evidence, having no special views to promote, I wish only to arrive at the truth. On this point my account differs from that of my reverend predecessors, and I must frankly admit that there is almost as much to be said on the one hand as on the other. Negroes are inclined rather to exaggerate than to underrate; I have examined a larger number of witnesses than probably Messrs. Wilson, Savage, and Ford did altogether, and I used double care in this examination, since it had become a controversial question. But these missionaries, on the other hand, possessed a great advantage over me, because they knew the native language, and therefore could not be imposed upon by interpreters; and they were better acquainted with native character than I was. The relative value of our evidence I can not precisely estimate, because I do not know from what tribe they derived their information. If from the Mpongwe, among whom they lived, and among whom there are no genuine gorilla hunters, my evidence will be the more trustworthy. But if they examined the same class of men as myself, their accounts, from their knowledge of native dialects and superior experience, will be entitled to the most attention.

That which I can attest from my own personal experience, in my unsuccessful attempts to shoot a gorilla, is as follows: I have seen the nests of the gorillas as I have described them; I can not say positively whether they are used as beds, or only as lying-in couches. I have repeatedly seen the tracks of the gorillas, and could tell by the tracks that the gorilla goes habitually on all-fours. I have never seen the tracks of as many as two gorillas in company. I have seen a young gorilla and a young chimpanzee in a domestic state. They were equally docile. I have seen the dung of the gorilla, which resembles that of a man. And I can say positively that the gorilla *sometimes* runs away from man, for I have been near enough to hear one run away from me.

I heard other stories about the gorilla, which, though not sufficiently absurd to be put aside as incredible, were not so thoroughly corroborated by other witnesses as those which I have just related.

One of these is, that sometimes a family of gorillas will ascend a tree, and will eat a certain fruit till they become gorged, like turkey-buzzards. The old father remains seated at the foot of the tree. If you can approach close enough to shoot him, you may then kill the rest of the family at your ease.

The second story is the one so often told, not only of gorillas,

but of all large monkeys—of women being run away with. At a
village on the right-hand bank of the Fernand Vaz, the women
are said to have been frequently chased by gorillas as they went
to fill their calabashes at the spring. A woman was brought to
me who stated that she herself had excited the passion of a gorilla,
and had hardly escaped him. In all this, however, there is nothing wonderful. We know that monkeys are susceptible animals.
But when one hears of a woman being carried off to the woods
and living among apes in a semi-domesticated state, we are justified in thorough disbelief.

The chimpanzee is said to be more intelligent than the gorilla.
If you throw a spear at the *njina*, say the natives, he will spring
out of its way; but if you throw one at the *nchigo*, he will catch
it in his hand and throw it back at you. In the interior country
of Sierra Leone it is commonly reported that the natives tame
the chimpanzee, and teach him to pound maize in mortars, and to
fetch water from the spring. This is as badly authenticated as
that rumor of the people in the Lower Soudan who have tame
giraffes; but it is not very improbable. Monkeys were tamed
by the ancient Egyptians, and taught to pick fruit off the trees,
and to do other kinds of work. In some parts of Abyssinia they
are still taught to hold torches at feasts. The chimpanzee, it is
known, is very docile and intelligent in a state of captivity.

When I asked if the gorilla made a noise like a drum by beating on his breast, I was told "No;" but that the chimpanzees had
drums, and often came to beat them near the village. As may be
supposed, I did not pay much attention to this story; but I afterward mentioned it to Etia, who replied that to say the chimpanzees had a drum like theirs was not true; but it was true that the
chimpanzee had a drum, and that he beat it with his feet. I said
that I should like to see this drum. He took me into the wood,
and showed me a large tree called *oreva*. It was hollow, for I
could see where a porcupine had burrowed in it. This was the
chimpanzee's drum, he said; and, catching hold of two young
trees, he swung himself in the air, and beat with the soles of his
feet against the tree. I must confess that I heard no sound like
that of a drum; but he told me that the chimpanzee did it "so
strong-strong-strong" that one could hear a booming noise ever so
far away.*

---

* It has been said on good authority that they occasionally assemble in large
numbers in gambols. My informant asserts that he saw once not less than fifty so

GORILLA AND NEST.

The third variety of ape in Equatorial Africa is the koolookamba. M. Du Chaillu has asserted that it gives the cry of *kooloo*, whence its name. When I asked the hunters to imitate its cry, they made a noise like *ee!—ee!—a-a-a!* I asked them if they could tell me any thing in its way of life which made it different from the chimpanzee and gorilla. They said that there was only one thing which it did different from them. If the mother had its young one in its arms, and saw a little string of red ants crossing the path (which has really a very pretty appearance), she would think that they were playthings for the child, and she would put it in the midst. When the child cried, she would take it up again. Then the *drivers*, as these ants are called, would begin to bite her; she would think it was the child, and would dash it down upon the ground, so that sometimes it was killed then and there.

In the gorilla dance which I saw performed at Ngumbi, and in which the dancers imitated various attitudes of the gorilla, two of these struck me as peculiar. One of them was a sitting posture, with the legs straight out and the arms upon them; the other was also a sitting attitude, with the arms folded over one another on the forehead.

. I have not been able to discover that the habits of the gorilla differ in any material respect from those of the chimpanzee. Both animals build nests; both go usually on all-fours; both attack by biting;* both change their dwelling-places in search of food and solitude; both, without being gregarious, sometimes seem to assemble in large numbers, as Dr. Savage was told respecting the chimpanzee at Cape Palmas, and I respecting the gorilla at Fernand Vaz. A white man has never yet bagged a gorilla or a chimpanzee. The wariness of these animals, the uncertainty of their haunts, and the jealousy of native hunters, will always render ape-shooting a difficult task, and one which offers more interest to the naturalist than to the sportsman.

At present we possess only the evidence of native hunters, as collected by Messrs. Wilson, Savage, Ford, and myself. From

---

engaged, hooting, screaming, and drumming with sticks upon old logs, which is done in the latter case with equal facility by the four extremities.—*Observations of the External Character and Habits of the Troglodytes Niger, by Thomas N. Savage, M.D., Boston.* "Journal of Natural History," vol. iv. 1843-4.

* *Biting* is their principal act of defense. I have seen one man who had thus been severely wounded in the feet.

this, which I have just placed at some length before the reader, it
will be seen that the great apes of Equatorial Africa differ but
little in their habits from one another. Nor does it seem that
they differ much from the orang-outang, which also, as is well
known, builds a nest to sleep in, goes on all-fours, sits with its
head bowed, loves the densest and most sombre of the forests, and
when wounded, will rush raging upon its enemies, whose sole
safety lies in instant flight, as they are sure to be killed if caught.

CHAPTER XIX.

DETAINED.

Leave Ngumbi.—Am brought back.—Imprisonment.—The false Ananga.—Great Palaver.—Deputation of Bakělěs.—Set at Liberty.—Dangerous Bar.

ETIA, under pretense of making a detour, had led me so carefully out of the gorilla's way that I abandoned the chase in disgust. I saw that it had been by the merest accident that I had so nearly succeeded, and doubts respecting the integrity of my Caliban began to arise. These were confirmed by Oshupu, who came up to me that evening in great wrath (for I had promised him a handsome present if I killed a gorilla), and said that Quenqueza had given orders to Etia not to introduce me to the mighty anthropoid whose acquaintance I was so desirous of making.

This was, of course, very annoying and disheartening, after all the trouble I had taken. I went to the king, and told him that I should leave his town the next day. I had previously dispatched a canoe to Captain Johnson at Brooklyn, asking him to send me goods, and I received that evening several pieces of cloth, and a gallon or two of rum. I gave the rum to Quenqueza, and spent almost all the cloth in buying billets of ebony, partly to keep up my character of trader, partly to do a good turn to the king and his people, all of whom had been very kind to me.

The next day the king and his people were supinely drunk. The king begged me to wait till the next day. He would then accompany me in person to Brooklyn. Much as I might have felt flattered by this offer, I at first declined it, for I wished to reach the Gaboon in time to sail to Fernando Po by the vessel which went to meet the mails there, and I had not many days to spare; and negro princes do not love rapid traveling. However, the old man was so polite, so humble even, that I graciously yielded, and remained another day.

The next day I had my boat loaded with the ebony which I had bought and with my other effects. I then went to the king, and announced that I was ready. He said that he must go with me, because he was my dear friend. I requested him to come, then, immediately. He said that he would eat his breakfast, and then he would go. After he had finished breakfast, I reminded him that my canoe was waiting. He said I must please speak to his cousin before I went. I asked him where his cousin was. He replied that he was in the plantation. I said, in broad English, that I would see his cousin farther before I waited for him. This was translated by Mafuk into polite Mpongwe. Then the king promised to come down to the canoe as soon as he had arranged some domestic matters with his steward. I went down before him, and waited half an hour in a boiling fidget. The king did not come. This increased my exasperation. I cried *Kabbi* in a savage voice. Mafuk and Oshupu began to remonstrate. I would not listen to them. The men grinned, and bent their backs. We shot out into the middle of the stream; a cluster of natives on the bank looked at us with open mouths. When Ngumbi was hidden from sight, I felt like a man who had escaped from prison, and stretched myself luxuriously on my mat.

A large black and white eagle was perched upon a tree above the river, and, contemplating the stream which flowed calmly past, was digesting the heads of fishes (which alone he eats), or trying to devise a second course to his repast. I placed my rifle to my shoulder, and knocked away the branch from under him. He gave a scream, and vanished.

On we went through the water shadowed by the high trees, while the river on the other side shone like molten silver in the sun. I was lying at full length on my back, with my hat over my eyes, building castles in the air. Suddenly my men stopped, and looked at each other with anxious faces. Lazily raising myself, I looked back, and could see, at a great distance, a large black spot, and something rising and falling like a streak of light in the sunshine. The men put their hands to their ears: I listened, and could hear now and then a faint note borne toward us on the wind.

"What's that, Mafuk?"

"King, sir."

"Oh, he's coming, is he?" said I, laughing. "Well, he can easily catch us now he's so near. *Kabbi!*"

My stewards gave an uneasy smile, and did not answer me.

The men dipped their paddles into the water, and that was all. Every man was listening with bent head, as if trying to detect

DETAINED.

the words or the tune. I looked round again. I could see that it was a large canoe, manned by about twenty men, with a kind of thatched house in its stern. The song still continued, and could now be heard plainly. My men flung their paddles down, and began to talk to one another in an excited manner.

" What is the matter?" said I, pettishly.

The sweat was running down Mafuk's forehead. He knew what he had to fear, if I did not.

"*It is the war song!*"

On came the canoe, low and dark, black with men, the paddles tossing the white water in the air. On it came, shot swiftly past us, arched round, and came close alongside. Then arose a storm of angry voices, Quenqueza's raised above the rest.

" What does he say, Mafuk?"

" Says we must go back, sir."

" Does he?" said I, and looked at his canoe. They were more than double our numbers, and I was afraid that my men would not fight very well against natives of the same river as themselves. However, I knew that my rifle (though it could not speak, for it was empty) would nevertheless exercise a tacit influence in the palaver, and I had placed my hands upon it, when, happening to look round (I can not imagine why), I saw something which made me sink gracefully back in my seat, and put my umbrella up. The next moment a canoe filled with well-armed men came on the other side, and two men, springing into the bow, began to turn our canoe. Oshupu, who had remained quiet enough as long as there had been only one canoe to deal with, now that escape became impossible stirred himself up to war, his courage rising with the danger. Knife in hand, he ran forward in the boat; there his friends held his hands, while his foes knocked him down with their paddles edgewise—a sight which afforded me infinite amusement. But when a youth at my right hand seemed anxious to join the scuffle with a drawn sword, I had to place my hand on his shoulder, cry *Nyawhi, nyawhi* (No, no) in a most impressive manner, and shake my head as if I wanted it to fall into the water. The fact is that your fine dashing fellows are very dangerous company: fights, like breakers, should be avoided as long as tact or skill can contrive; and then pluck, which is a quality the brutes possess in common with ourselves, should be used only as a sword in the hands of system.

When I saw that resistance was useless, I adopted the only

N

course which was left to me. I sat under my umbrella and calmly surveyed the row. I knew that if I showed signs of fear I should be in danger. Negroes are like monkeys, which will caress you as long as you confront them; but shrink from them in fear, and they will bite.

My men were taken out of the canoe, and assigned places in those of our captors. Quenqueza came to sit beside me, and embraced me with his treacherous arms. I shook my head surlily, and gave him the cold shoulder. But, with the exception of Robert, who was sulky over his wounds, and I over my indignity, every body was joking and laughing. It was wonderful how quickly good humor was restored. The men, who had still the black war-paint on their foreheads, were affably slapping the breasts of those who were now polite prisoners of war.

I set two men to sleep in the canoe and to guard its contents. I knew that it would be bad policy to take my things back to the house, as that would imply an intention of continued residence. When I went up into the town I expected to find a crowd in the palaver-house. But it was empty; the streets were deserted; the king was asleep. This reliance in their own power, and in my inability to escape, hurt my pride more than if they had chained me hand and foot. I returned to the boat, and made Oshupu (who was so fond of fighting) an insensate offer of going off again, and of contesting any attempt to bring us back. But this time it was Oshupu who was wise. His bloodletting had wonderfully cooled him down, and he condescended to pronounce this prudential sentence: " These people hurt we properly if we go again."

I went and sat down in my house. Presently the door opened softly, and Ananga came in. She tapped her bare feet lightly against the lintel to shake the red dust from them, and tripped toward me, her anklets tinkling gayly. I turned my head. She placed her hand softly on my shoulder. She laid her little cheek against mine. She brought to me with her lips one of those sweet lessons she had learnt from mine. But I went through this ordeal of enticement with unchanged features and an obdurate mien. When she found that I took no notice of her, she pretended to go out, raised the latch, made a terrific noise, and slammed the door. Thinking that she had gone out, I turned round, and there was the little impostor crouched beside me. She burst into a wild and musical laugh; at the same moment the sun disappeared; there was a moment of twilight; the darkness fell upon us like a sudden cloud; the fires blazed forth, and the sweet notes of the harp arose. Ananga, springing from me in coy revenge, danced with inimitable grace, her arms rising and falling like the wings of a beautiful bird; and as she danced she murmured forth her favorite song, which she had sung before me till I knew it well.

It was a song of the Bushmen describing the white man, according to their mythology.

> In the blue palace of the deep sea
> Dwells a strange creature:
> His skin as white as salt;
> His hair long and tangled as the sea-weed.
> He is more great than the princes of the earth;
> He is clothed with the skins of fishes,
> Fishes more beautiful than birds.
> His house is built of brass rods;
> His garden is a forest of tobacco.
> On his soil white beads are scattered
> Like sand-grains on the sea-shore.
>   *   *   *   *   *   *   *

Pleasures should be cherished, but never analyzed. Dandle the cherub in your lap, and take it for granted that its roses are not false, and that its little teeth are all its own.

Although I could only speak to Ananga through the voice of Mafuk, and though I was aware that the white complexion inspires negroes with disgust, since it appears to them to be the result of disease, I yet had the vanity to believe Ananga when she said that she loved me.

That night, wishing for a little conversation, I sent for Mafuk. Ananga and I sat on the mat side by side. Mafuk perched himself on a stool in a dark corner, so that his voice alone might obtrude upon us. A torch was stuck in the ground before us. Sometimes its gleams were so feeble that I could not see her form, as black as the night; then only her bright eyes, her shining teeth, and her brass ornaments gleamed upon me. At other times the torch burned well enough, and made the whole room light as day.

I had spent a little fortune in trade-goods upon my princess. From her neck fell a cluster of beads which I had hung there with my own hands. Round her waist, arranged in elegant folds, she wore her best dress—two fathoms of satin-stripe cloth. How well I remembered the day on which I had given it to her! She had immediately begun to hem it with some fine plantain fibre—which makes good thread, except that it is brittle—and a needle made from a small fish-bone. There she had staid all the day, and would scarcely speak to me till it was finished. And when it *was* finished, how her eyes sparkled as she put it on! how she tossed her little head, and turned her coquettish eyes upon it, and received with a proud smile the envious looks of the king's wives!

"Mafuk," said I, "tell Ananga that I am going away to-morrow."

Ananga gave a pert smile when this was translated to her, as much as to say, "If my father lets you." But she answered,

"When you go away I shall be sorry."

"And why will you be sorry?"

"Because I love you very much."

"Do you love me better than your own people?"

"Yes."

"Would you like to come with me to my country?"

Ananga sighed. "I am a bundle," she answered; "if my father tells you to take me, I am taken; if my father tells you to leave me, I am left. Man is the master."

This recognition of our superiority came with double grace from her lips, since, to tell the truth, she had rather tyrannized over me lately. I was in the habit of treating her as a lady, while hitherto she had been only treated as a slave. But I regret to say that this kindness on my part had appeared to lessen her affection for me, and to develop her self-esteem.

I felt a fatal curiosity to know why it was that Ananga loved me better than the people of her own race. I burned to hear the artless confession of this child of nature; to fathom the thought-secrets of her young soul. From the tender and untrained mind, thought I, of this guileless girl I shall hear, for the first time, the unsophisticated language of the heart; having wandered through our social desert of withered passions and spurious affection, I can now refresh myself with a draught at the sweet fountain of purity and candor.

"Why do you love me better than black men, Ananga?"

She hesitated to answer. At last she said faintly that she loved me better than them, she could not tell why. But I made her fond of me; perhaps it was some fetich which I had given her. She was only a poor black girl; how was she to know all the arts of a great white man?

Ah! thought I, not without a little self-complacency, love is indeed a fetich which no philosopher can define, and which may be concealed in a look, in a smile, in a word; which—

Ananga's musical laugh interrupted my meditations. She was chattering something to Mafuk with vast noise and volubility.

Now savages can not speak without a pantomime of eyes and hands, which often renders language superfluous. Ananga was touching her beads and cloth, glancing at me, and laughing immoderately.

"What is she saying, Mafuk?" said I.

My grave tone warned Ananga. She said something in a low, quick tone to Mafuk; but as she put her fingers on her lips at the same time, I easily guessed the meaning of her words.

"She is asking you not to tell me, Mafuk; but I am your master: do what I order you."

Mafuk, alarmed by my apparent knowledge of Mpongwe, and by my imperious tone, confessed what Ananga had just said, viz., that she thought a white face very ugly; that having her face wetted with a man's lips was very improper, and not nice at all; and, finally, that she only liked me because I had a fine canoe and servants, and because I had given her plenty of beads and some fine satin-stripe cloth.

Upon this I went into the house of the slaves, and began to take down some words of the Mchâgâ dialect.

I had always shown, as the match-makers say, "a marked attachment" for Caliban. It was natural that at such a moment I should seek relief in his sweet and intellectual society. I began to look upon him as an old and valued friend. Even his extreme ugliness disposed me in his favor; there, at all events, could be no deceit in that.

The next morning a grand palaver was held. The king, and his cousin, who was heir to the throne, sat on stools; the rest squatted on their heels. The king had a long staff in his hand. After he had spoken he handed it to his cousin, who passed it on in the same manner. No one interrupted the man who held the staff, and the whole meeting was conducted in the most orderly way. All spoke without that hemming or hawing by which the mass of our orators are distinguished; and even when very young men rose to speak, their opinions were listened to in strict silence.

After the king had spoken, his cousin rose and declaimed with great energy. Mafuk, Oshupu, and I were sitting at a little distance from the palaver-house, and I observed that they seemed to listen with great interest to the prince's speech. When they explained its purport to me, I was not surprised that they should. It was, in fact, proposing that Mafuk and Oshupu, my two interpreters, should be killed.

I had at first been a great deal too indignant to think about danger; and it was now with a sense of relief, notwithstanding the wound to my vanity, that I found I was not held responsible for my escapade. This clever cousin of the king's represented that affair as a deep-laid scheme of my stewards to take me away like a golden goose from this town, that I might set up my factory near the mouth of the river. He therefore brought forward a bill for the extinction of these two traitors. Oshupu did not show signs of discomposure: as a Gaboon man, he considered himself superior to these people, and did not believe that they would dare to do such a thing. But Mafuk remembered the fable of Njabi and the fate of Seringiba. He saw himself already tied to an imaginary stake, and wept aloud.

I went into the midst of the assembly, and through the mouth of the impassible Oshupu I informed the king, his cousin, and their people that I was the master of these two men, and that in leaving the town they had only obeyed my commands. "If you must kill some one," said I, addressing myself pointedly to the king's cousin, "you must kill me." Upon this I gave a lofty kind of laugh, as if the slaying of a white man was too absurd an idea to be entertained for a moment. Upon this the Makagas laughed too.

"Now," said I to the king, "you wish me to stay here because I am your dear friend, and because you wish to give me and my men goats and plantains to eat. I wish to go away, that I may bring you cloth and tobacco, and white beads for your women. Now listen to a story which I will tell you. A man lived with his wife. His wife loved him because he had plantains, cassada, and ground-nuts plenty." (This was a touch of nature, and there was a murmur of applause.) "But she loved him so much that she never wished him to leave her. But one day he said to her, 'My heart, I must go to the plantation to-day. I must get ground-nuts from my slaves who work there.' And she said, 'You must not go yet.' But he said, 'I must go,' and he went. Then she was angry, and she said to her two brothers, 'Go, bring back my

husband; he wishes to see another woman.' They brought him
back, and he staid. But one day she said to him, 'Sir, I am very
hungry; nothing lives in my stomach. Please go and get me
something to eat from your plantation.' But he said, 'My wife,
this plantation it is far away. In three days I go; in three days
I come again.' So he went. But when he came back he found
her dead from hunger.

"So, my friends, the plantation where I get cloth and tobacco
is far away. I go now; in a moon I come back. But if I stay
here, you will smoke all your tobacco, you will wear out all your
cloth. Then you will say, 'Go,' and I will go. But while I am
gone away you will have no tobacco, and you will die."

The Makagas applauded this speech much in the same way as
Tories praise Macaulay's History for the beauty of its style, with-
out allowing themselves to be influenced by his treatment of facts.
In other words, I was to be kept a prisoner.

At the close of the palaver, I sent Mafuk to the king to ask
when I could go. He replied that I could go to-morrow. To-
morrow! a negro's to-morrow! The morrow came, and with it
the same promise. I saw that I was likely to be detained a long
time. I knew what I had to expect. I should be treated well;
but time, the treasure of which I was so avaricious, would be
wasted away by these spendthrifts, who know not its value—who,
like children, do not know that it has any value at all. You will
naturally ask what the motive of the king could be, since he could
gain no real advantage by making me a prisoner. But this system of keeping white men prisoners of hospitality is common
enough in Africa, as all those who have studied the manners of
this continent are well aware. Vanity is its root. The chieftain
who has a white man in his town is looked up to by all his neighbors. He invites his friends to come and see *his white man*, as
lion-hunters in England would invite you to meet a great statesman or author at dinner. Possibly, also, he wished to show—not
me, the golden goose, but those "who had taken me away by
force"—that he was not a man to be jilted so contemptuously.

I had resigned myself to my fate, when the aspect of affairs
very suddenly changed. Twelve men had entered the town, and
were assembled in the palaver-house. Their features were ferocious; their hair thick and rough; and they were armed with
spears. They were a deputation of Makagas from a neighboring
tribe of Bakělěs. At a meeting of river-chieftains some time be-

fore, Captain Lawlin had proposed a law for the abolition of those intestine wars which are so fatal to commercial interests. The law enacted that whatever chieftain shed blood, or caused blood to be shed, should pay a fine to all the other chieftains. These Bakĕlĕs had heard of our little skirmish, and of the shedding of Oshupu's blood—chiefly from the nose. They came to demand sundry fathoms of cloth and articles of crockery-ware. If these were not immediately paid, they would burn the town.

These simple-minded but resolute men were paid what they asked, and I was once more free. The next morning I was ready to go. Quenqueza wished to sit with me in my canoe. I told him that I would have nothing to do with him. He might go in the canoe he brought me back with. He accordingly took his big canoe, which he could only man with a few slaves, as he was now afraid to leave his town in a defenseless state. He dogged me all the way down the river with a pertinacity which made me watch him closely. At every village which we passed a large crowd was collected on the bank. At each we were requested to stop and bear witness to the infraction of the law; at each the king's canoe was detained, and he was duly informed that he was fined so many fathoms, mugs, and dishes. A perfect unanimity prevailed as to the king's guilt. There was no party spirit. Every village was entitled to its mulct, and every village demanded it on the spot. If the cabinets of Europe were to form such a treaty, there would be an end to all armed neutralities, to all luke-warm intrigues, and perhaps to all warlike aggressions.

At every village Quenqueza requested me to stop and pass the night; at every village I refused, in the most decided terms, to do any thing of the kind. Mafuk was all for conciliatory measures. Quenqueza had the reputation of being a powerful magician, and Mafuk acknowledged that as long as he remained in the Rembo he (Mafuk) was a boy, although he was an old man. I pointed out to him what an excellent reason this was for getting out of the Rembo. I told the men that I was well acquainted with the king's magic arts, but as long as we kept moving they would be ineffectual against us.

That night, as I sat with my rifle across my lap, not daring to sleep, I saw the great canoe creep stealthily past us. Two miles farther on I saw a light gleaming through the trees. It was the king's encampment. We passed close to it. The sight of those cheerful fires, and of the king's men as they lay round them eat-

ing their supper, was a powerful temptation to my weary men.
Quenqueza's stately figure rose in the midst, the ruddy glare of
the flames playing on his face. "Come," he cried, "you are
tired. Here are mats spread on the ground, and the supper is
prepared."

And then Ananga's voice, melodious and enticing as those of
the ancient sirens, was heard from the dark background, as, softly
singing, she entreated us to come.

My men wavered, but I would not yield to them. "You must
paddle till daybreak," I said; "or, if you sleep, it shall be in the
canoe, and I will keep watch." Upon this they regained their
courage, and cried out that they were not Bushmen to sleep in
the wood. Then Ananga's song ceased, and the king cursed us
heartily. Mafuk trembled. I laughed at him. "Ah!" he said,
"to-morrow I shall be a man, but to-night I am a rat."

I thought that we were now fairly rid of our man, and was beginning to doze, when I heard again the low plash of the paddles,
and the king's canoe, gray in the moonlight, again shot by. I
was "on guard" instanter. This pertinacity perplexed me; nor
have I yet been able to understand it. When we reached the
open river we were favored with a fair breeze. I hoisted mast
and sail, and soon left the king's canoe behind us in the distance.

On arriving at Brooklyn I was compelled to remain a day there,
in order to obtain a more seaworthy canoe. As the south wind
blows through the three months of the dry season without intermission, I resolved to take the open sea and attempt to round
Cape Lopez—an enterprise attended with some little danger in a
crank canoe under heavy canvas; but I was too much pressed
for time to think of adopting the usual route, viz., by paddling
through the creeks, and running up under land.

As we were beating down to the mouth of the river, the villagers on the shore called out to us that we could not cross the
bar, as the sea-breezes had been so strong that it was in a dangerous state. In the afternoon we made a small sandy point on the
south side of the river. Here my men landed, spread my rug under some shrubs, and told me that we must wait till the bar had
subsided, which might possibly be by five o'clock or so the next
morning. A more abominable place there could not have been.
There was not a village within miles of us.

I calmly calculated certainties and probabilities. During four
hours I should be certainly exposed to a burning sun; during a

whole night I should be certainly bitten by mosquitoes if I staid. If I did not stay I should probably be drowned. I preferred taking my chance, ordered the rug to be taken back to the canoe, and told the men that there was not the least danger, and that across the bar they must go. I spoke with a perfect assurance, as if I knew more about the matter than they did. They looked at each other in a very perplexed manner, and ended by yielding to the superior mind. We paddled round the point.

As we approached the bar, the frightful roaring of the waters, the foam which dashed incessantly in the air hanging over them like a white mist, and the uneasy faces of the men, made me doubt there being a probability in the matter. The boatmen took off their shirts, and bound their cloths tightly round their thighs, evidently preparing for a swim. As I did not know how to swim, I was saved that trouble, at all events.

I had often observed the skill and judgment displayed by these men in crossing bars: on the other hand, I knew that in moments of extreme peril they frequently lose their nerve.

But in Oshupu I had great confidence. Unfortunately, he did not know the channel, and could only hold the sheet. Mafuk, on the other hand, knew the bar, but his face was already a dingy blue. I sat close to him, resolving that if he mismanaged matters I would throw my arms round his neck and drown him. Possibly my eyes expressed some such intention, for he seemed alarmed when I changed my seat. The men were talking loudly as we neared the white water, probably declaiming on the impossibility of getting through it. I told them to hold their tongues. Mafuk pointed out the channel with a trembling finger. Oshupu, with an easy smile on his lips, turned his eyes on the water and the sail by turns. He is the only courageous negro whom I have yet seen. For escape was not a certainty even for these able swimmers. The bar was at some distance from the land; the waves might dash them upon the rocks; and the water abounded in sharks.

As we mounted the first roller, a funny idea seized me of *lounging* into death, if I had to die; so I laid myself at full length on my bed, and, with my face resting in my hand, regarded the army of waves which we had to encounter. By the skillful management of the boatmen we had almost got through, when a giant roller loomed before us. It was *a third wave*, which is always the worst. Wrenching the rudder from Mafuk, who had wildly op-

posed our broadside to it, I cheered the men to their work. If it
broke before we topped it, we were lost. I put her head straight
at it, like a horse at a stiff fence. The canoe sprang toward it in
great leaps like a horse's gallop. I never had such a moment of
intensity. Now the wave was above us like a huge precipice.
Up, up we went, as if we were mounting to the sky, and then
down, down, down on that dark smooth wave, like sliding down a
mountain side. Behind us there was a terrific crash, like the
bursting of a water-spout. The wave had broken, and we were
skimming through the open sea.

Then I burst into a profuse perspiration all over, and one of my
legs had a fit of trembling which I could not stop for some time.
And it is singular enough that since that, whenever I am startled
or excited, even by such trifles as a slammed door, or by any
one speaking to me suddenly, this limb is subject to the same sensation. As for the men, they clapped their hands and said that
white men knew every thing. They attributed to superior intelligence that which was really an ignorance of danger, and an in-
temperate rashness which is far inferior to true courage.

When the time came for the evening meal, the men found that
they had put their water in a leaky cask, and that all the store we
had was in a gallon jar which I had filled for my private drinking. I told them that I could not land, and that, as they had been
fools, they must put up with a little privation. With this moral
exordium, I filled a small pannikin and handed it to one of the
men, telling him he must not drink much. To my amazement, he
simply filled his mouth with water, rolled it round his palate, and
spat it out again. The others did the same. I have since been
told that such is their invariable habit when stinted in their supply.

In three days, the wind being always on our beam, we had
made our voyage of two hundred miles, and having stretched my
cramped limbs, I walked up to Baraka Mission.

CHAPTER XX.

THE EQUATORIAL SAVAGE.

His Education.—Religion.—Witchcraft.—Government.—Code Moral.

AMONG the natives of Equatorial Africa one finds as little variety as among its features and natural productions. There appears to me to be no difference between the Mpongwe, Benga, Bakali, Shekani, etc., except such as can be attributed to circumstance and climate. Their strength, stature, complexion, manners, and dialects are modified by their locality, their food, their isolation from their fellows, and their intercourse with white men.

The dialect of a great city is usually more soft than that of a provincial town; the latter less harsh and rugged than the scarcely intelligible sounds which one hears in remote mining or agricultural districts.

The court lady is tall and elegant; her skin smooth and transparent; her beauty has stamina and longevity. The girl of the middle classes, so frequently pretty, is very often short and coarse, and soon becomes a matron; while, if you descend to the lower classes, you will find good looks rare, and the figure angular, stunted, sometimes almost deformed.

The Mpongwe, with their melodious dialect, their courteous manners, and their graceful forms, inhabit Gaboon, the metropolis of *Equatorial Africa*. Securing the best situations on the rivers, they laugh at the poor Bushmen who plant their villages so far from these high-roads of commerce, and who, with their guttural tongue and their degraded appearance, are the rustics of the country. The Benga of Corisco and the Commi of the Fernand Vaz form the middle-class link between the two.

The Fans would appear to be the exceptional race, and to have descended from the north; while the others, as far as I could learn, had originally migrated from the south. In their manners and customs the Fans do not appear to differ much from the rest: like them, they are circumcised; like them, the women wear brass rings on their legs and beads in their hair. But their appearance, with their light complexions and rabbit-mouths, is peculiar; and when I first entered a Fula village, I was much struck by the resemblance of the races. They have a metal currency similar to that which is used on the Niger; their method of killing elephants I have already proved by Leo Africanus to have been practiced in Nigritia; and it seems to me extremely probable that these Fans are an offshoot of that powerful race who have extended their conquests over so great a part of Africa.

I shall now attempt to describe the real existence of the savage; his progress from the womb to the grave; the woman whom he rules; the laws which he obeys, and the gods whom he worships.

If a negro of Equatorial Africa possessed an entailed estate, and detested his heir-at-law, he could not wish more earnestly for children. Owing to the evil climate of this country, to the poor food and vicious habits of its people, propagation is a perfect struggle; polygamy becomes a law of nature; and even with the aid of this institution, so favorable to reproduction, there are fewer children than wives.

The child is introduced into the world without medical assistance, and is cordially welcomed. It is rubbed every day with palm-oil, especially on its neck, back, and loins. The mother is treated with great respect, and is exempt from all labor while she continues to suckle her child, which she continues to do while her milk lasts—generally two or three years: I have seen a child tall enough to take the breast standing by its mother's side; but that, I imagine, must be an exceptional case. During this time, and also from the moment that impregnation becomes apparent, the mother no longer cohabits with her husband. Otherwise, say the natives, the child would be born sickly or crippled (in which case it would be killed), and the milk would be spoiled. There are, unfortunately, no such sanitary precautions for the preservation of the child when once born. Carried in a sling across the breast, or perched on a bustle behind, it is exposed to all weathers; and a large proportion of infants perish.

Babies, which in England resemble skinned rabbits, soon lose that carnation hue in Africa. It rapidly changes to a yellow frog-color, and then deepens into black. After a certain period they are released from the sling or bustle, which is their only cradle, and are left to crawl about on the ground till instinct teaches them to walk. Then a string is tied round their waist, and their education commences. Both sexes are taught at the tenderest age to drink palm wine, as if intoxication were a virtue; and little girls are given lessons in dancing. I no longer wondered at the intricate steps which these women perform when I saw a child of two years old circled by women, who were clapping their hands and singing the nursery refrain, *Fear the he-goat, ya! ya! ya! Fear the he-goat! ya! ya! ya!* while it wriggled its little body into the queerest shapes imaginable.

These children are absurdly precocious. Africa is a great hot-house, in which they are forced by the sun, and in which they perish prematurely. They can always talk when they are twelve months old. At four or five years I have seen them listening with twinkling eyes to the immoral songs of their seniors, and at eight or nine nature permits them to put in practice those theories which, incredible as it may seem, they have actually studied beforehand.

So much for savage chastity; and I fear that I can say as little for parental affection. The father wishes to have a child partly because nature has planted within his breast an instinct for reproduction second only in power to that of self-preservation, and partly because that child, if a son, will help him to hunt or fish, or paddle his canoe, and will give him food when he is old: if a daughter, he will sell her to a suitor, and will receive sufficient in return to make him a man of status in his tribe. He kills the sickly or crippled child because it will cost him one more mouth to feed without affording him any thing in return.

The maternal instinct which we see so powerful in the mere animal creation is not absent from the negress. Ananga accompanied her father, Quenqueza, when I left Ngumbi. She and her mother both cried very much when she went, although it was only for a few days. By secluding mothers during the nursing period, the child has no rival, while the respect which is paid to the woman because she is a mother must increase her love for her offspring, as the miseries which some poor girls endure in our own country have been known to sour all those feelings which nature has planted within their breasts.

The prettiest song which I ever heard was sung by a mother to her child in the Balengi country. If we can believe it, fathers also have sometimes a little love for their infants:

Why dost thou weep, my child?
The sky is bright; the sun is shining: why dost thou weep?

Go to thy father; he loves thee: go, tell him why thou weepest.
What! thou weepest still. Thy father loves thee; I caress thee: yet still thou art sad.
    Tell me then, my child, why dost thou weep?

Before they are permitted to wear clothes, marry, and rank in society as men and women, the young have to be initiated into certain mysteries. I received some information upon this head from Mongilomba, after he had made me promise that I would not put it in my book—a promise which I am compelled to break by the stern duties of my vocation.

He told me that he was taken into a fetich-house, stripped, severely flogged, and plastered with goat-dung; this ceremony, like those of masonry, being conducted to the sound of music. Afterward there came from behind a kind of screen or shrine uncouth and terrible sounds such as he had never heard before. These, he was told, emanated from a spirit called *Ukuk*. He afterward brought to me the instrument with which the fetich-man makes this noise. It is a kind of whistle made of hollowed mangrove wood, about two inches in length, and covered at one end with a scrap of bat's wing. For a period of five days after initiation the novice wears an apron of dry palm-leaves, which I have frequently seen.

The initiation of the girls is performed by elderly females who call themselves *ngembi*. They go into the forest, clear a place, sweep the ground carefully, come back to the town, and build a sacred hut which no male may enter. They return to the clearing in the forest, taking with them the *igonji*, or novice. It is necessary that she should have never been to that place before, and that she fast during the whole of the ceremony, which lasts three days. All this time a fire is kept burning in the wood. From morning to night, and from night to morning, a *ngembi* sits beside it and feeds it, singing with a cracked voice, *The fire will never die out!* The third night is passed in the sacred hut; the *igonji* is rubbed with black, red, and white paints, and, as the men beat drums outside, she cries *Okanda, yo! yo! yo!* which reminds one of the *Evohe!* of the ancient Bacchantes. The ceremonies which are performed in the hut and in the wood are kept secret from the men, and I can say but little of them. Mongilomba had evidently been playing the spy, but was very reserved upon the subject. Should it be known, he said, that he had told me what he had, the women would drag him into a fetich-house, and would flog him, perhaps, till he was dead.

It is pretty certain, however, that these rites, like those of the Bona Dea, are essentially of a Phallic nature; for Mongilomba once confessed that, having peeped through the chinks of the hut, he saw a ceremony like that which is described in Petronius Arbiter.

I do not think that Mongilomba's fear of the *ngembi* was affected. They are really a powerful body, and are held in great respect, perhaps in a little terror, by the men. They pretend to find out the secrets of their enemies, and to detect thieves; and I am inclined to believe that the origin of this institution was to protect wives from being harshly treated by their husbands.

During the novitiate which succeeds initiation, the girls are taught religious dances, the men are instructed in the science of fetich. It is then that they are told that there are certain kinds of food which are forbidden to their clan. One clan may not eat crocodile, nor another hippopotamus, nor a third buffalo. These are relics of the old animal worship. The spirit *Ukuk* (or Mwetyi, as he is called in the Shekani country) is supposed to live in the bowels of the earth, and to come to the upper world when there is any business to perform. He is then supposed to dwell in the fetich house, which is built in a peculiar form, covered with dried plantain-leaves, and is always kept perfectly dark. Thence issue strange sounds, like the growling of a tiger, which make the women and children shudder and run to their houses. When the mangrove-tube is thus heard to be at work, the initiated repair to the house, and "a lodge" is held.

The natives of Equatorial Africa worship also the spirits of their ancestors, a worship for which their minds are prepared by the veneration which they pay to old age. Young men never enter the presence of an aged person without courtesying,* and passing in a stooping attitude, as if they were going under a low door. When seated in his presence, it is always at a humble distance. If they hand him a lighted pipe or a mug of water, they fall on one knee. If an old man, they address him as *rera*—father; if an old woman, as *ngwe*—mother. It is customary for only the old people to communicate bad news to one another; and it is not to be wondered at that we find the negroes such perfect courtiers, since it is the etiquette of the country that the aged should only be addressed in terms of flattery and adulation.

When they die their relics are honored. In the Congo country

* A genuine courtesy like that of a charity-school girl.

their bodies are dried into mummies. Here, their bones are some-times stored up and visited at set periods. Or, when a person noted for his wisdom has died, his head, when partially decom-posed, is often cut off and suspended, so as to drip upon a mass of chalk placed underneath. This matter is supposed to be the wis-dom which formerly animated the brain, and which, rubbed upon the foreheads of others, will communicate its virtue.

The worship of their spirits follows the veneration of their rel-ics naturally enough. They believe that the shades of their an-cestors exercise a beneficent influence over their lives and for-tunes. They will send messages to their relatives by those who are dying; and a son has been known to kill his old mother, un-der the belief that she would be of more use to him as a spirit than as a substance. This is the *ne plus ultra* of utilitarianism. The words which they hear and the sights which they see in their dreams come to them from spirits. Always talking of these dreams, and relating them to one another, they dream the more. The higher type of negro, with his nervous temperament, and his imagination lively and vivid as that of a woman, would make an excellent "medium."

In times of peril or distress one may witness a very touching sight among these people. They will assemble in clans on the brink of some mountain brow or on the skirt of a dense forest, and, extending their arms to the sky, while the women are wail-ing and the very children weep, they will cry to the spirits of those who have passed away.

There is also a curious ceremony which Mongilomba thus re-lated to me: "The people which are dead, when they are tired of staying in the bush, then they come for one of their people which they like. And one ghost will say, 'I am tired of staying in the bush, please to build a little house for me in the town close to your house.' He tells the man to dance and sing too; so the man call plenty of women by night to dance and sing."

He told me that the next day the people would go to the grave of the *obambo*, or ghost, and make a rude idol; then take the bam-boo frame on which the body had been carried to the grave, and which is always left there, and some of the grave-dust itself, and carry them into a little hut which they build near the house of the visited, and the door of which they cover with a white cloth.

It is worth while mentioning that during the singing and dan-cing which accompany this ceremony, like as in all their religious

O

ceremonies, there is one line which is remarkably striking, for it
makes us conclude that they have a legend like that of Charon
and the Styx. They are singing to the ghost, and the verse is,
"*You are well dressed, but you have no canoe to go over to the other
side.*"

These natives have their Naiads and Dryads; their spirits
which inhabit lakes, and mountains, and forests, and high places.
They have also their Typhon and their Osiris, their Evil Genius
and their Good Spirit. The former (*Mbwiri*) they worship pi-
ously, being always anxious to deprecate his anger. They regard
him as the Prince of this world; as a tyrant whom they hate, but
before whom they must prostrate themselves. The Good Spirit,
on the other hand, they do not deem it necessary to pray to in a
regular way, because he will not harm them. The word by which
they express this Supreme Being answers exactly to our word of
God. Like the *Jehovah* of the Hebrews, like that word in masonry which is only known to masters, and never pronounced but in
a whisper and in full lodge, this word they seldom dare to speak,
and they display uneasiness if it is uttered before them. Twice
only I remember having heard it: once, as I have related, when
we were in a dangerous storm, the men threw their clenched
hands upward and cried it twice; and again, when I was at
Ngumbi, taking down words from an Ashira slave, I asked him
what was the word for God in the language of his country. He
raised his eyes, and pointing to heaven, said, in a soft voice,
Njambi.

Among most illiterate nations, diseases of an epileptic character
are ascribed to demoniac possession. In Africa it is Mbwiri
which enters the possessed, and who can only be driven out by
the assistance of the fetich or medicine-man. A shanty is built in
the middle of the street, and this is occupied by the patient, the
priest, and his disciples. Then for ten days or a fortnight there
is one perpetual dance to the sound of flute and drum, every body
who is invited eating and drinking as much as he can, Mbwiri being peculiarly averse to good living. All this is done at the expense of the next of kin. The patient dances, usually shamming
madness, till the real fit comes on, with its wild stare, convulsions
of limbs, gnashing of teeth, and foaming at the mouth. Whatever the man does at such a period is supposed not to be done by
the man, but by the demon which possesses him. When a cure
has been made, real or affected, the patient builds a little fetich

house, avoids certain kinds of food, and performs certain duties. Sometimes the patient has been known to become quite insane; to run away to the bush, hide from all human beings, and live on the roots and berries of the forest. Such cases, as I have been credibly informed, are by no means rare.

These fetich-men are priest-doctors, like those of the ancient Germans. They have a profound knowledge of herbs, and also of human nature, for they always monopolize the real power in the state; but it is very doubtful whether they possess any secrets save that of extracting virtue and poison from plants. During the first trip which I made into the bush I sent for one of these doctors. At that time I was staying among the Shekani, who are celebrated for their fetich. He came attended by half a dozen disciples. He was a tall man, dressed in white, with a girdle of leopard's skin, from which hung an iron bell, of the same shape as our sheep-bells. He had two chalk-marks over his eyes. I took some of my own hair, frizzled it with a burning-glass, and gave it him. He popped it with alacrity into his little grass bag; for white man's hair is fetich of the first order. Then I poured out some raspberry vinegar into a glass, drank a little of it first, country fashion, and offered it to him, telling him that it was blood from the brains of great doctors. Upon this he received it with great reverence, and, dipping his fingers into it as if it was snap-dragon, sprinkled with it his forehead, both feet between the two first toes, and the ground behind his back. He then handed his glass to a disciple, who emptied it, and smacked his lips afterward in a very secular manner. I then desired to see a little of his fetich. He drew on the ground with red chalk some hieroglyphics, among which I distinguished the circle, the cross, and the crescent. He said that if I would give him a fine "dash," he would tell me all about it. But as he would not take any thing in reason, and as I knew that he would tell me nothing of very great importance in public, negotiations were suspended.

The belief in the supernatural powers of the fetich-man is general among the natives. "When a Mpongwe," said Mongilomba, "wants to get a white man to come to his house to trade, he goes to Camma, where the best fetich live, and he says, 'Doctor, I want a medicine for white man.' 'What will you give me?' 'I will give you two slaves.' 'Your mother is alive?' 'Yes.' 'Then you must give me your mother.' 'No, I can't give you my mother.' 'Then you must take hold of the branch of that tree.' He

takes hold of the branch, and it jumps up and takes the man into
the tree—fetich, sir, Mr. Reade. 'Now,' says the doctor, 'will
you give me your mother?' 'Yes,' says the man, 'you must
have my mother.' So he comes down, and the doctor shows him
his mother in the looking-glass. This is called okundu. Then
the doctor ties together a branch, a stone, an iron bar, and a long
stick, and tells the Mpongwe to put it in water, what place white
man's ship come for anchor. When he come back from Camma
no man gives him *mbolo* (the salutation), for they think that he has
gone to Camma to get bad fetich. Proper bad fetich live at Camma. But when the white man comes to his house, then all people say, 'He has mbumba.'"

The fetich-man is not only a doctor and a priest, he is a witch-
finder, and that is perhaps his most important office.

It is a curious thing that, though these people, if you speak to
them about death, will acknowledge that it is a natural visitation,
as indeed may be seen by the verse of a song—

> Rich man and poor fellow, all men must die:
> Bodies are only shadows. Why should I be sad?—

yet when a man of rank dies they say that he has been bewitched,
and a victim is chosen with the aid of a fetich-man. This custom
is *universal* in Africa, and, as I shall show you, is interesting on
account of the striking analogies which it presents with the witchcraft of mediæval Europe.

I shall begin in the words of Mongilomba. "When a man is
sick a long time," said he, "they call *ngembi*, and if she can't make
it well, the fetich-man. He comes at night, in white dress, with
cock's feathers on his head, and having his bell and his little glass.
He calls two or three relations together into a room. He does
not speak, but always looks in his glass. Then he tells them that
the sickness is not of Mbwiri, nor of Obambo, nor of God, but that
it comes from a witch. They say to him, 'What shall we do?'
He goes out and says, 'I have told you; I have no more to say.'
(It seems that there are consulting physicians in Africa.) They
give him a dollar's worth of cloth; and every night they gather
together in the streets, and they cry, '*I know that man who witch
my brother. It is good for you to make him well.*' Then the witch
make him well.

"But if the man no get well, they call Bush doctor from Shekani country. He sings in the language of the Bush. At night
he goes into the street; all people come about him. He has tiger-

cat skin in his hand. He walk in and out among the people, and lay the skin at the feet of the witch, singing all the while. When the song is done, the people seize the witch and put him in chains, saying, 'If you don't make our brother well, we kill you.'"

One evening, as we were sitting in a mission-house at Corisco with the windows open, we heard a wild and piteous cry rising from a village at a little distance. My friends immediately became grave and silent. The school was in the next room, and two girls who belonged to that village began crying too. I was told that it was the death-wail, and that it was the knell of more lives than one. A chieftain had been some time in a hopeless state, and a woman had been accused of bewitching him. She had a son about seven years of age, and, fearing lest he should avenge her when he grew up, they had accused him also of the crime. They were now prisoners, and as soon as the chief was dead they would be killed.

The next morning, which was Sunday, I went up with Mackey to the village. The man was not yet dead; he had suddenly become speechless, which had made them believe that he had died. I went into the house, and found him lying in a state of stupor on the bamboo bedstead. The house was completely filled with women, who had taken off their clothes and shaved their heads in token of mourning, and who were *raining* tears in their hired and admirably acted grief. Sometimes one of them would sit by his side, and, throwing her arms round him, would cry, almost in the very words of the Irish death-lament, "Why did ye die, darling; why did ye die?" for they looked upon him as really dead, since he could no longer speak to them or look at them.

In grave contrast with their shrill sorrow sat the men, also naked, in the chief house of the town, silent and fasting. On the ground, in their midst, crouched the child, the marks of a severe wound visible on his arm, and his wrists bound together by a piece of withy. I shall never forget that child's face. It wore that expression of dogged endurance which is one of the traditional characteristics of the savage. While I was there one of the men held an axe below his eyes: it was the brute's idea of humor. The child looked at it without showing a spark of emotion. Some, equally fearless of death, would have displayed contempt, anger, or acted curiosity; but he was the perfect stoic. His eye flashed for a moment when his name was first mentioned, but only for a moment. He showed the same indifference when he heard his life being pleaded for as when, a little while before, he had been taunted with his death.

We did not see the mother. I was told afterward that she had been flogged till she had confessed that she, and she only, had bewitched the man. Her son had confessed the crime as soon as he was taxed with it. Though confessions extracted by torture are easily explained, it is a remarkable fact that the *witches* (I use it as a generic term for both sexes) frequently accuse themselves of the crime, as every body knows they used to do in Europe: they will even enter into minute details, such as directing the people to look in some particular place, where they will find the witch-power, which is usually a buried spider or a bundle of dried plants.

Mr. Mackey said that he had come to speak to *Okota*, the nearest of kin, upon whom, in such cases, all responsibilty devolves. Okota came from the midst, and, taking a stool near the feet of the missionary, listened to him with great attention.

"Death," said the missionary, "must come to all. It is foolish to think that if a man dies he is bewitched."

"Death must come to all," said Okota, "but not always from God. Sometimes it comes from the hand of man."

"But how do you know that this comes from the hand of man?"

"The woman has been given *quai* to drink." (This *quai* is the drink of ordeal.) "The *quai* says that she has bewitched him."

"But *quai* can sometimes be wrong. When Cabinda went to the Muni, he was lost a long time. All people said that he was dead. A man, you said, was the witch; you gave him *quai*; *quai* said that he had killed him; but Cabinda came back alive, and *quai* was wrong."

At this there was a roar of laughter.

"It is not only *quai*," said Okota. "The woman confesses that she has bewitched. What man comes to you and says 'I have stolen your fowl,' if he has not stolen it? This woman is killing my brother; when my brother is dead I will kill her."

It was the first time, so Mr. Mackey told me, that a man had ever spoken so plainly. They generally pretended to be convinced by his arguments, and endeavored afterward to kill the witch without his knowing of it.

The ordeal-drink of Equatorial Africa is not the famous red water of Northern Guinea. It is prepared from the root of a small shrub called *Nkazya*, or *Quai*. Half a pint of this decoction is

given to the accused. Small sticks are laid down at the distance
of two feet apart, and, after drinking, he is required to step over
them five times. If it acts upon him as a diuretic, he is pronounced innocent; but sometimes it produces vertigo: the sticks
rise before him like great logs, and in his awkward efforts to stride
over them, he reels, falls to the ground, and is considered guilty.

THE ORDEAL.

The chief died after I had gone to Bapuku. The woman and
the boy were both killed: Oshupu was present, and described
their execution. The woman was taken out to sea in a boat,
killed with an axe, and thrown overboard. The boy was burnt
alive; bags of gunpowder were tied to his legs, which made him
"jump like a dog," as Oshupu expressed it. I inquired why the
boy should be subjected to a death so much more cruel than that
of his mother. Oshupu was astounded: "Burning more bad!
No, Mr. Reade, burning and drowning all the same."

This explains well enough the cruelty of the negro: it is the cruelty of the boy who spins a cockchafer on a pin; it is the cruelty of ignorance. A twirling cockchafer, and a boy who "jumps like a dog," are ludicrous sights to those who do not possess the sense of sympathy. How useless it is to address such people as these with the logic of reason, religion, and humanity! Such superstitions can only be quelled by laws as ruthless as themselves.

Among these equatorial tribes the government is patriarchal, which is almost equivalent to saying that there is no government at all. The tribes are divided into clans. Each clan inhabits a separate village or group of villages, and at the head of each is a patriarch, the parody of a king. They are distinguished from the others by the grass-woven cap which they wear on their heads, and by the staff which they carry in their hands. They are always rich and aged, therefore they are venerated. But, though they can exert influence, they can not wield power: they can advise, but they can not command. In some instances, as in that of Quenqueza, king of the Rembo, the title and empty honors of royalty are bestowed upon the most influential patriarch in a district. This is a vestige of higher civilization and of ancient empire, which disappears as one descends among the lower tribes.

And in the lowest of all that I have seen, in the small and expiring tribe of the Bapuku, occupying their patch of coast to the north of the River Muni, I had the rare privilege of studying that Utopia of philosophy—a republic in which there existed no invidious distinctions of rank or wealth, where the men were all equal, and where all property was common.

In this commonwealth, were it not for the women, the men would have starved. There the woman is cook, gardener, woodcutter, porter, and makes herself generally useful when there is any hard work to be done. Her lord swings in a hammock, smokes tobacco, drinks palm wine, and talks scandal with his friends. These people are the most indolent aud dishonest middle-men upon the Coast. If one of them does bring ebony and rubber from the interior, he carefully hides it, and sells it on the sly, so violating the principles of the constitution. And even then his wealth is useless to him. If he builds a house of better materials than the others, or if he indulges in the foreign luxury of a new cloth, his brothers, with pious indignation, pull the one down or tear the other off his back.* When men are equal, therefore, the women become their beasts of burden and their slaves. Where goods are common there can be no progress, for how can there be progress when every incentive to industry is carefully removed, and when every spark of ambition is stifled in its birth?

Among the wealthier Mpongwe the married women do not lead so laborious a life. The Bush-man can generally afford but one wife, who must find him his daily bread, and who is robustly beaten if she fails to do so; but the rich man can indulge in the institutions of polygamy and domestic slavery, which render the necessary work light enough among so many. It will seem strange to us that the women should be the stoutest supporters of polygamy; but, to be able to judge of these matters correctly, you must look at them from an African, and not from a European point of view. The wife in Africa is sold by the father to the husband, to whom she becomes a valuable possession. She is his servant; she can give him children, which he can sell, or which will also become his servants. If she is tolerably good-looking, she can be used to entrap young bachelors, who have to pay through the nose for their indiscretion. Matrimony is there a very practical institution. They have not in their language any words either for *jealousy* or *conjugal love*, passions which probably do not exist among them. If a man marries, and his wife thinks that he can afford another spouse, she pesters him to marry again, and calls him "a stingy fellow" if he declines to do so. These women live together, as far as I could judge, in great amity, but unite in cordially detesting their common husband.

There are few vices of polished life which are not vulgarly represented here. Elopements, for instance, are common enough; and the husband, who is as sensitive as he is brutal, suffers under a great indignity. Among the semi-civilized tribes the separation is sealed by "damages;" among the Bush tribes by a melodrama.

The Bush-man who has thus lost the wife of his bosom, or, more properly, of his plantation, walks out with his gun and shoots the first person whom he meets. He then proclaims that he has done this because a man has run away with his wife. The clansmen of the murdered man are enraged, not against the husband—who has simply complied with a usage of society—but because the duty of the avenger is now cast upon them. As the gay Lotha-

---

* The same illiberal conservatism prevails among the Aniya of Fernando Po, in the Benin River, and in many other parts of Africa.

rio is out of their reach, they kill a man belonging to the next village; his friends retaliate on their unsuspecting neighbors; and so rolls on this ball of destruction till the whole country is on the alert. The gates of all the villages are closed and barricaded, and some luckless clan can gain no opportunity of washing out their wrong in somebody else's blood. The chief of that clan then summons a council, and puts forward his claim against the man who has run away with the wife. The husband has no longer any thing to do with the matter. The chief of the culprit's clan offers pecuniary compensation, and general concord is restored.

This practice may appear not only barbarous, but absurd.* But it is only by some means of this kind that private ills, in such a lawless community, can be made public wrongs.

Even among these savages there is something which corresponds with our ideas of a code moral. A girl who disgraces her family by wantonness is banished from her clan; and, in cases of seduction, the man is severely flogged. Theft is also punishable by flogging, and adultery by the payment of a large sum of money, in default of which death or slavery is at the option of the husband.

It is curious that these people should have a remarkable antipathy to widows. Women never marry twice; they are compelled to go on the town on the death of their husband, and to pay all their earnings to their brothers.

It is an error to suppose that vice is an exotic, and that it can only flourish when fed with artificial manure. Besides those brutal habits which, vices among us, are simple customs among savages, they have real vices, recognized as such among themselves, and among themselves openly paraded. Public opinion has no terrors for the culprits of society; they fear only the anger and revenge of those whom they have wronged.

That a husband should offer one of his wives to a visitor, as he offers him a seat in his house and at his table, argues a want of refinement only. The custom was anciently common enough. But the husband who uses his wife, as is done all over Africa, to decoy young men to ruin, slavery, and death, practices a vice which seldom occurs among civilized nations.

In the most disgraceful period of Venetian history, we learn from Daru that mothers used to sell their daughters to wealthy

---

* Among the Indians of the Musquito Shore a similar custom prevails in cases of theft. If a man has an ox stolen, he takes the first he finds, and so on.

patricians publicly and without shame.   But even then it must have been regarded as a vice; while, not only in savage Africa, but in semi-civilized Sierra Leone, this disgraceful commerce is at the very root of their social institutions.

Adultery is regarded by the Africans as a kind of theft.   It is a vice, therefore, and so common that one might write a Decameron of native tales like those of Boccaccio.   And what in Boccaccio is more poignant and more vicious than this song of the Benga, which I have often heard them sing, young men and women together, when no old men were present?

> The old men young girls married.
> The young girls made the old men fools,
> For they loved to kiss the young men in the dark,
> Or beneath the green leaves of the plantain-tree.
> The old men then threatened the young men,
> And said, you make us look like fools;
> But we will stab you with our knives till your blood runs forth!
> Oh stab us, stab us, cried the young men, gladly,
> *For then your wives will fasten up our wounds.*

Such is the child of nature!   Such the noble savage!   Such the primitive condition of man, which philosophers, who had never studied it, have dared to hold up to our example!

What is it, then, that they would have us imitate?   Must we instruct our children in vice at the tenderest possible age, and sell them for marriage as soon as they arrive at puberty?   Must we make our wives mothers when they are scarcely girls; treat them as slaves when they are women, and kill them when they are old?   Must we place no restraints upon our passions, but abandon our youth to dissipation and debauchery, that we may have gray hairs on young heads, and all the foul diseases which spring from the diet and habits of a brute?   For so does man in an uncivilized condition.   The savage lives a life without a future or a past, without hope or regret, and dies the death of a coward and a dog, for whom the grave brings darkness, and nothing more.

CHAPTER XXI.

VOLCANIC FLOWER-GARDENS.

Prince's Island.—African Champagne.—Mulatto Politeness. — St. Thomas.—The
Dutchman's Church-yard.—Senhor Pereira.—I become a Spy.

THAT night, Saturday, June 2, I slept between sheets, in all the
dignity of civilization. The next day I gave up to a Sabbath repose, which I had, for once in my life, fairly earned, and which I
devoutly enjoyed.

The morning after, at daybreak, my labors began again. That
day I was to leave Equatorial Africa. In a few hours all my
preparations must be made. So I called my men together, culled
a few necessaries from my outfit, stowed them in a couple of stout
bullock-trunks, cleaned my rifle and locked it up in a leather case,
and packed up my very modest toilet apparatus, with my precious
MSS., in a small valise.

The rest of my property, less valuable than voluminous, I left
with my good friends, who offered to sell that which was salable,
and to send the rest home for me. In the middle of the day the
time came for me to go, and I bade them farewell, hoping that
which I scarcely dared to hope, that we might meet again.

The barque "Guilford" was bound for Fernando Po. It was
my intention to go to that island, where I should find a man-of-
war come there to meet the mails, and to beg a passage to the
South Coast.

It happened, however, that a Mr. Sparrhawk, a very intelligent
American trader, discovered before we sailed that he had left behind him a box of important papers at the Ilha da Princa, from
which he had come a few days previously. Mr. Knight, agent of
the firm (Messrs. Hutton and Cookson) to which the barque belonged, consented to touch there, as it was but little out of the
way, and as fair winds at this time of the year can always be de-
pended on going north.

In less than twenty-four hours we "rose" the island, and by
evening we laid at anchor in its harbor. There was a schooner

lying near us, a beautiful, wicked-looking jewel of a craft, with rakish tapering masts, and a fluttering top-sail like a white bonnet. Ships have their physiognomies, and this seemed a *lorette* of the ocean—a *traviata* of the high seas. I fell in love with her on the spot, and asked what her name was, and where she was bound, in the same way that I would have inquired the name and address of a handsome girl who had suddenly inspired me with "the divine passion." When I heard that she was the Mondego, bound for San Thomé, I felt an irresistible inclination to offer her my company. From San Thomé I could go by a Portuguese line of steamers to Loanda. Mr. Sparrhawk, who knew the captain, said that the matter could be easily arranged; the schooner would sail in four days' time; the passage would take about four days, and I should have to pay about four pounds. He would introduce me to a gentleman at whose house I could reside while I remained in the island.

Accordingly, at 10 P.M., I found myself standing on Portuguese land. A light was glimmering in the distance, growing smaller and smaller, till it became a twinkling speck and disappeared. This was the "Guilford" sailing before the wind, and bound for Fernando Po. I then remembered that I had only £20 in cash; that I could not speak Portuguese; that I had letters for no one in Loanda; that, in short, having with me no credentials of any kind, an amount of luggage which was not imposing, and very indifferent wearing apparel, there was nothing in the world to distinguish me from a *chevalier d'industrie*. However, reflecting that it was useless to waste thought on such trifles, I took my companion's arm, returned to his house, and soon forgot my little difficulties.

The next morning I had leisure to look about me. I was in the town of San Antonio. Its bay is the arena of the loveliest amphitheatre one can conceive. Tier over tier of forest trees form the sides, and a volcanic peak, also covered with trees, might be regarded as a kind of gallery. The continuous rustling of the leaves in the wind, and the dull moan of the waters falling on the beach, reminded me of the hum of human crowds.

My host was a mulatto; a fact to be recognized not only by his skin and hair, but also by his curiosity respecting my relatives, his reiteration of the same remarks, and the pompous nature of his hospitality. He kept a small shop, and had two plantations, with about seventy slaves. This enabled him to live on the produce of his farm. He drank his own coffee, of which and of cocoa he sold sufficient to buy him clothes and other necessaries. He ate baked yams as a substitute for bread; also great quantities of *farinha*, a flour made from cassada or manioc, and which closely resembles sawdust. His farm afforded him fowls, sheep, and pigs in no great quantity; but the food of the poor people is principally vegetable—

For beef is rare within these ox-less isles, etc.

I found only six white men on this island, three of whom were government officials. The houses of the town are well built, but execrably furnished: bare, ghastly rooms, with an isolated chair or sofa sprinkled here and there, and looking as if they never had been sat upon, nor were meant to be. On the unpapered walls hung some of those solemn portraits which one meets in England in the dining-rooms of the middle classes, and which are said to be striking likenesses of individuals, but bear little resemblance to human beings generally.

There was a profusion of churches, and it was curious to see the black priests walking about in their bombazine gowns and lace collars. They have a school, in which they teach the small negroes to read and write; those who are intended for the Church are also instructed in dog-Latin. Many novices are sent forth from this island (but more still from San Thomé) as missionaries to various parts of the Coast, and so contribute their mite to the great work of civilization.

It is true that these priests, from all that I have heard, are not models of virtue, but this may partly be owing to the charming laxity of public manners. Plato has been much blamed because in his Republic he made the wives common. In this little island I had an opportunity of studying this system, which there exists and flourishes.

I have certainly never seen so many happy people in Africa as I saw upon Prince's Island, nor so many pretty girls. A very large proportion are slaves; but they are required to do but little work, for the fertile soil requires small assistance; and the domestic slaves are more numerous, idle, and tyrannical in a merchant's house in Princa than the servants in Belgravia. All day long one may see those fascinating creatures tripping about in the streets in long flowing cotton robes, with handkerchiefs bound elegantly round their heads; when they see one, they give a smile which would bewitch a saint (imagine the effect upon a sinner!), and prattle away to you with such gushes of girlish laughter that one's heart, which Africa has already a little deadened, warms and flushes into life. Then other black eyes shine upon you, and soft hands play at hide and seek in your European hair; and then you sit beneath some noble palm, as says Linnæus, a prince of the vegetable kingdom; and there one may sit and drink cocoa-nut milk, and take lessons in Portuguese patois, and enjoy one's noon-day siesta, feeling almost inclined at times to turn one's back on ambition and the passions of the world, and there to dream, dream, dream one's life away.

Having led a life of extreme self-denial for some little time, I suddenly fancied a bottle of Champagne; so I went into my host's shop, and asked him if he had any. He replied that he had, and, opening a Champagne bottle, poured me out a tumbler of a still, very sweet, dark brown wine, which I immediately recognized as a *viño branco* of the lowest order. To all my arguments that this wine was not Champagne, nor any thing like it, he replied by showing me the label on the bottle; and although, providentially, he could not compel me to drink it, I had to pay for it, and as dearly as if I had bought it at Cremorne.

Great men are never discouraged by difficulties. I had made the acquaintance of a young man named Francisco, who spoke English remarkably well, and whom I paid a dollar a day to act as my interpreter and general informant. He had taken me to several coffee and cocoa plantations, and had shown me the churches and the cemetery, the barracks and the fort. I asked him if it was possible to obtain a bottle of Champagne in the island. He said he did not think that it could be bought, but that his friend the collector of customs had some, and, if I went to see him, would be sure to offer some. Accordingly, we walked through the town, crossed a stream by means of stepping-stones, passed through a grove of cocoa-nut-trees, ascended a hill-path skirted by plantations, and entered the picturesque dwelling of the Collector of Customs.

He was a good-natured little mulatto, and was celebrated in the island as the possessor of an opera-glass. The view from his house was worthy of the glass, and appeared doubly beautiful to one who had passed five months among the dreary forests of the continent. These islands of Prinça and San Thomé may be called volcanic flower-gardens. With Annobom, they seem to belong to a range of mountains resembling in features the Sierra del Crystal on the main land. The peak of Cameroons is 14,000 feet high; that of Fernando Po (in the same latitude) is 10,000; San Thomé, 3000; Annobom, 2000. In the same manner, the Sierra del Crystal range, which may be said to commence with the Cameroons, appears also to dwindle as it runs south, and presents the same forest-crowned features, and, as far as I can judge, the same geological characters.

As Francisco had predicted, the collector asked me whether I preferred gin or Champagne, and, on receiving my answer, brought in a pint bottle with a large label on its side—*Fine Crab-apple Cider.* This he opened, and, with many fears of the colic, I helped to drink it; after which he asked me, with unblushing effrontery, if I liked the quality of the wine. The words *cider* and *cidra* being so much alike, and this same drink being afterward offered to me at other houses in the same manner, I concluded crab-apple cider at Prince's Island to hold the same position as gooseberry wine in England; and that among certain classes the most undisguised imitation is offered with audacity, and received with well-bred ignorance.

We dined with the good collector, who told me that the revenue of the island to government was about £1000. The taxes were very heavy, and one had lately been levied upon slaves. On returning to the town, we found it tastefully illuminated by means of oranges hollowed and filled with palm-oil and a cotton wick. It was some feast-day. Then we met a procession of young girls, playing musical instruments, and singing as they went. Joachim told me that every night the girls went to dance at one of the houses, a different house being taken each night, the host or hostess providing refreshments. I admired this genial custom, and wondered whether I was really in a land of slavery. Joachim, having spoken with one of the young ladies, told me that feasting and dancing would that night be kept up till daybreak, and with unusual vigor. Seven days ago a child had been born in the house they were going to. It was a popular belief that on the seventh day the midwife can transform herself into an owl, and will come to suck the child's blood. But, as the witch can not endure good company, these girls crowd to the house toward evening. There they watch and sing; also dancing, eating, and drinking till the dawn. This effectually disturbs the scheme of the witch and the slumbers of the neighborhood.

On the third day of my residence, my mulatto entertainer told me (he could speak a little bad French) that the "Mondego" would sail on the morrow; that it would be necessary for me to take a passport, which it would give me a great deal of trouble to get myself, and that, if I liked, he would arrange the matter for me. To this I consented; and he contrived to arrange it so ingeniously that I paid for my passport a price which I believe no son of Adam ever paid before. What with this petty larceny, and with the few things which I had bought from his shop, and for which he charged cent. per cent., I reckoned that I paid for his hospitality at the same rate that I should have paid at the Clarendon or the Clarges; but I preferred to do that rather than lie under an obligation to him. But the captain of the "Mondego," who heard of it afterward, was very indignant, and declared that he would expose the fraud to the governor: he also expressed an opinion that mulattoes inherited the vices of both races—a maxim which I had heard often enough before, and which is not altogether without truth for its foundation.

I found this captain and his first officer extremely agreeable and well-informed men. The vessel sailed close to the wind, which, as we were going south, was always against us, and we made the passage in four days.

There lay the island of San Thomé, with its peak towering to the clouds, and its sides dotted with Nature's richest mantle of leaves and flowers. A very pretty town, Santa Anna de Chaves, lay smiling in the bay, and the chimes from the bells of her seven churches made me believe that I once more approached civilization.

We landed, and our captain exchanged greetings with a number of merchants, who stood by the door of the custom-house watching the disembarkation of a cargo. I was then introduced to Senhor Pereira, the owner of the schooner, and the Monte Christo of the island.

He had begun life as mate or master of a slave ship, which was taken by an English cruiser. He was set ashore, in accordance with the regular rule, at the first place they touched; which happened to be Prince's Island. He had two dollars in his pocket, and he had only his pocket in the world. He came over to San Thomé, and speculated so cleverly in *black ivory*, and applied himself so closely to business—never touching wine nor taking any kind of pleasure—that he became rich, and was now the owner

P

of two fine vessels, and could lay his hand (so they said) on a n
lion of dollars when he pleased.

His house was furnished with a gaudy want of taste, and
drawing-room reminded me of those in which one is so often
ceived in small country houses, and which are evidently ne·
used except to receive visitors. He had, however, a good tal
and every day dined a dozen guests. On this occasion we w
served with a very excellent *purée*, to which the Portuguese a
ed black olives, like those which grow in the south of Fran
They laughed to distraction when I said that the English pref
red olives with their wine. Then came a grand *bouilli* (rare lu
ury in Africa), and a fair variety of *entrées* and *entremets*. A c
of home-grown coffee concluded the feast.

The coffee grown on these two islands is celebrated, and
bought up by the grandees of the Peninsula. It is kept till it
four years of age; for coffee, like port, improves by time. Th
it is prepared with the greatest nicety; you take it without sug
or milk, and you find that you have arrived at an epoch in yc
life: an exquisite aroma gently ascends your nostrils; you k
the dark potion with your lips; and, as it trickles across your p
ate, you feel an exquisite thrill throughout your frame.

I noticed that only one bottle of wine, and that of an ordina
kind (*vino tinto*), had been placed upon the table. Except m
self, scarcely any one had touched it. I had drank it all but
glass or so, which I had left for manners. I had heard that t
Portuguese on the Coast were hard drinkers, and was astonish
at this abstinence. But I was informed that, in the first pla
only the Portuguese traders in the Congo affect to keep pace wi
true Britons in the way of drink; secondly, that the island w
under a cloud, and that all were living in great temperance. Dy
entery in an epidemic form had raged during a month, and in
small population of white men the deaths had averaged five
day. That was why I saw so few white men, they told me.

"To live strictly by rule," says Rochefoucauld, "is one of tl
most troublesome diseases that there is;" so I lived as usual, e
cept that I took care to eat plenty of fruit; for I have observ
that dysentery is almost always preceded by constipation, of whi
it is, in fact, the result. The dysentery of San Thomé is of a p
culiar kind, which the French call *gras fondu*.

This island of San Thomé had always a bad name; and in the
days when the Hollanders and the Portuguese fought in the

dull seas, fleet against fleet, and won these colonies and lost them turn by turn, it used to be called the Dutch Church-yard. More fertile than Principe, it is also more malarious; and it is this terrible fertility which exhales life-destroying vapors, and which is too rich even for the sugar-cane.

John II. of Portugal in 1484, finding that the climate was so unhealthy, gave the Jews in his kingdom the agreeable choice of being baptized or of colonizing San Thomé. Great numbers were sent out, and married with women brought over from Angola. From this union arose a mixed race, which the Portuguese firmly perpetuated. I could detect no relic of the Jewish type, which is decidedly providential, for a union of the Jew and the negro would be, commercially speaking, dangerous to Christianity.

There is also an exotic race upon the island. In the year 1544 a slaver dropped her anchor off Sete Pedras Megras to water. The negroes, seeing land, assassinated their officers and escaped. They were well received by the savages who inhabited the south part of the island, and who called them *Angolares*, a name they have preserved. Requiring wives, this youthful republic had recourse to a rape resembling that of the Sabines. They hid themselves in the neighborhood of Santa Anna de Chaves, and carried off a number of women to the bush. In forty years' time, having become very numerous, they attacked the people to the north, and afterward the plantations of the Portuguese. During more than a century the depredations of these bandits continued. This had much to do with the emigration of the traders to Brazil, and the consequent ruin of the colony, then prosperous. At last, in 1693, General Antonio Pereira de Berredo, having commanded Captain Mathews Pires to attack them in their mountain strongholds, the expedition proved successful; two thirds of the enemy were killed or taken captive, and the *guerra do matto* (bush war) was ended. The remnant of the Angolares joined the people of Angora de San João, entered semi-civilized life, and took to the city wares to sell, consisting of large canoes, fruits, birds, calabashes. The purity of this race is preserved by their intermarriages, and also by their pride, for they will do no menial work. They form a colony within a colony, and they have customs which are said to be extremely curious.

The eight days which I was forced to pass at this island were not spent very profitably. I lived on board the "Mondego" all the while. There was a very simple reason for this: the resi-

dents would not receive me in their houses, and there were no
public hotels.   It seems that I had become a secret emissary of
Lords Palmerston and Russell, having been sent here to watch
the *modus operandi* of the slave-trade; to send secret intelligence
to the commanders of the cruisers; and to communicate to the government some Utopian plan for the abolition of the slave-trade.

The Portuguese can not understand, and will not believe, that
a man can leave London, to visit this plague-spot of creation at
his own expense, from motives of enterprise and curiosity.   It
was plain to them that I was not a trader.   Having already learned to swear fluently in Portuguese, and having plainly no preten-
sion to superior virtue, I could scarcely be a missionary—even a
heretic.   Argal, I was a spy; I was a Fosco, a Machiavel, a Me-
phistopheles; I was a serpent who desired to warm myself in their
confiding breasts, that I might distill the poison more freely from
my fangs!

When this conviction had forced itself upon me, I remembered
what a number of little things I had said (as one always does in
such cases) which must have confirmed their suspicions.   I had
asked questions about the slave-trade out of pure curiosity; these
they doubtless thought had proceeded from a set system; and my
apparent artlessness was the result of deliberate and careful acting.   On our passage, too, we had been boarded by a cruiser.
One of the officers had seen me at Sierra Leone, and we chattered
away like magpies after we had shaken hands.   I remembered
with what a keen and peculiar look the captain had watched us
while we were discussing the last news from home.   Of course he
supposed that we were concocting schemes for the ensnarement
of some innocent slaver, and that our laughter arose from triumphs which we were recording.   I remembered also with what
earnestness Senhor Pereira—his thick eyebrows knitted into one,
and those stern eyes flashing fire—endeavored to impress upon
me the fact that if the slave-trade were abolished, cultivation
would cease, heresies creep into the Church, and the whole world
revert to barbarism.

Principe was a perfect little island of hermits.   There were no
vices there, since there were no restrictions; no crimes, since there
were no incentives; no paupers, since there were no wealthy men.
They were shut out from the world; no Archimedean screw disturbed the peaceful waters of their bay, and they received their
Lisbon letters at rare and accidental periods.

But San Thomé was a go-ahead island, because it possessed one go-ahead man—Pereira. The soil was fertile; he wanted to till it; for that he wanted men; for men he must have slaves. He had been in the habit of receiving them over from Loanda, where they were packed on board the mail in a manacled state, and registered as passengers. But the treaty specially prohibiting the conveyance of slaves from one colony to another, this was put a stop to. It certainly seems hard that slaves might not be sent from a land where they were not required, to an adjoining territory where they could be turned to account; but so the treaty stood, and so it was enforced. Pereira was now doing a smart trade with the Cape Lopez country in cutters, and, taking them a boatful at a time, he accumulated multitudes. He feared that this unassuming method of smuggling would draw the attention of cruisers: of course he desired to get me "off the premises" as quickly as possible.

In Africa hospitality is claimed as a right rather than requested as a favor. If you are not offered a bed, you must sleep in the street in this hotel-less, lodging-house-less land. The captain of the "Mondego" regretted that, as I had not brought letters of introduction, no citizen desired to receive me, but begged me to look upon his vessel as my home. Accordingly, I remained on board —a prisoner in a polite way, for I could scarcely ever get ashore. The mail was not due for three weeks, having touched at the island just before we arrived; but there was a fore-and-aft schooner which would sail for Loanda in a few days. I was very strongly recommended to take my passage in her; and, seeing myself manifestly *de trop*, I had no choice but to adopt the kind suggestion.

After ten days the "Emilia" received me, and at four o'clock in the afternoon I heard the hoarse cries of the sailors as they hoisted up the anchor.

CHAPTER XXII.

AT SEA.

Animal Vegetation.—Short Commons.—Boarded by a Cruiser.

At sea, where all the days are alike, one invariably keeps a diary. It is one of the foibles of human nature. In that villainous Portuguese schooner I spent fifty-six days, and the same number of nights. Looking back at my journal, I find that I went through three stages of existence.

August 1st. The "Mondego" was a rakish little coquette, who tripped over the waves with the feet of a fairy. The "Emilia" sails along as slowly and gravely as a matron.

More Dutch than Portuguese in her build, she as nearly approaches a washing-tub as the principles of naval architecture will allow. If she possesses any value, it can be only on the ground of her antiquity.

The winds are light and contrary. I fear that it will be a long voyage. The prospect is not agreeable. The second mate (also steward) is the only man on board who speaks French. No one can speak English. But I have the tiny cabin all to myself. I write up my narrative, and I study works on languages and science, which I have fortunately brought from England.

There are bunks here, but no bed-linen. The first night I "turned in" as if I had been in the bush, taking off my coat and stockings, and covering myself with my rug. In the middle of the night something woke me. I saw by the light of the swinging lamp a huge rat perched on my hip, and composedly cleaning his gray whiskers. I shuddered. Our eyes met. He bolted. Again I slept; again I was awoke. This time I became conscious of a rank and peculiar smell: something nasty crawled upon my face, and glued itself to my lips. I tugged at it; it came off, and writhed in my fingers. Ah! it was a cockroach—a tropical cockroach, fetid, slimy, and enormous. As I sprang up several more ran off me. I found my toes bleeding where they had been nibbling. I rushed on deck, laid my bed on the deck, and slept without farther interruption.

So my life passes. At seven o'clock I rise from this delightful couch, and wring the dew out of my rug. I eat a breakfast of fish, or salt junk, and coffee. I read and write till midday. Then I sit on the ship's side; for the decks are so choked with logs of wood and casks that there is no room to walk. I look alternately at the water and the clock till three, the hour of dinner. This consists of hot water slightly oiled, salt junk, and preserved fruits. Afterward I do some more work. We take tea and biscuits by moonlight. Then the second mate sings. He has a fine voice, and sings Portuguese words to Italian airs with taste and correctness. This is the only pleasure that I have, and I look forward to it through the long and weary day. Nothing is so cheerless and disheartening as this great water-desert. I often wish that I was back in that "land of hunger," the gorilla country. Monotony is the worst of hardships. *L'homme n'est jamais malheureux que par l'ennui.*

August 14*th.* We are becalmed. The sails are flapping the masts, and making all kinds of ugly noises. We don't advance. On the contrary, we recede. The current is taking us back to San Thomé. I don't care. It is quite immaterial to me where we go, or how long we stay. Evohe! I am an essence of viño tinto. You may bottle a dozen from my jugular. I am a victim of oinomania, and I have taken to drink.

Praise be to Bacchus! he has kicked Minerva out of the cabin. My studious mania soon passed away. West End tastes began to revive. As old maids put a spoonful of souchong into a pot, and attempt to stir it into tea, I, on the smallest materials, endeavored to gain excitement. I got up at twelve, persuading myself that I had a morning headache. At dinner-time I put on an old shooting-coat, sat down as if full dressed, and spread a brown napkin over my knees with the dignity of an alderman at a banquet. After dinner I would go on deck, persuading myself that I was "on town." The celestial bodies were my gas-lamps, the deck my Regent Street. I would sit up till the small hours, by which time I had always succeeded in getting drunk—on reminiscences. Having called on the binnacle for a song, I would reel to my bed, in the full belief that I was being carried by a fat butler and three powdered footmen.

It then occurred to me to clothe the dry bones of the past with reality, and to fill their shriveled veins with wine. The first day of a dead calm the captain became furious. I challenged him to mortal combat. The second mate was bottle-holder. We drank a strong red wine provided for patients. As we drank the captain's nose grew redder and redder, till it assumed gigantic proportions, and his eyes resembled phosphoric tea-saucers. I took wine with him. Presently I saw two captains. I took wine with both. Then came a fog, a thick London fog, through which his face glared for a moment and disappeared. When it cleared away he was lying on the ground, a bottle in each hand. To my heated imagination he appeared a maiden in a swoon. I poured some wine into my hat, and threw it over him. He breathed again, and muttered imprecations. "Drink, poor victim of man's perjury," I cried, and deluged his shirt bosom. "Drink, confiding angel," I murmured, and emptied the bottle in his eyes. He rose, dripping like a mermaid, and tried to clutch me. I escaped to deck. I saw all the stars dancing, and Jupiter waltzing indelicately with the moon. At the same time the ship reared up on its stern, and the deck, striking me violently on the face, deprived me of sense and consciousness.

August 25th. All the wine is drunk, all the provisions are eaten. We are placed upon an allowance of water. .

I thought it curious that there should be any scarcity of that when there were so many casks on board. I asked the captain how it was that there was no water in them. He glanced at the mate, laughed in an odd kind of way, and said that it had been forgotten. Afterward I recollected that a superfluity of water-casks is the surest sign by which an empty slaver can be detected.

We should certainly have been starved had we not caught a great quantity of albicores. When a shoal of these fish passed us, an ancient mariner, noted for his skill, squatted on the bowsprit, and danced on the top of the water a hook made up with blue and white cotton to resemble the flying-fish. The albicores rose at this like trout at feathers. After being played a little, the fish (weighing sometimes eighty pounds) would be hauled to the ship's side, and a sailor, holding the shrouds with one hand, would pass a rope through its gills with the other. As soon as the fish was landed on deck, it would be cut up into fids, salted and barreled. Thus great numbers were caught; but we had previously been hard put to it, having had to exist on old shark, which, being a scavenger fish, does not afford a delicate repast. I was often interested in watching these albicores as they swam past, sometimes turning on their sides, which flashed like flakes of green fire. It was a ludicrous sight to see one pop into a shoal of fly-ing-fish. They would get up like a covey of partridges, flying in all directions; the albicore, taking a huge leap, would swallow one *on the wing*, and often be caught itself by the frigate-bird hov-ering above.

Three or four times goat-suckers, when we were at least forty miles from land, perched upon the vessel in midday. As they are properly birds of the dusk, they must have been migrating; and it reminded me that once at Bapuku I observed two night-jars flying round the village all day, and sometimes perching, as swal-lows do with us before they start on their aërial tour.

One day we were favored with a gladiatorial entertainment. I was sitting on the ship's side, watching the sea-worms as they glit-tered past, when I saw a white speck upon the horizon. This grew into a little cloud of white foam. Then I heard a dull thud, which was repeated at brief intervals. Presently I saw something black appearing and disappearing, and something which rose in the air for a moment and seemed to cause the sound. The sail-ors left their work and crowded on the rigging. It was a whale being killed by a thresher.

The poor monster passed us rolling his great black sides, and blowing silver water into air. By its side rose a large flat tail, which descended upon him, making a sound like that of a flail on a barn floor. The whale already appeared " distressed," but that remorseless weapon rose and fell with the regularity of a machine.

They say that the thresher never leaves his victim till he is killed, and that, if the whale attempts to dive, a swordfish stabs him till he spouts blood. Naturalists have not yet discovered the cause of their virulence against an animal so much greater than themselves. It is probably the same which induces critics to at-tack celebrated authors.

Now my pleasures are all of a sober and contemplative kind. Isolation, like all evils, has its good results: it forces a man to de-scend into the depths of his own soul to study the anatomy of mind; and on these sad and solitary nights my heart first opened to the beauties of Nature. I spend hours looking upward at the sky of God—that scroll of shining characters—that archipelago of floating worlds. Here the moon beams with a lustre unknown in frosty skies; the Southern Cross, that mysterious symbol of hope and redemption, glimmers softly in the dark blue vault; and the Clouds of Magellan, most strange and beautiful of all, are suspend-

ed like a fairy veil on the sublime and swarthy countenance of
Night.

August 27*th*. Yesterday afternoon we sighted land. The officers
displayed great anxiety. It was clear that they had lost their
reckoning, and had not expected to find themselves so near the
coast. During the whole of the voyage we had kept well out at
sea, although "kedging" under the shore and sailing with the land-
breeze is considered the best method of making the voyage.

A sailor cried out that there was a sail in sight. We could see
without a glass the masts of the vessel, which looked like tiny
twigs above the horizon. A quarter of an hour afterward something rose above them like a small cloud. Upon this the captain
uttered a savage oath and gave an order. The men, also swear-
ing, ran to the yards. Our course was changed. We no longer
beat against the wind—we ran before it. I now began to understand matters. The distant vessel was a British cruiser. She
had seen us, and had got up steam, which is done only when they
chase. I was on board a slaver, and we were making a run of it.

It was late in the afternoon, and I could gather from what they
said that if she did not board us before dark there was a chance
left. Their papers were all right, but the water-casks were sufficient to damn them.

The man-of-war crept toward us: we could see her white sails
above, and below her black and thin hull, like the body of a
snake. But the wind was fresh, and the sun was already setting,
when suddenly the breeze dropped as if by enchantment. The
captain, who was steering us himself, bent his head upon the
wheel. The men collected in a knot, and looked at the coming
ship in blank dismay.

We could see the white water dashed up by the paddles. Then
a man gave a cry. The captain span the wheel round. The
wind revived, and with it the slaver's hopes. In ten minutes
more the sun disappeared, and darkness descended to bless young
lovers and my slaver friends.

Then, looming through the gray, vaporous air, we saw a sloop
of war, which grew upon our eyes without perceptible sound or
motion. When she came nearer we heard the splashing of her
paddles and the water which she dashed from her bows. A lantern was hung over our stern that she might not run into us.
She glided past, her hull blazing with lights, and, winding gracefully round, abated her speed.

Then came a clear, commanding voice out of the night—
"What vessel's that?"
To which I answered, having been requested to act as interpreter,
"The 'Emilia,' of Lisbon."
"Heave to."
"Ay, ay!"
We squared our yards. We heard the harsh barking voice of
the boatswain, and the cries of the sailors as they lowered the
boat, which fell with a thud into the water; then the sound of
oars, and something dark which approached us through the blazing sea. The lantern was hung over the side, and two officers
sprang on deck, their sword-hilts glittering in the light.

I showed the lieutenant the way to the cabin, where the captain
had his papers ready to show him. The water-casks, of course,
were not visible. The "young gentleman" who followed him
said, in rather a faint voice, "Shall I come down, sir?" Poor little fellow! I dare say he imagined that slaver's cabins were peaceful repositories of assassination, and every thing that was bad.

The papers were shown to the lieutenant, who examined them
very carefully, especially the Custom-house clearance. He took
the boarding-book out of the midshipman's hands, and filled up
the usual forms: the vessel's name and port, tonnage, number of
crew, cargo; asking especially what ports she had touched at, and
whether she had any guns.

Having finished this—not to his satisfaction, for they had a long
chase for nothing—the captain desired me to ask him where we
were. The midshipman was called upon to write down the latitude and longitude, whereupon the captain and mate abused each
other fiercely, one having supposed that we had been more to the
north, the other more to the south—neither of them any where
near the mark.

Having discharged my duty as interpreter, I asked the name
of their ship, and inquired after various commanders whose acquaintance I had made in the Bights. To these questions the officer replied with great caution. He plainly supposed that I had
something to do with the "Emilia," which, of course, he knew to
be a slaver, though not seizable, and attributed my curiosity to
any thing but disinterested motives. I certainly could not have
presented the appearance of a man who had ever been in good society, clothed as I was in a decayed dressing-gown, and with my

hair all moppy and tangled; for João had stolen my comb, and my very tooth-brush I had been obliged to carry about in my pocket, wrapped up in a bit of old newspaper; but I, not wishing to be taken for a slaver, mentioned my name, and said that I had been lately spending a few months after the gorilla.

Upon this the face of the British officer gleamed with sudden intelligence, and he said, with an ah!-you-can't-take-*me*-in kind of smile, "Well, I don't think gorillas are likely to come much in your way, but" (here his face beamed with triumph) "*you may pick up a few bits of black ivory.*"

CHAPTER XXIII.

BLACK IVORY.

The Slave-trade.—Its Results.—Its present State.—Its future Suppression.

WHEN the early Portuguese voyagers first commenced to trade on the Libyan coast, sealskins, gold dust, and " black ivory" were the articles offered for sale.

It is an error to suppose that the slave-trade was invented by the Europeans. In the time of Herodotus, and perhaps ages before his time, negroes had formed part of the tribute which Ethiopia paid to Egypt. From Egypt these slaves passed into Europe with the lions, the giraffes, and the other wonders of Africa. A large interior slave-trade has always existed between the Moors and the negroes, and is likely to exist for some time to come.

But slavery was never thoroughly reduced to a system till the Europeans took it in hand in the fifteenth century. And those who study history must allow that the African slave-trade has done its work in assisting the progress of civilization. It is to the slave-trade that we owe the first spirit of enterprise in Africa. It is to the slave-trade that we owe the writings of such gallant seamen and careful historians as Hawkins, Drake, Dampier, Bosman, Jannequin, and Barbot.

By means of the slave-trade, the dangerous classes of Africa, the destitute and the criminal, were carried off to the New World, which their hands raised, in an incredibly short space of time, almost to a level with the Old.

Even in those days the philanthropists of Europe cried out against the slave-trade, and several popes issued bulls against the practice, which were as impotent as the one against tobacco. But, as refinement became more general, the cry became stronger, and it was England—the philanthropist of nations—which first took active measures for its suppression.

Carthago est ruenda. The slave-trade must be abolished. Excusable or inexcusable at a ruder period of society, it has now done its work. Africa has not felt the loss of those who have blackened half America; but to take more away is to commit a dangerous and foolish error. In the first place, the blacks have already become the bugbear of the New World; in the second place, we wish to cultivate Africa, and to rob her of her laboring population is to dig up her future by the roots.

I therefore advocate the suppression of the slave-trade—not on moral and philanthropic grounds, but simply on those of political economy. The slave-trade, once so instrumental to civilization, is now one of its greatest obstacles. I will admit willingly that my experiences among savages have proved to me that there is no cruelty in a child being torn from the bosom of its family, since mothers will always sell their children; and since, like the beasts, however tenderly they rear them, they abandon them with indifference when once they are able to take care of themselves. I will admit that the tales of white men entering villages, killing some, and taking others to slavery, which are so frequently published in tracts, are quite untrue. Such things were done in the old days; but, after the slave-trade was regularly established, a slaver would no more think of stealing a negro than a tooth of ivory. I admit that the Africans are constantly at war among themselves, and, àpropos of mere trifles, in regions where the captives can not be disposed of as slaves. I admit that the generality of the slaves which are brought down are either criminals or captives, and that, if not sold, they would be killed; that it is thought wicked to sell one's own slaves unless they have committed a crime; and that the negro is often happier as a slave to a white man than as a free man in his own country.

On the other hand, I know from personal observation what one would naturally infer, that in those places where the slave-buying still goes on, the people are more disposed to go to war, to convict criminals, and to make use of any pretense to procure slaves. And it is also certain that there are regions where an almost constant war is carried on for the purpose of obtaining slaves. Up the Fernand Vaz, for instance, I was informed that I could not possibly pass a certain tribe six journeys distant from Ngumbi, because they were always at war with the tribe beyond, from whom they procured their slaves. I have been credibly informed that pretty much the same kind of thing exists on the Congo. Putting humanity out of the question altogether, I need not explain what obstacles are thus opposed to explorers—the pioneers of civilization.

The slave-trade is a drag on the wheel of commercial progress. "Black ivory" will always be brought down from the interior in preference to other commodities. A few men can drive a herd of slaves; it would require a hundred to bring down ivory, ebony, or palm-oil of equal value. When in 1852–53 the slave-trade was totally suspended in the Congo, an unusually large quantity of palm-oil, ivory, and ebony was exported. Statistics, however, are not necessary to prove that the export of slaves for the sole benefit of the Spanish planters is the reverse of beneficial to the rest of the world.

Having thus shown that the slave-trade is not only a little inhuman, but also perilous to the safety of the white population in the Americas, and that it is a systematized plunder of a continent in which we have an interest, I shall consider the means which are now taken to suppress this trade, and the props by which it is supported.

As every one knows, the coasts of Africa are blockaded by a large and expensive squadron.

The same kind of objections have been made against the squadron as have been made against the slave-trade—on the philanthropic ground that it increased the sufferings of the negroes, and that it led to much cruelty and bloodshed.

I have read in popular magazines two or three tales intended to illustrate these facts: of slaves being thrown overboard to delay the capture of the vessel; of their being drowned, so that none might be detected on board; of a vessel being run on a reef in despair, and all on board perishing, etc.

Such scenes might possibly have occurred at some remote period of slave-trade suppression, but I can safely assert that nothing of the kind is done now, and that a slaver, to whom I related the last episode, laughed till his sides ached again. Indeed, their absurdity is patent enough. A vessel which has a slave-deck or planking for the same, which is provided with an undue quantity of water-casks, provisions, mess-kits, etc., receives the same condemnation as the vessel which is full of slaves.

When the slaver finds that she can not escape, she does not run on a reef; she lies to. The captain becomes a passenger; the sailors belong to every nation under the sun excepting to those which have created laws against the trade. Ballast is tied to the bunting and ship's papers, and all signs of nationality disappear over the side of the vessel. Some officers come on board, holding scented handkerchiefs to their noses, cursing the stench of the slaves, and counting them with glee. The slaver's officers and crew have all their goods packed up; if they had any arms, they have thrown them overboard; they are shipped on board the cruiser in a state of desperate submission, and are landed at the nearest point of Africa.

Such scenes of cruelty and bloodshed might, however, readily ensue were the law against slavers to be carried out in England or America, and were such executions as that of the unhappy Walker to be often repeated.

I do not wish to enlist sympathy on behalf of slavers, but I should be glad to know why a slaver should be punished more severely than a thief, a forger, or an adulterer. To hang the one when the others are only condemned to suffer imprisonment or to pay a fine, is to place an Act of Parliament before the Decalogue. And it does appear to me an extreme measure, which savors rather of petulance than either of justice or mercy, to oppose barbarity to barbarity, and to punish with death that which a hundred years ago was rewarded with honor, and three hundred years ago with knighthood.

Among all the residents on the Coast with the exception of the missionaries, I never yet found a man who regarded a slaver as a criminal. The slave-trade is regarded by those who engage in it, and by those who look on at it, and who understand the system upon which it is worked, as simple smuggling, and that not of a very bad kind. I hope that I am not deficient in humanity, but I must own that I can look at it in no worse light. I have known a great many Portuguese slavers, and in all cases I found them treat their negro sailors and servants more kindly than the skippers of our traders do.

According to English law, a slaver is a pirate. Such a law is brutal and absurd. The slaver may take the utmost care of the slaves, who are shipped by agents in the Congo on board a vessel which has been consigned to his charge by owners in Havana. He may take every possible precaution that the health of those negroes is preserved, as, indeed, his own interests and his duty to his employers demand; for every life lost is money lost to them and to him. He may even attend to them in sickness with solicitude, and punish with the utmost severity any barbarous acts against them of which his crew may be guilty. He may have been induced to undertake the command of this vessel by some sudden misfortune, and by a desire to regain his losses; he may have a wife at home (as Walker had) whom he loves—for even slavers may be able to love—and to whom his life is precious. But if he is found on board this vessel by naval officers, he is sent home; he is tried under the same law as that man who has scuttled ships, who has devoured fortunes, who has wantonly murdered hundreds in cold blood. This cruel, blind law can not distinguish between the two, and he dies the death of a pirate.

I say so much upon this subject because I know that an English slaver would (unless it was proved that he was guilty of real cruelties) receive such sympathy from mercantile seamen that others would be actually encouraged (such is the proneness of man to imitate notorieties) to follow in the same path. Besides, when did barbarous laws ever check, far less abolish, crime? Was there less theft in those days when men were gibbeted by dozens at the old Bailey? The decrease of crime is owing to the superiority of Prevention, not to the severity of Punishment.

Thus I have endeavored to prove that no acts of cruelty to the slaves are caused by the efforts of the squadron to check the slave-trade, but that the existing laws of England and America are liable to drive men to despair and to great crimes, as in former days, when the pilfering of a few pence and the crime of the fratricide were punished in the same manner.

The next objection against the squadron is more reasonable. The slavers are now built for fast sailing, and are generally American clippers, with the exception of a few useless vessels like the "Emilia," which, as I shall presently explain, are used as decoys. In these clippers the slaves suffer inconceivable miseries from want of air and proper food.

The mortality is ten per cent. per voyage, which is certainly very high, although it must be taken into account that the slaves come down to the sea-side in a diseased and feeble state, and that the sudden change of temperature must of necessity prove fatal to many. There can be little doubt, too, that these sufferings have been exaggerated. The slaves are carefully aired and fed, and every precaution is taken to preserve their lives, which have now become so precious. But, after all, the question really comes to this—"Were the squadron to be withdrawn, would the negroes be better treated?" We know that the cupidity of agents will make them freight a ship so heavily that, in a heavy sea, she is scarcely manageable. One can scarcely expect them to take more

Q

precautions for the safety of negro slaves than of white sailors. I also find, in reading the old authors, that, in the time when the slave-trade was legal, the slaves suffered as much as they possibly could in the clipper vessels of the present day. We may therefore conclude that the suppression of the slave-trade alone can prevent the sufferings of the slaves, unless, indeed, the trade were to be licensed, and the vessels inspected by commissioners; but that, I think, can scarcely come to pass.

The last objection is, to a certain degree, unanswerable. It is that the squadron will never be able to suppress the slave-trade.

Sir Charles Hotham being examined by a select committee of the House of Commons, and being asked whether the slave-trade was regulated by the strength and efficiency of the British squadron on the Coast, or by the commercial demand for slaves, replied that it was "entirely dependent upon the commercial demand for slaves, and that it had little or no connection with the squadron."

This is a fact which no one who is at all acquainted with the trade can deny. It is indeed palpaple that a perfect blockade over such an extent of coast is an utter impossibility. As Mr. Crawfurd, the Commissioner of Havana, has shown in figures, one "run" will pay ten empty captures and five full ones. A trade will never be suspended, a blockade will never remain impregnable, while such profits as these can be obtained.

Besides the coast-blockade, we make feeble and somewhat ludicrous efforts to suppress the slave-trade by sending embassies to native kings.

In the first place, we can scarcely hope to prove to savages that the slave-trade is inhuman, when we can not convert Europeans to that belief. The most wealthy and respectable citizens of Havana in Cuba, and of St. Paul's de Loanda in Angola, are at the present time actively engaged in the trade. Portugal, the valet of England, affects an enthusiasm which it does not feel. But in Spain the feeling in favor of the slave-trade is but little disguised, and appears to be every day less carefully concealed. One of the Spanish penal laws has been framed for the protection of slaves by affording them a loophole to escape. It is the policy of Spain to fill Cuba with negroes, who may be armed against republican planters, and on whom a lucrative poll-tax is levied. The Spanish authorities receive from the slave-importers so much for every slave whom they permit to be smuggled into the island. Many of these officers, notorious for having made their fortunes by the "head-money," as it is called, have, by their wealth, obtained the honors of decoration and even of nobility.

Thus, if diplomacy is to avail us—and it is certainly our best weapon—it is to Madrid, and not to Dahomey or Ashantee, that missions should be sent.

In 1852–53 Brazil prohibited the importation of slaves, and took sufficiently active measures to enforce the law. The consequence was that in those years the traffic was completely paralyzed. St. Paul's de Loanda, which appears to depend entirely upon the slave-trade, was in consternation. The slave-merchants became bankrupt; foreign coin disappeared; paper money was issued by the provincial treasury, and guaranteed by the public revenues; and people began to talk of cultivating cotton, coffee, and ground-nuts.

In the Brazils, the slave-owners invested their money in the line of packets which now run on the River Amazon. A hundred and forty Portuguese returned to their country and embarked a sum of £1,200,000 in a bank at Lisbon.

But in 1854 arrangements were made with the Cuba merchants, and the trade, concentrated on that island, has now revived, and is as active as ever.

If the importation of slaves into Cuba could be prevented, the slave-trade would be suppressed. The hearty co-operation of the Spanish authorities alone is necessary for this purpose, but this there appears little probability of our obtaining.

During the last twenty-five years the slave-trade has greatly diminished. This is owing, not to the efforts of the squadron, but to the spread of colonization, and to the increase of lawful trade. On the Northwestern Coast, and in the Bights of Biafra and Benin, the slave-trade is almost extinct. The coast is thickly dotted with colonies and trading stations, and the palm-oil trade is flourishing. The Congo is the true lair of the slave-trade, which can only be cleansed by the planting of English settlements, and the establishment of lawful trade on a firm basis. This day is, I trust, not far distant; and, before many years are past, we may see the slave-trade banished from Africa, or at least from its Western Coast.

In this essay I have attempted to prove:

1. That the slave-trade is ruinous to Africa, perilous to America, and profitable only to a certain class in Cuba.

2. That the evils caused by the squadron have been much exaggerated; and that, were the squadron to be withdrawn, there would be no certain alleviation of negro suffering.

3. That the squadron stationed on the Coast has little influence upon the activity of the slave-trade.

4. That the severe laws against slavers are calculated to drive them to real crime, and are impotent in the cause of slave-trade suppression.

5. That missions to African kings are utterly useless.

6. That, were the Spanish authorities in Cuba to take the same honest measures as those in Brazil to prevent the importation of negroes, the slave-trade would be at an end.

7. That the export of slaves from Africa can only be prevented by the Coast being walled with civilization. That the trade is now confined almost entirely to Congo, and that English settlements in that country would drive it entirely from the Western Coast.

CHAPTER XXIV.

THE METROPOLIS OF AFRICA.

San Paolo de Loanda: its Description.—Pecuniary Embarrassment.—Ride in a
Palanquin.—Welcomed by Mr. Gabriel.—Portuguese Society.—A Reminiscence.

WHEN next we sighted land, our intelligent navigators found
that we were a matter of forty miles south of Loanda. We had
to coast back again, and on the evening of the 5th of September
lay outside the harbor of the metropolis of Africa.

This harbor is formed by a low, flat sandy island called Loanda, from a native word meaning *bald.* According to Pigafetta,
Merolla, and other ancient authorities, this island was in their
days more than double its present size. Two hundred years ago,
a fort, called "Our Lady of the Rose," stood upon the point of this
island, which is now only marked by a heap of stones a mile and
a half from the shore.

This island was formerly the cowrie-mine of Congo, to whose
king it belonged. These shells were the currency of Congo, the
females being preferred; and there is a tradition that the early
discoverers, observing that the royal slaves always sailed in one
direction for them, had the curiosity to sail after them, and so discovered the finest harbor on the West Coast of Africa. This harbor, however, is now becoming so choked with sand, that, unless
it be soon dredged, it will cease to be a harbor at all.

A black pilot came on board at daybreak the next morning,
and, running us close inshore on account of some dangerous shoals
at the mouth of the harbor, brought us to a safe anchorage among
about a dozen craft of the same nation.

The bustle of the harbor, the appearance of the city, and the
number of white faces around us in boat and vessel, made it for
me a scene of excitement and novelty.

Having seen only our own wretched colonial villages on the
Coast, I looked upon this great city as a young man brought up
in a secluded rural district looks down upon the grand chaos of

houses as he skims over them on his way to Shoreditch or Euston Square.

First built by the Portuguese, San Paolo was taken from them by the Dutch, and taken back again one Lady's Day, whence it was called San Paolo da Assumpção de Loanda.

As far as things African can resemble things European, Loanda resembles Lisbon; but it is not a flattering likeness. There are some fine churches and public buildings, which, like prepared dowagers, are seen to most advantage from a distance. Their appearance is decidedly *imposing*. The native huts, which form the suburbs of the city, afford a good contrast with their dark thatch against the glaring whitewashed buildings of the Portuguese, but in themselves are too uniform to be picturesque.

San Paolo, now fading into ruins, was two hundred years ago a city which deserved the admiration of the world. Father Cavazzi, who wrote in 1667, says that it was surrounded by temples and monasteries instead of bastions, and that it possessed a cathedral, a convent, a hospital, and a college of the Company of Jesus.

It was one of the most cherished colonies of that Order, and when the Jesuits fell, their palaces of religion also crumbled away. The discovery of the Brazils injured this colony by turning all enterprise to the New World. Angola was made a slave emporium, and for a time prospered; but since the laws of abolition have come into force, Angola has been dying away into poverty, and is now on the brink of utter ruin.

After we had been "visited," three young gentlemen connected with the firm to whom the ship belonged came aboard and ate a breakfast, which, supplied from our small stores, they did not appear to enjoy. The appearance of these youths did not give me a favorable impression of the climate. Father Carli's description of the colonists, "that their voices were broken, and that they looked as if they had been dug out of their graves," was not altogether inapplicable to these. Have you ever seen the genuine face of a woman who has spoiled her complexion with mineral paints? It is probable that you have not, for such faces seldom come to view unclothed. But if you have, imagine it also in a high state of yellow jaundice. Then you behold the faces of these three young men.

The captain asked me if I had any friends in Loanda. I replied that I knew nobody, but that I was going to call on the English consul. He said that if no one offered me bed and board, he hoped that I would return and stay with him on board, when he would be able to give me better-dinners than he had done during our voyage. Now this was after we had spent fifty-six long days in one another's company, and had every right to be mutually en-nuyés. But he saw that I ran a good chance of being houseless and homeless. He knew that my money was all gone. And he made me this offer with a delicacy and a thoughtfulness which would have done honor to a woman. Even slavers, therefore, must have some sparks of humanity.

Now attempt to understand the position I was placed in. I had passed two detestable and dreary months on board this schooner, and at length I had finished a voyage which in a steamer would have occupied me four days. I was in the unlimited possession of three and sixpence. I had no letters to the consul. There were no English houses of business in Loanda. I had the shadow of a hope that I might find a letter containing money, the proceeds of some goods which I had ordered from England, and which the missionaries of the Gaboon had agreed to send to me. At all events, there might be a letter from Captain Burton, to whom I had written from San Thomé, and which would serve me in some measure as a letter of credit. Personal security I felt convinced would do little for me. Having taken an unbiased look at my-self in a glass, I felt inclined to mistake myself for a costermonger "who had seen better days."

To be obliged to return to Fernando Po was not a cheerful prospect, especially as I should only be entitled to a deck passage as a distressed British subject. However, Dr. Livingstone's ac-count of Mr. Gabriel's kindness, and the manner in which the Portuguese all spoke of him, gave me hopes of a better fate, and I inquired, with great anxiety, whether that gentleman was still at Loanda.

A Senhor Isaac, whom I met on the custom-house quay, told me that he was at home, and called a palanquin for me, saying that I could not walk there in the sun. I refused, partly because I disdained that luminary, and partly because one desires to be economical when one has only three and sixpence in one's pock-et. However, the senhor insisted, the *machilla* was brought up by two stalwart negroes, and I was requested to get in. The ma-chilla, or African palanquin, is a carpeted board hanging from a pole, with a pillow for the back, and curtains at the sides. On to this board I crawled clumsily enough, amid a fire of well-bred smiles and of Portuguese compliments. The men started off at a jog-trot, singing, and I, oscillating in the air, concentrated mind and body on the preservation of equilibrium. After a ten minutes' ride I was set down at the door of a very handsome house, which they told me was that of the Senhor Gabriel. I got out with a sense of relief, gave them a shilling (which, being double their fare, they were discontented with and abused me), and mounted a stone staircase which led me to a large terrace. There a negro servant met me, informed me that Senhor Gabriel was out, but said that if I wished I could see the secretary. I did wish to see the secretary, and was introduced into a room furnished like an English drawing-room. The secretary came in, said that Mr. Gabriel was not at home, and asked me if it was any thing that he could do for me. I said that it was nothing very particular (!). I only wished to know if there were any letters for me. When I told him my name, I received the agreeable news that some letters had arrived for me, and that they had been sent back to Fernando Po, the secretary having fancied that he had seen my return announced in one of the papers.

Mr. Hewett, however, made me ample amends for this mistake by inviting me into his bedroom, where ivory-handled brushes and all the resplendent paraphernalia of a young man's toilet announced to me that I was once more among Englishmen who were not traders. I enjoyed my first night between the sheets— the first time during four months (except two nights at Baraka) —very well; but my grand sensation was on that morning when I washed in spring-water with perfumed soap.

Mr. Gabriel came in after a little while, and gave me a hearty welcome. In a few hours I was perfectly at home. Extremes meet; and it is curious that Dr. Livingstone had also come to Mr. Gabriel's house in a state of extreme indigence. Mr. Gabriel extended the same hospitality to the pigmy as to the giant; and, when I stated my difficulties, relieved me in the handsomest manner. In cashing my bill for £100 (the identical sum which Livingstone also required), he of course did so at a considerable risk.

I remained ten days with him, which I spent partly in studying the Bunda dialect, but chiefly in genial relaxation. In an ordinary way I used to go to a café, where the "men about town" (pardon this desecration of the term) resorted to play billiards, and to drink political toasts in bottled beer. And occasionally there would be a fête, with military music, fireworks, and mulatto flirtations.

The streets of Loanda are ankle-deep in sand; the public buildings are either decaying or *in statu quo;* oxen are stalled in the college of the Jesuits. All that remains of poetry and of power is dying away in this colony. It is in its Dark Age—in the interregnum between two civilizations. When will the second begin?

The town is garrisoned by convicts, who wear uniforms, and are called soldiers. They are strange guardians; but a low diet of beans and rice, with meat once a week, and occasional attacks of intermittent fever, would appear to be sanitary from a moral point of view, and to reform them completely. Crimes are certainly very rare, and those who commit them are usually sent to certain malarious localities in the interior. If they return from these (which is not invariably the case), their emaciated appearance is a far better bugbear than a skeleton on a gallows. Disease is more frightful than death.

There are but few ladies in Loanda, and those do not seem to mingle much in society. The Portuguese, speaking generally, have adopted the manners of the aborigines. They have their seraglios, and concubinage is there looked upon as a custom of the country, which one need not conceal in practice nor avoid in conversation. We may regard it as a vice, but it certainly extinguishes a worse one, for there are scarcely any courtesans in Loanda; and to bring a white woman to such a country as this is something more than a vice—it is a crime. It is to kill her beauty, her health, her happiness, and perhaps her life.

But let us excuse those who, even without ignorance for their plea, bring their wives with them to Western Africa. In this detestable land, where one's only society is masculine, and that usually of a low order, one yearns for the company of a woman—of a *lady*. It is true that there are girls here who have such sweet smiles, such dark, voluptuous eyes, such fond, caressing ways, that one can not help loving them, but only as one loves a child, a dog, or a singing-bird. They can gratify the desire of a libertine, but they can not inspire a passion of the soul, nor feed that hunger of love which must sometimes gnaw the heart of a refined and cultivated man. The negress has beauty — beauty in spite of her black skin—which might create a furore in our demi-monde, and for which fools might fling their fortunes to the dogs. And she is gentle, and faithful, and loving in her own poor way. But where is the coy glance, the tender sigh, the timid blush? where is the *intellect*, which is the light within the crystal lamp, the genius within the clay? No, no, the negress is not a woman; she is a parody of woman; she is a pretty toy, an affectionate brute—that is all.

I loved to steal away from empty-minded man, and listen to the military band which played three nights a week before the governor's palace. The instrumentalists, who were all blacks, did not belie the musical instinct which is attributed to the negro, and which, although it never ascends to genius, becomes a talent when drilled. It seemed strange, though, to hear *Ah che la Morte* and *La ci darem* in that barbarous place. What a contrast with the scene in which I heard them last! A *sandy* street in Africa —Her Majesty's Theatre in the Haymarket!

The sweetest pleasure which one can enjoy in the wilderness is reverie. With a vivid imagination and a poetical taste, what is there which one can not enjoy? But Reverie is a capricious angel; she will not come when she is called: like all her sisters of happiness, she prefers to descend upon us when we least expect her.

One afternoon I had wandered a little way out of the town to look at the grand earthworks which the Dutch had cast up in former days, and I chanced to find the ruins of an old convent of the Jesuits.

I entered a melancholy quadrangle choked with grass and flowers. It was encircled by gray and solemn cloisters. It was buried in a tomblike silence.

Its architecture reminded me of the colleges, those convents of my country. Will those relics of a past age ever perish? thought I. Will future travelers ever wander, as I do now, among the graves of learning and of an obsolete age?

Now the sun, sinking in the sky, reddened the jagged summits of those mouldering walls, and now the chimes from the distant city told me that the hour of vespers was at hand. At this sound, for which I had so often listened in my boyhood, a crowd of sad and gentle recollections poured upon me. I was once more in my little room, poring over my books for the schools; with tasseled cap in hand, I was once more in the holy chapel, which the organ filled with its swelling and melodious tones; and the voices of white-robed choristers rose caroling to the carved oak roof; and the evening sun, bathing them in its radiance, turned the brown saints of the painted windows into gold.

A young man may satirize the follies of the under-graduate, but he soon learns that there are worse sins than folly in the world. He may jeer at the monkish seclusion and ignorance of his seniors, but ere long he may wish for that peace and simplicity which they enjoy. He may rail against his gentle mother, but when he has left her he may find that he still loves her in his heart; for it is while she holds us to her breast that life smiles most sweetly, and the cheek of pleasure has not lost its bloom. The phantom of Life beckons; we embrace her; she withers and turns hideous in our arms. No longer a fair vision which entices us to manhood, she becomes a spirit with a flaming sword, which drives us onward to old age.

CHAPTER XXV.

BY OX AND HAMMOCK.

Joachim the Swiss.—His best Friend.—En Route for Ambaka.—Bloodthirsty Mus-
quitoes.—The Senhor Mendez.—Routine of Journey.—Mountains à la Suisse.—
Arrival at Amhaka.—The War with Cassange.—Governmental Plunder.—The
Fashion of secret Poisoning.—The Bœuf-cheval.—The Doorkeeper of Matiamvo.
—Joachim is drunk.—Is impertinent.—Loses two front Teeth.—Post-haste.—
The Story of Franz.

I HAD laid it down as my *programme de voyage* to visit the Congo on the north, and afterward Benguela on the south, thus making Loanda my head-quarters in the centre; but, being desirous to
visit the interior of Angola, in order to gain some idea as to the
capabilities of the province as a colony, to study the negro in a
semi-civilized state, and the workings of domestic slavery, I resolved to go as far as Ambaka, which is at the distance of a hundred and fifty miles from Loanda.

But here an obstacle arose. I could not speak Portuguese, and
I had no interpreter. This was a serious difficulty. There is perhaps no European colony in which so little English is spoken as
in Loanda.

That same evening we were sitting together in the drawing-
room, when a young man came on the terrace and knocked at the
door.

"Come in, Joachim," said Mr. Gabriel.

Joachim came in. I looked at him with some attention. He
was neatly dressed, but not in a manner that suggested opulence.
His handkerchief was tied by a hand which had once been a sail-
or's. His face expressed intelligence. This is the man for me,
thought I. He probably wants money. He has been a sailor,
and can therefore turn his hands to any thing; and he has evidently enough brains to carry out ideas.

Joachim came to request Mr. Gabriel to buy some oxen from
him, which he (my terrestrial angel) might sell to the cruisers.
Mr. Gabriel regretted that he could not oblige him by doing so,
for to sell oxen to the British government would be to interfere

with the rights of the contractor, Senhor Freites, and of course he himself found it more convenient to buy his meat as he wanted it from the butcher.

Joachim turned round despondingly. I resolved to strike.

"Perhaps," said I, "Joachim knows somebody who would act as my interpreter to Ambaka?"

Joachim's eyes gleamed. I saw that I had my man.

"Yes," said Mr. Gabriel, innocently. "Joachim, this gentleman is going as far as Ambaka. He wants somebody who can speak Portuguese, and English or French, to go with him as his steward and interpreter. He will pay him liberally, and will let him have a hammock to ride in."

Joachim reflected a little while. "I think," said he, "that my best friend would like to accompany this gentleman. But he would perhaps ask me for more particulars. For instance, he might say, 'What does this gentleman propose to give his steward?'"

"Three pounds a month," said I, "on certain conditions of obedience, adherence, and so on."

"Three pounds a month; yes, that is strong money. And if he asks me when the gentleman will start?"

"You will say that he will start immediately."

"Then my best friend will be very happy to become your interpreter."

"And who is your best friend?" said Mr. Gabriel.

"My best friend, that is myself," replied Joachim, mildly.

"Very good," said I; "come to me to-morrow at ten o'clock; I will give you your agreement, and tell you what I wish you to do."

Joachim made a gentlemanly bow, and left the room.

"That is fortunate," said I.

"Ye-es," said my host, with a little hesitation. And when we were alone he said, "I must not let you decide upon any thing without telling you that Joachim is a very bad character—so bad, indeed, that I shall not feel easy in mind so long as you are with him."

"He is intelligent, I think?"

"Oh, he is a very clever fellow, but—"

"Well," said I, "I have been accustomed to travel with my life in other people's hands, and I can generally manage to make it their interest as well as mine to preserve it."

However, I went to bed in a very anxious state of mind. One can generally divine a negro's intentions, not by his face, for he is a good actor, but by induction. A sameness of education and of purpose gives one a clew to their character. But with us it is so different: one may spend years before one learns the heart of one's nearest friend, and even then one gains no key to man in general. The grand distinction of the white man is individuality.

I resolved to watch my interpreter closely, and to irritate him, as one does with serpents, to see if they have fangs.

The next morning I gave him my directions, which he carried out with intelligence and industry. He obtained our passports from the Portuguese secretary, hired fourteen *carregadores*, or bearers, purchased two *tipoias*, or hammocks, and obtained such supplies as we needed for the road, viz., packets of tea, coffee, sugar, and brandy, and a bag full of copper coins called macoutas, of the value of twopence, which each man would receive as his rations, and so save us the trouble of providing food. There was a fifteenth man, who was a kind of sub-steward, head man to the gang.

At ten o'clock in the evening, Joachim, bowing himself into the room, announced that all was ready. I wore my old uniform, with a sword and revolver in my belt. My heart bounded at the thought of again visiting the interior, and I was soon comfortably reclining in my tipoia. "*Pront!*" I cried, and off went the men, singing, at a butter-and-eggs trot. I felt as if I was seated on an easy ambling horse, and the noise which the hammock made as it swang was like the creaking of a saddle.

The road ran close by the sea-shore, and once we were carried on the wet sands under some high cliffs, the feet of the bearers turning up phosphoric sparks. Then they came to a halt beneath a baobab, which sprawled its grotesque and gigantic branches in the eccentric manner peculiar to that tree. Here the relay came up; two fresh bearers raising the poles on their shoulders, having a double piece of cloth like a porter's knot between the wood and the bare skin. After we had made eight miles, we entered a small, straggling village, and awoke some of the authorities. I and Joachim were given mattresses on the floor, and the carregadores slept peacably by the road-side. At daybreak we were off again, and I now amused myself by watching the camel-like shuffle with which the bearers got over the ground. The leader had a small stick in his hand, which he flourished with a motion similar to that of a band-master, and sang or rather howled,

Shove him on!
But is he a good man?
No, I think he's a stingy fellow.
Shove him on!
Let him drop in the road, then.
No, he has a big stick;
Shove him on!
Oh matta-bicho! matta-bicho!
Who will give me matta-bicho?

Matta-bicho is a Bunda compound meaning *kill-worm;* the natives supposing that their entrails are tormented by a small worm, which it is necessary to kill with raw spirits. From the frequency of their demand, it would seem to be the worm that ever gnaws, and that their thirst is the fire which is never quenched.

At Kifangonda we stopped to breakfast. It is a pleasant little village on the banks of the Bengo River. There was a market-place in the centre of the village, where women squatted in front of miniature stalls, furnished with fruits, fish, and farinha. These were for the accommodation of caravans, which passed continually, being long files of negroes carrying the produce of the interior in baskets on their heads. One caravan was reposing under a large tree, upon which was posted an official notice in writing.

Having breakfasted, I ordered my tipoia to be brought round, and we passed along a road near the river, with rank, high grass on both sides. Here the musquitoes had not even the decency to wait till it was dark, but attacked me in broad daylight. When we had got clear of the river, we entered an undulating plain, which looked as if some gigantic sea had suddenly turned to dry land, the "rollers" being hundreds of yards apart.

The close of day found us at another station. The mulatto commandant received me with great cordiality. Joachim displayed his culinary talents, and made an *omelette au fromage* to a marvel. But when I went into the chamber which had been prepared for me, I stood aghast. There were no musquito-curtains.

The musquitoes of Angola are of a peculiar malevolent species. This was also remarked by Livingstone. In no part of Africa was I ever attacked by them in the daytime; in no part of Africa did I ever suffer so much by night. This voracity of carnivorous insects in certain localities, and the rage with which they attack man, is a curious problem in natural history. On board a palm-oil vessel the musquitoes seldom annoy one, and their little bags, when examined, are found full of oil. This can be understood; but it is impossible to explain why musquitoes should be more savage in the Bengo than in the Gaboon. It is curious also that the alligators of Equatorial Africa have never been known to attack men, while people both in Angola and Senegambia have often been attacked while on the banks.

The musquito is only found in moist localities; at an earlier period of its existence it wriggles in the water, a kind of worm. After its metempsychosis it becomes an insect very much like our common gnat, but twice as large. Perching on the skin, it draws its proboscis, which it inserts gently and gradually up to the hilt. Not content with drawing blood, it infuses a poisonous essence into the wound, which, in an unhealthy system, has even rendered necessary the amputation of a limb. One would think that they were surgeons of the old school in a state of transmigration, for they will bleed you to death, if you will let them.

The "flies" which plagued Egypt could only have been musquitoes, and the land of Goshen would naturally be exempt from the scourge, as its soil is dry and sandy.

In the first hour of the night I heard their low, sinister hum. They serenade one first and then make one pay for it, as if they were Italians. All night that song continued, which I accompanied by slapping myself violently on the cheeks and forehead. But after a while their humming became very incoherent (they were getting drunk on my blood), till, to my diseased fancy, it began to resemble "We won't go home till morning," which, at all events, they did not. I rose covered with red spots.

I received a formal introduction to Senhor Mendez, a mulatto who believed that he was civilized, who was an advocate, and the chief landowner of Ambaka. This gentleman offered me his company *en route*, and his house when we should arrive at Ambaka; so we joined cavalcades; his consisted of thirty slaves, who, being badly fed, had not half the stamina of my free bearers, and they delayed us considerably. As a kind of rear-guard he had two poor relations with muskets, who were supposed to shoot any slave who attempted to run away. In Africa, however, slaves only run away from real ill usage, for experience has taught them that to do so is only to change masters. When a runaway slave goes to a native village for protection, the chief imprisons him, endeavors to find out his master, and, if he succeeds, offers to restore him for a certain price. If unsuccessful, he sells him afresh. This appears to be law throughout Africa. Some slaves who had escaped from San Thomé with a canoe, landed on Corisco. As soon as they landed they were claimed as slaves by the first person who had seen them, and in slavery they were kept all their lives. In the Portuguese colonies the runaway slaves work in a chain-gang by themselves; and though the colonists of San Thomé had a bad character as masters, it is but justice to the Portuguese for me to state that I never witnessed a case of corporal punishment; nor, out of the hundreds of naked slaves that one sees here, have I ever seen a single scar which flogging could have caused.

Those who know what slaves are will immediately infer that 'those of Angola are really the masters, and not only masters, but tyrants. Such is unfortunately the case with negroes, school-boys, and all inferior beings. It is useless to appeal to any thing except their epidermes.

We crossed the winding Bengo that afternoon, ferried over by canoes. These are the turnpikes of the Angola roads; but those who do not carry merchandise can pass freely. A boat laded with ripe oranges, a beautiful sight, passed by; for this is the thoroughfare by which fruit descends to Loanda. The city is also supplied with water from the Bengo; and when, as sometimes happens, the bar is impassable, the Portuguese have to drink a brackish liquid and to dine fruitless.

The next day we passed through a barren and thinly-populated country, and at nightfall halted at a government caravanserai. These are shanties built of clay, resembling in their architecture the buildings of white ants, divided within into three compartments, each containing a wooden frame or bedstead of the rudest character. They are, however, admirable institutions; a policeman is provided in each, who attends to the wants of travelers, and who is bound to have fire and water always ready. A paper is posted on the wall, stating the legal regulations under which these stations may be used; and within hangs the monkey-bread, or fruit of the baobab, a huge pod filled with an edible pith which is glutinous enough to make excellent sealing-wax. The tree, in other respects, is almost as useful as the cocoa-nut; an admirable cloth is made from its inner bark, cords from its coarser fibres; and many of them, in desert districts, when hollowed in the centre, make excellent cisterns, and so save whole tribes from perishing of thirst.

R

As the rainy season had not yet commenced, the high grass of the plain made good straw beds, upon which we laid ourselves out for slumber. In the morning I made my first experiment upon Joachim by leaving three or four sovereigns on my bed; not that I expected him to fall into so glaring a trap, but in the hope that I might gain some clew to his character from the manner with which he brought them back. When he did so he gave me a look which betrayed itself by its very keenness. He wished to know whether I had left the money by accident or on purpose. But he could have read no expression in my face beyond stupidity, and during our journey I carefully shammed the fool.

I must own, however, that he was too much for me. I believe that I succeeded in making him "write me down an ass;" but he remained impenetrable: long habits of dissimulation were not quickly to be broken through. I was sure that he was a dangerous man. His very voice was pitched in an artificial tone, and infused with an artificial accent; he also cultivated that profuse artlessness, to be perfect in which is to arrive at the acme of human finesse. Beyond this I could see nothing. I wished to gauge his villainy, partly because it served me as good study in the dull desert, partly because I wished to know if I could trust myself with him in Congo and Benguela. Setting duplicity aside, he was an admirable cook, an attentive valet, and a charming *compagnon de voyage*. At first I had treated him as an ordinary servant, but after joining Mendez we breakfasted and dined at his table (or rather at his table-cloth, for we usually dined upon the ground); and Joachim was always invited to the repast as my equal, which indeed he was in manners and education.

Joachim was by birth a German-Swiss, and had been educated at St. Petersburg; he therefore knew French, German, and Russian perfectly. He had then studied medicine at Heidelberg. He had become tired of his studies, he said, and had a mania for the sea. He had his little patrimony. He bought a schooner, made a voyage in her; she was wrecked in the Gulf of Genoa, she had not been insured, he lost all. But he cared little for that, he said, with his inimitable imitation of simplicity, since the lives of all his men were saved. So far all seemed true enough; but now came the ugly hiatus. He had evidently been almost all over Europe; he could speak Italian, Spanish, Portuguese, and English. He appeared to have a horror of Switzerland, and said that he would never return to his family again, though he seemed very proud of possessing some sub-prefect as a relative. What had he been doing all that while? Upon this point he was mysterious, perhaps a little confused. He told me anecdotes about the great cities of Europe, and their *on dits*. But when he spoke of London, I soon perceived that he had been living in the filthiest localities of our filthy metropolis, and keeping the worst of the very bad company that is to be found there.

Next he had entered as able seaman on board Russian, English, American, and French vessels. He had been twice round the world. He cheered my evening hours with anecdotes of the islands of the Pacific, of Peru, and the Spanish girls; of the Californian gold mines, where he had dug, and played at pitch-and-toss with doubloons; of the Sitka Islands, where the ice-ships go; of pirates in the Chinese Seas; and of one terrible tempest off Cape Horn.

Owing to circumstances which he did not deem it worth while to explain, he had come to the West Coast of Africa—that refuge for the destitute, whether criminals or debtors; he had entered his name on the books of a French emigrant ship, and had made the voyage from Congo to Bourbon with a cargo of negroes; the vessel returning to Congo, he had requested the captain to put him ashore; he had become clerk in a factory at Loango, and afterward at Congo, and finally had come down to Loanda. There, I knew his history. He had done very well by bum-boating till he had been tabooed from all the English men-of-war, having repeatedly been caught trying to smuggle spirits on board; he had set up a small shop in the town, and become bankrupt.

Joachim was still very young. His high and classic forehead seemed the abode of a fine intellect; his hair was long, and fell upon his neck in luxuriant curls. Nature, in giving him his face, had bestowed upon him a mask for his character, and had ushered him into the world as one of her own fair frauds. He had a virtuous expression of countenance, a white and delicate skin, showing all the veins, finely chiseled lips, and eyes so pure, so bright, so limpid that you might read (or fancy you might read) all the secrets of his heart therein.

Joachim had not only the features, but the accomplishments of a gentleman. He knew the polite languages of Europe, and often helped me through a difficult passage in the Bucolics of Virgil, which I used to read in my tipoia. He was a musician, and played Handel on the *marimba* or calabash-harmonicon of the natives.

He had a fine tenor voice; he could use that quiet, cynical wit which passes so well in society, and, in spite of his poor clothes and mean position, he possessed the elegance and *aplomb* of a man who is accustomed to the world, and who is always at his ease.

So we went on for some time, and, except that I discovered some amusing insincerities, I gained no farther insight into his character. I had thought it best to affect absolute ignorance of Portuguese, though of course I had not passed two months in a condensed atmosphere of Lusitanians (or rather Lousitanians) without learning something of it, and could generally gather the sense of any thing that I heard. This was the means of affording me much entertainment; to hear Joachim, as he jeered Mendez for a bigoted papist, pathetically deplore in Portuguese that fate had condemned him to serve a heretic; and after satirizing the baboon element, which (ever retained in the mulatto) was strongly marked in Senhor Mendez, turn round and in the same breath caricature the grave imbecility of the Englishman.

Sometimes I thought that, after all, Joachim was only a brass medal, with flatterer on the one side and slanderer on the other. A fickleness of character, which usually accompanies versatility of talent, might fairly account for the vicissitudes of his life; and it was quite possible that he was one of those men with whom honesty is really the best policy, since they have neither patience nor talent enough to be successful knaves.

But he spoke of Switzerland and his family with peculiar abhorrence; nor were they the only ones whom he denounced. According to his own account, he had been ill-treated in many parts of the world. Although I often laughed at myself for the belief, I could not shake off an impression that he had committed crimes in those places of which he complained, and to which he declared, with an air which struck me as being really sincere, that he would never return.

But that which surprised me most was the hatred which this handsome young man displayed against the sex of whom we see so little. I shall never forget the bitterness with which he said, "I have been twice round the world, and I have found dogs and women every where the same."

I associated a woman with his first crime.

These real (or as I thought real) sentimnets, which escaped from Joachim from time to time, were but momentary, and they served to render him doubly careful afterward. I had almost despaired of finding the clew to this human labyrinth, when an accident gave it me. Being troubled with a slight attack of diarrhœa, I told him to bring me the brandy which I reserved for such emergencies. He brought it to me; as I filled a glass I happened to glance at his face. His eyes were riveted on the amber-colored poison as it trickled out. I knew that look. One. sees it often enough, God knows, especially on the Coast. He was now in my power: I could tear the mask from his mind, and read it like a child's primer; I could set a charm on his tongue which would make it babble forth the secrets of his brain. Joachim was a drunkard.

In the mean time, let us continue our journey. At daylight he would bring me a cup of prepared cocoa with an egg beat up in it. I would drink it, put on my coat and boots, and walk till the sun became powerful, then jump into my tipoia, which would be close at my heels. About twelve we would halt, usually at a station, and breakfast. This was always prefaced by a monologue from Mendez, who seemed to prefer talking to eating; so that, as Joachim once remarked, "if it was possible to eat words, we had made a very good breakfast." But after a deluge of compliments came a rainbow in the shape of a fowl or duck, accompanied with *pirão*, a kind of pudding made of lard and farinha, and a bottle or two of *viño tinto*. Before proceeding to business, one of my men would bring me a bowl of potter's earth, in which I would perform my ablutions.

This part of Africa is very different from the forest-mountains of the equator, which abound with rippling streams. Here the atmosphere of the early morning is perceptibly clearer and drier than that of the gorilla country, which is loaded with moisture. It was the end of the dry season; every night one might see a hundred grass-fires burning in all directions; sometimes our narrow road lay between heaps of ashes; and once a fire smouldering by the path burst out so suddenly, that I had to spring from my tipoia, which the flames, impelled by the wind, almost caught with their long yellow tongues. Another time I was astonished to find a canoe lying in the middle of the road, at a place where it was intersected by a small ravine covered with pebbles. I was told that this was the bed of the River Lelunda, which in a month's time it would be impossible to cross without this canoe.

It happened that the rain was a week or so late that year, which saved my caravan a great deal of discomfort, but which was a serious trial to the animated kingdom. Sometimes we found birds

which had perished apparently from the drought; one of them
the beautiful hoopoe, which, with the green woodpecker, the red-
legged partridge, and the quail, is common to England and Angola.   One day, having stopped at noon in a shed by the road-
side, and having filled our pots with water from calabashes which
we carried with us, a swarm of bees entered the house bodily and
buzzed round the pots.   The natives, who did not seem surprised
at this intrusion, placed some water in a large flat pan at a little
distance; upon this, the bees, as if understanding that it was meant
for them, collected round the edge of the water, and even on the
water, six or seven deep, remaining there for a few minutes, when
they would fly away, and their places would be taken by others.
Although they buzzed round us and settled on our faces and
hands, either from their thirst or their repletion none of us were
stung.

The country from undulatory became hilly, and after we had
made about a hundred miles we passed over a range of hills, and
then over another range a little higher.   These seemed to be a
continuation of the two ranges of the Sierra del Crystal, only
much dwarfed in height, the soil and the character of the trees
being very similar.

But afterward we entered a fine open country of hills and valleys, and Joachim repeatedly pointed out scenes which reminded
him of the minor views of the Alps.   At length, having come to
the summit of a hill, we saw a beautiful country stretched before
us, yellow with corn, green with groves, till it became mazy and
gray on the borders of the horizon.   It was the first time that I
had seen inland scenery in Africa: in the dreary forest-land of
the Gaboon the view is always circumscribed.   As for Joachim,
his Swiss heart warmed, and he cried, " C'est parfaitement un can-
ton de Berne!"

Joachim had another passion—that is to say, he had another
vulnerable point—he loved his country.   I laid my plans accordingly.

On the tenth day we arrived at Ambaka, and "put up" at the
house of the advocate.   This Senhor Mendez, who was really rich,
lived in a house which was little better than a large shed, with
its unpapered walls, uncarpeted floors, and a mere sprinkling of
bad furniture.   His wife, who was an invalid, lived in a small out-
house, which was almost comfortable by comparison, and took

her meals with only the company of her female servants. One frequently finds this isolation of the wife among the mulattoes; and I am told that even among the Brazilian planters the guest is seldom introduced to the ladies of the family.

This Mendez was a type of the educated mulatto. He had a quickness which might pass for penetration—a volubility which was almost eloquence—hospitality tarnished by ostentation—a penchant for his children—a veneration for himself. He united profuse good nature to the narrowest selfishness, and a heart which was almost womanly to manners which were almost apish.

He was one of those bustling men who are always in haste, who have not a moment to spare; who invariably carry papers in their hands, and who must read them as they walk, since to sit down would take up time; who, in the midst of their "pressing engagements," will talk to you for an hour about themselves; and who, when the day is gone, discover to their surprise that they have done nothing. He affected to be omniscient, and gabbled absurdities on all topics. He took great interest in English politics, he said, and asked me whether the Russian war was over, and if Mr. Palmerston was alive. We breakfasted usually about eleven o'clock, when Mendez would come in reading a letter, shake hands with me absently, and eat his beefsteak with a meditative air. When he had taken a little wine he would become communicative, and would read the letter out at length to the *clients* who surrounded his table. He would ask their opinion about the matter, and, without waiting for their answer, would declare his own; after which he would sing snatches of songs while yet at the table, and would exclaim that when a man's belly is full, life becomes supportable.

These little peculiarities afforded secret enjoyment to Joachim and myself. There was some old family plate, too, which he brought out one day to astonish us; and the air with which Joachim turned it over and over close to his eyes, pretending to be lost in admiration, but in reality looking for the hall-mark, was extremely comical.

But the crowning absurdity arrived at our final dinner. The oranges and guavas having been placed on the table, Mendez asked me if I would like some Champagne; and then cried, "Oh moleka! Champagne!" and grinned affably at the rest of the company, who responded with hideous grimaces. I was regretting that he should bring out an expensive wine on my account before

so many (there were twelve at table), when I saw, to my astonishment, *liqueur-glasses* placed before the guests, and a solitary pint
bottle introduced.

I had hoped to have gained some interesting facts respecting
these Ambakistas, who are industrious workmen and enterprising
traders, and who have even established schools, where they teach
one another to read and write. But I found that Mendez would
not be drawn out upon any subject but himself, and that Joachim
was a very bad interpreter in all matters except those in which
he was personally interested. As for the Ambakistas themselves,
they were all dispersed abroad. A war had been raging for some
time at Casanje between its natives and the Portuguese; the manner in which it originated, as well as the measures adopted to conclude it, are strikingly illustrative of Portuguese misrule.

The King of Casanje, who is about three hundred miles distant
from the Coast, was a vassal of the Portuguese, and had been in
the habit of paying to them ten slaves per annum. The Commandant of Casanje demanded tithes of all the property of the
king and of that of his subjects. The king replied, "I will pay
my lawful tribute. I will promise to protect your traders, and to
assist them in whatever they require; but to give you a tenth of
my kingdom! that I can not do." Shortly afterward a usurper
sprang up: the Portuguese supported him, and the king was compelled to abdicate. It was not long, however, before the usurper
died. The king was again elected to the throne, where he sat
without showing any desire to revenge himself upon the Portuguese. But when the commandant announced his intention of
appointing a minister for him—and a minister in African courts
has the same real power as an English premier—the king refused
flatly to accept their interference. The commandant sent an officer and a file of soldiers, who cut off the head of the king's minister. The king sent a crowd of warriors, who cut off the head of
the officer. Then began the war. The Casanjes took the fort
and its artillery, and drove the Portuguese back to Malanji, the
next station, where they were now strengthening their position
with earthworks. The commandant had been killed in the first
skirmish; and this war, which his brutal folly had occasioned,
had already ruined more than one firm in Lisbon. The Portuguese cabinet sent out a new governor general, a new command-
er-in-chief, and a new secretary. In the mean time the war remained in *statu quo*, the Portuguese behind their wall, the natives

in their huts; and the poor people of the province kept them in clothes and food, and were pressed as "carregadores" whenever they were wanted.

There had long been a scarcity of palm-oil in Loanda, much of the regular supply having been stopped by the war, those who had oil to sell fearing to enter the town, lest they should be sent to fight for their country, and against their countrymen.

I had frequently wondered why the people scowled at me so often on the road, but not after a young captain had passed me, his hammock-bells ringing gayly, followed by a crowd of chained negroes driven by soldiers toward the seat of war. I wore a braided coat; they naturally supposed that I was the leader of such another press-gang.

While I was at Ambaka I wished to buy some shoes, which they make there of untanned leather, and sell at a shilling the pair. But there had been an official razzia of these shoes for the soldiers of the royal army, and the shoemakers had wisely hidden the rest of their stock—and themselves. I wished to buy a couple of *bœuf-chevaux* for my journey back, and had great difficulty, owing to whole herds being also *cachés*. Finally, one day, when we were at breakfast, a native entered and said that he and his wife had been dragged away to Malanji in chains; but his wife having attracted the attention of one of the officers, a mulatto, he was graciously liberated, and she was retained for the exigencies of the service.

It is certain that a residence in Angola would not impress one with favorable ideas of human nature—of Portuguese mulattoes least of all. In this dark and dirty corner of the earth, where there are no coroner's inquests nor *post-mortem* examinations, secret poisoning is by no means of rare occurrence. Indeed, I had not been long in the interior before I found that poisoning was the stock article of conversation, as the weather is with us, and as fever is in our colonies of the Coast. The Bishop of Loanda died suddenly. The priests were to be seen crying like children, and declaring openly that he had been poisoned. A few days afterward a priest died—also suddenly. And on the public quays, in the open streets, by the stalls of the market-place, men said to one another, "*The murderer of the bishop is dead.*" Such was the story told to me: it was probably mere scandal; but we have not such scandal in England.

I saw sufficient with my own eyes to prove the prevalence of

the custom. Mendez was on bad terms with the chief of Ambaka, and his son having occasion to go to the latter on business, I
heard Mendez warn him in the most solemn manner not to touch
a drop of any thing as he valued his own life. On our return we
dined with Senhor Monção, a large planter, and who was at that
time governor of Golungo Alto, the principal station of the interior. Joachim had had an accident which I shall presently describe, and his mouth was very sore. The governor ordered his
"consort" to prepare some kind of liniment, which Joachim (who,
like all knaves, was suspicious) declined, but without any show of
distrust, merely saying that it was better to leave these things to
nature; upon which the governor cried, " What! do you think it
is poisoned, then ?" and rolled some of it round his mouth to prove
to us that it was not.

This Monção had been exiled in his youth to Angola at the
time when Portugal was so unsettled. He gave me no worse poison than some very fine wine of Oporto, of which we each drank
a bottle and a half. I have some recollection of drinking Republican toasts with him, our arms locked together and our hands
crossed; probably a bacchanalian emblem of conspiracy and com-
bination. He spoke to me of Livingstone, and expressed his admiration of a man who could travel so many miles on an ox. He
had then received him at his farm at Trombêta. Livingstone had
marked the latitude and longitude of Golungo Alto on the floor
of one of the rooms, which he showed me. When I told him that
his name was mentioned in Livingstone's book, he appeared intensely gratified.

Finally, Mendez, like the other planters, preferred stale, musty
tea to their own fine native coffee, which Joachim and myself
drank by preference. They say it is unwholesome, but they refuse it because "the chandler loveth not the smell of his tallow."
When Mendez saw that we were drinking coffee by ourselves, he
ordered one of his poor relations to be quick and finish his tea,
and then take some coffee; "so that," he added, turning to us with
a smile (as if he were saying some commonplace phrase of the table), "if you should be poisoned on the road, you shall not think
that it was here."

This was not agreeable, for I knew very well that there was little love lost between the Portuguese and myself. As a sample
of what small spite could do, the mulatto commandant at whose
station I had slept the second night of my journey had purposely

taken the musquito-curtains off my bed because I was an accursed Englishman. The illiterate supposed that I was a Portuguese officer searching for men, oxen, and shoes of untanned leather. The educated thought that I was on a secret mission from our government; that we wished for an estimate of the resources of the province, with a view to the ultimate seizure thereof. This belief was not exceptional; it was universal; and shows how this wretched nation fear us, and how we stamp upon them with an iron heel—or rather with a *golden* one. It was in vain that I assured them that the Colonial Office was not so much in love with West Africa; they only shook their heads with a sage smile, and asked anxiously whether England would indemnify them for the loss of their slaves. So I gave up arguing the matter, and promised to mention Senhor A. favorably at home, and to take care that Senhor B.'s claims were put in their proper light. The incredulity of fools is like the soft wood of African stockades, in which cannon balls can only inter themselves.

While I was at Ambaka I had some conversation with a slave who had run away from the unvisited kingdom of Matiamvo, a powerful African king of the interior. He came to me playing on a fruit which had been hollowed, and through which a few holes had been bored. He said that he had been *cambua*, or doorkeeper in Matiamvo's palace; that he had committed a fault, and had run away to escape death. The name of Matiamvo's people was *Boloni*. Their country had neither mountains nor high trees. The animals found there were lions, elephants, leopards, crocodiles, jackals, wild cattle, giraffes, and small monkeys. The great river Kikapa ran through it from the rising sun to the north. Another river, called the Matiamvo, joined it, running from west to east. A large river, called Ru, passes from east to west close by Matiamvo's palace. In this last river hippopotami are found; in the others only crocodiles.

When the king travels he is seated on the clasped hands of slaves. He punishes those of the vassal chieftains who perform human sacrifices. There are no cannibals in that country. The fetich-men are very powerful, dragging elephants, attracting animals to a certain place, and making wooden dolls which could spring several yards.

Having staid two days at Ambaka, I resolved to return; but wishing to enjoy the luxury of riding on an ox, and Joachim having entreated me to admit him to the same privilege, I purchased

a couple of oxen. One of them, a red ox, was, when once mounted, tractable enough; but the other, a small black bullock, with a
satanic eye, was "playful," as dealers say of vicious horses which
they want to sell. When I mounted the brute it ran backward
with crab-like rapidity, and performed two or three pirouettes. I
kept my seat with some difficulty. It feels very awkward at first
on an ox: you sit so far forward on his shoulders that you sometimes feel as if you were going to slip over his head. The black
bullock bounded savagely about, and, twisting his head round,
tried to gore my legs. This amusing exercise had gone on for
some time, when I felt the crazy country-made saddle gradually
slipping round under the bullock's belly. Disentangling my feet
from the copper stirrups, I sprang off in the midst of a trot, and
alighted on my feet, as they do at Astley's, though not with quite
the same grace.

I rode the red ox for the first two days, but found that this animal is unfit for quick traveling. He can not endure much work
in the middle of the day, and is at any time liable to sicken in
this part of Africa. But for steady, not too speedy work—day
after day, week after week—the ox, as has been proved by Livingstone and Andersson, is the best of beasts. He leaps well if
you give him time, and can get over broken ground with much
less danger to his rider than a horse can; but he is a slow, cold-
blooded, sulky kind of beast. If you insult your horse with your
spur, he tries to throw you on the spot, and, failing there, after a
few tosses of the head and champing of the bit, usually returns
to good temper; but the ox ruminates mentally as well as physically: he chews the cud of revenge. Once, being rather hurried,
I drubbed my ox heartily. He took no notice of it at the time;
but about ten minutes afterward we came to a place where there
was a fall of some feet on each side of the road. Suddenly, and
without the least warning or excuse, the brute jumped off the
road, and down we went into the bushes below. Luckily, I was
uppermost, with my legs round his neck. He got up snorting,
tried to kick me when I mounted him, then climbed the banks,
and went on peaceably.

When I bade adieu to Mendez, he threw his arms round me,
and kissed me on both cheeks. What a strange thing is fashion!
thought I. When I part with my dearest friend in England I
shake him by the hand, while this dirty mulatto, who makes a
show of me, and who gives me Champagne in a liqueur-glass, I

BY OX AND HAMMOCK.

must embrace as if he were Jonathan and I David. However, I congratulated myself that I was not in Lapland, where we should have rubbed noses, nor in the Philippines, where etiquette would have compelled me to shampoo my face with his foot.

The first day of our return journey I made Joachim ride in his tipoia, as I saw that the black ox was sufficiently unmanageable to cause delay; but Joachim, who had been drinking a great many *matta-bichos* with Mendez, having some Dutch courage supplied by Brazilian rum, insisted at our midday halting-place on mounting the black bullock, and riding him for the rest of the day. As he did not seem able to recognize the relative positions in which we stood, and as I thought that nothing would sober him so quickly as the bullock, I gave my assent (which Joachim, I must own, had not requested), and, after a quarter of an hour spent in arranging the girths, Joachim mounted. In a quarter of a minute a loud crash in the high grass announced that Joachim had fallen.

He was not to be beaten by an ox, he said, and he would mount again. But he was so long fiddling about with the saddle that I lost patience, and told him to be quick, or we should not reach Sainji with daylight.

"If we do not reach Sainji with daylight, we shall reach Sainji in the dark," said Joachim, thickly. "It is all the same. I prefer traveling by night."

"Who cares what you prefer?" said I, purposely baiting him, in order to draw him out. "Do you forget that I am your master?"

"I do not forget that you are my master. Remember also that I am a Swiss."

"The Swiss are a tribe of valets and couriers."

"The English," retorted Joachim, "are purse-proud idiots."

"If you don't get up on that bullock immediately, Joachim, you shall not ride it at all."

"The Swiss," said Joachim, with a hiccough, "is a faithful servant: he will not disobey the master whom he despises."

"Get up, then," said I, taking him by the scruff of the neck and shaking him.

"When one drinks Portuguese rum, it is necessary to eat English bread," said Joachim, sententiously. "You like to travel by day; I, on the contrary, prefer to go by night. It is true that by night there is danger: there are bandits; there are wild beasts;

it is necessary to have courage to travel by night. All people have not courage. They are wise, then, to go always with daylight. I am courageous, therefore I prefer the night."

"Very well," said I, "Joachim, you shall travel by night; you shall even ride the ox all night if you please. Now are you contented?"

Joachim made a polite and flowery speech. I chuckled inwardly. I knew that he was a coward; that he was always in an uneasy state when we were on the road at night: he had even asked me, as a great favor, not to travel after dusk. I knew that he would return to sobriety before we reached the station beyond Izanga, and that he would suffer torments. As part of our road would be very much broken, I thought it not impossible that his ox might fall down and break his neck, which would have subjected me to temporary inconvenience, but which would have been a benefit for society at large.

Instead of stopping at Izanga, therefore, I said that I should go on to the next station, which was about six miles off. Not wishing to punish my men on account of Joachim, I let them carry my hammock empty, and, getting off my ox, which I had no desire to ride in the dark, I walked on in front with sword and pistol at my belt. The road was execrable. On arriving at the station, I woke the people up and had a fire made. It was a long time before they came. At last I heard the tinkling of my hammock-bells, and the two oxen, both riderless, loomed in the distance. Joachim entered the house with his handkerchief to his mouth. Though burning to know what had happened, I took no notice of it, and ordered him to have my supper cooked directly. Joachim made some tea and boiled a couple of eggs with his usual industry. When I had finished I asked him whether he had looked after his own. He said that he could not eat any thing. Affecting surprise, I asked him why. Taking away the handkerchief, he showed me his mouth badly cut, and his two front teeth wrapped up in a piece of paper. It seemed that the ox had stumbled, that Joachim had fallen violently forward with his face against the bullock's skull, had smashed his teeth, and had then slid off, fallen under the bullock's nose, and had been nearly transfixed by his horns.

As nothing was to be gained by loitering on our road back, I traveled as fast as I could, and (as I had done in the gorilla country) got over ground, in a general way, faster than any body had done before me. I found that traveling through the middle hours of the day was bad policy, for the sandy soil then became scorching, and those men wearing no sandals began to have sore and swollen feet. My plan of march, therefore, was to have tea made overnight. This I took the first thing in the morning, before it was light, and, starting off the men with the oxen first, and Joachim in his tipoia to have breakfast ready at an appointed place by the time that I arrived, I made the other men make up their burdens; I coming behind them all, and whipping-in stragglers. We would be on the road from six till twelve. From twelve to four I let them rest; and from four we traveled till some indefinite hour in the night. Already acquainted with the route, having marked the distances carefully in my note-book, I was no longer at the mercy of guides, and could sketch out my own itinerary. Joachim did not approve of this rapidity. He thought it strange that I should wish to visit a country where there were no railways. One day he asked me:

"When you are in the tipoia, do you ever hear something go 'Cluck—cluck—cluck—cluck?'"

"Yes," said I.

"Then you must take care," said Joachim, "how you travel too fast. That is what we call in medicine *borborygmi*."

The carregadores themselves, as may be supposed, took a violent dislike to this velocity; not that it was too much for their *physique*, but because they have an African love of dawdling and talking scandal at every village they come to.

When we had first started they were in my debt. They had refused to engage themselves unless they were paid half their wages in advance. During the first part of their journey I was obliged to treat them with great politeness. They were generally drunk, and the shadow of an affront would have been sufficient to have made them leave me. But now the tables were turned. These men, who had been so arrogant as debtors, as creditors became servile. It is true that they mutinied over this forced march of mine, which I made in the hope of catching a cruiser bound for the Congo, that would first bring the mails to Loanda. A solemn deputation approached me, to represent that the Portuguese did not travel like that, and that "it's not the distance, but the pace that kills." I replied by thrashing the deputation with a whip made from the skin of a manatee. Upon this they became cheerful and agile, and profoundly grateful for any matta-bichos I might

S

choose to give them. "The stick," says the Moslem maxim, "came down from heaven, a blessing from God." And man resembles a spice, which, the more it is beaten, the sweeter perfume it exhales.

When we had arrived at the last station before Loanda, I determined to solve Joachim, that human enigma. After I had taken my dinner of fowl and farinha, I told him that I felt in low spirits, and should take a glass of grog. He brought me the materials, and watched me furtively as I drank. I invited him to join me. With that diffidence which confirmed drunkards so often assume, he replied that he seldom touched spirits, but that he would take a *demi-goutte* just to keep me company. I drank enough to have turned my head at any other time; but when one determines not to be drunk, it is as when one desires in cold blood to be drunk—one remains sober.

After I had unbosomed several secrets of an imaginary nature to Joachim, he began to be garrulous and communicative, the subject which he chiefly dwelt upon being the number of injuries he had received at other people's hands, and the remarkable manner in which the Fates had always conspired against him.

"I am now in Africa," he said; "it is my prison; I do not know how I shall escape from it. I am a Swiss; here there is no Swiss consul. It is true, I can work my passage in a vessel to Lisbon—but then?—what am I to do?"

"You will return to Switzerland and your family, without doubt."

"Return to Switzerland! Never!"

"You do not love your country, then?"

"I do not love my country! Oh, *mon Dieu!* he says I do not love my country. Switzerland! Switzerland! oh, I would kiss your dust were I with you. I would sit on your hill-side, and I would look all day at your blue lakes, and your cultivated fields, and your mountains of snow, which lose themselves in the clouds. Do not I yearn for you in this filthy land? And I must never, never see you again!"

"But what is there to prevent your seeing Switzerland again?"

"What is there to prevent me? Well, I will tell you," said he, clenching his teeth. "I have made a vow. It is that which prevents me."

"Oh, a vow! You are romantic, Joachim."

"Yes, I am very romantic," he said, bitterly. "Listen. I love

Switzerland; I hate the Swiss. I had a friend; that brutal people drove him away. I made a vow that I would go among them
no more."

"Drove him away!"

Joachim swallowed a glass of neat brandy, and now spoke thickly and rapidly, as if afraid of being interrupted. "You wish me
to tell you this story. I will tell it you. This young man, my
friend, he was a student; he was young and handsome; he was
un peu galant; when he was merry, he sang; when he was thoughtful, he wrote verses to pretty women; he led the life of a bird which
has a gay plumage and a sweet voice.

"His parents were Swiss, but not pure Swiss; there was Italian
blood there. He went to see them, for he had his money from an
uncle who had made him his heir, and he was independent of
them. He gave them a visit; they were proud of him when they
saw his fine clothes and his French manners; and the girls of the
village they thought him very handsome, and they called him
' Monsieur.'

"He had another uncle in that same village. He was a bear-
hunter, a huge brute of a man, with a black beard, and limbs like
a giant's. But he had a very pretty daughter—the cousin of my
friend. You know, monsieur, that custom which they have in
Switzerland on Saturday nights for young people to pass the night
together: in French we call it *se-veiller.* One Saturday night his
cousine came into his father's house. She had a new cap on, and
gay ribbons, and for a Swiss she was charming. His mother—
yes, it was his own mother who said it—told him that such a pretty couple must *se-veiller* that night; and Pauline clapped her little
hands, and kissed my friend on the cheek, and—"

"But what was his name?"

"His name! Eh, sacre Dieu! his name! Oh, the name of this
young man, it was Franz.

"You know, monsieur, that a custom is nothing because it is a
custom. In Switzerland the young people do not think it strange
to *se-veiller;* they are stupid, besides: they are not men and wom-
en—they are swine of the mountain. But this Franz, he was a
young Parisian. He had hot blood—he did not understand this
custom: you can easily understand, monsieur, why Pauline had
such pale cheeks the next day. She was a child, this Pauline. A
woman knows how to hide a folly, but the tongue of a child is
quicker than her thought. When the bear-hunter came home that

night he called her to him, and sat her on his knee, as he always did, and kissed her. And she began to cry, and twisted her fingers in his beard, and then she hid her head in his breast, and told him all. And what did this wise father do? In France, and in Russia, and in England too, I dare say, they understand these things; they do not foul their own nest—they keep still tongue, and they make a marriage. Franz was not a bad man then; he would not have refused to marry her. But no, this man talks to every body; when Franz enters the village, the girls who used to bring him flowers turn away their eyes and look at him after he has passed; the old people whisper together, looking at him. He does not understand this; he does not know why the people come together. Ah! now that man, whose daughter Franz has known, he rushes from the crowd; he seizes him by the neck, and beats him with the wood of mountain ash. He beat him—he beat him like a dog; and when he fainted away, he left him like a dog to die!"

"And did Franz die?" I asked.

Joachim, who had sunk his face in his hand, raised his eyes, which shone like those of a hyena.

"No, he did not die. In the night he crawled to his father's house. A hand was put outside the door and gave him food; a voice told him to go from them and to return no more. He went away, and to return no more. But he would stay a little—yes, a little while in the mountain. He went to the place where he had been beaten; his alpenstock still lay there; no one had touched it; it was his; it would have tainted them. He climbed up the mountain till he came to a small chasm in its side; he walked along its side till he came to the path of the hill-goats: it was by this path that the hunter of bears always went to seek his sport. It was a wide place to leap, but a large flat stone jutted out from the mountain side, and was imbedded in a soil of gravel. When Franz had first sprang upon it in chasing the chamois, he had feared that it would yield beneath his feet. This fear was the instinct of his revenge. He labored all night, though his limbs were cramped and tender, and loss of blood had made him faint. But every pain which he felt reminded him of his insult, and urged him to his task. It was scarcely dawn when his work was done.

"He hid himself behind a bush some feet above the stone, which tottered in the very wind. He heard a step. Was it a goat, which would come and spoil his snare? No, it was the firm tread of a man upon the rattling stones. Yes, it was he; no one could mistake that form of a giant: he came on and on—to his doom. It was scarcely light; he could not see that the earth had been touched; he did not even examine the leap he had to make; he had leaped it a thousand times. Franz saw him running forward —saw his body as it bounded in the air. The giant stood quivering before him as the stone rolled from beneath his feet and fell crashing in the ravine below. With a yell which made the hills echo all around, the giant sprang up in the air, athlete that he was, and seized a plant which grew from the mountain side: it slowly—oh, how slowly!—tore itself out root by root, fibre by fibre. But his active feet were searching for a resting-place—another moment, and he was saved—when Franz held out the alpenstock, and cried, 'Quick! quick! take this, and you are saved.'

"When a man struggles for life he does not suspect a snare; he seized it with both his hands. Those hands had lost their brown and healthy color; fear had made them all white and mottled. And oh! his face, that was horrid to see. 'I see it sometimes now,' said Franz; 'his mouth covered with foam, and his eyes bursting from his head. But that only pleased me then. I laughed in that fearful face; I let go the pole; I saw him fall, the blood spurting as he struck against the rocks; and after I could see no more, I heard something faint and dull fall in the invisible depths below.'"

Joachim was silent.

"And what became of Franz?" I asked.

"Franz left Switzerland," said Joachim, in a dull, dreamy tone. "He returned to Paris, where he spent all his money like a madman. When it was gone his friends left him, his mistresses insulted him. He became a vagabond, and while a vagabond he was a criminal."

"Well, Joachim," said I, "that is a very interesting story, but I do not see why you should hate your family because Franz has had reason to detest his. Now make my bed. We must be off early to-morrow."

The next morning Joachim told me that he had made up this story to amuse me, because he saw that I was dull. There was not a word of truth in it. My Cognac had inspired him; for certainly it was dramatic, was it not? I complimented him upon his powers of imagination; at the same time, I took pains to impress upon him the fact that I had not been taken in, and that I knew very well all along that there was no such a person as his friend Franz.

CHAPTER XXVI.

FEVER AND FLIGHT.

Three Dreams.—Fever.—Mr. Gabriel's Sickness.—His Death.—S. S. Don Pedro.
—The White Lady.—The Language of Cigars.

On the morning of my arrival in Loanda I felt unwell, which I
ascribed to the brandy and water overnight.   When I sat down
to copy and arrange my note-book memoranda, according to my
custom on returning from a journey, I found that I could not settle down to work, although I felt a restless inclination to do so.
As the evening approached my spirits became quite elastic; my
veins seemed no longer filled with blood, but with quicksilver;
and my brain was filled with thoughts so fantastic that they resembled dreams.   I sent out Joachim to inquire if I could get a
boat to take me to the Congo.   In spite of Mr. Gabriel's advice
that I should enjoy a little civilized repose, I determined to set
off to the Congo in a couple of days.   When I went to bed that
night I had never felt in such buoyant health.

I got to sleep with great difficulty, and not before I had built
quite a city of castles in the air.   My imagination having been
already so excited, it was natural that I should dream.

I dreamt that I was at home—my bachelor's home in London.
It was a winter's night.   The fire was blazing in the grate, and
threw flickering shadows on the walls.   I was reading by the
light of two candles.   Suddenly these became extinguished; the
fire died out; I felt in my dream as if I was cold.   Out from the
walls, as they faded away, came tall, dim, shadowy trees, and a red
moon rising above them.   Water splashed round me.   I was in a
canoe, and before me were my men bending to their paddles.   We
glided along with inconceivable swiftness, till my brain seemed to
turn, and the trees and the moon were left far behind.

I awoke, but soon fell asleep again.   This time I was in the forest.   This impression was so vivid that the tints of certain leaves,
the rugged appearance of the bark of the trees, have never yet left
my memory.   I was there, standing alone, with my double-barreled rifle in my hand.   I heard a rustle in the wood.   I started.

Something huge and black burst through the screen of leaves and confronted me. It was the gorilla which I had bought from the Shekani. He was not lying dead in a canoe now; he was standing before me, as I had seen him then, with his hideous mouth open, with vacant eyes, with a wound in his head, and the blood coagulated upon it. It seemed to me that he was dead, and yet that he was alive. I raised my gun and took aim at him; I pulled and pulled, but the hammer would not fall. At last it fell with a dull snick; the sweat poured down my cheeks; and there stood the beast, never moving, with its eyes covered by the gray film of death, its great yellow teeth displayed, and its arms hanging powerless by its side. I thought that if it moved it would break the charm. I looked at it fixedly as if fascinated. It did not move; but *the wound burst open*, and blood, not like our blood, but black as ink, oozed forth. I followed the stream with my eyes. It slowly trickled down that hairy body, leaving a trail behind. It streamed down the leg till it came to the knee, over which it poured quickly, and so to the ground. There it formed a puddle. I looked at the wound shuddering. Again it yawned like a mouth, its lips quivering—again the black stream was vomited forth. It swelled the puddle till it overflowed, and till it began to creep like a reptile toward me. I awoke, uttering a gasp of fright. My mouth was dry and parched. When I got out of bed I found that I was giddy. I emptied the water-bottle, and, drawing the curtains, looked out. I could faintly see trees and houses through the dusk; it was nearly morning, therefore. I determined not to go to sleep again; but I slept in spite of myself; and my last dream was as follows:

I was *en route* from Ambaka. I had just arrived at a lonely caravanserai, in a certain part of the road, where for nearly fifty miles few habitations are met with. I descended from my ox, and lay down on one of the settles, or benches, which are provided there for beds. Joachim also lay down opposite to me, leaving, as was our custom, a palm-oil light burning on the floor. I dreamt, as one often does, that I went to sleep, and that I awoke. The palm-oil light was nearly out, but I could see a dark body gliding backward and forward before me. The light flamed up. I caught sight of a white face and two green eyes, which shone like live coals. I tried to move. I could not. Something black squatted on my face and tittered at me. I tried, in vain, to shake him off, my eyes always fixed on the moving form. The light flickered again. I saw a hand and a glittering knife-blade. The form slowly, slowly came toward me. At the same moment the light also rose into a clear and brighter flame. The room became quite light. Above me I saw Joachim's face. My tongue clove to my mouth. He raised the knife and plunged it twice into my breast. Immediately I felt myself covered with blood. Then he bent close over me, and said to me in a polite tone,

"Are you not well this morning, sir?"

These words awoke me. Joachim was standing over me with a look of deep sympathy impressed upon his face. One of his hands contained a roll of paper; and he had awoke me by placing his hand twice upon me. This was the knife of my dream; and I was drenched in perspiration, which I had mistaken for blood.

I was giddy and languid, with a strong feeling of nausea. I had fever, that was very clear; and it had commenced overnight, as frequently happens, with an excitability which simulates the liveliness of health, and takes the unhappy patient in before it does for him.

While in the gorilla country I had had frequent attacks of fever, but none of them severe. They recurred once a month, making me unfit for mental exercise for two or three days; but during the five months which I had spent in Equatorial Africa, I was never confined to my bed for a single hour beyond my usual time. But now it was very different.

The climate of Angola is less unhealthy than that of Equatorial Africa. But in the latter I had always been extremly temperate, and had never enjoyed a pleasure of any kind. In the former I had, unhappily, yielded to the allurements of civilization. I had gone to cafés. I had drunk bottled beer. I had even been guilty of late suppers. I had breakfasted at noon, as if I had been at St. James's instead of in San Paolo; and, as a crowning folly, I had regularly taken my matta-bicho or *petit verre* of Brazilian rum before every meal, after the fashion of the Portuguese colonists.

Having taken large doses of quinine without success, I abandoned drugs altogether, and gave myself up to Nature and cold water. I had a huge earthen jar by my bedside, and drank immense quantities. This made me perspire, etc., profusely, and so the poison gradually ebbed out of me. My mind remained always in a cheerful state, which in febrile diseases, and, indeed, in most others, is of very great importance. Mr. Dickens must have been my best doctor, for I find among the notes which I scribbled in my pocket-book between the paroxysms, *Read Pickwick—an actual medicine.*

My host was ill at the same time as myself, but with a far more dangerous disease—*dysenteria mucosa.* A naval surgeon (there happened to be a cruiser in the port) attended us both. I heard him say to Mr. Gabriel, after I had refused to take any more quinine—a proceeding which he considered equivalent to suicide—that he had known pluck keep a man alive in the last stage of the disease, and that that alone could save me. He little thought then that the patient whom he was addressing, and who, even in his own sickness, showed such anxiety respecting mine, would be the first to go. Poor Gabriel! He had worked his way up to the top of his little tree. He had only two years more to spend on the Coast, and he would have retired on full pension. He often talked to me of what he would do and how he would live when he went back to England. A little cottage in the country, with a good service of plate, and a few nice people round him, he said, that was all he wanted. Perhaps they might make him a C. B. after his long and faithful services.

As soon as he was able to rise he came into my room, and, sitting by the bedside, he would talk to me of these trifles, but which are now so touching since he is gone. When I left Loanda, ill as he was, he went down with me to the beach. Even then I was looked upon as the worse invalid of the two. "I hope that you will soon be all right," said I, carelessly enough; he thanked me in the same manner; and we wished each other an *au revoir* in England. But dysentery is a stubborn and terrible disease. When, three months afterward, I went on board a mail steamer in the Gambia, I was shocked to hear that he was dead. He had had a relapse: the doctor had ordered him a change of air, which he had required long before, but which his duties, to which he was always so faithful, had prevented him from accepting. He was actually on board a cruiser and outside the port, when another entered with a prize in tow. It was a disputed case: his presence was demanded in the court of mixed commissioners—the first time for years. "The Fates seem to be against me," he said, in the last letter which he ever wrote. They were. Had that prize been brought in a few hours later, his life would probably have been saved.

Such is Western Africa. It is not like other tropical countries.

One never becomes acclimatized. The old residents are as liable to disease as the new-comers. Out of the few European friends whom I had in Africa and Angola, four have since died; three of these—the doctor of the mail steamer, one of the missionaries at Corisco, and Mr. Gabriel—had spent most of their lives upon the Coast; while the captain, Johnson, with whom I had sailed to the Fernand Vaz, had been in the habit of previously trading in that river.

Restored to my legs, I found myself very weak; but I felt a necessity for locomotion. I desired to go either to the Congo or to Benguela. In order to go to Benguela, I must wait for the Portuguese packet; to Congo, for the chance arrival of a man-of-war. To go to Benguela by open boat, with the surety of a head wind, would involve a voyage of at least a month at the commencement of the rainy season. This was not to be thought of. To enter the Congo by boat was equally out of the question. A certain tribe at the mouth of the river had robbed a schooner there shipwrecked. They had gutted her, and had kept the sailors in captivity till ransomed. The squadron had retaliated by burning some huts and destroying a few canoes. The natives then seized the factor, who had complained to the commodore, stripped him, stabbed him, cudgeled him, dragged him through bushes of a poisonous character, and left him to all appearance dead. He revived, however, and established his factory in another part of the Coast. Another Englishman they took prisoner, and told him that, if he was not ransomed by a certain time, he would be killed. He was led about in the daytime with a string; at night he was made to sleep in some locality famous for musquitoes; and, as is the custom with prisoners in the Congo, he was *smoked:* damp leaves, mingled with red peppers, were set on fire. He was told to talk; if he refused, he was pricked with a spear; if he consented, the hot, poignant smoke entered his mouth and throat, and made him suffer torments.

As it would be impossible to enter the Congo in a boat without being taken prisoner by these people, who had declared that they would in future kill any Englishman they could get hold of, I felt little inclination to go. I was thoroughly perplexed. I did not dare to take Joachim with me to any out-of-the-way place, since I should also be obliged to take with me a good deal of money. I did not know how to get another interpreter. I did not see my way out of Loanda, in which I felt that stagnation would be dangerous, except by a steamer which was homeward bound; so I took a step which I have since greatly regretted, though possibly it saved my life. I gave up my Congo enterprise, and took a passage to the islands of the Cape de Verd.

When (on October the 18th) I embarked on board the Dom Pedro, a Clyde-built steamer, I found the passengers in a state of European excitement. I was informed that a white lady was expected. Here a white lady is a black swan. I grooved my stomach on the side-railings, and waited anxiously. First installment—three green monkeys, five gray parrots, and two black girls. Second ditto—bandboxes, feminine trunks, and a live crane. Third ditto—an old gentleman with the countenance of an amiable baboon, a young lady wearing no bonnet, but a very pretty cap, with peach-colored ribbons flying in the air. She mounted the ladder, disdaining masculine assistance, and was soon seated on the quarter-deck surrounded by admirers.

To these she dealt out murderous smiles, and I had my heart assassinated on the spot. She was pretty, at least for Africa, and possessed eyes remarkable for their beauty even among the dark-eyed Portuguese. When we were fairly off she no longer remained an isolated star. She became simply one of ourselves. She mingled among us with the sang-froid of an actress in the green-room. But if she did not always receive from these men, who usually caricatured politeness, that empty homage current in society, she enjoyed, in compensation, the noblest prerogative of our sex. She would smoke a cigar to the ash with any man on board, and disdained cigarettes as effeminate. She would take her glass of Cognac or Geneva after dinner with the air and *aplomb* of a *bon vivant*, and would use her toothpick between the courses with the nasty nonchalance of a true Portuguese. Her hair prevented her from doing that which is considered the correct thing among this refined race—that of carrying a cigarette behind one ear and a toothpick behind the other. But she had her cigar-case always in her pocket, and her toothpick adjusted in her hair-net.

The use of this little instrument was her only fault. In other respects she was vastly superior to most Portuguese women. She washed her face every day; she always declined garlic; she took her nails out of mourning (don't ask me what with); and she was not *lic*entious—an epithet which I heard a palm-oil trader apply to the women at Madeira.

As for her smoking, the time will come when tobacco will be
enlisted into the artillery of a lady's charms. I observed that her
eyes seemed to flash with double fire through the smoke which
issued from her lips (or nostrils). In raising the cigar to her
mouth she was compelled to display a white arm to the elbow;
and there were all kinds of pretty gestures which she used to assume, and which ladies who travel in the Peninsula would do well
to study.

As far as *we* are concerned, let us remember that smoking is
conducive to silence before we set ourselves too sternly against it.

I did not dare address her frequently with my mutilated Portuguese. To speak a language badly is to render one's self ridiculous and to fall. How can a woman return the affection of a
man who calls himself her "loafer?" At first we conversed with
our eyes. We then invented a new language of love—the language of cigars.

She used to smoke excellent Cubas. I had only some detestable Bahias. But she never refused when I offered one to her.
Was it economy? Perish the thought! It was noble self-denial. She would press my hand as she took it, smile, and smoke.
Thus she accepted my vows and breathed them from her lips
again. These vows were not permanent, but they were warm;
they were quickly dissolved, but they were as speedily renewed;
and even when they finally melted away, a fragrant memory was
left behind.

The cigar affords the finest illustrations of human emotion.
Sometimes she would smoke without looking at me, criticise the
ash of the cigar with a little sneer, and exhale the smoke with a
pah! This expressed coldness and contempt. Sometimes, biting
off the end of the cigar with a savage nip, she would smoke in
rapid puffs, injecting the smoke into my eyes. This was petulance and anger. But sometimes she would give the cigar a coy
kiss as she put it to her lips, and looking at me with her bright
and coaxing eyes, she would murmur, *O que cigarro benito!* words
which expressed love and tenderness for me. And when at length
we had to part, she brought me a delicious Havana, and offered
me a light with a trembling hand. In our little dialect this was
to say that thus she gave me her heart, and that soon after we
were separated it would be reduced to ashes.

CHAPTER XXVII.

THE CONGO EMPIRE.

African Revolutions.—King of Congo.—Benediction of the People.—The Bed-tax.
—The royal Harem.—The Pontiff and Priests of Congo.—Religious and Civil
Institutions.—An African Napoleon.—The Queen of the Jagas.—Her Valor and
Cruelty.—Her bloodthirsty Laws.—Her cannibal Amours.—Her violent Death.

In Africa, as in Europe, revolutions take place. The empires
of Ashantee and Dahomey have sprung up within the last two
hundred years, and within that time the great empire of Congo
has been broken up into a thousand petty principalities.

The writings of the Jesuit and Capuchin missionaries have
made us well acquainted with the ancient constitution of Congo.
Its study is not only curious, as displaying several remarkable
customs, but useful as affording us a clew to the inland empires
of Matiamvo and other potentates as yet unvisited.

When a new king is elected his first duty is to give his subjects the Benediction. An immense square is filled with people,
who come there from all parts of the kingdom. The king comes
out of his palace covered with blue aggry stones, gold ornaments,
and small looking-glasses, so that it is impossible to look at him
fixedly in the full sun-glare. He is followed by a long train of
priests and nobles, who range themselves round him. He then
addresses the people, exhorts them to be faithful and obedient,
and assures them of his love. He rises, and all the people prostrate themselves before him. He stretches his hands over them,
and makes gestures with his fingers without uttering a word.
This is the Benediction, which is followed by cries of joy, the fir-
ing of muskets, and a long jubilee of banquets.

Before the Portuguese traders had imported those Spanish hats,
silk jackets, damask coats, and velvet slippers, which afterward
were worn by the Congo aristocracy, the king and nobles wore
petticoats of fine grass cloth, dyed black, hanging from the waist
to the ankle, with aprons of tiger-cat's skins; on the head a cap
like a hood, or a small square red and yellow cap like those which
the marabouts wear in Senegambia. Next to their skin they wore

a kind of shirt, made also of grass cloth, and worn like the Roman toga, leaving the right arm bare. The poorer people went
barefooted, but the king and nobles wore sandals made of the
wood of the palm-tree.

The king is a despot, secretly controlled by his ministers. His
revenues consist chiefly of tributes paid to him by his vassal lords.
Sometimes he finds it necessary to levy taxes; and as the negro
never commits an act of oppression or treachery without some excuse, however ridiculous, the king will go out with his cap placed
loosely on his head. The wind will blow it off, and the king will
pretend to return to his house in a furious rage, and will send two
or three hundred tax-gatherers out the next day to seize goats,
fowls, slaves, and palm wine.

Our legislators once taxed windows, and many were bricked up
in consequence. In Congo they are more ingenious; they tax
beds. This is levied specially for the maintenance of the king's
concubines; each bed is taxed at a slave the span's breadth. A
broad bed is therefore a luxury in Congo, and a sign of great
wealth.

When the king takes a fresh concubine her husband is put to
death. She is forced to give the names of her lovers (for it seems
that all the married women have lovers), and these are also executed. She then enters a seraglio, which resembles the Oriental
harem, except that its inmates have more liberty. When the king
dies his wives are buried with him.

The king eats and drinks in secrecy. If a dog enters the house
while he is at meals it is killed; and an instance is recorded of the
king's son having accidentally seen his father drinking palm wine,
and of his being executed on the spot.

The king has a large army, composed of different companies,
who serve under the banners of their respective lords. They
have reviews, like the Dahomans, and fight with bows and arrows,
knives, spears, and muskets.

Civil suits are brought before a judge who sits on a piece of
carpet under a large tree, with a staff in his hand. These judges
are not incorruptible; but those who have lost their suit have no
power of appeal, and never complain against the injustice of a decision. Criminal cases are usually brought before the priests, and
are tested by various kinds of ordeal. The two commonest are
those of the drink, which I have already described, and of the hot
iron.

A hot iron is applied to the prisoner's skin, and if it burns he is pronounced guilty. One would imagine from this that he has no more chance of escaping from such an ordeal than a poacher from a bench of sporting magistrates. But it is said that the priests have a preparation which they rub over the part about to be touched, and which completely counteracts the effects of the heated metal. It is curious that this same ordeal was practiced in Europe in the Dark Ages, and that the same story was told of the monks who applied it.

Nowhere can the ancient African religion be studied better than in the kingdom of Congo. In Abyssinia, Christianity, and in Northern Guinea, Mohammedanism, have become so mingled with pagan rites as to render it extremely difficult to distinguish between them.

The inhabitants of Congo, whom I take as a true type of the tribes of Southern Guinea generally, and of Southern Central Africa, believe in a Supreme Creator, and in a host of lesser divinities. These last they represent by images; each has its temple, its priests, and its days of sacrifice, as among the Greeks and Romans.

There is one particular sect in the Congo country who are distinguished from the others by their recognition of one God, whom they call *Deus caca*, which means "one God," or *Desu*, which means "God of heaven," but on whom they have bestowed as attributes their own dirty vices.

Father Cavazzi mentions a most remarkable invocation which these people use when sick or in trouble, viz., *Desu, Nghesu fumami*, which means "God of heaven, Jesus my lord." Those which he heard among people who could not possibly have received instruction from other missionaries, he ascribes to intuition; and observes that this invocation is only used as a last resource, when prayers and sacrifices to the grosser deities have failed. It is probable that this tribe has wandered across the continent from Abyssinia, and that this invocation (if it really exists) is a relic of the Christian ceremonies which their ancestors performed.

The chief of the priests occupies the position of pontiff in the state. Even the king fears him, and seeks his favor. The populace look upon him almost as a god. He receives from each family the first-fruits of the harvest, which are brought to him by the pater familias and his head wife, chanting a hymn. He receives them with dignity, and tells them that their next year's crop will be increased by this act of piety. The *Chitomé* also lives on a special diet, consisting of delicate fishes and small animals, which form the offering of the hunters and fishermen.

In his house burns a sacred fire, which is never suffered to go out, and embers of which he sells at a high price. No one is allowed to approach his house except upon matters of importance and bringing a handsome present. When a new king is elected, he repairs to the pontiff's house, attended by a crowd of people who utter piercing cries. He kneels before the house and entreats the favor of the high-priest. He enumerates some of the presents which he has brought. A stern voice from within tells him to go away and not to trouble him with such paltry matters. But, as the king continues his catalogue of gifts, the voice loses its harshness, the door opens, and a venerable man, clothed in white, with feathers on his head, and a mirror on his breast, appears before them. The king prostrates himself. The priest sprinkles him with water, scatters dust over him, and tramples on him. Then making him lie on his back, he extends himself upon him, and makes him swear that he will always obey. After this ceremony the king is established on the throne, and soon extorts from his subjects the value of the presents which he has been compelled to make.

When the Chitomé leaves his house to make his circuit for the settling of disputes among the minor priests, criers proclaim the fact, and a fast of continence is enjoined till he returns. Those who break this law (which is a most severe one for such a people) are instantly condemned to death; for it is believed that by such continence they preserve the life of their common father. In such cases, only the man being punished, wives who are tired of their husbands very often accuse them of an imaginary amour, by which stratagem they obtain their liberty and a reputation for virtue.

They believe that, were the Chitomé to die a natural death, the universe would immediately be demolished. Accordingly, when their pontiff falls dangerously ill, the priest who has been appointed as his successor enters his house and beats his brains out with a club, or strangles him with a bow-string.

The priest second in rank to the Chitomé is the *nghombo*. When he appears in public he walks on his hands, with his body straight and his feet in the air. He can walk in this manner, through constant practice, with great ease and rapidity. He is the medicine-man or fetich-doctor, and is consulted in cases of sickness and witchcraft. To the cunning of this priest may easily be traced that superstition which I have described as prevalent in Equatorial Africa, that no one dies a natural death. If any one dies in spite of the medicines of the *nghombo*, he preserves his reputation by declaring that the patient has been bewitched, and obtains more money by discovering the sorcerer. There is another priest named *npindi*, who officiates as *rain-maker;* for this, a knowledge of the seasons, which in Congo never vary more than a few days, is all that is required. The ceremony of rain-making is that of covering mounds with branches of trees and ornaments of fetich, and of walking round these, muttering incantations. It is said that an insect of unknown form will then issue out of the mound, and, rising in the air, bring thunder, lightning, and rain. Besides a great number of priests of different denominations, some of whom pretend to have the power of taming animals, others of raising the dead, but who are merely conjurors and doctors, all dwarfs and albinoes are elevated to a priesthood, who maintain their rule by appealing to the vulgar senses of the mob.

The condition of the women is pretty much the same as in other parts of Africa. The husband, however, sometimes deigns to confer marks of affection upon his wife, which he imprints upon her with a whip made from the skin of the sea-cow. *Chacun à sa fantaisie.* If the Congo wife is not soundly flogged every now and then, she considers herself an injured woman, and her relatives remonstrate with her husband.

In Congo, however, there is no Salic law; and instances are frequent enough of women ascending the throne. One of these became as famous in her own country as Elizabeth of England or Catharine the Great.

Shinga came to the throne in 1640. As she refused to adopt the ceremonies enjoined by the Portuguese priests, they aided her nephew, and she was forced to fly from her kingdom, having lost three battles.

She settled about a hundred and fifty miles up the country, and made war toward the Jaga country, subduing many towns and villages. Encouraged by this success, she again marched against the Portuguese, by whom she was completely routed and her sisters taken prisoner. But in 1646 she regained her kingdom, and concluded an honorable peace with the Portuguese.

Shinga had become so accustomed to war that she cared for no

T

other occupation, and led an Arabic life with her followers, roving
after plunder and conquest. Before she undertook any new enterprise, she would sacrifice the handsomest man that she could
find. Clad in skins, with a sword hanging round her neck, an
axe at her side, a bow and arrows in her hand, she would dance
and sing, striking two iron bells. Then taking a feather, she
would put it through the holes in her nose as a sign of war,
would cut off the victim's head with her sword, and drink a deep
draught of his blood.

She kept fifty or sixty male concubines, and while she always
dressed herself as a man, they were compelled to take the names
and garments of women. If any of them denied that he was a
woman, he was immediately killed. The queen, however, was
charitable enough to let them belie their words by their actions;
they might have as many wives as they chose, but if a child was
born the husband was compelled to kill it with his own hands.

But Shinga was a mere milksop in comparison with *Tembandumba*, queen of the Jagas.

These Jagas appear to be the Arabs of Western Africa. According to Cavazzi, they first appeared in Congo in the beginning
of the sixteenth century, and fell upon the indolent and luxurious
Conghese as the Goths fell upon the Romans. With their king,
Zimbo, at their head, they made the kingdom of Congo a desert.
The Conghese yielded in despair, and joined him as tributaries.
He then held a review of his immense army, and, as food began
to fail them, he divided it into bands. One of these he sent to
ravage the countries of Abyssinia and Mozambique, under the
command of his captain, Quizzuva, who carried his conquests to
the sea, but was defeated by the Portuguese near Tete. Zimbo,
on hearing this, came to his assistance ; the Portuguese were defeated ; their general killed : the skulls of the white prisoners
paved the ground before his house ; and a Dominician who fell
into his power he murdered with frightful torments, and, putting
on his sacerdotal robes, danced before his troops, holding the sacred chalice in his hands.

Zimbo is even said to have taken the island of Mozambique—
a European fleet which bore up to its relief having been dispersed
by a tempest—and only to have abandoned it when he found it
impossible to obtain provisions for his army. But this Napoleon
of Africa found his Waterloo in the kingdom of Melinda, where
he was completely routed, and, having lost all his riches, escaped

with a small body of followers. Not daring to return to the countries which he had laid waste as a conqueror, he took unfrequent-
ed routes, and is said to have passed from the East Coast by the
Cape of Good Hope to the equator, and to have settled on the
banks of the River Cuneve, which takes its source in the province
of Scella, and enters the sea in 17° lat. There he built a town
(called in their language *Chilombo*), and divided his little army
into companies, over which he appointed captains. One of these,
named *Donji*, settled in the kingdom of Matamba with his concubine Mussasa. There he had a daughter, whom he named after
Tembandumba, the celebrated wife and companion of Zimbo.
Some years afterward Zimbo died. No one was fit to succeed
him, so the empire dissolved into petty principalities, each governed by its chief.

Donji having also died, his wife Mussasa continued his enterprises and conquests. She was a skillful warrior, and extremely
cruel and bloodthirsty. She gave her daughter the education of
a warrior; and these two women, at the head of their army, were
always the first to charge the enemy, and the last to retreat.
Mussasa was so struck with her daughter's courage, wisdom, and
endurance, that she gave her the command of half the troops, although at that time she was only a girl. Tembandumba, having
gained several victories, and now confident of her superior genius,
no longer deigned to listen to her mother's advice. A lion in
war, she became a tigress in passion; savage in her wantonness—
at once voluptuous and bloodthirsty—she admitted a crowd of
lovers to her arms, and killed them with the cruelest tortures as
soon as her lust was satiated. Her mother having remonstrated
with her respecting these excesses, she openly rebelled against her,
proclaimed herself Queen of the Jagas, and founded laws so barbarous and cruel, that only the abject fear in which this young girl
was held, and the veneration she had won by her marvelous valor,
insured her the obedience of her subjects, savages as they were.

It is commonly said that women are always at extremes, and it
is difficult to imagine any constitution more barbarous than that
which she proposed.

Following in the footsteps of the great Zimbo, she would turn
the world into a wilderness; she would kill all living animals;
she would burn all forests, grass, and vegetable food. The sustenance of her subjects should be the flesh of man; his blood
should be their drink.

She commanded that all male children, all twins, and all infants whose upper teeth appeared before their lower ones, should be killed by their own mothers. From their bodies an ointment should be made in the way which she would show. The female children should be reared and instructed in war; and male prisoners, before being killed and eaten, should be used for purposes of procreation.

Having concluded her harangue, with the publication of other laws of minor importance, this young woman seized her child which was feeding at her breast, flung him into a mortar, and pounded him to a pulp. She flung this into a large earthen pot, adding roots, leaves, and oils, and made the whole into an ointment, with which she rubbed herself before them all, telling them that this would render her invulnerable, and that now she could subdue the universe. Immediately her subjects, seized with a savage enthusiasm, massacred all their male children, and immense quantities of this human ointment were made; and of which, they say, some is still preserved among the Jagas, and is called *Magija Samba.*

It is clear enough that Tembandumba wished to found an empire of Amazons, such as we read of as existing among the Scythians, in the forests of South America, and in Central Africa. She not only enjoined the massacre of male children; she forbade the eating of woman's flesh. But she had to conquer an instinct in order to carry out her views; she fought against nature, and in time she was subdued.

Mothers used so many arts to preserve the lives of their male infants—which women usually cherish more than those of their own sex—that she was obliged to appoint officers who were to be present at all accouchements, and to enforce obedience to her law; but when the disaffection became general, she permitted children taken in war to be sacrificed, and the *Magija Samba* to be made from their bodies instead.

She subdued immense territories only to lay them waste, to depopulate them, and to bring the scourges of famine and disease upon her own army; but she prevented rebellion by keeping them always at war, in which her valor, her perseverance, and her military genius preserved for her the admiration and adherence of her followers.

As she grew older she became more cruel, more lustful, and more capricious. She embraced a lover one day, she dined off

THE QUEEN OF THE CANNIBALS.

him the next. But, in spite of this inconstancy, she was at last entrapped, and those passions which she had rendered so fatal to others were adroitly turned against herself.

She fell in love with a man named Culemba. He was a private soldier in her army, but he possessed all the qualities which such a princess would admire. He was young, strong, and finely proportioned; cruel, bloodthirsty, and remorseless. He possessed all the arts of flattery and insinuation. He studied the nature of this extraordinary woman, and gained such influence over her that she married him publicly, and gave him the half of her throne and kingdom.

But in the course of time the queen found married life a little dull. She yawned sometimes; and it was well known that such yawns swallowed young men's lives. Culemba used every art in his power to retain her affection, and succeeded in postponing her determination.

But when he saw his death-warrant written in her face, and observed that she now studied his beautiful form with the eyes of a gourmand rather than with those of a lover, he invited her to dine with him—the highest compliment which one Jaga can pay to another. He entertained her magnificently (probably with male infants); Lisbon wine and ratafia, from the budding colonies on the Coast, were handed to her in the skulls of her enemies. She drank, and died upon the spot.

Culemba displayed such violent grief, being scarcely restrained from killing himself upon her body, that no one supposed that he had poisoned her. She was buried on a high hill, where a large vault was excavated and divided into several cells, which were furnished with the finest trade-stuffs, mats, and skins. Her favorite drinks and dishes were placed there. Clothed in her warrior's dress, she was buried sitting on her throne in a commanding attitude. Her body was accompanied to the grave by an army; a herd of victims were sacrificed; the musical instruments made a sound like thunder; and above all rose the cries of the unhappy Culemba, who succeeded to the throne.

CHAPTER XXVIII.

THE ISLANDS OF THE GREEN CAPE.

Santiago.—Trip into the Interior.—A rough Lodging.—Negro Modesty.—San Vincenti.—Character of our Consul.—San Nicholão.—The Town of the Wild Stream. —Quail-shooting.—Boã Vista.—Sal.—Salt-pits.—The Charms of Solitude.

I HAD a return of the fever in a fortnight. It was short and sharp. The healthy influence of the sea exorcised the evil spirit, who went out of me in devilish paroxysms, and I rejoiced at my safe delivery.

On November 10th we anchored off Villa da Praya, the capital of Santiago, the most important island of the Cape de Verds.

The bay is formed by two headlands, one of which is called the White Woman, the other the Timid Woman. The town is built on a table-land perched over the sea. It is half a mile long, and about seven hundred feet broad; is clean and compact, and has a much more civilized appearance than Loanda: the population, too, composed chiefly of whites and mulattoes, gives it the semblance of a European rather than of an African town.

The old capital is about nine miles distant, and is situated on the banks of the Ribeira Grande, or Great River, a small and muddy stream, which in the dry season dwindles to a gutter. The ruins of a cathedral, a bishop's palace, a collegiate school, and a nunnery may be seen there; but, as with all these colonial ruins, they are barren ground to the archæologist.

I went ashore as soon as I could, and, having walked round the town and heard the military band, which is superior to that of Loanda, I went in at a door, above which was painted, in large yellow letters, HOUSE. BILLIARDS. COFFEE. There I made arrangements for hiring a horse and guide, with a view to visiting the interior of the island. I also filled a large bag with boxes of sardines, preserved fruits, and penny loaves; then, having mounted horses of Moorish breed imported from the main land, we cantered over the sandy road toward the mountains.

My guide, who of course commenced the conversation by asking me if my father and mother were alive and well, went a step farther than the savage negro could do, requesting to be informed how old they were, if they were rich, and whether they were good Catholics. This was, of course, unbearable; and as, in spite of my silence, he persisted in urging these inquiries, I solemnly warned him that, if he did not hold his tongue, I would send him back to the town. As he still went on, I took the bag and gave him " the sack." He rode off, looking terrified, not having received it in the gentlest manner, and I was left in solitude and peace.

But, after the first moment of relief, I began to see that my position was not enviable. It was nearly sunset; I was alone in a semi-civilized country (which is far more dangerous than a savage one), without arms, and with a bag which had all the appearance of containing valuable property. I could not speak a word of *Creole*, as the *patois* of these islands is called, and which is sometimes unintelligible to the Portuguese themselves. Prudence suggested my return; pride compelled me to go on. So, resolving to shun mulattoes, and to defend myself with the sardine end of the bag, if necessary, I rode on at the sharpest trot of which my gifted steed was capable. When it was twilight—for there is a little twilight in these islands—I saw a group of cottages a short distance out of the road. On arriving among them, I observed a fat, good-natured looking negress standing before one of the doors. I tied my horse to a pulga-tree, and approached her with an amiable smile. It had not occurred to me, however, that, though her round face and large mouth were sufficient to prepossess me in her favor, my physiognomy might not be so assuring. I gave her a small silver coin by way of commencing negotiations; she looked at me angrily, evidently supposing that my intentions were not honorable, *pocketed the money*, and sent a little girl round a corner as fast as her thin black legs would carry her.

She came back with a negro who had a drawn knife in his hand. Without allowing myself to be embarrassed by this circumstance, I entered the hovel, sat down on a bench, and began to open my bag. Curiosity conquered distrust, and they permitted me to do so. *Je connais les nègres, moi.* The mouth of the bag being sewn up, I gestured to the negro to lend me his knife. He hesitated. I looked at him with gentle determination. He gave it me. I drew forth my *trésors de cuisine*, handed the woman some coffee, which I made her understand she should prepare, and gave a biscuit to the girl with the thin legs. The man with the knife retired; the girl made up a fire; and a boy, leading my horse to a shed, put him up for the night.

While I was taking my coffee and sardines, the master of the house came in. He could speak a little English, having been a voyage to the West Indies, and said that I must stop there that night, which I had previously made up my mind to do. After we had spent an hour or so in conversation by the light of the kernels of the pulga nut—which, strung on a stick and full of essential oil, afforded a good light—it was bedtime among these simple people, who rise at dawn. A mattress was spread on the floor, and, covering myself with a ragged blanket, I experienced that feeling of "roughing it," which, as every traveler knows, is not without its relish.

The little girl now came in and recited a prodigiously long prayer, which lasted several minutes, and which was interspersed with as many yawns as genuflexions. Her father sometimes "gave her the word," but she repeated it, on the whole, with surprising fluency. Afterward the boy came in and went through the same ceremony. The man showed me his religious library, which consisted of a Breviary and of the New Testament translated into Portuguese. The whole family then strewed themselves around me in the most sociable manner. But you need not be shocked. Every country has its anomalies, and in Africa a woman dresses to go to bed. Having covered themselves with their *pannos* (large shawls made of cotton or wool) to keep out the wind, which entered very freely through various gaps and crevices, they slept the sleep of the peasant and the pig. Then all was silent; the struggling flame of the pulga cast fluttering shadows on the wall; and a sandy-colored cat walking to and fro preserved our slumbers from the rats—disturbers of nocturnal rest.

At daybreak I drank a cup of milk, warm and frothing from the goat, and then I proved (not for the first time) the truth of that axiom, "Give a nigger the ship, and he'll ask you for the long-boat." I had a considerable quantity of preserved fruits, bread, and coffee in my bag, and, as they had treated me very well, I gave them all that there was, except a small box of figs, in addition to a gratuity in money.

At first they were so astounded by this act of liberality that they could scarcely speak. When they did find their tongues, no gratitude could be more profuse. "God would reward me for my kindness to the poor; the Holy Virgin and the saints would preserve me; they would ever remember me in their prayers, and bless the day when I entered their humble roof." But I had not ridden ten yards from the door when the girl with the thin legs came running after me, and asked me, with her father's compliments, whether I would not give them half the figs!

I was surprised to hear that there is a system of squirearchy and entailed property on this island. It seems that when this island was first colonized, the government portioned it forth in grants to certain residents, chiefly colored, securing it to their successors by entail, and under certain conditions, viz., that they should keep a certain number of mules or horses; that they should live in houses with a certain number of rooms; keep a certain retinue, and give a night's lodging and board withal to all *bonâ fide* travelers who demanded it.

Whoever framed this clause was well acquainted with the mulatto character, as the result has proved; for, unfortunately, it has not been enforced. These *mulgrados*—who, as I am credibly informed, have some of them a rent-roll of as much as £2000 a year, and the average £1000—live in detestable hovels, containing not more than a couple of rooms, which are far less neat and clean than those of a small negro trader on the Coast. They contrive to spend their money by assiduously drinking and gambling from morning till night. If they have any other diversion, it is to frequent the company of low negresses to enjoy the *batuka*—a favorite and slightly indecent African dance.

This is another of twenty other groups of instances which might be cited to prove that the negro does not care about making a fortune. If he can eat, drink, and be merry, he desires no more. Ambition may be a vice, but without its element man must remain on a level with the brute.

Having remained at Santiago four days, we steamed over to St. Vincent's, the finis of my voyage. A sea-captain having been asked his opinion of this island, said he thought it was "hell with the fire gone out." Physically speaking, the metaphor is not so bad, for it forms the base of an extinct volcano.

Even desert islands, however, can be done wonders with, as is proved by the waterless example of Ascension. Fever is not indigenous at St. Vincent's, which is therefore an excellent sanatorium, although, like all hospitals, it is rather dull. It is barren, but it is amply supplied with provisions from the neighboring isl-

and of St. Antonio, as Ascension is supplied from St. Helena. But
that which renders it wealthy is its port and its central situation.
On the grand highway of commerce, three lines of packets and a
large number of steam-ships touch here for coals, besides sailing
vessels for provisions. All their wants are supplied by one firm
(Messrs. Visger and Miller, of Bristol), whose acting chief has
achieved the triumph of making negroes labor. One might have
fancied one's self at Newcastle or Cardiff. It astonished me to
see in Portuguese Africa piers and wharves, trucks running on
rails, and tiny steam-boats tugging out huge barges of coal; still
more, when I landed, to see the black men and women working
with an industry and with a method which I had never seen in
them before, even in slaves under the eye of the overseer. The
mystery was partly explained when I saw English artisans also
busy on board the tugs and at the blacksmith's forge; and more
fully when I met the presiding genius—a man with the head of a
mathematician and the eye of a hawk. He told me afterward
what a cruel struggle he had had with their inborn propensities
for sloth and theft; and how, by severe and unchanging discipline, he had at length subdued their natures, as with repeated
kindness (though *he* did not tell me this) he had won their hearts.

I went to the Hôtel de France, where one can receive moderate
accommodation at an immoderate price. I was saved in great
measure from the talons of extortion by the hospitality of the English consul, with whom I breakfasted and dined every day. This
gentleman—and I say it not from gratitude for his dinners, but
from a real esteem for his character—is one of those three or four
men who are now assisting the progress of Western Africa by
their individual efforts. It is true that they can not do much, but
that little should obtain our warmest admiration.

Mr. Thomas Miller has two hundred laborers under his charge.
For years there has been no medical man on the island, and it is
to him that all come when they are sick; it is to him, also, as
"the king of the island," they come when they are in trouble.
For years there he has labored without ostentation, and reaping
only those silent rewards which, rising from one's own conscience,
are the sweetest of all.

In times of general misfortune, such men as these rise above the
surface under which they have worked so long. The Cape de
Verd Islands, surfeited with population, have always been liable
to epidemics. One of these was a famine. Crowds of these poor

people laid themselves down to die. The negro does not resist the enemy, whether hunger or disease; he resigns himself without a struggle. Mr. Miller, having obtained the sanction of the authorities, furnished large numbers with the means of emigration to the West Indies. Afterward the cholera came, and swept off *two thirds* of the inhabitants! Here, again, the labors of Mr. Miller, whose own family was not spared a loss, obtained from the Portuguese government one of their highest orders—that of the Tower and the Cross. And when, on another occasion, the small-pox had shown itself, he vaccinated a thousand people with his own hands.

As the French mail was not due for three weeks, I determined to spend that time in making a tour round these islands, and embarked on board the "Aurora," a small schooner, which was bound for St. Nicholas. She was a terribly dirty little craft, overrun with vermin, and managed by a negro crew, who also sustained a large parasitical population. In the night we had a good run; but I was awoke the next morning by the whistling of the sailors. Then I knew that we were becalmed. I went on deck, and found that we were lying under a mountain, which closed all the wind against us. The vessel rolled heavily from side to side, and, while I was looking at the island, the main boom, swinging over, hit me on the back of the head, and sent me sprawling on the deck. I was picked up, slightly stunned, and put below out of the way. There, eating dried figs, I cursed the tardy wind, as Milo at Massilia cursed lukewarm Cicero.

In the evening we had a light breeze, and anchored the next morning in the Port of Laziness (Porte da Preguiça). It was a village of a few fishermen's hovels, one or two stores, and a custom-house. A boat took me to the rough stone quay, on which a negro in blue trowsers and a red shirt walked majestically to and fro. As the landing was bad, I held up my hand, and asked him in villainous Portuguese to help me up. He replied in detestable English that he must first see the ship's paper of health. Having read it very carefully, he permitted me to land, informed me that he was the captain of the port, and said that, if I liked, he would introduce me to the mayor. I had some tea and biscuits with the latter dignitary, and two hours afterward his wife came down on horseback, accompanied by a slave, who carried breakfast in a large basket. After breakfast I told them that I wished to visit a family named Dias, to whom I had a letter from

the English consul. He said that I must go to the Town of the
Wild Stream (Villa da Ribeira Brava), and that he would lend
me a horse, as it was more than three miles off. I accepted his
kind offer, and hired a woman to carry my traps. This young
person, carrying a huge weight on her head, but unretarded by
superfluous clothing, trotted alongside of me, and chattered to me
as if she had known me for years. As she spoke *Creole*, I scarcely
understood a word that she said, but threw in exclamations of assent or surprise with instinctive judgment.

This, by-the-by, is very good practice for society. One can not
listen to all that people say to one, and the art of appearing to
listen with the closest attention, and of laughing at a joke which
one has not heard, is perhaps the highest social accomplishment
to which man or woman can attain.

We went for a couple of miles or so over a country of hilly
moors and stone inclosures, with a patch of maize or grass-land
here and there. Then the country rose higher and higher from
the sea, the roads became goat-walks, the hills precipices. On we
went. All signs of civilization had now passed away. We were
in the heart of the mountains, which appeared more desolate and
barren than before. I began to despair of finding this concealed
city, when suddenly, on mounting the brow of a hill, I saw it lying in a ravine below my feet. A mountain brook, the Wild
Stream, ran through the midst. I could see the women washing
their clothes and the horses drinking there, and I wondered how
on earth a town containing 4000 inhabitants could have been built
in such a hole.

But tradition explains it. Years ago the Cape de Verd Islands
were a grand resort of pirates, who repeatedly sacked the ill-forti-
fied sea-ports. So in all these islands the coast was abandoned
by the inhabitants, and towns were built in the fastnesses of the
mountains, where in this island, St. Antonio, and others, they still
remain.

Having introduced myself to Senhor Dias Leite, a young gentleman who had lately graduated at the University of Coimbra,
he showed me over the family mansion, which was well furnished,
and reminded me a little of an English country house. He then
told me that, at the close of the rainy season, the water which had
poured down the hills into the town putrefied, and bred fevers.
At that time of year, therefore, the upper classes resorted to their
mountain houses, where his family were now staying.

So we rode through the town, which, with its narrow streets, gray houses, and rough paving-stones, reminded me of Lerwick; the gaunt barren hills, and the stone walls in the fields, were also highly suggestive of Shetland scenery; even the women were not unlike, the dress consisting in both of a chemise, a petticoat, and Nature's stockings. In other respects, these tawny black-eyed wenches were very different from the blondes of Thule; and, instead of carrying peat on their shoulders and knitting stockings, they were bearing loads of pulga nuts and spinning cotton.

The mountain house was in itself cold and cheerless, but it was warmed by pleasant company and good fare. I found it quite a farmer's board—cheese, milk, eggs, fruit, coffee, beef-steaks, and legs of mutton, all from the plantation and the field. Some three thousand feet above the level of the sea I found a Scotch appetite, and afterward had the pleasure of getting into *a cold bed* for the first time since I had left England.

The next morning before breakfast we went out shooting quails. The dogs were well bred (a cross between English and Portuguese), but had not been trained at all. After chasing a donkey and almost murdering a pig, we at last induced them to enter the clover. Each took a separate field, found the birds well, but made strenuous efforts to catch them on the wing. One of them, seeing me come up solus to a point, left his bird, evidently possessed of a deep-rooted antipathy to foreigners. However, when he had seen me walk the quail up and kill it, he formed a better opinion of me, and kept by me till breakfast-time.

The birds were very plentiful, but there was no variety; and quail-shooting *per se* is little better than shooting larks to a pointer. There are Guinea-fowl on the island; but these birds, which on the continent are found only in the jungle, frequent here the most inaccessible rocks.

I spent ten days with these hospitable people, and admired their simple and happy lives. There the slaves were treated as if they were free, while in our country the free are too often treated as if they were slaves. The young people mingled with innocent freedom. The aged were revered. Crime seldom came to disturb their peaceful homes; and vice was driven forth—with an indignation which was real, and which was therefore irresistible.

The "Alerta," a trim little schooner, which might have served as a gentleman's yacht, carried me off, bound for Sal. I had a fellow-passenger, a Frenchman, who was a merchant in a small way

at Boã-Vista; and we went on comfortably enough till sunset,
when the wind, as if to apologize for its absence on the previous
occasion, blew hard in our teeth. A wave entering into the cabin
at midnight announced this fact to me. The next morning we
were both in a miserably drenched condition; but a steaming
Irish stew being brought to me, my heart revived, and I stirred
it gayly round. As I was in the act of dipping my spoon into its
solid fragrance, I heard a shout; the schooner shuddered, and a
huge wave plumped in among us, and completely spoiled my
breakfast. Great waves always go in trinities; the second put
out the fire in the caboose; the third carried away our jib-boom.
We had to put into Boã-Vista.

We received a *visite* in the due form, as I saw to my disgust.
I had not expected to find custom-house officers, captains of the
port, and such abominations among these minor islands, and I had
not taken a passport. However, you can imagine the feelings of
a man who has been rolling about for hours in a small vessel, who
has had no breakfast, and who sees little prospect of a dinner.
The harbor was merely a large bay, in which the sea was tolerably, or rather intolerably high, and I could not think of remaining there for twenty-four hours. I went down into the boat. The
officer asked me for my passport. I replied calmly that I had
none. Then followed an interesting colloquy, which they little
thought that I could understand.

"Is it worth while to take him ashore?"

"Yes, I think so," said the Frenchman (who had a few hours
before sworn eternal friendship); "I fancy that he's a fool, with
plenty of money."

"Has he any luggage?"

"Oh yes, he has luggage."

"I think, senhor, you had better stay aboard," said one of the
sailors in English, putting his head over the side.

The custom-house officer guessed the meaning of this remark,
and told him savagely to mind his own business, and shut up.
Then he smiled upon me in a most benignant manner, and, taking my hand in his, drew me to his side—the viper—with every
demonstration of friendship and esteem.

The governor was on the quay when we landed, and it was arranged between them that the Frenchman should say that I had
come ashore for a walk, and that I was a friend of his. The
Frenchman gave me a bed that night; the officers came in, chat-

ted about the passport in Portuguese to my host, and paid me a few compliments in bad French. The next morning I was officially summoned before the mayor, and was condemned to pay 10s. only for being without a passport; but the skipper was fined the amount of £4 for taking a passenger who had none; and as I had to settle this too (he being a poor man, and the fault being mine), I paid pretty dearly for having landed at so disagreeable an island. As I was going down to the boat in the evening I saw the mayor, the custom-house officer, and the captain of the port in close confabulation, and apparently dividing money. I had not, therefore, the satisfaction of believing that my modest contribution had been added to revenues which so much require augmentation.

The next day I landed and spent a night at Sal, an island which, like Boã-Vista, has been a good deal frequented for its salt-trade. I went to see the salt-marsh at the latter island. It is a small plain covered with salt, which, in various stages of formation, looked like ice powdered with snow. Art had been made to assist nature by small square pits, which had been dug in the plain. These, when filled by water, were pumped on to the land, where it evaporated, leaving its residue of salt. The pumps had sails like those of a wind-mill; and, what is still more rare and curious, cars were *sailed* upon an iron tramway from the marsh to the port, being provided with canvas wings of the same kind. This contrivance is said to have been invented by a Dutchman in the sixteenth century, and to have been applied to public vehicles.

Sal and Boã-Vista are mere insular deposits of sand and stone. As sometimes years pass without their tasting a drop of rain, nothing can be done in the way of cultivation. There is also a scarcity of firewood, which is supplied from the Gambia in exchange for salt.

I had the pleasure of meeting in Sal the judge of these islands, who was then on circuit. He lent me some numbers of *Le Revue de deux Mondes*. How I devoured them, and what a long healthy chat we had about German, French, and English literature, with all of which he was well acquainted! I could not but pity the isolation of such a man from the world of intellect. His family I knew well by name: it is one of the oldest in Portugal; but the entail system has not passed away in that country, as it has passed away in France, and is passing away in Spain; and the judge was a younger son. "But I am very happy," he said. "I have a

U

young wife; and I have money enough for my necessities. I do not hanker for that life of excitement which is not unknown to me, and to which you will soon return. I have my own tranquil pleasures, which now, perhaps, you are unable to understand; but they resemble those which invalids and old men enjoy when a tender wife or a loving daughter wait upon them, and read all their wishes in their eyes.

I pitied him less after he had told me this. I believe that I almost envied him—for a few moments. How charming it must be, I thought, to turn one's back on the strife and struggles of the world, and to enjoy those pure and peaceful pleasures which fame can never bestow! It however occurred to me, after a little deeper reflection, that such contentment is often mere apathy, in-dolence, and habit; that the horse in his stall, and the pig in his sty, are none the less inferior to man because their lives are more tranquil, and because they are disturbed by fewer passions; and that, if all young men were to turn hermits and philosophers, we should stagnate, sink back into savage life, and end by dining on each other.

CHAPTER XXIX.

UP THE CASEMANCHE.

Return to the Continent.—To the Casemanche in a French Schooner.—Fort Caraban.—The Jolas.—Rice and Palm Wine.—A Shift for a Divorce.—A Scene from
the Desert.—A Shot at Antelopes. —Sedhu.—The traveling Marabouts. — The
tree Self-Fire.—The Djikijunka.—Journey in Search of it.—Senegambia Scenery.—Mandingo Village.—Native Courtesy.—Edible Earth.—The Trumpet-bird.
—Missera.—Description of Djikijunka.—The Feast of Lanterns.—A Christmas
Breakfast.—An Evening on the Water.

A MONTH in this tropical but comparatively healthy climate
made me a new man, and again I yearned for Continental life.
The French line of packets to the Brazils work a small steamer
across to Senegambia, and on the 8th of December I left the Cape
de Verds. I was now to enter on quite a new field of studies;
and I had the satisfaction of knowing that, after I had mingled
with the ingenious Mandingoes, with the jet-black Wollofs, and
with the powerful Fulas, my tour would have embraced all the
types of negro races, and the principal features of negro life; and,
having already visited the English and Portuguese settlements, I
had only to visit those of the French to add the finishing touch to
my colonial experience.

After a voyage of two days I landed at Goree, a small island
which in Park's time belonged to the English, and from which he
was supplied with men for his last and ill-fated enterprise.

It is now a town the most compact in Western Africa. Its
streets are narrow, for there space is precious, but it is well stock-
ed with shops; it is disgraced by no hovels; its fortifications are
in fine order; and opposite the governor's palace is a large sand
square, ornamented with small trees imprisoned in palisades.
These are the *ficus religiosæ;* and before these, at noon and eve,
one may see negroes prostrating themselves, and curiously min-
gling the rites of the Mohammedan and pagan religions.

Goree is the grand dépôt of French trade in Senegambia. A
number of ships are always lying in the harbor, and are as exclusively French as those at Loanda are exclusively Portuguese. At

Dakar, on the main land opposite, a new town is being built, as there is no more building-room on the island.

As soon as I arrived I presented myself at a pension, which in French Africa is something between shop, boarding-house, and tavern. I was shown into a chamber, and an anomalous little being, sex unknown, came in. It had its head clean shaven except a few stray rat's tails on the scalp; it was dressed in a short robe, open at the back, and made a tinkling noise when it ran. It looked at me with intelligent eyes, and then, as I supposed, cleared its throat somewhat coarsely. I afterward understood that it had addressed me in Wollof, the most guttural language in existence.

Then entered a tall grave matron, in turban, sandals, and flowing cotton robes. She made my bed with nonchalance, and regarded me—an infidel—with contempt. I felt abashed, and went down into the shop, which was café, haberdasher's, bookseller's, green-grocer's, Italian warehouse, fancy toy, and ready-made clothes' shop, and where, in fact, they seemed to retail every mortal thing. There, one might see at the same time sea-captains drinking absinthe at a little marble table, a young lieutenant trying on a pair of patent leather boots, and a negress choosing, with staring mouth and eyes, some garish pattern in cotton prints.

M. Rapet was a trader in the Casemanche, a French colony which lies to the south of the Gambia. He invited me to accompany him to this river, which he described as a terrestrial paradise; so the day following my arrival at Goree I went aboard his schooner, a vessel of ninety tons, and in the evening we set sail for the south with a fair wind. A voyage of two days brought us to the mouth of our river. We had to beat across the bar, the vessel stirring up the sand with her keel, and leaving a yellow track in our wake. But our progress became so slow that we took to the boat, and after three hours in the sun were landed at Caraban, the fort which commands the entrance of the Casemanche. It is a small island, like Bathurst on the Gambia and St. Louis on the Senegal, and affords to the view a flat surface of sand, with a few cotton-trees, and mangroves in the distance. We paid a series of rapid visits to traders and officials, and found the cold brandy and water of the English colonies was here represented by vermouth and absinthe, and that one was obliged to drink in every house which one entered.

We escaped in the evening, when a light wind bore us up the

river. The scenery was rich, but, like every thing in Africa, monotonous.

It was not long before we were becalmed, and we went ashore to a village of the Jolas or Felloops, a pagan tribe which inhabit the southern bank of the river. The Balengi, who are scattered along the north side near the mouth, are of the same order. They are typical negroes, diseased in body, debased in mind; singing and dancing all the night, drinking and dozing through the day. They possess the great rice-lands of Senegambia; and having slaves and wives whom they compel to be industrious, they supply the native tribes with this favorite article of food. They grow six or seven varieties, the finest of which, a large white grain, grows best in a dry soil. Their country also abounds in the palm-wine-tree, and the Jola women carry thousands of gallons every year on their heads to Bathurst. This wine, or juice of the tree, when fresh, tastes like sweet turnips, and is then wholesome; but, after being fermented in the sun, it becomes sour and heady, and induces dysentery in Europeans, and a painful local disease in the natives. The tapping of these trees is a distinct trade in itself. The tapster ascends the tree by means of a hoop round his waist and the trunk; he bleeds the tree, places a calabash underneath, and finds it filled the next morning with a liquid resembling cocoa-nut milk. A glass bottle is preferred for this purpose, as monkeys and palm cats often empty the calabash before the proprietor's arrival.

The houses of these people are square, and built of four clay walls. Above these, but not resting on them, is a thatched roof, supported by a pole which occupies the centre of the building. Their instruments of music (?) are the reed flute, the buffalo horn, and the tam-tam. Their fetich-rites and their customs are those which I have already described at length in other portions of this work. Throughout pagan Africa there appears to be little variety, physical or psychological.

They have a matrimonial arrangement, however, which is worth relating. As soon as a child is born it is betrothed to another as near its own age as possible. When the pair arrive at the age of puberty they are married. The boy presents the girl with a shift and waist-cloth. When the shift is worn out she is at liberty to go where she likes, and marry whom she chooses. She is taught to believe that if she commits an infidelity before that time, the Evil Spirit will run off with her. These wives, therefore, remain rigidly constant; but it is not unusual to see one pounding her shift between two stones.

One evening, being again becalmed, we went ashore at a part of the country which is totally without inhabitants. We entered a plain, of which the grass was high above our heads, and through which we walked with difficulty. I saw a patch of water shining to the left, and, making my way toward it, found ample proofs of the existence of the nobler fauna. I recognized the tracks of antelopes, gazelles, wild boars, leopards, and hippopotami. I remarked an antelope's footprint much larger than any of the others. This, he told me, was *un solitaire;* an antelope who was separated from his wife and family, and who seemed to have grown larger under the infliction. Such misanthropes are found among all gregarious animals, from the " rogue" among elephants to the "old bachelors" among partridges.

Then I found a firm large track which was unknown to me. It was the footprint of a lion.

Leaving the pond, we came to a large savannah of short grass, over which we could look to a great distance. My companion showed me two brown spots a quarter of a mile off. They were antelopes feeding. We crept toward them through the belt of forest which skirted the prairie; but they were quite four hundred yards from cover. I fired at them, but without success. Rapet, who carried a fowling-piece, killed a brace of black and white ducks, and we returned to the vessel delighted with our little promenade.

On the sixth day we anchored off Sedhu, a thriving station a hundred miles up the river. I found that M. Rapet had a grand establishment, and was lord of a whole village. I also found, to my delight and surprise, that he had a good library; and when I read on his shelves the names of Corneille, Molière, Rousseau, Pascal, and Voltaire, I saw that I could agreeably occupy my spare time.

But Rapet, a veteran of twenty years in the Casemanche, was the best book for me to read. He spoke Wollof and Mandingo as he spoke French, and was as much at home among the marabouts, who came to see him every evening, as if he had been entertaining merchants of Marseilles. These men would come into the large bare room where we took our meals, would seat themselves on the floor, smoke their pipes, and talk scandal with a grave and puritanic air.

They were dressed in blue and white usually, and sometimes in black or yellow robes. These robes are made of cotton, and are shaped like surplices. They are dyed blue with an extract of indigo; black, with the refuse of forged iron thrown into water and mingled with millet flour; and yellow, from the tenderest roots of a tree called *fayar*, and from the barks of three trees, the *ratt*, the *kreule*, and the *aurô*. This color is the most highly prized of all, being worn by princes; and so potent is the dye, that if the robe is worn too soon after it is applied, its poison enters the pores of the skin, and causes death.

These marabouts were all of them commercial travelers. Most of them had been to Timbuctoo, some of them to Mecca even. They pack their wares on donkeys, which they drive before them, setting out at daybreak, resting in the heat of the day, and traveling late into the night when there is a moon. When they arrive at a town they establish an impromptu shop under some large tree, and remain there two or three days, according to the traffic. Thus beads, powder, and cloth are carried into the unknown heart of Africa.

My host, always anxious to please me, would make them talk of the countries through which they had traveled, and of the strange sights which they had seen. They told me of the lions which had long manes near Timbuctoo; of the antelope which was striped like a zebra; and of the tribe near Segdo, on the Niger, which could live hours under the water, and whom the sultan employed to catch crocodiles alive.

In addition to this they described the tree *Self-fire.* It was found near the water. It bore a fruit which closely resembled the anana, but which was uneatable. When this fruit became perfectly ripe and dry, the heavy dews of the night caused it to explode, which it would do with a sound like a musket-shot, and flames bursting forth would consume the tree, from whose ashes a young shoot, phœnix-like, would arise. The belief in its igneous qualities is so deeply rooted in these people's minds, that M. Rapet (who seemed to believe it himself), wishing to plant one near his house to ascertain the truth, was implored by them not to do so, as they feared that their village would be burnt down. He informed me that he had seen the tree charred by fire. It grows in the Gambia as well, where it is called by the English the burning bush. The fruits of trees which belong to its order frequently do explode as described, and this explosion probably suggested the fable of the conflagration.

Then they told me of an antelope called *Djikijunka*, larger than a buffalo, and double the size of a native bullock, with a black mane, spiral horns, and white stripes on its sides. It was found in the great bamboo forest of Bambouka, distant about fifty miles from Sedhu. I resolved to go there, and to make inquiries of the hunters in that neighborhood. Having engaged a Mandingo named Hassan, who had come from the Gambia and could speak a little English, I borrowed a horse from Rapet, and took two men into my service, who were to carry my necessaries, and to guide me to the village of Missera, on the borders of the great bamboo forest of Bambouka.

My little nag had the blood of the Barbs in its veins, and having been mounted but once before, made me fear that its pranks would delay us considerably; but after it had plunged and reared for a little while, finding a whip of hippopotamus hide no less active, it became suddenly docile, and my tiny caravan set forth for the bush.

We crossed alternately belts of jungle, and prairies rendered swamps by the recent rains. In the depths of the jungle we could hear the pigeons cooing, as you may of a summer in an English beech-wood; monkeys chattered from the trees, blue jays flew across the path, and sometimes a rustling in the bushes told us that the serpent, timid and harmless till trod upon, was rapidly gliding out of the way.

On the green plains were flocks of white egrets, which, never having been shot at, sat looking at me as I rode past them, gun in hand, with a virgin and touching confidence.

We found villages every five miles, and their neighborhood would be announced by a clearing in the forest, or a patch in the plain reduced to cultivation. Either it would be a crop of ground-nuts, with women pounding them out of the earth; or crops of maize and millet, which they would be reaping with a small knife, cutting off the ears close to the stalk; or fields of cotton. These last excited my chief attention; indeed, it is curious to see, bursting out from the yellow flowers of a small plant, a bunch of that which has all the appearance of a manufactured substance. The cotton of Senegambia is poor (chétif), and inferior to that of Angola. At present, however, it has scarcely received a fair trial; both natives and traders appear to prefer the certainties of the ground-nut trade, which is in a flourishing condition.

In the evening we stopped at a Mandingo village. As in the

Gaboon country, we 'went to the patriarch's house, who is here called *Al Mami*. He received us politely, though not, I thought, with the same cordiality as a Mpongwe would have done. Some grass and corn were brought for my horse, and a large calabash of rice and milk was placed before me. Hassan and the two guides joined me, and their three dingy hands and my white one mingled in the bowl. I lived three days upon this fare, which is that of the Mandingoes generally. I had been in the habit of dining rather freely with Rapet, who kept an excellent table, and always found that a total change of diet was the best medicine in cases of digestive and biliary disarrangements. The Mandingoes never touch milk or butter till the one has been soured, and till the other has been salted and reduced to a kind of oil. It is, I do not doubt, a useful sanitary precaution, as the natives of Angola also use it in respect to milk.

The houses of the Mandingoes are of the bee-hive shape so common in Africa. The roofs look in the distance exactly like the tops of hay-ricks: the body of the house is quite round, and is lightly built of rods interwoven together, as in withy hurdles; but those of the marabouts or priests, and of the men of rank, are built of clay, and have a double wall. Between these walls is a passage which is cool and protected from the glare of the sun. Here the elders sit during the day, receive visitors, and interchange the news of the day. The interior of the house is quite dark. On the thatch one may see bundles of corn and huge slices of cassada drying in the sun. Small circular store-houses, raised on piles, contain their ground-nuts.

On the thatch of one house I saw some lumps of yellow earth, and on asking Hassan what it was for, he replied that these people took it sometimes as a purge, eating it raw. Curiously enough, M. Rapet had never heard of this custom, and flatly avowed his disbelief in my statement, or rather in that of Hassan. The children of Goree, he said, would eat a kind of clay which is found there, and which is of a glutinous character, being used for polishing buttons, etc.; but only while they were children, in the same manner as puppies eat dung. However, on examining some veteran Mandingoes, he found that this was really the case. I was not so much surprised, as I knew that there were earth-eaters in South America, in some parts of North Guinea, and in Lapland; but I do not think that a case of its being used as a medicine has been brought to light before. I could easily understand its being eatable, for it had a most piquant and agreeable odor.

I lay down on a rude wooden frame, like those of Southwestern and Equatorial Africa, and attempted to sleep; but, though the people did not dance all night to the tam-tam like the Fans, I found that their religious exercises were no less noisy. Half a dozen theological students were intoning the Koran, as if they had been public criers. When at last they ceased, I was wrought to such a pitch of excitement that I gave up all ideas of sleep, and waited anxiously for the morning. After a couple of hours I heard a sound, which proceeded, as I thought, from a horn. I got up, and went out over the prostrate bodies of my men. It was pitch dark; there was no sign of the gray dawn; and, to my astonishment, I heard the horn again, this time above my head. I looked up, and could dimly descry between me and the stars the figure of a huge bird. It was evidently the trumpet-bird, which makes a sound like the blast of a cornet-à-piston with a hair in it. I turned in again, and was in due time aroused by the muezzan, or prayer of the faithful, an hour before daybreak, at which hour the sun is supposed to be rising over Mecca.

That day, at the village where we stopped to breakfast, I saw a marabout and his school. It was held under a tree in the middle of the village. Each pupil had a board, on which he wrote the Arabic characters with a charcoal pencil. Almost all adults are taught to read and write Arabic free of expense, the marabouts receiving certain dues from the field and fold. They have also the exclusive privilege of making and selling gris-gris, or amulets, consisting of scraps of the Koran in little leather cases, beautifully tanned and worked. As far as I could learn, they were a more estimable body of men than usually constitute a priesthood, especially among savage nations.

These Mohammedan negroes do not follow the strict letter of the ceremonial law, nor are they intolerant. When they saw me reading my volume of Voltaire's " Dictionnaire Philosophique" (which Hassan told them was the Koran of my country), they crowded round me with simple curiosity. I was always received by them with courtesy; they offered me their right hands; and when I left them, the chef de village would accompany me half a mile or so on the road, carrying some article which belonged to me, before he bid me farewell. It is true that this was a mere form of politeness, but it would be difficult to invent one more delicate or expressive.

On arriving at Missera I found myself disappointed in the ob-

THE DJIKJUKKA (OREAS DERBIANUS).

ject of my search. A *Djikijunka* skin had lately been in the town, but the Mandingoes are great tanners and curriers, and it had been cut up long ago for sandals and *gris-gris*. In the evening I called two or three of the principal hunters to my lodgings, and asked them about this animal. Their description of its size tallied with that which I had heard before. They said that it went in families; that it was found only in the forest; that it never grazed; and that the male tore down branches from the trees, upon which the does and fawns would feed. I asked them whether I could possibly get a shot at one. Had I asked this of a Gaboon man, he would have replied without hesitation that he could show me one the first day. But the Mandingoes are a higher race. The hunters replied that sometimes they happened to come across a stray Djikijunka, but at this time of year it would be useless to hunt them. The bush was *dark* now, they said, but in a month's time they would set fire to the high grass of the plains, and to the tangled undergrowth of the forest. The people, collecting from all the neighborhood, would form a vast semicircle, and animated nature, toward the close of the day, would be driven into a large plain. Then there would be a grand battue of gazelles, porcupines, antelopes, and boars. Most of the animals would be so exhausted as to let themselves be killed with sticks; and, indeed, few guns would be allowed, on account of accidents. I then made them promise me to send the first specimen which they killed to M. Rapet, who would buy it for me from them; and it was in this manner that I obtained a good specimen of a female, which he kindly forwarded to me at the Gambia. In that river I obtained two other specimens less complete, which had been killed in the neighborhood of Macarthy's Island. A part of the skin of this animal had been previously brought to England by an employé of the Earl of Derby. It had been named by Dr. Gray *Oreas Derbiana*. The French naturalists, however, had denied the existence of this new species of eland, and, oddly enough, it is to a Frenchman that we owe the proof. Superior in size to the eland of South Africa, it is therefore the largest antelope in the world.

The following morning I started before daybreak, and rode the whole distance, reaching Sedhu at eight o'clock P.M. Those who know what it is to ride a young and unbroken horse by night over forest paths and through pathless swamps, can easily understand that I had a nice time of it. But it was Christmas Eve, and

I wished to spend some hours of that night in Christian company. I arrived just after dinner, covered with mud; but my horse was still fresh, and my men showed no great signs of fatigue.

I was well rewarded by my haste with the sight of a most singular ceremony. We English once possessed the Senegal, and there, every Christmas Eve, the Feast of Lanterns used to be held. The native women had picked up the words and airs of the carols; the custom had descended to the Gambia, and even to the Casemanche, where it is still preserved. A few minutes after I had ridden up, sounds of music were heard, and a crowd of blacks came to the door, carrying the model of a ship, made of paper, and illuminated within, and hollowed pumpkins also lighted up for the occasion. Then they sang some of our dear old Christmas carols, and among others one which I had heard years ago one Christmas Eve at Oxford.

> Nowel, Nowel, the angels did say
> To certain poor shepherds in fields as they lay;
> In fields as they lay keeping their sheep
> One cold winter's night, which was so deep.
>   Nowel, Nowel, Nowel, Nowel,
>   Born is the King of Israel.

You can imagine with what feelings I listened to those simple words sung by negresses who knew not a phrase of English besides. You can imagine what recollections they called up as I sat under an African sky, the palm-trees rustling above my head, and the crocodiles moaning in the river beyond. I thought of the snow lying thick upon the ground, and of the keen, clear, frosty air. I thought of the ruddy fire which would be blazing in a room I knew, and of those young faces which would be beaming still more brightly by its side; I thought of—oh, a hundred things, which I can laugh at now, because I am in England, but which in Africa made me more wretched than I can well express.

The next morning I went out with a native hunter, and, having concealed ourselves behind trees in the jungle, he took his nose between his fingers, and emitted a horrible noise like that made by a gazelle who is looking for his mate. One of these pretty little creatures came running up, and then stopped and stared us in the face with her great startled eyes. We fired together; she rolled over like a hare. But when I ran, flushed with murderous excitement, to take her up, she turned upon me

CHRISTMAS EVE IN THE CABOOSE.

those eyes, those tender eyes, which were closing fast under a
thick gray film.   The blood frothed to her lips; her poor little
body shook convulsively, and then, with one low womanish wail,
her soul—for surely gazelles have souls—left the body, which
still shuddered, though the life was gone.   We had her cutlets
dressed *à la papillote*.   Exquisite as her beauty, I ate them to in-
digestion.

That Christmas morning I enjoyed a stupendous repast.   The
mouths of members of the Acclimatization Society will water as
they read.   It was a collection of gastronomical rarities—a tissue
of eccentricities *de cuisine*.

We commenced with snails, brought from France in barrels
filled with flour, which had preserved them admirably.   They
were prepared *au gratin*, and we forked them out of their retreats
with instruments unpleasantly resembling toothpicks.   We had
also oysters torn from trees.

Our fish consisted of African soles, carp, and mullet.   Detestable in themselves, they illustrated the skill of the cuisinier.

Then followed the gazelle cutlets *à la papillote*.   Two small
monkeys served cross-legged and with liver sauce, on toast.   Stewed iguana, which was much admired.   A dish of roasted crocodile's eggs.   Some slices of smoked elephant (from the interior),
which none of us could touch.   A few agreeable plates of fried
locusts, land-crabs (previously fattened), and other crustaceæ.   The
breasts of a mermaid, or manatee—the grand bonnebouche of the
repast.   Some boiled alligator, which had a taste between pork
and cod, with the addition of a musky flavor.   And some hippopotamus steaks *aux pommes de terre*.

We might have obtained a better dessert at Covent Garden,
where one can see the bright side of the tropics without the trouble
or expense of traveling.   But we had pine-apples, oranges, roasted plantains, silver bananas, papaws (which, when made into a tart
with cloves, might be taken for apples), and a variety of fruits
which had long native names, curious shapes, and all of them
very nasty tastes.   But I must not omit the famous palm-cabbage.

It is erroneously supposed that it is peculiar to one tree which
is called the cabbage palm.   It is, however, the bud of the tree,
so to speak, and is found in all the palms, though in some it is
red, in others white.   It is a great luxury; indeed, to eat one is
like eating a whole tree, for the palm always dies when the cabbage is cut out.   Throughout this country, therefore, it is for-

X

bidden food; but Europeans may sometimes infringe the law by paying a large sum. When raw it tastes like celery, but when stewed *au sauce blanc*, as upon this occasion, it is not to be compared with any vegetable of mortal growth. It must have been the ambrosia of the gods.

That was certainly a ❂ble Christmas feast, with a wild boar's head grinning on the table, and a bottle of recherché Bordeaux at each man's elbow. Another meal on that day was simply impossible, so my friend and I went out on the river in the evening.

It might have served Etty for a painting. The rosy wine had rouged our yellow cheeks, and we lay back on the cushions, and watched the setting sun with languid, half-closed eyes.

Four men, who might have served as models to Apelles, bent slowly to their stroke, and murmured forth a sweet and plaintive song.

Their oars, obedient to their voice, rippled the still water, and dropped from their blades pearl-drops, which the sun made rubies with its rays.

Two beautiful girls, who sat before us in the bow, raised their rounded arms, and tinkled their bracelets in the air; then, gliding into the water, they brought us flowers from beneath the dark bushes, and kissed the hands which took them with wet and laughing lips.

Like a dark curtain the warm night fell upon us; strange cries arose from the forest; beasts of the water plunged around us; and my friend's honest hand pressed mine as he spoke of my departure.

It was my last night in the Casemanche, and such nights as these I love to dwell upon. In Europe they are effaced by brighter ones, but here they are so rare. Do not laugh at me if sometimes I seize some little spark of romance, and try to fan it to a flame; if I try to paint those softer emotions which should not be extinguished in a young man's heart, but which this isolated savage life can so seldom awaken.

And yet these wanderings of mine have taught me lessons in the love of men. How many simple unselfish tokens of affection have I received from those who knew that we should not meet again! Dear friends whom I have known in Africa, whose hearts I could not even claim as a compatriot, believe that your kindness is not forgotten, although it can never be returned!

CHAPTER XXX.

UP THE GAMBIA.

Colonial Life.—On Board the "Dover."—Ground-nut Diplomacy.—Massacre Christianity.—A day's Shooting.—The nondescript Animal.—African Palavers.—Mr. Rooke, the Apostle. — Missionary Labors. — The dog-faced Baboons. — Strange Story of Sergeant Bonvin.—The Falls of Barraconda.—An angry Hippopotamus.

ONE French man-of-war conveyed me with the mails to Caraban, another was to take me from Caraban to Senegal. We put into the Gambia for letters, and, as we were to remain a few hours, I went ashore to see some old acquaintances. Some of these had gone home on sick leave, suffering from severe attacks of cold brandy and water; but I found a civilian, Mr. Primet, who received me with the same hospitality which he had shown me a twelvemonth before.

He advised me, before ascending the Senegal, to go up the Gambia, and he showed me a little colonial steamer, the "Dover," which was about to make her annual trip to the Upper River. I was very desirous to go, but, not having seen a tailor for more than a year, I had nothing fit to wear in genteel society. Besides, all the money I had was at Goree. I was ragged and penniless. However, Mr. Primet gave me the loan of his wardrobe and his purse, so I rode off to the governor's, Colonel D'Arcy, who courteously gave me permission to join the expedition free of expense, and every thing was arranged.

Some officers of the **th West India Regiment were going up to Macarthy's Island; there was also a Mr. Rooke, a Wesleyan missionary; and we were all under the orders of Mr. Mantell, a nephew of the great geologist, and chief justice of the Gambia.

Our departure would take place in two days. During these I had some opportunity of observing the routine of colonial life, which will not take long to describe. Before breakfast one rides or drives along the sandy roads of this flat and loose little island; and even at that early hour of the morning one can not but remark in the oscillatory movements of the horsemen, and in the *degagé* style of the driving, something which savors strongly of Cognac and Moselle.

The breakfast is a heavy meal, at which nobody thinks of drinking tea. Beer is considered the correct thing, though some prefer cold brandy and water. After breakfast the duties of the day commence, at least for civilians; military men go to sleep in their shirt-sleeves, and drink cold brandy and water whenever they wake up. In the evening there is something going on in a languid way out of doors; at dusk there is dinner, and afterward, at a late hour, they "go the rounds"—that is to say, they knock up their friends. If one is docile and lets them in, they drink a few glasses with him and leave him in peace. If, on the contrary, he does not desire to receive them, they burst all his doors open, drag him out of bed (whether he has fever or not is of little consequence), and not only make him give them something to drink, but compel him to drink as well. Such freaks are excusable in young collegians, the intermediate type between boys and men; but with those who have not extreme youth to plead in their favor, they are simply brutal—and worse, for they have destroyed the prospects of more than one young man who (a *rara avis*) has appeared in West Africa with an undamaged reputation.

Mr. Primet's house was built upon a principle which, I believe, is West Indian. The ground floor is not inhabited by Europeans. The first floor is portioned into the bedrooms, and into one large sitting-room elegantly furnished. This is inclosed between two piazzas; one looks out on a square court tenanted by domestic and domesticated animals—pigs and monkeys, fowls and gazelles. It is in this piazza that one breakfasts and dines. The other has a sea-view, and makes an agreeable promenade during rain or in the heat of the day.

Before starting I hired a boy as my attendant for the voyage. These Gambia boys, the descendants of liberated Africans, are a handy set of rogues, being able to swim a river, clean a gun, paddle a canoe, wait at table, pipeclay uniforms, and wash any thing admirably except themselves. They are honest if you watch them strictly, and are patient, obedient, and industrious—if thrashed every three days.

On the afternoon of the 10th of January the "Dover" got up steam, and we were fairly off. We anchored that evening in the Surra-warra Creek.

I must now explain the object of our voyage. All along this river from Bathurst to Barraconda there are trading stations, the traders paying certain tribute or customs to the native owners of the soil. Every year the governor, or (as on this occasion) his deputy, ascends the river, encourages the kings and chieftains with words and presents to protect the traders, and attempts to settle any disputes that may have arisen between them.

The Gambia trade consists almost entirely of ground-nuts, an article of commerce which has entered Europe only of late years. The olive-oil with which Parisians dress their salad has been expressed from a nut shaped like an almond, which grows under the ground, and which is raised by the savages of Senegambia.

The agriculture of the ground-nuts is principally performed by a tribe called the Sera-woullis, whose country lies toward Timbuctoo. They come down in hordes, as Irish reapers come to England in harvest-time, and, having sold a crop or two, pay the rent for their ground, and go home with their earnings.

Now it so happened that a religious war had broken out in Senegambia. It was raging close to Sedhu, on the opposite side of the river, when I was in the Casemanche.

It was this same war which was being waged in the Gambia between the Mohammedan and pagan Mandingoes. The mischief of it was that the Mohammedans had pressed the agricultural Sera-woullis into their service, and from these crops of ground-nuts sprang an army of fighting men.

It is true that their pitched battles are rather different from those of civilized nations, who have a better-regulated system of slaughter. If a village is to be stormed, the army, surrounding it at a careful distance, fire shots in the air all day long. The besieged estimate the number of besiegers by the quantity of shots, and, if they think that their foes will be too much for them, evacuate peaceably; otherwise it becomes a matter of blockade. The others follow up their victory, and shoot or capture stragglers in the forest. But, on approaching the desert, one finds a different race of men; in the Senegal they fight harder than they do in the Gambia; in the Gambia than in the Casemanche.

But, in any case, all trade is stopped during a native war. The crops are burnt with the villages, and the country lies desolate. The towns are surrounded by earthen walls, with round towers at intervals for archers to fire from. Skeletons lie scattered round, and the country presents every where the *facies belli* of Tacitus. *Vastum ubique silentium, secreti colles; fumantia procul tecta; nemo exploratoribus obvius.*

In such a case as this, it is usually the policy of the European power to request the rival tribes to "make it up;" and if they decline, to go to war with both—an amicable way of settling difficulties. It was therefore part of Judge Mantell's mission to reconcile the followers of fetich with the disciples of Mohammed; and if this failed, it was owing to no want of skill of the English emissary, but to the difficult, almost impossible nature of the undertaking.

The Mohammedan power in Senegambia is rising and ambitious. It has even awakened the jealousy of the English authorities, who hoped by the cunning of diplomacy to tear from them the Sera-woullis, in whom lay all their strength. But what are the promises of a white man who comes to them for a few hours in a steam-boat, compared with the cajolements and the threats of those who dwell among them, and whose swords are above their heads. The Sera-woullis said, "We are a peaceable people; we do not come here to fight; we come here to dig ground-nuts; but what are we to do? The Marabouts say, 'If you do not join us, we will burn your crops; and we will kill you; and we will take your women and children.' We love our women and our children; we love our own lives; the Marabouts are strongest, and we join them."

"Whose ground are you on?"

"The Mandingoes (pagan)."

"And why do you not join the Mandingoes?"

"Because the Marabouts are more strong."

"You go with the oppressors against the weak. Then you are cowards."

The Sera-woulli chieftain bent his aged head, and said gently, "People who come from a far country are always cowards."

They knew how to answer sense with sense; for in this instance, caring nothing for either party, they were right in joining the stronger of the two. And when the baffled barrister descended to sophistry, he found that he had to encounter a whole council of special pleaders. So matters stood when I left the Gambia. It was generally agreed that nothing could stop these wars but an aggressive movement.

The Badibú war, however, had been a grave lesson. It had cost the Home Office many thousand pounds. The result had been half a dozen bamboo villages destroyed, and a fine of some tons of ground-nuts, which was never paid.

European interference is of little avail in this country except when both parties are predisposed to reconciliation. It must be remembered that we are simple tenants in their country. We pay them rent for the land we hold; we have therefore no right to interfere between our landlords if they quarrel, and we have not yet been able to display the might.

I shall be blamed by ignorant persons when I say that, if war is waged against savages, it must be a massacre, or it is useless. Cruel as this maxim may appear, it would, if followed out, be the cause of less misery and bloodshed afterward. It must be remembered that the minds of savages are as differently constituted from our minds as are their bodies from our bodies. "Few people," says Fielding, "think better of others than of themselves, nor do they really allow the existence of any virtue of which they perceive no traces in their own minds." Forbearance these negroes ascribe to fear, and mercy to personal interest. Those who are spared are not grateful. They are only inflated with a sense of their own importance, and are the readiest to offend again.

Such was the system of the great Faidherbe, the "Napoleon of the Senegal." Profoundly versed in the nature of the lower men (itself a separate study), he had the wrath of a lion in the field, the tact of a woman in the council. By waging war as a pitiless scourge, he made them understand that there were blessings in peace.

While all these weary palavers were going on, we used to amuse ourselves shooting. We would take our boys, and go ashore as early as possible. We would hear the birds "calling" as soon as we got ashore, and we would sometimes see them in the dusky light running over the clods, with their heads perked in the air. As they disappeared in the long grass, our boys would rush in and beat vigorously. Up they would get and whirr away with a familiar and pleasant sound. Then one would collapse in mid-air, his feathers ruffled, and fall twirling to the ground. We would pick him up, and would find a bird rather larger than the English partridge, handsomely mottled on the chest, and with two spurs on his legs.

The covey is marked down. We come to the place and beat about. Nothing rises. Are you sure that this was the place? Yes; but partridges are not fools, *mes enfants*. It is now that we stand in need of dogs. Mark! there goes one, a long shot. He has run. What is that I see in the grass? a little brown twink-

ling eye.　As soon as it meets mine there is a whirr that startles
my fever and quinine shaken nerves.　I "feather" him; he makes
a long flight of it toward the river, and perches in the mangroves.
These partridges "tree" when walked up once or twice, and always roost in the wood.

Another whirr, this time not so loud, and a covey of small red-
legged partridges fly round us.　The novices shoot behind them,
the more experienced turn round and make a straight shot of it.
These are the best eating birds of all.　Then a grayish-colored
hare is kicked up and missed, and one or two quail go to the bag.
Besides these little birds there is the Barbary quail, a bird resembling the woodcock in plumage and flight, but which is worthless
for the table.

We cross a barren piece of ground, with a few thorn-bushes
scattered here and there, and we bag a solitary sand-grouse, the
handsomest game-bird that flies in Africa.

Then we come to a kind of meadow, with a stream half covered
by flags and rushes.　*Sceep !* goes a snipe; and while floundering
in the mud after these old acquaintances, we come across a couple
of ducks, which give amplitude to the bag.

We try the wood, where we might shoot pigeons by the sack-
ful, and where we find one or two stray partridges.　What are
those birds with blue feathers a hundred yards off?　A flock of
Guinea-fowl, and wild as blazes.　Up they get with a perfect roar,
and we return to the plain in disgust.

As I am struggling through a patch of high grass I hear a rush,
and out bounds a graceful antelope.　I feel tempted to pepper
him with No. 5, but reason interposes.　He turns round when he
has run (or rather sprung) a hundred yards, and looks at me in-
quiringly.

It was the first time that I had been in a real game country, for
Equatorial Africa and Angola are equally desolate in that respect.
But we did not stop long enough at any one place to organize a
regular hunt of the larger animals.　One day, however, three of
the passengers had a little adventure.　They shot at a quadruped,
which charged them, and from which they only escaped by climbing up into a tree.　When I asked what animal it was, the first
replied that it was a wild boar, the second that it was a buffalo,
the third that it was a young hippopotamus.

All three of them, I must observe, were tolerably experienced
sportsmen.　The first, having acknowledged to me that his boar

had black tusks, which he attributed to the influence of the sun, I put his theory at once aside. The second, having killed buffaloes in South Africa, I was inclined to accept his evidence; but the third, who seemed to prefer the ocular evidence of other people to his own, said that he had met two natives immediately afterward who had told him that the beast lived in the water, and all allowed that he had gone in the direction of the river; so I could come to no definite conclusion, except that my friends were not in a very calm state at the time. "If," said I, "there existed a species of water-buffalo, I could easily reconcile your statements."*

We were all of us very glad when on the tenth day we arrived at Macarthy's Island. African palavers bear such a family resemblance to one another that three would suffice the most curious man for his lifetime. The palavers of politeness, which were held at every village where there was a trading station, were managed in this manner. The steamer would anchor opposite the village; the judge would send his Mandingo interpreter ashore. The almami and other gentlemen of eminence would come off in a canoe, with their troubadours and minstrel girls. The officers would put on their uniforms, and in red coats and faces, with dark trowsers and boots, would look like half-boiled lobsters.

The judge would thank them for having protected the traders during the year, and would point out to them the substantial advantages of pursuing such a course by making them presents of cloth, beads, tobacco, and loaf-sugar, in proportion to their rank.   ✦

The almami would hope the judge was quite well, and after making a few remarks upon general subjects, would, if not a Mohammedan, ask for a glass of rum.

Sometimes an absurd incident will break the sameness of a palaver. There is a story told of a late governor who, having called

---

* I was much surprised afterward on reading the following passage in Dos Santos's History of Ethiopia (701 p., Pinkerton's Collect.): "Besides hippopotami in the rivers, other amphibious animals are found remarkable for horns similar to those of the bull, and having their hoof divided like theirs." And in Leo Africanus (ninth book): "The sea-oxe, being covered with an exceeding hard skinne, is shaped in all respects like unto the land-oxe, save that in bignes it exceedeth not a calfe of six moneths olde. It is found in both the rivers of Niger and of Nilus, and being taken by fishers, is kept a long time alive out of the water. I myselfe saw one at Cairo led up and downe by the neck in a chaine, which (they say) was taken at the city of Asna, standing upon the bank of Nilus about four hundred miles from Cairo."

together some powerful chieftains, addressed to them a set and rather pompous speech, which he always used on such occasions, and which began:

"Where blood is shed no corn will grow."

Here the populace roared out laughing, and even the grave marabouts giggled a little.

"Sons of the burning soil of Ethiopia—"

Here there was a deafening yell, and the rival chieftains, forgetting all hostilities, looked at each other and laughed till they nearly cried.

Silence was only restored after some minutes, and the governor was about to resume his speech, though a little perplexed by their hilarity, when again every face lost its African gravity, and five hundred rows of white teeth met his eyes. He turned round to ask his aid-de-camp what it all meant, when he saw that gentleman with his wig in one hand and a false tooth in the other, performing rapid evolutions, and making the most horrible grimaces behind his back. The reconciliation between the chieftains was most complete: no stroke of diplomacy could have been more happy.

Some of our visitors were dirty enough, but the most unclean of all was a king, who came on board to receive his present at some place in the Upper River. His features displayed none of that high intelligence which one frequently finds among the Mandingoes. A face more brutish it would be difficult to conceive. He took enormous quantities of snuff, placing it under the tongue, and the whole deck was bespattered with brown spittle.

While the usual interpreter business was going on, we made remarks very freely upon him, and I, who sat opposite him, exclaimed, "Did you ever come across a more perfect specimen of a savage? Now, can't you see in that man's face that he has never mingled with higher beings?" As I said these words I looked at him with disgust. He winked at me deliberately. I must own that I was astounded. This, thought I, is an African salutation that has escaped me. He could see that I was talking about him. I dare say he thought I was paying him a compliment. So, as I am never behindhand in politeness, I winked in return, at which he seemed intensely gratified.

When the present had been made—including six cola nuts, which are used in token of amity among these people, and are also highly prized all over Africa as a fruit, though bitter as horse-chestnuts—the king made a long speech in Mandingo: it was a request that the judge would give him a few more colas.

"Well, I suppose we can not refuse the dirty ruffian," said the judge. "Give him four more; that will be ten."

"*Make it twenty!*" said the king, eagerly; and then joined the roar of laughter which greeted his inadvertence. He had lived in Sierra Leone some years, as we heard afterward, and could speak English as well as any one when he did not wish to hear the *asides*.

A tame baboon and a missionary afforded us the most genuine amusement on our voyage to Macarthy's. The latter must have held originally a very humble position in life; but he had had a "call," and had made a good thing by it. He was a large-jointed young man of stunted stature, with codlike eyes. His delivery combined a broad Devonshire accent with the traditional snuffle. He shaved and brushed his best clothes on Saturday night, that he might not break the Sabbath day. He refused not only to eat hot meats on Sunday, but to sit at the table where they were eaten. Retiring below with a cheese and a tray of biscuits, he performed feats of gluttony. He forbad our boys to bathe on that day, and threatened us once a week with hell-fire as fiercely as if it lay in his power to send us there. His ungrammatical denunciations served to amuse us all, with the exception of an Irish officer, who said, twisting his mustache, that Rooke preached most *ungentle-manly* sermons.

Taking, as I do, an interest in missionary effort as one of the civilizing influences, I asked him how the station at Macarthy's Island was getting on. He replied that it was not doing very well; that all the buildings were out of repair; and that, as the subscriptions were so small, he thought that it would be hardly worth while to continue the mission there. This I thought rather a Stock Exchange view to take of the matter, and then asked him if he had made many Moslem converts.

"Oh," said he, "we don't labor among them pollygimmists."

"Among the pagans, perhaps?" said I.

"Naw, naw, we confine our labors to the liberated Africans."

I found Mr. Rooke not only ill informed, but quite uneducated. He was ignorant of the principles of the Mohammedan religion; and when once I asked him what he thought of Calvin, he replied that he had met Mr. Calvin in London, and that he liked him very well.

I take the liberty of suggesting to the society who can send such missionaries as Mr. West to this coast, that it would be as well if all their ministers were educated, and if the question of their sincerity in heart was examined as closely as their delivery from the pulpit. I beg also to inform them that the missionaries now in the Gambia, who profess to be spreading the Gospel among the heathen, do not know a word of the dialects of this country, and confine their "labors" (if that be the proper word) to a limited population of English negroes.

After three days passed at Macarthy's Island, which is 180 miles from Bathurst, we entered the Upper River. The voyage now became much more agreeable. The river was so narrow that we shot on either side at the crocodiles, which slumbered on the mud; at the Guinea-fowl (which the old writers on Africa used to call peacocks), which came down to drink; and at the patta-parras, a beautiful red monkey, which sprang gayly from tree to tree, and which is said never to descend to the ground.

Sometimes a shoal would render the channel so narrow that our masts would become entangled with the boughs, and scatter leaves upon the deck. The country here and there was *almost* picturesque; and these dwellers in alluvial deposits hailed some small round hills as if they had been the very Apennines.

One day there was an unusual commotion on deck. I was informed that we were approaching a hill which was the residence of a mountain spirit named Manidungabi. No native of the country passes this place for the first time without making a salutation to the spirit, which he does by exposing his *podex* to the hill, bowing with it, and repeating a formula to the effect that he has inherited this part of his body from his father and mother, and that he hopes Manidungabi will look upon it with favor. A certain horrible story is told of a man who passed without performing the ceremony, and who, visited by the wrath of the spirit, could never sit down again. The aft passengers who had not passed the hill procured deputies at half a crown apiece, and you will easily understand that more than a dozen men and women performing this rite on the bridge and in the forecastle was a most impressive sight.

When we had arrived at Yaba-tenda, the *Thule* of steamer exploration, we took to the boats to visit the Falls of Barraconda. We went early, and shot a few great-eyed plovers as we went along. Sometimes we would shoot at a crocodile; but these animals always lie with their heads to the water, and even when the balls tell loudly on them, they plunge in, as if you had but "knuckled" at them with a marble. One which I had shot in the Casemanche as it floated in the water, looking like a dead log of wood, had sunk, and turned up in a decomposed state opposite the factory three days afterward; but I should imagine that it would be almost impossible to "bag" them as they lie on the shore.

It has often been asserted that hippopotami and crocodiles are mortal foes, the latter nibbling the feet of this elephant of the water. But that I am disinclined to believe. In the Ncomo, where the stream was only fifteen yards wide, I found on a little island the egg-shells of the alligator close to the tracks of a hippopotamus. In Gambia and Senegal they are found in the same parts of the river. But in the Fernand Vaz the river-horse is found only near the mouth, and the alligator above Ngumbi. There they sun themselves, not on the bank, but on branches of trees which overhang the river. When disturbed they give "headers," showing their mottled yellow bellies as they dive.

In this part of Africa they are the bugbears of the native laundresses. These women always turn their backs to the water, finding it more convenient to wash up hill; the alligator glides behind his victim, sweeps her into the water with his tail, and usually makes off with a leg or an arm.

Almost all over Africa there is a superstition resembling that of the wer-wolf. In Equatorial Africa men can transform themselves into leopards and gorillas; in Prince's Island the midwife can become an owl; and in Senegambia malice can assume the shape and ferocity of a crocodile. When I was in the Casemanche a man was severely bitten by an alligator; on being restored to consciousness, he said that he knew perfectly well who it was: it was Abdalla, whom he had offended a few days before.

We had rowed some miles when we heard a bark from the forest. That was a strange sound in Africa, where dogs do not bark, but howl.

It was a distinct canine bark, like that of a spaniel, and was taken up by others till the woods echoed again. Then we saw on the bank above our heads a troop of animals with faces like dogs and bodies like men. They galloped on all fours, turning their inquisitive faces toward us; some of them mounted the trees ahead of us, and barked to give notice that we were coming. I saw females too, who carried their young, lodged in the small of the back, exactly as negresses carry theirs.

Now I knew that these were the dog-apes of Philostorgius, the "Ἄνθρωποι κυνοπρόσωποι (dog-faced men) of Ælian, and the *Gorillæ* of the Periplus of Hanno.

The ferocity of these cynocephali is extraordinary, and was remarked by all the ancient writers. Native hunters whom I conversed with, both in the Senegal and the Casemanche, agreed in asserting that they are more savage even than the buffalo. Sometimes, I was told, a leopard would climb a tree and kill one of these baboons. On such occasions they unite till they resemble an army; the forest resounds with their barkings; on finding their enemy, they surround him, still uttering their cries; then, pouring on him *pêle-mêle*, they spring on his back, and, seizing his flesh between their hands, tear it out with their ferocious teeth. The leopard fights hard, kills several, but never escapes.

The manner in which they usually attack man, when one of their number has been shot, is by throwing stones. These they "lob underhand," as do cricketers, say to the distance of twenty yards or so, with great force and precision. This fact, I believe, is not generally credited; and Sir Andrew Smith informs me that the baboons of *South Africa* can not throw stones, though he has seen them kick stones with their heels off a rock upon people below, aud though they attack other animals in the same manner by springing on the back. Upon this point, however, not only is the evidence of the natives perfectly unanimous, but Europeans who have kept these animals in captivity have remarked this habit.

Mr. Miller, H. B. M. Consul at the Cape de Verd Islands, upon whose good faith I can fully rely, informed me that he once kept a baboon in a kennel in his yard, and that he had to get rid of it on account of its ferocious temperament, and its habit of throwing stones at visitors, or on slack days through windows. He showed a great fondness for the woman who fed it, but if she passed with plates and dishes in her hands without giving him any thing, he would throw a stone at her on the spot; and, with a foresight which is not always found in human *simiæ*, he would raise a pile of stones near his kennel ready for action.

A difficult and rather delicate question, though of great importance in natural history, is that of the rape of women by baboons and apes. When I was at the town of Ñgumbi (not Quenqueza's town, but one of the same name about thirty miles up the river), I was assured that the gorillas had frequently chased women who went to a neighboring stream to draw water. A woman was even

brought to me who asserted that she herself had escaped by running from this ape, who is not capable of swift movement.

A number of instances were given me by natives in Senegambia. I will, however, quote an anecdote which was told me by
Sergeant Boivin, of the 2d Company of Tirailleurs at St. Louis. I
repeat this extraordinary story without vouching for its truth. I
will merely observe that Boivin assured me on his honor that it
was true; that he was a man who had distinguished himself in
several campaigns; who by this time has probably received his
Legion of Honor; and who, like many *sous-officiers* in the French
army, is a gentleman by birth and education. He gave me permission to print his statement and to use his name. He had the
command of a block-house some distance up the Senegal, in a
country which was much infested by these dog-faced baboons.
One day the villagers came to him entreating his assistance, saying that a troop of baboons had come down from the hills with
sticks, and had driven their herd of goats in all directions. They
said nothing to him of the girl who was tending the herd. He
took a file of men, and, on being conducted to the place, found the
goats had all disappeared, and the baboons collected together in
one place. They fired at these animals, which retreated; and on
coming up to the spot, they found the corpse of the girl, who had
been violated, *et stupri vestigia in oculis, in auribus, in naribus, in anu.*

We came to a part of the river where one or two rocks raised
their jagged heads above the stream. Finding plenty of water,
we passed between them. The other party, who were behind us,
called out to us to land. We supposed that they were tired of it,
and went resolutely on, little thinking that we had actually gone
over the Falls of Barraconda. This pompous name is given to a
small ledge of rocks which crosses the river at this point. In the
rains they are completely hidden, and it is only in the depth of
the dry season that they present a real barrier. Yet there are people at Bathurst who will tell you that it is a magnificent cataract.

At Barraconda we had fallen in with a herd of hippopotami,
and had popped at their heads for some time without success—a
kind of sport as unsatisfactory as crocodile shooting. We had
left them some way behind, and I had just remarked that we
ought soon to find some more, when there was a great bump under the stern of the boat, which almost pitched us off our seats.
The men stopped for a moment panic-stricken, and then gave way
with a will. The river-horse, or river-mare rather, did not rise

till she was a hundred yards astern; but when she rose again she was not so far from us. "I believe that she is chasing us," said I, though I had not the least idea that such was the case. When she "spouted," however, throwing two little jets of water into the air from her nostrils, she became unpleasantly near. Negroes on such occasions are always birds of ill omen. One of the boatmen said that she had a calf and was angry. Another added that two men had been killed by a hippopotamus at that very place.

Our skipper who was in the boat turned very white, and steered the boat to land, where terror acted upon his system in a manner which I can not describe. At the same time the cow, her temper evidently not improved by parturition, raised her head close to the boat. I had never seen such grand ferocity in an animal. The hairs of her ears were bristling, and her huge round prominent eyes glared furiously upon us.

We stood on the beach, she passing backward and forward before us like a sentinel. It was now almost dark. We knew that if we wounded her without killing her we should have the boat smashed to atoms. We therefore agreed to let her alone, and not "stir a fire with a sword." The cow doubtless supposed that the boat was a rival monster of the deep, and her fears and her fury had been awakened on account of her offspring.

When she was under the water we laughed and cut jokes about the irritated dame; but when, with a mighty rush from below which sent the water dashing in the air, that grim and massive head appeared, there was a dead silence, which was only broken when, with her eyes fixed upon us, her head slowly disappeared.

After this had gone on for a little while, she changed the angry snort with which she occasionally saluted us for a kind of braying sound. This we could hear faintly re-echoed from the distance; then we heard some low grunts from under the water, being mother and child engaged in conversation, and a smaller head appeared. When next the lady showed herself it was with a placid countenance; so we returned to our boat, and reached the "Dover" about midnight.

I find it difficult to explain my emotions during this little incident. It was a refined, a very refined sense of danger, accompanied with a cold sweat and a nervous tingling of the extremities. If, as they say, "Discretion is the better part of valor," I am sure that we all displayed the quintessence of intrepidity.

CHAPTER XXXI.

THE THREE DOCTORS OF MACARTHY'S ISLAND.

Description of the Island.—The Harmattan.—The Rainy Season.—Deaths of Staff
Assistant Surgeons Beale and Trestrail.—Appearance of Beale to Campbell.—
Death of Campbell.—The Sentry and the Apparition.—The haunted House.—
The Sounds in the Piazza and the Centre Room.—The Man in White.—The
Footsteps on the Floor.—The Science of the Spirit-world and its Study.

MACARTHY'S ISLAND is situated about a hundred and eighty miles from the sea. It is six miles long by two broad. There are two factories there; a village of liberated Africans; and a garrison of forty men, one subaltern, and two surgeons.

In the dry season this island presents an agreeable aspect, and is not unhealthy; but before the rains set in the two hot months (May and June) occur. I was there in January, and, although I had passed days under the line in an open boat without awning or umbrella, it was there that I suffered from heat for the first time.

What the heat of the hot months may be I can not understand. A surgeon who had traveled a great deal told me that it possessed a close, stifling character which the thermometer could not express, and that it was of a different heat from those which he had experienced in Australia and the two Indies.

It must be remembered, too, that they have not the "doctor," as the sea-breeze has well been called. It is this sea-breeze which, blowing at noon and eve, preserves the vigor and the lives of the residents upon the Coast.

At the commencement of the rainy season of 1860, Mr. Beale, a staff assistant surgeon, was seized with malarious fever. The 'Dover" arrived soon afterward, bringing a Mr. Campbell to relieve him. The relief came too late. Mr. Beale was taken on board the "Dover," shook hands with the captain on deck, went below, and expired almost immediately.

Mr. Trestrail, his colleague, sat down to write out the case. It is still preserved in the medical report-book at the surgeons' quar-

ters. Toward the end the hand-writing changes its character, becomes uneven, and sometimes scarcely legible. A few hours afterward Trestrail was a corpse. The two surgeons were buried
together.

Mr. Campbell wrote out a report of Mr. Trestrail's case. He
slept alone in the surgeons' quarters, in the same bed in which
the two others had died.

A palisade was being erected around their grave.

Mr. Savage is a mulatto trader on the island. A few days afterward Campbell came to him and asked him to give him a bed.
Savage complied with his request.

"Don't you like your quarters?" he said.

"No," replied Campbell. "*I have seen Beale.* And, Savage,"
he added, "I shall never see my poor wife and children any
more."

As the palisade round the grave was finished Dr. Campbell also
died. He was buried outside it. No importance was attached to
his words, *I have seen Beale.* It was supposed at the time that it
was merely a dream of which he had spoken. The words themselves would have been quite forgotten had it not been for that
which afterward occurred.

The commandant's quarters, a detached building, stands about
fifteen yards from the surgeons' quarters, also a detached building. A sentry is stationed over each. Captain Wilcox and Dr.
Bradshaw were sitting one evening in the piazza of the commandant's quarters, when they heard a shriek from the dectirion of the
other building. A few moments afterward a soldier, livid with
fright and without his musket, rushed into the piazza. Captain
Wilcox, supposing that he was drunk, put him under arrest.

The next morning, being examined, he declared that while on
guard at the surgeons' quarters a gentleman, dressed in black, had
come toward him. He had never seen him before. He challenged him, and received no answer. The gentleman continued
till he was close to him. He (the sentry) threatened to run him
through if he did not answer the challenge. Receiving no answer, he thrust, and saw the bayonet pass through the body. The
figure gibbered at him, and turned away. It was then that he
had shrieked, dropped his musket, and ran away. Examined by
Dr. Bradshaw, he described the figure closely; the face, height,
and dress tallied precisely with those of Dr. Beale, whom the sentinel had never seen.

Drs. Bradshaw and Hind slept in the building in separate rooms. They heard noises, the cause of which they did not understand, but to which they paid little attention at the time.

Doctors Macarthy and Fox came up. They heard nothing. Dr. Macarthy remained there a month, and during that month he had a severe fever. He went to Bathurst, and returned afterward in company with Dr. Duggan. Both of them were in good health at the time. Neither of them had heard the ghost story. They slept each in an end room (there were three *en suite*), and Dr. Duggan's servant, a boy of about sixteen, in the centre one.

Dr. Macarthy (from whom I received these particulars) now heard peculiar noises in the night. In the piazza or passage outside there was a table, on which they placed their tea-things after they had done with them. He would hear the cups and saucers clashed together, and the plates, as it seemed to him, dashed forcibly to the ground. Several times he went out in the morning, expecting to find every thing broken; but in no instance had the position of the plates, cups, or saucers been altered in the least. He ascribed these noises to some mischievous fellow who had climbed into the piazza without having been observed by the sentry below.

He also heard noises in the middle room, as if heavy pieces of furniture were being moved about.

And often all night long he would be annoyed with a pattering sound upon the floor all round his bed. He thought at first that these were bats which had fallen on the floor, and which had been unable to rise. But he could never find them in the morning. Then he supposed that they were mice.

One night, instead of going to bed, he kept his candle alight, and sat on a chair, with a stick across his knee, waiting for these mice to come out.

He heard a sound at the farther end of the room. It was like that of a man walking cautiously on tiptoe. The sound came toward him. He strained his eyes, but he could see nothing. *Then the footsteps passed before him, close to him, and he could see nothing.*

Doctors are essentially materialists. Dr. Macarthy knew that the strangest sights and sounds can spring from a disordered stomach or a checked secretion. But when he mentioned his hallucination to Dr. Duggan, and when Duggan replied that he had been troubled in the same manner, they became perplexed. Still it did not occur to them that these sounds were supernatural. The mind of man is averse to believe that which it can not grasp. No one seriously describes a phenomenon of this kind if he can account for it in any natural manner.

In the course of conversation, they happened to speak to Savage about it. He replied as if it was a commonplace matter. "Oh, don't you know that the house is haunted?" and related the affair of the sentry.

On returning to their quarters, Dr. Duggan observed that his boy was looking ill. He asked him what was the matter with him. The boy said he did not know, but perhaps sleeping in the open air had made him sick.

On being asked what he meant, the boy replied, with some reluctance, that he had gone to sleep on the flat roof of the house, because a tall man in white used to come and wake him up, so that he could get no rest. This boy I afterward examined myself. He told me that it came and pulled him by the ear, and said, "*Wake, wake.*" When he awoke he could see something white moving off in a manner which he said was not walking, nor running, nor flying, but something different from what he had ever seen.

I offered to give him five shillings (which to him would be a large sum) if he would sleep there that night, even offering to keep him company. He looked frightened and refused.

Doctors Macarthy and Duggan, after that, slept in the same room. And now here comes the part of this story which is so extraordinary—which is, I believe, unparalleled among instances of its kind.

These two men, materialists by education, lying broad awake, with a light burning in the room, would both hear those noises, and would call each other's attention to them at the time; the heavy bodies moved in the centre room, the rattling of plates in the piazza, and the light tiptoe footsteps passing between both their beds.

This story will interest children and the vulgar, as all ghost-stories do. To them, of course, I have nothing to say. But to those who are studying the science of the spirit-world, I wish to point out the futility of their investigations. Purposeless in themselves—for they can pave the way to no system—they are perilous by reason of their action on the brain. You waste your precious essence of thought, and will, and electricity, that you may touch ethereal rubbish.

A sentry is frightened, a boy's ear is pulled, plates are clashed, furniture moves. This is mysterious, but it is far from being sublime. These glimpses are degrading, disheartening, and would soon prove deleterious. Men would not be likely to lead better or more careful lives if your researches should prove (that which alone they can hope to prove) that futurity has its comic element.

CHAPTER XXXII.

UP THE SENEGAL.

Calomel and Jaundice.—The Senegal.—Cumar the Pilgrim.—The Moors of the Desert.—Up to Podor.—Mohammedan Negro.—Return from the Campaign.— On the Var.—Farewell.

IN the Casemanche I had not suffered from malarious fever; but in this agreeable country, if you escape one disease, it is only that you may contract another. By the time that I reached Macarthy's Island I had acquired a rheumatic habit, which has now become second nature.

At Macarthy's Island I suffered from a cold in the head.

At Barraconda this was replaced by a sore throat and a cough.

On returning to Macarthy's Island I had yellow jaundice.

Colchicum, cough mixture, jalap, and blue pill proving futile, I was indulged with a violent course of calomel. I took eighteen grains of the latter in one day, with no result save those of a disheartening nature. The next I should probably have been offered thirty-six. But I preferred a natural death. So did Mr. Mantell, who had been treated with equally ill success for dysentery.

On arriving at Bathurst, he was prescribed for by a resident of fifty years' experience in the Gambia: three rusty nails made red-hot were to be put into a *petit-verre* of Cognac, which was to be drunk off as hot as possible (without the nails). As we returned to Bathurst on the sixth, and I escaped from it on the eighth, I do not know whether it proved efficacious.

But the remedy which I received from an ancient mulatto lady saved my life, or, at all events, my liver. It was the native remedy for jaundice, and is, I believe, a species of cassia. It grows abundantly in Senegambia. A few slices from its yellow root are put into a jug of cold water. After it has stood a little, the patient drinks whenever he feels thirsty. A few glasses of this infusion conquered the bile, which had resisted a potent mineral, and I felt that I was safe. The yellow tinge gradually departed from my eyes, nails, and skin, and I am now just beginning to recover from the colchicum, the blue pill, and the eighteen grains of calomel. The French doctors would have given me a *tisane de carrottes*. But I do not blame my medical attendant. Had he prescribed so simple a remedy, and I had afterward died, he would have been censured for neglect; but when one is treated with mercury, and plenty of it, one's friends have the melancholy satisfaction of knowing that no " effort was spared," and that up till the last moment one was gratuitously given medicine which costs two shillings an ounce. One must legislate, write, and physic down to the level of the mob. If the French doctors dare to prescribe carrot-tea for yellow jaundice, it is because their patients are more enlightened : we won't have faith in any thing that has not a long name; argal, our lives are saved by simplicity in disguise, or we perish by kill or cure calomel.

Having spent a month in the Gambia, I really enjoyed my seavoyage to the Senegal.

This river has a mouth as narrow and insignificant as that of the Gambia is broad and majestic; but in the rainy season it is navigated to a much greater distance by small steamers. Whether such steamers as the " Dover" could pass over the Falls of Barraconda in the rains has yet to be given a fair trial. In that river we appear to have receded rather than progressed; for Marmol, an ancient writer, relates that an effort was made in his time even to blast that ledge of rocks which opposes a barrier to navigation.

The Senegal, having changed hands several times, was finally assigned to the French in 1817. The commencement of this colony was not propitious. The ship which carried the officers and troops to take possession of it was *La Méduse*, whose shipwreck has become historical.

The city of St. Louis is built on a small island, and is chiefly fortified by its position. It has more than 12,000 inhabitants, and though not equal in size to San Paolo de Loanda, it is in a far more flourishing condition. The barracks, hospitals, and other public buildings would disgrace no city in Europe; and this is the only spot in Western Africa where one can find tailors, hairdressers, confectioners, and a public library.

At one end of the town is a large and elegant mosque, but *the* civic institution of St. Louis is the market-place. As the tears came into Joachim's eyes when he saw in Angola mountains which reminded him of Switzerland, so watered my mouth at the sight of butchers' stalls—real butchers' stalls—in the open air, like

those in the Whitechapel Road. An Englishman's heart, they
say, is in his stomach, and I found this a touching sight after my
weary wanderings in vegetarian Africa. The contemplation of a
raw rump-steak almost overpowered me, and it was with a chok-
ing voice that I asked how much it was a pound.

There were fish-stalls, too, and corn-stalls, and spice and sweet-
meat stalls, and fruit-stalls, the last very indifferently supplied.
Among these moved the elegant Mandingoes, the jet-black Wollofs, the red-skinned Foulas, with hands and feet small as those of
a demoiselle, and the Moors of the desert, with thin wiry forms,
long tangled hair, and eyes which glared round them with a sin-
gularly wild expression.

As soon as we had landed at St. Louis I was taken to the best
pension and introduced to its proprietor. For two pounds a week
I obtained a couple of large rooms, a breakfast and dinner en famille, and the honor of being waited upon (for the first time in Africa) by a European maid.

Marie was a buxom Provençale—a brisk, noisy, merry, hard-
working, romping wench, such as one may still find sometimes (a
rare relic of the past) in public houses in the country; who gives
a kiss to her sweetheart which sounds like a smack on the cheek,
or a smack on the cheek like the report of a small pistol; who,
like the heroine of an old play, calling things by plain words, and
dealing in jokes as broad as any man's, preserves always her coarse
chastity, and her heart pure and bright, though hidden in a dirty
shell.

I passed a few days at St. Louis working at the library, and
visiting acquaintances, military, commercial, and ecclesiastical.
There is no regular society in this city, although it possesses more
European ladies than the rest of Western Africa put together.
No balls are given except now and then by the governor general as a kind of levée. The reason is that the French officers, military and naval, usually live on their pay. They indulge in no
heavy mess entertainments. If they have a mind to make fools
of themselves, they have the taste to wait till they return to Paris,
where folly is almost wise. In the same manner, the traders come
out to spend a certain number of years, to gain so many thousand
francs, and to return to their native land with a small fortune.
They therefore exercise a rigid economy. Every napoleon saved
is so much of their exile shortened.

The English alone have a word for *home;* and yet they will

take root in a foreign land, become essentially foreigners, modifying their tastes, their habits, their very natures, and live and die there. The French, who have no domestic tastes, and who may be said to inhabit *cafés*, won't bear transplanting beyond a certain time. Always pining, eventually they return or perish. This they account for by saying that it is impossible, in traveling, to find a country more charming than France or so detestable as England. We must accept this explanation, I suppose, for want of a better one. During my little travels I have, of course, wished to see absent friends, but, had some revulsion of fashion cast them all from London into the Boulevards, I should not have been deeply grieved. Unfeeling as it may seem, I have never sighed for a November fog, or yearned to wade through a slough between hedgerows.

While I was at St. Louis, the governor, with a body of 1800 men, was engaged in a campaign in the interior. These inland tribes are sufficiently fanatical to hate Christians, and sufficiently warlike to become dangerous, when urged and directed by genius. This has already once occurred within the short period of colonial history. The reader will understand that the negro kingdom is divided into petty principalities, like that of the Jews before Saul, and of the Britons before William.

Al Aguy Oumar—Oumar the Pilgrim, was born at Podor, on the Senegal, toward the end of the last century. In his youth he was distinguished by his devotion, and even then had dabbled in miracles with success.

In 1825 he came to St. Louis. He wished to make the pilgrimage to Mecca. The Mohammedans of influence subscribed the means. He started in 1826, and crossed Central Africa to the Holy City. Nothing is known of his life there. It was not till 1842 that he reappeared at Segou, on the Niger, with a large caravan, preaching Islamism from village to village, and selling Korans and *gris-gris* at a high price. He gained the reputation of a devout man, possessed of the gift of miracles. He also gained gold, shawls, embroidered surplices, and a throng of slaves, all of whom he compelled, under pain of death, to become Mussulmans.

He built a village in Fouta, and established himself there. The marabouts made pilgrimages to the hadji. None presented themselves to him without bringing presents, according to the Oriental custom. Oumar, who refused nothing, converted all his riches into arms and ammunition.

The doctrine which he preached was a kind of Puritanism—the rigid observance of the ceremonial law.

"You Foutas," he said, "think that you have performed your religious duties when you have made your salaam. But I am going to convert Africa."

Again he said: "You are like the infidels; you eat and drink injustice; and you violate the law of God by oppressing the weak."

It will be easily understood that he incurred the hatred of the Fouta chieftains. One of them laid a plot for his assassination. Oumar was warned of this, and left that part of the country, having first written to the chieftains: "You have refused to follow me to convert infidels; but the day is not far off when you will come to me without being called."

In the same year he had an interview with M. de Grammont, the commandant of Fort Bakel. He was then a short spare man, with a thoughtful face, and keen, sparkling eyes. To this officer he made very fine promises. "I am the friend of the whites," he said. "I want peace; I detest oppression. When a Christian has paid his 'custom' he should be allowed to trade in safety. When I become Al Mami of Fouta you must build me a fort. I will discipline the natives, assist you in your wars, and a friendship will be established between us." It will be needless to say that the French did not build him a fort. It was not difficult to see that under the cloak of religion he was scheming for empire in Senegambia.

In a mountainous nook between the countries of Dgialon, Bambouk, and Boudon lay a town called Tamba. Its inhabitants were independent. They had laws of their own, and could dictate them to some of their neighbors. Oumar sent an embassador, commanding them to turn Mussulmans. They sent him back with a message of contempt. Oumar made a brilliant repartee by taking the town by storm. This was in 1852.

In 1853 he invaded Bambouk. This country, filled with gold mines and superstitions, afforded fine food to his two passions—proselytism and power.

By turning intestine troubles to account, his battles were all victories. And now, all over the Soudan, nothing was talked of by the evening fires but of Oumar the Pilgrim, who had come to deliver his brethren from the oppressions of the Moors. Crowds swarmed to him. He soon commanded a large army; and in 1854 he marched against Farabana.

Farabana was a city of refuge for runaway slaves. It was inhabited by men whom despair had rendered valiant. It was fortified by a *tata* or mud wall, which had hitherto proved itself impregnable. Oumar sent for the chiefs. He spoke to them of his Holy War, and inflamed both their zeal and their ambition. Detaining them, according to his Napoleonic policy, he sent one of his own marabouts to govern in their absence. When this man had gained a certain amount of influence, he followed out his master's instructions, and proposed to them to pull down the *tata*. There were some who did not recognize the divine legation of the hadji, and felt little inclination to place themselves at his mercy. But the fanatics prevailed; the *tata* was destroyed; and Oumar proclaimed himself, without opposition, Emperor of Senegambia.

Hitherto he had not experienced a reverse, and, inflated by his success, he determined to attack the French—a shallow policy, for it was to attempt to root out wealth from his dominions. He sent to Bakel to purchase arms, ammunition, and even cannon. These were refused to him. The French government wisely prohibits the sale of powder and muskets to the natives. It would be as well if we had always followed their example.

Oumar made this an excuse for throwing off his mask, and seized the property of some whites at Medina. At the same time he wrote to the Mussulmans at St. Louis, informing them of what he had done, warning them of the sin which they would commit in aiding the infidels against him, and boasting that ere long he would sit in the governor's house in St. Louis.

But if, in the war which followed, he suffered no disastrous defeat, he gained no decisive victory. Religious enthusiasm began to cool as soon as the continued excitements of success became wanting. Then famine and disease began to thin his ranks; his men deserted him by hundreds; and he found himself one day alone, like Zimbo the Jaga, with a few faithful followers. He is now said to be intriguing among the Moors; but he is no longer dangerous.

From this outline of his history, and from anecdotes of his character which I heard from those who had served against him, Oumar seems to have possessed courage, finesse, and pertinacity in a very remarkable degree. It is impossible to analyze the character of a man who was known to my informants only at a distance. But it is clear that he had the foible of all his countrymen, and which can only be expressed by the French slang phrase—*la blague.* If it was his intention to attack a *poste*, for instance, instead of making a forced march upon it, and saving some of his men's lives by their legs, he would warn the French of his intention in a polite letter to the officer in command; giving him greeting in pure Arabic, and informing him that on such a day he (Oumar) would destroy the fort, and tear out his (the officer's) eyes.

But it will also be clearly seen, from this little biography, that in the Lower Soudan there is stuff for an empire; and it is not impossible that some day a black Mohammed may arise.

I obtained a passage on board a steamer which was going up to Podor to fetch the mails. On the evening previous I was invited to a military convivial meeting.

Three *sous-officiers*, who had just been promoted lieutenants, were giving a farewell party to their old comrades. There is not, of course, the same gulf between commissioned and non-commissioned officers in the French army as in ours. In the first place, the lower classes in France are, on the whole, as civilized and intelligent as ours are ignorant and brutal. In the second place, the conscript system falls alike upon all orders of society, and young gentlemen of good family and refined education, but not rich enough to purchase a substitute, are frequently obliged to enter the ranks. There is only one type of the English soldier, and that, though one of the most debased, is perhaps the most *useful* in the world. A stolid, clod-brained, beef-eating animal; a drilled and disciplined flesh-and-blood machine; insensible to danger, incapable of reflection, he marches when ordered to march, and only halts or retreats when he receives the command. With his drilled, dogged step, with his square, stupid, vacant face, which even battle can scarcely brighten, he goes on, on, on. If it is a mountain which opposes him, he surmounts it, or faints on its side. If it is a river, he swims it, or drowns like a pig. If it is an army, he penetrates its phalanx, or perishes upon its skirts.

The Frenchman, if he fails in his first impetuous charge, becomes a general, and reflects. He thinks that he can secure a better position. He retreats, and the retreat becomes a rout.

The brutal insensibility and the blind obedience of the British soldier have gained us all our victories, as the genius of the French officers have gained them theirs.

It is not uncommon to see a French private in a public library sipping Horace or working out a mathematical problem. But he soon receives his promotion as *sous-officier*, and after a certain period of service and a severe examination, becomes lieutenant.

The *officier* may shake hands with the *sous-officier* in public; he may invite him as a guest to his own quarters; but etiquette forbids the two classes to mingle: they must not dine at the same *table d'hôte*, nor frequent the same *café*.

This wine-party, therefore, was a polite adieu to old comrades in arms.

One of the entertainers ushered me into a long room, where about fifty non-commissioned officers were seated. He thoughtfully announced me as M. Rêde (*ride* meaning wrinkle), and even then I heard a *sotto voce* pun about *raide* and *jaune*.

I found that they were regaling themselves with mulled claret, punch, Havre beer, coffee, and confectionery, and that I had entered a perfect atmosphere of *chansonnettes à boire* and *bon mots*. After a few hours of indulgence without drunkenness, and of banter without venom, the crowd dispersed, and a select party of us were invited (or, if I remember right, we invited ourselves) to some rooms in the town, which were furnished with an automatonic piano-forte. Out of consideration for the traditional gravity of our race, I was put safely away in a corner, with a bottle of beer and a glass. The proprietor whirled the handle of the instrument round with fury, dancing at the same time. The Frenchmen frantically waltzed, polkaed, formed masculine quadrilles, and brandished their legs round their heads, as you may see them at the *Jardin Mabille* or the *Château des Fleurs*. But there, alas! the simile ends. They could get nothing frailer to dance with them than the straw-bottomed four-legged "wall-flowers" which were scattered round the room, and which suffered severely at their partners' hands.

This physical gayety characteristic of the nation, so far from detracting from their pre-eminent wisdom, genius, and learning, may be regarded partly as their cause. At school the clever boys are generally good cricketers or foot-ball players. The philosophers of ancient Greece were almost always celebrated as athletes. Samuel Clarke, that profound logician, was fond of leaping over chairs and tables; Johnson committed similar gambols; Richelieu was caught jumping a match against his servant; the Jesuit Petavius, when engaged in his erudite work, *Dogmata Theologica*, used to twirl his chair for five minutes at the end of every second hour; and Socrates was fond of dancing.

There are no less than eight *Postes* or military stations on the
Senegal. During the dry season the river can only be navigated
by steamer as far as Podor. The mails are carried to the distant
Postes by natives overland; but in time of war even this communication is suspended.

The most remote of these stations are mere block-houses; and
in these, far away in the desert, encircled on all sides by savage
hordes, prodigies of endurance and valor are performed.

Near the sea, the country on both sides of the Senegal is parched
and barren. The first sight which interested me was that of a
Moorish encampment.

The tents were pitched close to the side of the river, which was
very salt, but of which the camels and horses were drinking, and
from which women were filling their vessels.

These tents are the only dwellings of the Moors of the Sahara.
They are double; the outer one is made of untanned hides, the
inner one of sheepskin tanned and dyed.

In these tents their horses come to sleep as socially as the Irishman's pig. They delight in being caressed, and lay their heads
upon the children, thus turning them into pillows. They are not
shod; they are fed at night with dry grass and a little millet, and
in the spring are put out to grass (when there is any), and are not
used for a month.

Their camels are one-humped, and are gray or brown in color.
As soon as a young camel is born they bind its four feet under its
belly, cover it with a cloth, and place heavy stones on the ends;
thus, its education commencing with its life, it is trained to stoop.
When it becomes old, it is, like the horse, brought to the table.
Its flesh is tough, but nourishing.

It is to this diet that the Arab naturalists ascribe the cruel and
revengeful nature of their countrymen. The camel is said to be
the worst-tempered of all animals. In the Canary Islands they
have camel-fights, which are, by all accounts, terrible affairs.
When I was at Teneriffe I saw one of these animals which was
muzzled. Something enraged him at the moment, and, protruding a kind of bladder from his mouth, which foamed with saliva,
he uttered a very peculiar babbling noise. The camel has, however, one redeeming trait. He has a passion for music. I have
been informed that in Morocco he is taught to dance; it is at least
certain that the spur for the brute among the Arabs is a song;
among the Moors, a tune on a musical instrument.

The Moors have Caucasian features, of which the complexion is tawny, and sometimes of a dirty white putty color. They are remarkably hardy, and can pass days without eating or drinking. On such occasions they wear, like the red Indians, a hunger-belt, which they gradually tighten. Unequalled in their powers of abstinence, they also stand supreme in voracity. An hour after a Moor has eaten his full he can dispatch a second meal, as if he had fasted for a month.

Among the Moors matrimony possesses a delightful freedom. Husbands and wives can be divorced from one another, without form or ceremony, as often as they please. It is, indeed, considered low for a couple to live too long together; and the leaders of fashion are those who have been the oftenest divorced. Polygamy, though legal, is not much in vogue; for the Moorish ladies do not live in amity with one another.

The Senegal forms a border between two countries, which are as totally distinct as if they were separated by a sea. Of this the Moors are the moss-troopers. They are forever descending upon the effeminate negroes, as the Picts scourged the Britons in ancient days. The Moors occasionally deign to have low amours with negresses. I have frequently seen the offspring, which, with thin straight hair just covering the head, and an unhealthy-looking complexion, neither black nor tawny, is abject in the extreme. The Moors obtain their slaves from negro-land. They despise them heartily, and a man who can afford it will cut off a slave's head to test the temper of a new sword. In return, they are cordially detested by the blacks, and there is a Wollof proverb: *Berkélé emboull gorr*—There is nothing good under a tent; *Loull narrou gowr betchié bountou ba*—Unless it is the horse which is at the door.

They come down to the Senegal in the dry season for trade. As soon as the inundations commence, Moors and ostriches take refuge in the desert. In the desert they have their granaries. These are wells called *matamors*, in which they bury their corn, lining the bottom and sides with straw, and covering it with straw above.

The wares which they bring to the Senegal consist of gold trinkets, daggers of fine steel, carpets worked by hand, and gum.

When the rainy season is over, and the Harmattan has begun to blow, the acacias give forth their milk, of which the aqueous part evaporates, and a ball-like excrescence remains, its size de-

termined by the vigor of the tree. These excrescences are torn
from the tree by means of hooked sticks; when fresh gathered,
they will open in two like a ripe apricot, and the inside is not
very unlike that fruit. The negro slaves fill bags of skin with
the gum, and these bags, packed on camels, are sent off to the
nearest trading station.

The only food of the slaves during this harvest is the gum itself, which they suck like sugar-candy. It is said to be very
nourishing. But large numbers of slaves perish in these acacia
forests every year.

The Moors believe that we possess the secret of turning gum
into gold; others assert that with us it is the aliment of princes.

They believe also that we white men (whom they despise) are a
race of merchants fearing war, and unable to endure fatigue. That
in our country, having neither oxen, sheep, nor horses, we live almost entirely on human flesh, and that by means of a compact
with the Fiend we are permitted to enjoy this luxury and others,
that we may be the more thoroughly damned hereafter.

On arriving at Podor, which is about as far up the Senegal as
Macarthy's Island is up the Gambia, I had opportunities of studying the Moors whom I have just described, and who had a large
encampment on the other side of the river; and also the manners,
customs, and characters of the negro Mohammedans of Senegambia.

This region, which lies between the Senegal and the Casemanche, bounded on the east by the Atlas Mountains, on the west
by the sea, is inhabited by three great nations—the Wollof, the
Mandingo, and the Fulah.

Djoloff, the country of the Wollof nation, lies between the Senegal and the Gambia, near the coast.

The Wollof are (excepting the Kru) the finest specimens of
true negroes in Africa. They are very tall, with thick lips, flat
noses, and short crisp hair; but with little prognathous development, and with high prominent foreheads. Their complexion is
the intensest black. They are very tall, and are sometimes robust; but they are much afflicted with pulmonary complaints,
and are frequently flat-chested and spindle-shanked.

The Wollof girls are very pretty; for there is nothing more
lovely than a black skin, soft, rich, and glossy as Utrecht velvet.
But when the first jet of youth is passed, the skin turns to a dirty
yellow, and creases like old leather; the eyes sink into the skull,
and the breasts hang down like the udder of a cow, or shrivel up
like a bladder that has burst.

The Wollof make good soldiers when led by a white officer, and good servants under a judicious mixture of kindness and hard flogging. But, in spite of their fine physique, they are far inferior to the Fulahs and Mandingoes. True negroes in mind and body, they are singers and dancers, gluttons and drunkards; averse to work; exorbitant both to Europeans and to inland tribes; importunate beggars whom nothing will repel or satisfy; adroit thieves, stealing things with their feet while they draw away one's attention with their eyes; bad Mohammedans, selling their own children into slavery, and becoming Christians for a bottle of brandy. Their dialect, which, like their country, is called Djoloff, is extremely guttural, and reminded me of that of the Kru, whom in many respects they themselves resemble.

The Mandingoes are the commercial travelers of Northern Central Africa. In no people is the migratory instinct so strongly developed. My man Hassan had left the Gambia to come to the Casemanche, and was about to leave the Casemanche (without reason) for the Senegal. "A Mandingo," he said, "can't live long in one place." As I have already observed, their merchants travel to Mecca and Timbuctoo. They also trade in Liberia, Ashantee, and Dahomey.

They are said to have originally come from a country bearing their name to the south of Bambuk, and occupy the inland country between the Casemanche and the Gambia. They also mingle with the Fulahs on the northern side of the Gambia. It is impossible to define their territory, which changes every year.

They are strict Mohammedans, and, so far from selling their own children, they consider it wicked to sell a slave against whom they have no just cause of complaint. They are extremely courteous and hospitable. Their mode of salutation is by shaking hands European fashion, which appears to be general all over Africa. But when a man salutes a woman, he raises her hand twice —not to his lips, but to his nose, and smells it ardently.

The Mandingo complexion is tawny; but it is common enough to meet with black Mandingoes. Their constitution is usually feudal or patriarchal, each village being governed by its *alkadi*, who has more power than the chieftains in other parts of Africa. Every village has two common fields of corn and rice; the *alkadi* appoints men to till the former, women the latter, and divides the crops among them.

The principal men among the Mandingoes are their traveling

Z

merchants, who perform considerable journeys, visiting Timbuctoo, and even Mecca. They pack their wares on donkeys, which they drive before them, setting out at daybreak, resting in the heat of the day, and traveling late into the night when there is a moon. When they come to a large town, they establish an impromptu shop under some large shady tree, and remain there two or three days. Thus Manchester cloths and Venice beads are carried into regions of Africa which may not be visited by white men for long years to come.

The Fouta, Fuli, or Fellatah compose a great pastoral and warlike nation, which have extended their conquests to the Niger, where they are known as the Pulo; and I believe them to be identical with the Fanh of the Sierra del Crystal, and with the Jagas of the Congo. Their origin is unknown, but there is reason to suppose that this is the great *Phout* nation mentioned in Genesis, and of which all traces have been lost.

They are skillful herdsmen, bold hunters, formidable warriors, and industrious agriculturists. Their color is tawny, or red; but, as with the Mandingoes, the nation appears to be turning black as it draws near the sea. They are Mohammedans, like the negroes, and are excellent Arabic scholars—a knowledge of this language being indispensable to the education of a gentleman.

Having thus distinguished the grand characteristics of these three nations, I shall describe some of their manners and customs.

These negro Mohammedans worship God under the name of Allah; they acknowledge Mohammed as a prophet, but do not pay him divine honors; they have some traditions respecting Jesus Christ, whom they call Nale, the son of Malek, and whom they speak of as a great prophet, who had wrought wondrous miracles; they denounce as impious the doctrine that God could have carnal conversation with a woman, but have a prophecy of their own that some day they shall all be subdued by a white people.

There are rudely-built mosques in most of the villages; in these divine service is conducted in this manner: the marabout extends his arms, and utters several words in a loud and deliberate voice, his hearers repeating them after him. Then he kneels and kisses the ground three times, the congregation following his example; after which he draws a circle on the ground with his finger, marks it with several characters, which he kisses, and, resting his head on the palms of his hands and his elbows on his knees, delivers himself up to profound meditation, with his eyes fixed on the ground. A few minutes having passed, he throws dust over his head and face, and prays aloud, touching the ground with his finger and raising it to his forehead, repeating several times *Salati Malek*—" Lord, I salute you."

The Ramadan, the Mohammedan Lent, was being observed when I was in the Senegal in February. They keep this fast very scrupulously, touching nothing between sunrise and sunset. The puritans will not even swallow their own saliva, and cover their mouths lest they should unconsciously masticate a fly. When the Ramadan is past they have their festival, the Taba-shet, which is solemnized with prayers, sacrifices, feasts, and dancing parties.

When the new moon of the autumnal equinox appears, they pay it great honor, saluting it by spitting in their hands and waving them round their heads three times. They have at all times a reverence for this chaste luminary, and ingeniously account for eclipses by saying that a celestial cat puts her paw between the moon and the earth.

The marabouts are the priests, merchants, and physicians of Mohammedan Africa, and are most important among the Mandingoes. They differ only in their dress from the others by their red, yellow, or blue caps. Like the ancient Druids, some of them are resident as school-teachers; others travel as merchant-missionaries, carrying with them articles of commerce and their sacred books; others join the retinue of noblemen and kings. They make their living principally by the manufacture of *gris-gris*, which are scraps of Arabic in leather cases. These are usually adjusted on the person in the form of a cross; but those who are rich enough will cover themselves so completely with these charms as to make quite a coat of them.

Chief among their religious ceremonies is that of circumcision. It is never omitted; for there is said to be a spirit which swallows uncircumcised boys, and carries them about nine days in its belly.

A number of boys about fourteen years of age being brought to the marabout, each accompanied by two relatives, who act as godfathers, a procession is formed. They march to the appointed spot, usually beneath some large tree; the patients dance along with indecent gestures, while women and girls following sing the details of this ancient ceremony.

While the operation is being performed with a knife or a sharp stone, the boy has to raise his right thumb, and to recite in a loud voice the Mussulman's creed—*La Allah ila Allah, Mohammed Re-sûl Allah.* For a month afterward the circumcised wear a pecul-iar dress, and an oddly shaped cap with two horns branching forth. During this month they can commit any violence toward girls short of rape or murder. After this period is passed they become men, and adopt the occupations of their fathers.

A somewhat similar operation is performed upon the girls by the marabouts' wives.

As one might expect, the women hold a less menial position among these tribes of Senegambia. Among the Foutas they ap-pear to enjoy a power scarcely inferior to that of ladies in good society.

These Fouta women have delicate features and fine forms. Their hair is adorned with amber; and a muslin veil gives them a *piquante* and voluptuous air. But they are as mercenary as they are beautiful: I could never speak to a Fouta girl in the Senegal for five minutes without her saying "*Donnez moû quelque chose.*"

They are the most tyrannical wives in Africa. They know how to make their husbands kneel before their charms, and how to place their little feet upon them. When they are threatened with divorce, they shed tears; and if a man actually repudiates his wife, they attack him *en masse.* Like the members of a priest-hood, they hate, but protect each other.

They go to this unfortunate devil of a husband, who has per-haps never enjoyed a quiet moment in his own house, and say, "Why do you ill-treat your wife? A woman is helpless; a man has all things. Go, recall her; and, to appease her just anger, make her a kind present." The husband prays for forgiveness, and when his entreaties take the form of a bullock or a slave, she consents to return.

These women, however, do not dine at the same table with their lords. Each lives in a separate house, and the famous handker-chief signal is here replaced by the order *to get supper ready.* The chosen wife gladly obeys the command, hurriedly lighting the fire and preparing the *cous-cous,* not so much from affection as from vanity. In fact, they sometimes make presents to their husbands to obtain this honor, and to spite the other wives.

Marriages always take place on a Friday, and it is usual for the bridegroom to have obtained the parents' consent; though, as with us, it is not indispensable. Accompanied by his relatives, especially by his sister, he goes to the mosque with his bride and her relatives. A *griot* or public minstrel sings an amorous song; the relatives interchange copious compliments. After reciting a few prayers, the marabout says to the girl, "Do you wish to take this man for your husband?" She replies in the affirmative. The bridegroom's sister then says to the marabout, "Here is the *tak* (yoke) which is to unite this woman with my brother." This *tak* is a pair of cotton drawers. The marabout receives them and gives them to the bride, charging her solemnly to keep them with care, and to put them on at any important crisis of her married life. The marabout then calls the spouses, recites a verse of the Koran, and says, "Go; you are united." The woman returns to her own house. Her husband builds a new one. When it is prepared, there is another procession; the bride is accompanied by young girls, who deplore the loss of their playmate in a low and mournful song. It is not only in Europe that weddings resemble funerals. At the door of the new house the sister offers to the bride a calabash containing corn, ground-nuts, and tobacco—a delicate mode of showing to her that her future must be agricultural. She enters the house on all fours, in token of submission; but, on reaching the bed, she seats herself proudly upon it. It is the throne of her sex, and there she will remain till it becomes her sepulchre.

The husband may beat his wife within reasonable limits; but if he breaks a tooth or a limb, she is entitled to a power of divorce. This can also be obtained by mutual consent, by the husband's desertion, by impotency, or by the wife's adultery. But as the latter can only be proved by seven respectable witnesses, evidence *de visu* alone being received, the law is almost a dead letter. To prevent brief and frivolous divorces on the grounds of mutual consent, it is necessary that the wife be married to another before her husband can remarry her. This law is, however, easily eluded.

It is the custom for a woman always to be delivered in the presence of her parents, who remain with her till her convalescence. The baby is washed with warm water, the bed is curtained with mats, and a fire is lighted to drive away the Evil Spirit. The mother lies in eight days, is fed lightly, and is not allowed to eat *cous-cous*, which is said to cause colic. The husband's sister (who appears to hold the same place in domestic economy as the English mother-in-law) has the immemorial privilege of washing the wife's linen and of naming the child. She brings a sheep with her. As she pronounces the name, the sheep's throat is cut, and the animal is cooked.

If her husband dies, his friends roast an ox whole over his grave; abundant alms are given to the poor, who there, like worms and undertakers, feed upon mortality. The widow remains in the house crouched upon the ground. Thence she must not stir till the terrible sister-in-law comes to knot her hair. If they have ever "had words," she, of course, finds unexpected obstacles which delay her.

Every Friday the widow goes out to solicit alms. Her knotted hair and the dagger which she carries in her hand warn all men to avoid her, because she is mourning and impure. She goes to a house. Its mistress brings out a bowl of *cous-cous*, holding it behind her back. The widow, having emptied it, hurls it away as far as she can, which in this land of emblems is possibly symbolical of gratitude. After she has mourned eight days she is married by her late husband's eldest brother.

When a king dies, his death is kept secret for eight days. During this time he is privately buried by members of his family; for it is believed that if a man were to obtain his shoulder-blade he could make a *gri-gri* with it which would dethrone the reigning house. A somewhat similar superstition prevails in the Gaboon.

The natives of Senegambia have among them skillful minstrels, blacksmiths, and sandal-makers; but these three crafts are held in great contempt, especially that of the *griots*.

There are three classes of these public minstrels: 1. those who play such vulgar instruments as the flute and drum; 2. those who play on the ballafond, which is the marimba of Angola and South America, and on the harp; 3. those who sing the legends and battle-songs of their country, or who improvise satires or panegyrics. This last class are dreaded, though despised. They are richly rewarded in their lifetime, but after death they are not even given a decent burial: if they were buried in the ground, it would become barren; if in the river, the water would be poisoned, and the fish would die. So they are buried in hollow trees.

Among the graver Foutas the tam-tam is forbidden, and the *griots* may only sing canticles in honor of Mohammed.

As specimens of these songs of the *griots*, and also as giving one some clew to native character and custom, I will give the following song, which I took down from the mouth of a Wollof *griot*, a soldier in the French army, and whom I invited to dinner at St. Louis. He sang in the sonorous, drawling style of our rustics, accompanying himself with his iron castanets and jangling anklets.

A WAR-SONG.

I go in front. I fear not death. I am not afraid. If I die, I will take my blood to bathe my head.

The man who fears nothing marches always in front, and is never hit by the murderous ball. The coward hides himself behind a bush and is killed.

Go to the battle. It is not lead that kills. It is Fate which strikes us, and which makes us die.

HISTORICAL.

The Tubabs (French) went against Galam. The King of Maïel said to a woman, "Take your child, put it in a mortar, and pound it to dust. From its dust I will make a man rise who will save our town." The woman pounded her child to dust; from the dust came a man; but the Tubabs took Maïel.

SONG OF A FREETHINKER.

Many years ago a Moor preached new doctrines among the Africans, showing them the frauds of their priests, and proclaiming himself as the Messiah. This song is supposed to have been sung by one of his disciples.

The false marabout is only fit to eat eggs and fowls offered to the dead. He never follows the men when they go to war: he can only mess about their wounds.

God is the greatest of all. None is great but God.

If you know how to write Marabout (Arabic) you will become one of the disciples of God. If you know Marabout you are the greatest of your family. You maintain them; if they commit a fault it is you who will protect them.

Now I know perfectly how to read and write Marabout. My parents have given me that custom. I follow the religion of Marabout because I had it from my parents.

If I make my salaam it is because I conciliate other people, but I believe nothing of what I say.

We follow you because you do good; we believe in you because you do good; and we love you because after you die there will be no more war.

PROVERBIAL SONG.

This is the commonest kind of song, and is general all over Africa. It consists of detached sentences, usually impromptu, sung by one and repeated in chorus by the crowd. Three verses will be sufficient.

When a woman has no good *gris-gris* she will go to hell.

When a woman does not clap her hands to her lover's dance she is a woman of stone.

When a fisherman catches a narwhal he can catch any fish in the world.

Lastly, as a fair specimen of their extravagant flattery and original talent, I will give in prose the song which this *griot* himself composed the next day in my honor.

I.

The man who had not feared to pass the seas through a love of study and of science heard of the poor Griot. He had him summoned. He made him sing songs which made the echoes of the Bornou mountains covered with palm-trees ring louder and louder as the sounds flew over the summits of the trees.

II.

The songs touched the heart of the great white man, and the dew of his magnificence fell upon the Griot's head. Oh! how can he sing the wonderful deeds of the Tonbab? His voice and his breath would not be strong enough to sing that theme. He must be silent, and let the lion of the forest sing his battles and his victories.

III.

Fatimata heard the songs of the Griot. She heard, too, the deeds which the Tonbab had accomplished. She sighed, and covered her head with her robe.* Then she turned to her young lover, and she said, "Go to the wars: let the flying ball kill thee; for Fatimata loves thee no longer. The white man fills her thoughts."

The commander of the "Serpent" introduced me to a French mulatto at Podor, who undertook to bed and board me while I was there. But my first breakfast was enough.

Mulattoes are always caricatures of their parent nation. The English mulattoes are absurd sticklers for etiquette, dress decently, and drink hard. The Portuguese mulattoes, fawning, servile, treacherous, will swindle one under their own roof, and poison him if it is worth their while. The French mulattoes have good manners; *blaguent* beyond belief; and, having cooked a dinner exquisitely, will serve it incrusted with filth.

The colonial French certainly appear to think that cleanliness is next not only to godliness, but to cooking. The English, on the other hand, serve one an uneatable dinner on a table-cloth white as snow, and in a plate as polished as a mirror. The just medium is not to be found in Africa.

Frenchmen in the Senegal have acquired a habit which must have been the result of severe experience. It is said that a newly-appointed governor, having arrived at St. Louis, invited several officers to breakfast. You can imagine the astonishment of this veteran, who was one of the old *régime*, and terribly sensitive on matters of etiquette, when all his guests, on sitting down to table, set to work polishing their plates with their napkins, holding them up to the light, and scrutinizing them, as he thought, in a marked

---

* This is a very fine image. To cover one's head like a widow is to invoke death upon one's head. If done intentionally, it is a crime.

and supercilious manner. He could only suppose that this was a studied insult, and rising, red with vexation, exclaimed, "I have not invited lackeys to come here and clean my plates." But when the custom was explained to him, profuse apologies were made, and the governor, having criticised his own platter, fell to like the rest, observing, "He saw that in Senegal every one must be his own servant."

The mulatto I allude to gave me a breakfast of several dishes, but could only afford us one plate apiece. These, therefore, had to be cleaned between the *entrées*. Acquainted with the carelessness of French mulattoes, I wondered to find the plates returned to us not only clean, but polished. But, happening to glance into the back, I saw the dirty little nigger that waited on us cleaning them with his tongue. My dinner came into my mouth; I felt myself turn white; I fled to the fort, and, having told them there this incident, threw myself on their compassion. These brave men sympathized with me, gave me a seat at their table, and offered me every possible kindness.

The fort at Podor is a fine building surrounded by spacious grounds. In these two hundred men were encamped, with their tiny triangular tents, and piles of stacked arms, and cheerful wood fires, round which they sat in the evening, like the Africans themselves. The French army was in the neighborhood, and a steamer was ready to take this detachment to any particular point, if orders should be received. One day we heard their guns; every thing was prepared; I obtained permission from the commandant to join as a volunteer; but the next news we heard was that the campaign was finished, and that the governor was returning to St. Louis.

Podor has the reputation of being the hottest place in the world. You may bake your eggs in the sand; and it is to the sand that crocodiles, as well as ostriches, leave theirs to be hatched. The discovery of the power of caloric which these intelligent animals could make probably suggested the hatching ovens of the Egyptians.

Senegambia is terribly plagued with musquitoes in the rainy season, and millions of these insects, each of which possesses a venomous and caustic poison, can not tend to purify the atmosphere. In the dry season they disappear, and provident Nature atones for their loss with sand-flies, house-flies, locusts, and ants.

The sand-flies are carnivorous. They creep through the finest gauze, and, settling on one's hands and face, render life bitter.

The house-flies fly into one's eyes when one is looking at any thing, and down one's mouth when one ventures to make an observation. They settle on one's food in swarms. After the first day of flies I sympathized with Domitian; on the second I began to emulate him.

Locusts, when flying, resemble *distant* flakes of snow. They settle on fertile districts and reduce them to a wilderness. The natives retaliate by dining on them. The flesh of these marauders is not disagreeable, and is as white as a lobster's; but the diet is not wholesome, for the insects are said to be capable of reproduction even after they are digested.

As for the red ants, they represent invaders. Led by some Alexander or Napoleon of their own, they sweep onward in thousands, and destroy all that they meet. If a house is in their way, the inhabitants must vacate it with all that they value, and, on returning, will find it cleared of all vermin, and of every particle of filth. If they encounter animals, they will frequently destroy them, eating the live flesh off their bones. Thus elephants, leopards, and even Scotchmen have perished.

The Scotchman I allude to was a trader in the Casemanche some years ago. M. Rapet was well acquainted with him. This gentleman used to get drunk every evening, which is not unusual among Britannic colonists. But, after his first bottle of brandy, he used to take another in his pocket, put on a pair of enormous boots, and wander about in the jungle till he had finished the bottle; then he would lie down wherever he happened to be, and go peaceably to sleep. One morning he did not return as usual. His people went into the wood to look for him. To their horror, they found that a swarm of drivers had fallen in with him. Even his boots had been eaten up. A ghastly and clean-picked skeleton, with a few scattered boot-nails, alone were left to tell the tale!

I left Podor in the "Crocodile," the commandant of which was M. Braouézzec, who had been one time commandant at Nengĕ-Nengĕ, in the Gaboon. We had a long chat about the cannibal Fans, and the Falls of the Ncomo, which he had also gone in search of. While I was on board, he received the news that he was appointed consul at Sierra Leone.

It was plain that the "Crocodile" had lately seen rough service. The wheel was shielded by large iron plates, which bore bullet-marks upon them. Braouézzec told me that in the floods he had explored the surrounding country in his little steamer. These inundations quite transform the face of the country. We all know that story in Munchausen, where the traveler ties his horse to something sticking out of the snow, goes to sleep beside it, and finds in the morning that, the snow having melted, he is lying in the street of a town, and that his horse is hanging from the church steeple. In the same manner (only this is strictly true), if a boat was to be moored in the rains to the top of an acacia-tree just projecting above the water, you would find it afterward in the dry season hanging forty feet above your head. When, ascending these two rivers—the Senegal and the Gambia—and seeing on each side of me high banks and trees on those, I was informed that the waters mounted up to their very tops. I could scarcely believe it. Fancy steaming into a forest! what can appear more romantic and incredible than such a voyage?

What becomes of the land animals in the floods, and of the water animals in times of perfect drought? These are two very interesting questions.

I was told that, when in Southwestern Africa the rivers dry up, the hippopotami and crocodiles will invade towns. I have already described how a swarm of bees took us by storm in Angola; and there can at least be no doubt that the migrations are entirely determined by seasons.

In Equatorial Africa the leopard never approaches the villages in the rains. This led me to suppose that it hibernated, and, on asking where it lived during the wet season, I was told that it made a bed under some large tree which had fallen to the ground, and that it slept there all the while. The tiger-cat also hibernates in the hole of a tree.

But in Senegambia it is in the rains that the lion approaches human habitations, and the ostrich flies to the desert. While the "Crocodile" was steaming over an inundated jungle, several snakes and monkeys, that had taken refuge in the tops of the higher trees, came on board the vessel, which they converted for a short time into a small Noah's ark. Three wild boars were also caught alive without difficulty.

Sergeant Boivin told me that, being engaged in boat-work at a distance of four hundred and twenty-three miles up the country, in the time of the floods, in company with several other white men, one of whom was the son of M. Carrère, the author of a work on Senegambia, they came to an island which was formed probably by the summit of a hill, and on which there were two hills.

On this island there were lying, huddled together, two lions, a leopard, some monkeys and hyænas, two antelopes, and a wild boar. All of these they killed without difficulty. None of them took to the water; the leopard only made an effort to escape by running up the tree. This is certainly an improbable story; but to those who know how danger will stifle ferocity in wild beasts, it will not appear impossible.

As we laid at Dagama, between Podor and St. Louis, we heard, toward midnight, a steamer puffing in the distance. It was the "Serpent" taking the governor back to St. Louis.

M. Braouézzec, having gone on board, received orders to return to St. Louis, and to put me on board the "African."

We met the "African" the next morning. She was so crammed with troops that there was no room to walk on deck. As I climbed the ladder I heard the doctor exclaim, "Here's an Englishman come on board to die," which reminded me that I still cut a very ghastly figure. However, the same officer kindly welcomed me to the dinner-table, and I ate with double appetite, because the beef and mutton had been taken from the enemy, and because I wished to prove that I had not come on board to die, but to dine.

There was a large assemblage of naval and military officers, none of whom seemed well contented with the result of the campaign. The governor had commanded the troops in person. He was a Protestant, and so puritanic that he did not allow his soldiers to fight on Sundays. This the natives in time discovered, and of course turned to their own advantage. Had Wellington had these scruples, Waterloo would never have been fought; and if a general is so careful not to break the fourth commandment, he should choose a profession in which duty does not compel him to break the sixth on so large a scale.

But now, happily for this colony, Faidherbe is restored to it. It was Faidherbe who organized the colonial infantry; who conquered the natives at a time when no man's life was safe three miles from St. Louis; and who established an electric telegraph between St. Louis and Goree. It was Faidherbe, in fact, who has founded civilization in this one corner of Western Africa, and who has commenced that great work which I hope ere long to see continued by system, and of which presently I shall treat at large.

I had now ascended the Casemanche, the Gambia, and the Sen-

A FLOOD IN SENEGAMBIA.

egal, the three great rivers of Senegambia. I had had some idea of going to Guinea, visiting Ashantee and Dahomey, and afterward descending to the Congo.

But I found that a tour in Africa, when one is always on the move, is as expensive as traveling in Europe. I also began to observe that the little dwelling which I rent from Providence was getting sadly out of repair. I was what the French call *fatigué*, and we *used up*. I resolved to return.

On the twenty-sixth of February I re-embarked on board the "African." The bar, which was one of the worst upon the Coast, was very bad that day. The vessel was old, and was so loaded with troops and stores as to render her almost unmanageable.

Two men were placed at the wheel; but, in spite of their efforts, she turned her broadside to the bar; we shipped seas, and struck three times. The pilot bawled furiously from the bridge, and the two men, with moist hands, whirled the wheel round like lightning: knapsacks were floating about on deck; we were nearly blinded by the spray; and more than one sailor turned pale. Every moment I expected to have seen the planks of the deck burst asunder, and the ship go into halves. And scarcely had we cleared white water when the engine broke down, owing to the shocks which the vessel had received. Had this happened a few minutes earlier, she must have gone to pieces, and nothing could possibly have saved us from the sharks.

As if warned by some ravenous instinct, the sharks are nowhere so numerous on the West Coast of Africa as at the Lagos and Senegal bars, which are the most dangerous on the Coast, and where so many lives have been lost. Similar cases have been observed by voyagers in different parts of the world.

A few days afterward I was enjoying my last look at Africa. It was the same spot which I had hailed fourteen months before with the enthusiasm of a youth *ætat.* 23.

I had hoped that I should make some great discovery in Africa, and I was not disappointed. I had made a discovery which few men succeed in making at so early an age, and which, though not profitable to others, will prove extremely useful to myself.

It was the discovery of my own ignorance.

During those days which I spent in the sombre forest—during those nights which I passed in a canoe on the lonely river, or in an open boat far out at sea, cut off from all the resources of art, from all the pleasures of civilization—I was compelled to taste the grand silence of the desert, the gigantic solitude of Space.

And then were laid open before me the three grand pages of the universe—the heavens, the earth, and the sea; but I could not read them; they were written in a language which I did not understand. I could only guess at their mysterious characters; I could only look at their pictures like a child.

And thus, dear reader, I have traveled a long way that I might be allowed to enter the Temple of Fame. But above its porch I have read the terrible Γνῶθι Σεαυτνό. I descend the hill which I have so prematurely mounted. I go to study with humble industry the elements of science, the grammar of Nature.

CHAPTER XXXIII.

MONSTERS AND FABULOUS ANIMALS.

Origin of Fables.—The Sloth in Africa.—The Roc.—The Unicorn.—Described by the Ancients.—Account of Barthema.—Account of Tellez.—Tailed Men of the Eastern Archipelago.—Tailed Men of Africa.—Tailed Men of Kent.

IT must be laid down as a certain principle that man can originate nothing; that lies are always truths embellished, distorted, or turned inside out. There are other facts besides those which lie on the surface, and it is the duty of the traveler and historian to sift and wash the gold-grains of truth from the dirt of fable.

It was a saying of the ancients that Africa is always affording something new. As in the days of Pliny and Herodotus, so now it still remains *par excellence* the land of mystery and of romance. It is true that some of the ancient myths have been sobered down to natural beings. The men with dogs' heads, of whom Herodotus speaks, are the barking baboons which I saw in the Senegal; the men with their heads under their shoulders, their eyes in their breast, are the ill-formed negroes, whose shoulders are shrugged up, and whose heads drop on their breasts; the mermaids of the Arab tales are the sea-cows of the African rivers, which have feminine dugs, and a face almost human in expression; the huge serpent which opposed the army of Regulus is now well known as the python; the burning mountains which Hanno saw, and the sounds as of lutes which were believed to proceed from the strife of the elements, are only caused by the poor negroes burning the grass on their hill-tops; the music being that of their flutes, as I have heard it often in those long and silent African nights far away.

But those who have studied African literature must confess that we know little more respecting the natural productions of this country than the ancients did. Many of the stories of Herodotus, which in the last century were ridiculed as absurd, have been endorsed by the experience of recent travelers. Is it not possible that some of those accounts which we still regard as fabulous may yet be cited against us by another generation?

A A

Incredulity has now become so vulgar a folly, that one is al-most tempted, out of simple hatred for a fashion, to run into the opposite extreme.   However, I shall content myself with citing evidence respecting certain unknown, fabulous, and monstrous an-imals of Africa, without committing myself to an opinion one way or the other, preserving only my conviction that there is always a basis of truth to the most fantastic fables, and that, by rejecting without inquiry that which appears incredible, one throws away ore in which others might have found a jewel.   A traveler should believe nothing, for he will find himself so often deceived; and he should disbelieve nothing, for he will see so many wonderful things: he should doubt; he should investigate; and then he may perhaps discover.

Many curious animals are made mention of by the old authors as existing in Africa—of an animal near Sierra Leone "which had a stone in his forehead, which gives him light to feed by, but, as soon as he hears the least noise, he covers it with a film or skin to prevent being discovered; of a water-ox which resembles a buffalo, having hoofed feet, but which is amphibious like the hip-popotamus; of white monkeys, winged dragons, and great sea-serpents.

One can easily understand that the animal with the glow-worm development is only some variety of the cat kind, whose eyes are remarkably powerful at night.   The water-ox is probably some buffalo, which, like the water-buck of Southern Africa, spends most of the day wallowing in the rivers.   The white monkeys, which are often mentioned by the early voyagers, and of which I was given a detailed account in the Muni country, are probably albinoes, like those which are found among buffaloes, elephants, and, indeed, most animals.   As for the winged dragons, it is not impossible that such an animal exists, as we have the type pre-served in the *draco volans*, a little lizard with a membrane like a bat's wing; but it is, to say the least of it, very improbable.

The flying squirrel exists in Equatorial Africa; and I believe that I have been the first to see this curious little animal in that country.   An antelope striped like a zebra is said to exist in Cen-tral Africa.   But the most curious type existing in Africa is that of the sloth, which has always been supposed to be peculiar to the New World.

Barbot mentions the *entigiengio*, a small creature very curious-ly streaked, slender-bodied, with a fine tail and legs.   "It never comes upon the earth; for the very touch thereof proves mortal to it, therefore keeps to the trees, and has always twenty black-haired creatures called *embis* attending it; that is, ten before and ten behind. They take the ten first in snares, and then the ten behind make their escape, by which means the animal, bereaved of its guard, is also taken. The skin of this little beast bears such a value that none but the kings may wear it."

This would appear to be a distorted account of a sloth, and the following description by Artus of Dantzic, and Bosman, two of the most reliable authorities on Africa, satisfactorily proves the existence of this animal: "Here is a creature by the natives called *Potto*, but known to the Dutch by the name of sluggard, a whole day being little enough for it to advance ten steps forward.

"Some writers affirm that, when this Creature has climbed up a Tree, he does not leave it till he has not only eaten up the Fruit, but Leaves also; then descending fat, and in very good Case, in order to get up into another Tree; But, before he can compass this, he becomes as poor and lean as possible; and if the Trees be high or at any Distance, and he meets with nothing on his Journey, he inevitably dies with Hunger betwixt one Tree and another. But the Author will not undertake for the Truth of this Story, though the Negroes seem to believe something like it."

This creature, according to Bosman, is so horribly ugly that he does not believe any thing in the world can come up to it. "Its fore feet are very like Hands, the Head most disproportionally large. When very young, it is of a pale mouse colour, and the Skin smooth; But when old it is red, and covered with a sort of Hair as thick-set as Flocks of Wool." Bosman knew nothing more of this animal than that it is impossible to look on it without horror, and that it has nothing very particular but its hideous form.*

The existence of the *roc* of Marco Polo and the "Arabian Nights" is now proved by the discovery of an immense egg in a semi-fossil state in Madagascar. This egg (a cast of which is in the British Museum) must have been emitted by a bird double the size of the ostrich. At present it would appear to be confined to that island: but I find in Father Lobo's account of Abyssinia

* Since writing the above I have been informed by Dr. Gray that specimens of these animals have been brought to England; that they are not true sloths, having lemur-like teeth; and that perfect specimens from Guinea would be gladly received by naturalists.

a description of this bird. He not only repeats the exaggerated
tales of the natives, who declare that it can carry away an ele
phant in its talons, but, like Marco Polo, he asserts that he had ac
tually seen one of its feathers, although he had not seen the bird
itself. "*In aliquibus autem regionibus vidi pennas alœ istuis avi.
prodigiosœ, licet avem non viderim. Penna illa prout ex forma col
ligebatur, erat ex mediocribus longitudine 28 palmorum, latitudine 8.'*

And in the narrative of the Lascar Isuf's voyage in Eastern
Africa, in Ehrman's "Collection," is a description of the *pyon*, a
bird ten feet in height.

Of all animals which have been classed as fabulous, the unicorn
is the most remarkable, since to this very day it is impossible for
a careful writer to make a positive assertion respecting its existence.

The ancients compared their *monoceros* to a horse with a stag's
head, which proves that they had seen an animal very different
from the rhinoceros. They also distinctly name the *unicorn-ass*,
an animal of great size, swift of foot, solitary in his habits, and
having a horn striped with white, black, and brown.

Garcias, a writer of the sixteenth century, relates that the Portuguese navigators saw, between the Cape of Good Hope and Cape
Corrientes, an animal having the head and mane of a horse, with
one movable horn. In this same region Sparmann and Barrow
saw representations of a one-horned animal. The rocks of Cam-
debo and Bambo are covered with them—a curious fact, setting
zoology aside; for it proves the ancient connection of Caffraria
with Asia; the unicorn, among the Persians and Hebrews, being
the symbol of kingly power. It is with this meaning delineated
on the monuments of Persepolis, and on the royal arms of Great
Britain.

The Dutch colonists also, according to Voight, affirmed that
they had seen these animals alive, and that they resembled the
quagga, while the horn adhered only to the skin.

According to Merolla, the real unicorn is extinct; though I
shall quote better authority to prove that it is living than that
upon which he makes his assertion. "Here," he says, writing of
Angola, "is also the unicorn, called by the Congolans *abada*,
whose medicinal virtue, being sufficiently known, needs not to be
taken notice of. These unicorns are very different from those
commonly mentioned by authors; and, if you will believe what I

have heard say, there are none of that sort now to be found. A Theatine missioner to the East Indies told me, at his return from Goa, he had endeavored to get one of these last; but, whatever diligence he used, he could by no means obtain it. He added, moreover, that he had heard several of the Eastern people, especially the Chinese authorities, say that, according to their computations, those unicorns all died the same day that our Savior died. What allusion these can have to our Savior may probably be from their chastity; but I must leave all to my good reader, who will condemn and approve, as he thinks fit."

In the fifteenth century, Barthema, or Verdomanus, who preceded Burckhardt and Burton in a pilgrimage to Mecca, gives a minute account of two unicorns which he saw there.

"By the side of the temple there is a large court inclosed by walls, where we saw a unicorn, which they showed us as a curiosity; and not without reason. For the larger one had the form of a colt eighteen months old, a horn in the middle of his forehead the length of three spans. The lesser one was the size of a colt a twelvemonth old, with his horn about four cubits long. The color of this animal was a dark gray, having a head like a stag, the head tolerably long, with a little thin hair hanging on the side; the legs long and graceful, like those of a deer. These two animals were given to the Sultan of Mecca (as a most rich and precious gift) by a king of Ethiopia, who wished to negotiate for peace."

The next authority is that of a Portuguese who had lived some time in Abyssinia, and is quoted by Father Tellez.

"It is certain that the unicorn is not to be confounded with the *abada*, about which they usually dispute; this one may see by the difference of their names, as well as by the difference of their body and parts, and it would appear by the *abada* which we have seen, and by the unicorn which we have seen painted. The latter has a long straight horn of admirable virtue; the *abada* has two crooked horns, which are not so sovereign, although they will serve as antidotes against poison. The country of the unicorn, which is an animal of Africa, where only it is known, is the province of Agoa, in the kingdom of Damotes, although it is occasionally seen in more distant places. This animal is as large as a fine horse, is a dark bay color, the mane and tail black, short, and thin, though in other parts of the province observed to be longer and thicker. On the forehead there is a beautiful horn five palms

long, as they are usually painted, the color being nearly white.
They live in woods and retired thickets, sometimes coming out
into the plains, where they are not often seen, because they are
timid animals, not numerous, and easily hidden in the wood.
The most barbarous people in the world have them, and perhaps
eat them like other animals.

"A missionary who was my companion, and who had spent
some time in that province, having been told that they had found
this renowned animal, did all that he could to get one. The natives brought him a very young one, but it was so delicate that it
died in a few days.

"A Portuguese captain, a man of years and good credit, and
held in great esteem by the princes of this empire, under whom
he serves, told me this story about unicorns. He said that once,
as he was returning from the army with twenty other Portuguese
soldiers, and they were resting one morning in a little valley encircled by very thick trees, getting ready their breakfast while
their horses grazed on the rich pasture, scarcely were they seated
when there sprang out of the thickest part of the wood a beautiful horse of the same shape and color that I have described. He
came so rapidly that he did not observe the people till he was
quite among them; then he was startled, began to tremble, and
suddenly bounded back, leaving, however, sufficient time to the
spectators to see and observe him with pleasure. The knowledge
which I have of this captain induces me to relate this as an un-
doubted fact.

"In another part of the same province, where it is stony and
mountainous, people have often seen this animal feeding among
several others of different kinds. This is the most remote part
of the province; that is why exiles are usually sent there by the
emperor. It is bounded by high mountains, below which are vast
plains and forests inhabited by various kinds of wild beasts. To
this place a tyrannical emperor named *Adamas-Segued* sent without cause several Portuguese, who, from the tops of the mountains, saw the unicorn feeding in the plains below, the distance not
being so great but that they could observe distinctly that it was
like a fine Spanish jennet, having a horn in his forehead.

"These testimonies, especially that of the good old man, John
Gabriel, with what the missionary, my companion, affirmed also
of his own knowledge, confirm me in the belief that this celebrated animal is found in the province, and that young ones are born
and bred there."

The latest traveler who has spoken of the unicorn is Dr. Baikie, who, when I was in Africa, had started on an incursion after this animal, the existence of which he must therefore have credited, and could only have done so upon reliable authority. That such an animal has existed, there can, I think, be little doubt; it is possible that he is extinct; but more probable that, flying from fire-arms (which, it must always be remembered, are used by tribes whom white men have never visited), he has concealed himself in those vast forest-wastes of Central Africa which are uninhabited and unexplored.

There are few works in the natural history of our race in which some reference is not made to the legends of tailed men, which are rejected by all writers (excepting Lord Monboddo) with more or less disdain. I shall now collect the evidence upon these beings in a more perfect manner than has hitherto been done, and shall add thereto the rumors which I heard on the same subject during my travels in Africa.

Blumenbach (De G. H. Var. Nat., sect. iii., § 76) proved that a certain engraving of a tailed man had the sketch of a monkey for its origin. Martini, in his version of Buffon, took it from Linnæus, who took it from Aldrovandus, who took it from Gesner, who took it from a German description of the Holy Land, "Reyss in des Gelbolte Land," Mentz, 1486, in which work a quadrumanous monkey is represented, and which, humanized a little by each of its borrowers, had been gradually transformed into a human being.

In the same manner, there can be no doubt that many of the accounts of tailed men have been simply descriptions of monkeys, which passed from mouth to mouth, and have gone through the same gradations per tongue as the drawing alluded to per pencil. But the reader will find that, in the mass of evidence which I shall bring before him, there is a unity and an appearance of truth which will stagger, if it will not convince.

The tailed men of the ancients, like their dog-faced men, were certainly baboons, with the exception of one race described by Pausanias (lib. ii., cap. 3). The account which he gives of these he received from a sailor named Euphemus. This man, upon a voyage to Italy, was driven by a storm into the Atlantic Ocean, and was obliged to anchor off a group of islands known to the sailors by the name of the Islands of Satyrs. These were inhabited by men with tails, some of whom wanted to come on board

the ship, but the sailors would not allow them; and as they knew
it was some women they had in the ship whom they wanted, in
order to satisfy them they gave them a barbarian woman that
they had on board, whom they used not only in the natural way,
but in every other way possible. They had tails, he said, not
much less than the tails of horses, but they made no use of speech.

The early European mariners to the East Indies speak continually of men with tails. Koepling relates that he had actually
seen them in the Nicobar Islands.

Barchewitz, a German traveler, in the sixth chapter of his voyages, gives an account of a tailed girl whom he saw in the Mo-
luccas.

Hesse, who went to Sumatra in 1680, describes a woman with
a short tail like-a goat in the island of Formosa.

Strauss, a Dutchman, who visited Formosa in 1650, describes a
native with a tail a foot long and covered with hair, whom he saw
burnt alive for murder. He concludes his description with these
words: *"That this man had a tail I saw as distinctly as I saw that
he had a head."*

Gemelli Carreri and Le Gentil mention similar cases in the Philippines, especially in the island of Mindeiro, on hearsay evidence.

Falk and Rytschkow relate that such *kuïrukli*, or tailed people,
are to be found only in Turkestan, and that this caudal prolongation is very slight.

Captain Samuel Turner, in his embassy to Thibet, 1806, gives
the following passage in his interview with the Daïb Raja:

"He told me of wonders for which I claim no other credit than
that of repeating with fidelity the story of my author. In the
same range of mountains north of Assam, he informed me that
there was a species of human beings with short straight tails,
which, according to report, were extremely inconvenient to them,
as they were inflexible; in consequence of which, they were
obliged to dig holes in the ground before they could attempt to
sit down."

Purchas, writing of the Philippine Islands, says, "Lambri, the
next kingdom, hath in it some men with tayles like dogges, a
span long." And of Sumatra: "They say that there are certain
people there called *Daragui Dara*, which have tayles like to
sheepe."

The great Harvey also published an account which he had received from a surgeon lately returned from the East Indies, and

whom he knew to be a man of strict veracity. This surgeon related that a tailed race existed in the island of Borneo, and that he had himself seen a girl who had a thick fleshy tail a span long: *intra clunes reflexa, quæ anum et pudenda operiebat, usque adeo velari ea loca Natura voluit.*

It is only lately that we have heard of tailed men in Africa. On the Egyptian monuments, it is true, the negroes are frequently represented with tails, which our best authorities have always regarded as caricatures. It is very probable, however, that such caricatures, if they are nothing more, had been suggested by such accounts of an interior tribe as those which follow.

M. de Castelnau is well known to men of science. He was selected as chief of the expedition sent out by the French government to explore the central parts of South America. He crossed the continent from Rio de Janeiro to Lima, returning by the Amazon to Pera in the years 1843–47.

M. de Castelnau having found at Bahia a great number of intelligent negro slaves, many of whom could read and write Arabic, and who were acquainted with the interior of Central Africa, was induced to examine them for the purpose of acquiring geographical information respecting these unknown regions.

One of these slaves, Mahammah, was remarkable for his intelligence, and had made extensive journeys. As a naturalist, M. de Castelnau could form a correct judgment of the truth of his descriptions, and had always found him careful and exact; till one day he spoke of the Niam-Niams, or tailed men, whom he declared that he had seen. In spite of M. de Castelnau's incredulity, he maintained the truth of his assertions, entered into minute details, and brought a dozen negroes from Soudan who also pretended that they had seen these tailed men. M. de Castelnau attached little importance to these statements till his return to France, when he learned that another traveler had heard similar stories in Arabia, and had even succeeded (it was said) in seeing a tailed man. M. de Castelnau therefore determined to publish the results of his researches, without asserting the reality of a fact which appears to be in opposition to the principles of zoology.

EVIDENCE OF MAHAMMAH.

"Mahammah served in an expedition which the Sultan of Kano sent against the Niam-Niams. The Haoussa army was mostly composed of cavalry. They bivouacked nine nights in

dense forests, through which they had frequently to cut a road for
their horses, and in which they did not see a human being. On
leaving the forest they climbed high mountains, and a few days
afterward discovered a group of the wild Niam-Niams. These
people were asleep in the sun; the Haoussas crept softly up to
them and killed them all. They had tails about forty *centimètres*
in length, and from two to three in diameter. This organ is without hair. Among the corpses were those of women formed in
the same manner; they were all quite naked. The following
days they met several other bands of the same kind of people:
some were eating human flesh, and the heads of three men were
still roasting at the fire, suspended on sticks stuck in the ground.
Mahammah was in the vanguard, and saw many of these people
killed; he examined the bodies, measured the tails, and does not
understand how their existence can be doubted.

"These Niam-Niams live in the holes of rocks, but some of
them build miserable huts of straw. The Haoussas were frequently attacked by these people, and killed great numbers of
them; they are of a deep black color, and their teeth are filed;
they are not tattooed; they make fire by means of a stone which
they find in their country. They used clubs, arrows, and asse-
gais. In battle they utter savage cries. They cultivate rice,
maize, and some other fruits and grains unknown to the Haoussas; they are fine men, and their hair is woolly.

"The chief of the Niam-Niams asked for quarter, but the King
of Kano killed all they found, *because they had tails*, and because
he supposed that nobody would buy them as slaves. They had
little oxen without horns, and large sheep and goats; their country is rocky and mountainous: the name of Niam-Niams is also
given to another cannibal tribe, but which have no tails. The
men go naked also, but the women wear a leaf before the waist.

"Adam, from Haoussa, had heard of the tailed men, but had
never seen them. Karo, from Bernou, described the Niam-Niams
as wearing a piece of wood in the lobe of the ear, and their wom-
en as wearing it in the lip. He said that they were cannibals.
Mammaron, from Bernou, had heard of tailed men inhabiting the
mountains, but had not seen them. So Allah, from the country
of Adamah, had seen children brought as curiosities from the
country of the Niam-Niams. They had tails; he had seen and
touched them. They were about as long and as big as his finger;
and the children might be eight or ten years old.

"Mahammad, from Haoussa, had left his country fifty years before. New-comers had told him that since his departure a new race of tailed savages had been discovered in the mountains to the south.

"Griss, from Haoussa, had witnessed the cannibalism of the Niam-Niams, but had not seen those with tails, although he had heard of them.

"Neidassara, from Haoussa, had served against the Niam-Niams, and had killed several. They had tails. When children were born they had tails about two inches long. He had seen a man who had one about seventy *centimètres* in length. Generally they were about eighteen inches long, and an inch and a half in diameter. These people are like negroes in other respects. They are cannibals. The tail has no movement; and they have seats to sit down, in which a hole has been pierced for the tail to pass through. Neidassara made this campaign under the command of the Sultan of Kano in person. The expedition brought back three Niam-Niams as prisoners to Kano. They excited great curiosity, but the sultan ordered them to be clothed. It was the first time that any of their lives had been spared."

I make no comment on this evidence, abstracted from *Renseignements sur l'Afrique Centrale, et sur une Nation d'hommes à queue, par Francis de Castelnau;* but refer the reader to that work for geographical information which appears to be valuable, but for which I can find no space here. I will only add the rumors, and in one case the trustworthy evidence, which I heard during my visit to Western Africa.

The natives of Equatorial Africa not only assert the existence of a tailed people, but of a hoofed or cloven-footed race. Captain Lawlin, who had traded during twenty years in the Camma country, believed that such creatures existed in the interior. When Mr. Mackey first visited the Fans, they crowded round him to look at his boots; for at first they believed that he belonged to the hoofed tribe of which they had heard so often, and which they said inhabited a country to the northeast of them.

Mr. Sparrhawk, an American trader who was well acquainted with the Congo, said that he had frequently been told of a tailed people living in the interior. He had spoken about it to a native who had traveled a considerable distance in the interior, and who was called the king of the slave-dealers. He answered, with some reluctance, that of course he knew that he (Sparrhawk) only wished to laugh at him.   But such people did exist; and as the slave-dealers always refused to buy them, they had sometimes been brought down to the markets with their tails cut off as close as possible, but with the stumps visible.

When I was at Ngumbi, Etia told me of a people in the interior who went with their heels forward and their toes backward, like the ὀπποδοδακλυλοι of the ancients, which were said to inhabit India, and like those of whom Humboldt heard in South America.

He also told me of a people that had feet like a deer, and assured me that he had himself seen one of them, who was on a visit from his own country, which was far away, and he treated with great reverence, because it was thought that his race was under the protection of the spirits.   This hoofed man was very short, but like a negro in all other respects, and had a language of his own.   I was struck with the indifferent tone with which Etia gave me this account: there was none of that warmth of voice and gesture which usually accompanies native exaggeration.   I asked him if he did not think it very wonderful that such a being should exist.   He said that he did not think it more wonderful than white men.   I told him, laughing, that I did not believe that he had seen such a man as that.   He answered, laconically, that when he had told the Bush-people he had seen white men they would not believe him.

Such evidence as that of negroes and of old voyagers it may be easy enough to reject.   But I was told by the captain of a trader, and, as far as I could judge, a most trustworthy man, that he had seen a woman at Masarado, near Cape Palmas, who had a tail. He described it as short, and without any hair—apparently a prolongation of the spine.   She spoke a language; and the Coast natives said that she came from the Bush, where there was a tribe of them.   This captain's name, I believe, was Neill; he was an *employé* of the house of King and Co., at Bristol.   I must own that I find it very difficult to reject the testimony of a person who gave it to me in so exact and moderate a manner.   Finally, a *sous-officier*, whom I met in Senegal, told me, without my having mentioned the subject, that two of his comrades in Algeria, having made an exploration into the interior, had also seen a people having tails short and smooth, as already described.

Whether such a race exist or not is of no importance in comparative anthropology.   It is simply a question of pathology.

This tail appears to be merely the external prolongation of the vertebral column, which in every individual, male or female, forms a tail of from two to three inches long. We are, therefore, tailed animals. These Niam-Niams and Philippine Islanders are animals with a fuller caudal development, that is all.

This tail is an organic peculiarity, which has been perpetuated by hereditary transmission. That children have been born with tails is a recognized fact in pathology, and instances have been quoted by Aldrovandus, Schenckius, and others. It is also well known that monstrosities can be perpetuated; for what, after all, is a monstrosity but that which in the lower kingdoms is termed a variety? and varieties can form a race. In 1731 the porcupine man was brought before the notice of the Royal Society. That monstrosity has been perpetuated; for the porcupine family is existing in its third generation. Similar cases might be instanced of six-fingered families. It will easily be understood that, in Europe, intermarriage with others would gradually extinguish such a character; but in a savage community, such a brood of monsters would be exiled, and breeding in-and-in would procreate a race.

There are, perhaps, few who know that a tribe of tailed men once existed in Kent, and became so notorious in Europe that it was at one time popularly believed that the whole nation were *homines caudati*.

There is an account of them in Bulwer's " Man Transformed, or the Artificiall Changeling:" a very curious old work; the passage I will quote at length :

" When Augustine the monke, being sent by Gregory the Great, came to preach the Gospell unto the English nation at Rochester, the vulgar, in derision of the Holy man, pin'd fishe's tails upon his garment, or, as some say, threw them at him ; whereupon Augustine prayed to God that their children might be borne with Tailes, and it pleased God to confirme his Doctrine by inflicting this punishment upon the Posterity of that incredulous people; so that these Kentish Long-tails proceeded not from the influence of Heaven, but from a miracle. And although *Antonius Neirembergensis* thinks that this punishment endured but for a time, and that this Miracle is now ceased, yet I am informed by an ingenious and honest Gentleman of good worth, who professed that he had read in some of our Chronicles, or other author whose name he could not very well remember, that there is at this day

(1653) a Family in Kent who have to Surname the name of a
village very neare Rochester, whereof all that are descended have
a Taile, insomuch that you may know any one to be rightly descended of that Family by having a Taile; yet I must suspect
some failing in my friend's memory, because I find in Debrio his
disquisition of Magick, that the originall of the Kentish Long-
tailes was after this manner. 'Thomas Becket, Arch-Bishop of
Canterbury, being in disgrace with Henry the Second, and riding
through Stroud, near Rochester, the inhabitants, to put an affront
upon him, cut off his Horse's Taile, which ever since was entailed
upon them, insomuch as you may know a man of Stroud by his
long Taile.' And to make it a little more credible, that the Rump-
bone among bruitish and strong-dockt nations doth often sprout
out with such an excrescence or beastly emanation, I am informed
by an honest young man of Captaine Morris's company, in Lieu-
tenant-Generall Ireton's Regiment, that at Cashell, in the county
of Tipperary, in the province of Munster, in Carrick Patrick
Church, seated on a hill or rock, stormed by the Lord Trichequine,
and where there were neare seven hundred put to the sword, and
none saved but the Mayor's wife and his Son, there were found
among the slaine of the Irish, when they were stripped, divers
that had Tailes near a quarter of a yard long; the Relator, being
very diffident of the truth of this story, after enquiry was ensured
of the certainty thereof by forty Souldiers, that testified upon their
oath that they were eye-witnesses, being present at the action. It
is reported, also, that in Spain there is another such tailed nation."

CHAPTER XXXIV.

FEATURES OF AFRICA.

The Mother and her Children.—Central Plateau after Buffon, Lacépède, and Ritter.
—Description of the Western Wall.—The Lowlands of Western Africa.

THERE is a woman whose features, in expression, are sad and
noble, but which have been degraded, distorted, and rendered repulsive by disease; whose breath is perfumed by rich spices and
by fragrant gums, yet through all steals the stench of the black
mud of the mangroves and the miasma of the swamps; whose lap
is filled with gold, but beneath lies a black snake, watchful and
concealed; from whose breasts stream milk and honey, mingled
with poison and with blood; whose head lies dead and cold, and
yet is alive.   In her horrible womb heave strange and monstrous
embryos.   Swarming round her are thousands of her children,
whose hideousness inspires disgust, their misery compassion.

She kisses them upon the lips, and with her own breath she
strikes them corpses by her side.   She feeds them at her breasts,
and from her own breasts they are poisoned, and they die.   She
offers them the treasures of her lap, and as each hand is put forth
the black snake bites it with his fatal fangs.

Thus, for ages and ages, this woman has continued to bring forth
her children, and to kill them as she attempts to nourish them.

Look at the map of Africa.   Does it not resemble a woman
with a huge burden on her back, and with her face turned toward
America?

"Ethiopia is stretching out her hands unto God?"

The redemption of Africa shall be the great work of this generation.

I will now attempt to sketch her features; to analyze the poison which flows from her lips and from her breasts; to write the
history of her unhappy offspring; to examine their origin, their
characters, and capabilities; and, finally, to show how they may
be taught to pour an elixir of life into their mother's veins; to
suck the poison from her system; to kill the reptile in her lap;

to reanimate the heart which lies dead and cold; and to restore the decaying frame to immortal youth and beauty.

Africa, the cradle of civilization, is now the last refuge of romance. The eyes of the world are turned upon its central regions —a white blot on the page of science—the *terra incognita* of this age of steam.

It is a continent within a continent. White men have never crossed its wide expanse. Their footprints and their skeletons are scattered round its skirts.

It was here that the pagan fabulists and the Christian fathers believed the terrestrial paradise to exist. The imagination of man is ever prone to clothe the distant with beauty, and to people the unknown with visions which in this little planet can never be realized. Even men of science can build their cities in the sun; latitudes and longitudes can afford their poetry; and figures be made to flatter. What hypothesis can be more seductive than that the heart of this poisonous Africa is an elevated table-land, where the climate is as pure as that of Quito, or of the Happy Valley of Cashmere? That here, encircled on all sides by cruel and treacherous savages, dwell a primitive and innocent race, skilled in those arts which have perished from the outer world, and enjoying the pure pleasures of the Golden Age?

It is now established as a fact in science that Central Africa consists of an elevated table-land. This discovery, like all others, was made by degrees. It was Buffon who gave the leading idea. He believed that Central Africa contained great longitudinal chains of mountains, and conjectured their general course and elevation in accordance with his theory of the earth.

Lacépède, accepting this idea, formed these chains of mountains into a grand plateau, of which he supposed the interior of Africa to consist. He ventured even to lay down its precise limits. It extended, he said, from the 20th degree of southern latitude to the 10th degree on this side of the equator; its length being upward of 660 leagues, or equal to the breadth of Europe from the port of Brest to the nearest land in Asia; it contained 132,000 square leagues; it was supported by numerous ranges of hills, situated nearly in the direction of the axis of the plateau, which, being inclined toward the west, formed, with the equator, an angle of nearly 60 degrees; the outline of its configuration is traced by the great waters which descended from it on every side. In some parts it approached the sea-coast, in others its boundaries were surrounded by vast deserts of sand; these being so situated that the east wind reached them after crossing the burning plains of Ajan and Zanzibar, and converted them into a perfect sea of fire.

Regarding the formation of the plateau, I will quote the words of this distinguished geographer (Mémoire sur le Grand Plateau de l'Intérieure de l'Afrique. Annales du Mus. d'Hist. Naturelle, tome vi. Par Lacépède).

"Nous ne devons pas considérer ce grand plateau comme une élévation régulière, comme une convexité plus ou moins arrondie, comme une sorte de plaine immense exhaussée au dessus des contrées qui l'entourent. Sa largeur, sa longueur, et le nombre des rivières qui en découlent, et qui ne doivent s'en échapper que par les vallées latérales plus ou moins larges et plus ou moins profondes, doivent vous faire croire que ce plateau est composé d'un système de montagnes."

Ritter, the greatest of German geographers, improved upon Lacépède as Lacépède had improved upon Buffon. He proved that the dimensions of the plateau, as given by Lacépède, were incorrect, and disapproved of his arrangement of the mountains.

According to Ritter, all Africa, from the Cape of Good Hope to the 10th degree of north latitude, is one continuous and immense plateau, which is formed by a succession of terraces rising one above another. This table-land is traversed by no great river. The Nile, the Niger, and the Congo are mere rivulets compared with the immense masses of water which descend from the steppes of Central Asia. He therefore supposed that the heights of the central region contain great lakes which absorb the running waters, a supposition which late explorations have partially proved to be correct.*

Central Africa, therefore, may be said to stand raised upon mountains, which present their sides, more or less lofty, more or less irregular, to the north, the south, the east, and the west.

I will attempt to describe the western wall, under almost the whole length of which I have passed, and the first terrace of which I have ascended.

* About seven years ago Sir Roderick Murchison put forward as his own this theory, which belongs to the last generation. I prefer to believe that this is one of those strange coincidences which have so frequently occurred in the history of science, and that the President of the Geographical Society is not acquainted with the works of Buffon, Lacépède, and Ritter, rather than suppose that he could be guilty of a gross and willful plagiarism.

The western side of the plateau rises to its greatest height at the Cameroons Mountain. This mountain is 15,000 feet high, and appears to be a spur thrown out from the longitudinal chain. It is an almost generally received opinion that at this point Africa is divided by a chain of mountains which have been called the Mountains of the Moon. Should this be the case, the central plateau would be made double, a mountainous partition being interposed between. I have not, however, been able to find a single proof of the existence of such a chain. From inquiries which I made in the Muni and the Ncomo, it appears pretty certain that very high, possibly snow-covered mountains are found in those latitudes; but that they are continued across the continent is, I think, extremely improbable.

From the Cameroons southward the terraced wall sinks lower and lower, and recedes gradually from the coast. In Gaboon the first terrace is less elevated than in the Muni; in the Fernand Vaz than in the Gaboon. In Angola it has dwindled down to a low range of hills, but toward Benguela it rises and approaches the coast. At a very short distance from the sea one can ascend the second terrace, where, at the Portuguese station Kakonda, the climate is European; and on the third terrace ice is said to form, whence probably this chain derived its appellation of *Serras frios*, the cold mountains.

The first and second equatorial terraces are clothed with virgin forest. They are extremely irregular in their formation, throwing out spurs in all directions; but in all the rivers which I ascended I observed that we were gradually mounting higher and higher above the level of the sea. In my incursion to the Falls of the Ncomo, the last mountain which I saw was higher than any of those which we had passed.

From these terraces pour down a vast number of streams, which unite into rivers; and between the ranges are longitudinal valleys of swamps, or of forests with bottoms of black mud.

Having carefully questioned the natives of the Ncomo respecting the country to the northeast, its rivers, its mountains, and its marshes, I am inclined to believe that a large lake exists in that direction, and that it is thence the northern branch of the Congo flows; and it is worth remarking that Tuchey's own observations led him to embrace that opinion. "Combining my observations," he says, "with the information which I have been able to collect from natives, vague and trifling as it is, I can not help thinking that the Zaire will be found to issue from some large lake, or chain of lakes, considerably to the northward of the line."

This idea was suggested to Tuchey by the quiet and regular rise of the river, such as would be caused by the gradual overflowing of a lake; while the rise of the water in the Senegal, which proceeds from the pouring in of mountain torrents, is sudden and impetuous.

I have already observed that there is a submarine range, which runs parallel with the Sierra del Crystal from the Cameroons downward. Fernando Po, Principe, San Thomé, and Annobome are the four mountains which protrude above the waters. Like the Sierra del Crystal, they dwindle as they run southward, and, like that range, they are covered with dense forest, and display volcanic characters.

The mountain wall, on leaving the Cameroons, is only found at some distance inland, a circumstance which renders the Niger navigable to a great distance. Toward Ashantee and Sierra Leone it approaches the coast, as is proved by the small size of the rivers, and then again winding inland, permits the Gambia and the Senegal to flow as large and useful streams from the far interior.

Thus this wall, or succession of walls, runs parallel with the sea along the whole western side of the continent. Between the mountains and the sea lie the lowlands of Western Africa.

These lowlands are watered by an incredible number of rivers, which descend from the mountain wall, and which, crossing and intersecting one another—their courses determined by the surface of the soil, and sometimes swallowed up by lakes—form a perfect labyrinth of streams, and constitute a water-system which can not be paralleled in the world.

It is this surfeit of water which renders the West Coast of Africa, from the Senegal on the north to Benguela on the south, the plague-spot of the world.

CHAPTER XXXV.

MALARIA.

Rains, Dew, and Winds malarious.—Human Infection.—Nature of Malaria.—Natural History of Fever.—Siestas and Stimulants.

THE region of Senegambia lies near the desert of Sahara. The Harmattan purifies its atmosphere, and it is only during the four months of rain that the country can be considered febrile. But on the southern bank of the Casemanche the scenery begins to change; the stunted jungles rise into timber; the arid plains become clothed with rich and tropical, but also dangerous luxuriance. In Senegambia malarious fever is an annual visitor; from the south of the Casemanche to the province of Benguela it is a resident. Between those two points there is not a colony on the sea-board of Western Africa which is free from it—not a single spot which might serve as a sanatorium.

The *rains* which fall in Senegambia have a peculiar and deadly character, as if the clouds had been supplied from poisonous swamps. Their action upon neutral substances and human beings is as immediate as it is severe. In forty-eight hours the leather of shoes will become mouldy and rotten. In all the houses at Bathurst, fires are kept burning to preserve the furniture from being mildewed.

Mungo Park writes: "The rain had not commenced three minutes before many of the soldiers were affected with vomiting; others fell asleep, and seemed as if intoxicated. I felt a strong inclination to sleep during the storm, and, as soon as it was over, I fell asleep on the wet ground, although I used every exertion to keep myself awake. Twelve of the soldiers were ill the next day." In the rainy season at Sierra Leone the horses are seized with a swelling of the legs, which in almost all cases results in death.

There can be no doubt, therefore, that malaria is contained in rain, which the natives allege to be pernicious if it falls on the naked skin. But the rains of Equatorial Africa do not appear to possess this character, at least in so mortal a degree. It is also worthy of remark that while in Senegambia two inches of rain will fall in an hour, that is a large quantity for a night's rain in the Gaboon.

The *dews* are universally considered dangerous in Western Africa, as in all tropical and intertropical countries. Des Marchais asserts that the dews which fall on deck before sunrise have been observed to produce immediately small insects resembling lizards, toads, and serpents.

There are *winds* in certain localities, which, flowing from a particular quarter, are well known to residents to be the carriers of malaria and the precursors of disease.

The commencement of the rainy season, when the rains, unable to penetrate the ground hardened by the sun, form puddles and putrefy, and the commencement of the dry season, when the sun is exhaling the noxious vapors from the soil, are the two most unhealthy periods of the year.

In some parts of the world malaria is engendered by unusual drought, but in the coast-lands of Western Africa the amount of malaria may be estimated by the amount of moisture.

It has been proved that malaria perishes at sea about three miles distant from the shore. In the island of San Nicolão, one of the group of the Cape de Verds, at a certain season of the year, owing to a very simple cause, viz., the stagnation of rain-water in the town, fever annually scourges the inhabitants. The better classes ascend the mountains, and are very careful not to visit the town after dusk. A Portuguese doctor informed me that, at a time when the fever was killing immense numbers of people in the town, not a case of fever occurred in the mountains; and it was found that houses on the mountain-side, about three quarters of a mile distant from the town, and possessing seven degrees lower temperature (about 65°), were quite exempt from the disease, excepting a few cases of infection; for he assured me, as did also Mr. Miller, our consul at St. Vincent's, that malarious fever is infectious. Both of them gave me a number of instances in which persons from the town had visited persons in the mountain, and had given them the fever.

All who have written on the malarious fever of Africa have denied that it is infectious. But it is not, I think, unreasonable that the breath of an infected person should possess the same qualities as the exhalations of the marsh by which he was infected. And it can easily be understood that, though those who live with him in a malarious atmosphere might breathe it with impunity, those who have been habituated to a purer air would be liable to receive disease.

Without presuming to make any assertion upon this subject, except that the physician from whom I received this information had studied at London and Paris, and had practiced at the latter city, and that the instances which he gave were of a remarkable character, I would suggest to our naval surgeons the propriety of examining into this question, since I have certainly met with cases of malarious fever in persons who had lived on board their vessel, and had never set their feet for a moment upon the shore.

Rains, dews, winds blowing from malarious localities, marsh exhalations, and possibly the human breath, may therefore be considered as the proximate causes of fever.

Those of a nervous temperament, of light hair, and of fair complexion, of strumous habits, or a plethoric disposition, are the most liable to suffer from fever. There are also many predisposing causes, such as sedentary habits, the reaction which follows drunkenness or licentious indulgence; in females, the condition of system attendant upon the menstrual flux; a prior attack of fever, such not being a protection, but an initiation; a change of place, even to one more salubrious; and any kind of mental excitement or physical privation.

The fever usually makes its appearance at night, and this circumstance has served as the basis of many curious theories. But it ceases to be a mystery if it is true that our systems are subject to a fever every night. This *evening-fever*, as it is called, is said to be caused partly by the accession of new chyle to the blood, partly by the absence of the sun, and by that alteration in the atmosphere which is connected with it.

It comes on at the close of day, and, like all simple fevers, has its excitement, its lassitude, and its crisis by perspiration, sensible or insensible. This takes place at midnight.

To speak from my own experience, I have often remarked that, in Africa, as the sun was setting, a complete revolution has taken place in my system. From a state of the heaviest lassitude, I have become active and restless, and have experienced an indescribable sensation, as if my brain were bursting out of bonds. This is the reason that nervous people can study better at night; and it is for this reason also that it is so dangerous to avoid sleep, and prolong this fever by the use of stimulants.

Such are the principal proximate and predisposing causes of
fever. But what is the real cause of fever? and what are we to
call the fever itself?

The real cause of fever is *malaria*. Having studied all the authorities upon this subject from Lancisi downward, I find that
nothing whatever is known of the nature of this poison, of its constitution, or of the circumstances under which it is engendered.
This is proved by the confessions of the wise, and by the contra-
dictions of the foolish writers on the subject.

I will therefore spare the reader the immense mass of evidence
which I have collected upon this topic, since I can cite it to no
purpose. I will simply observe that it is for chemistry to unveil
these mysteries of the air; at present it would be idle to guess at
the origin of a principle, the very properties of which we are un-
acquainted with.

Passing by this question, therefore, I shall write in a few words
the natural history of fever, its effects upon the human system,
and the method by which it should be treated.

Let us suppose that malaria consists of minute and invisible
particles of poison, gaseous or animal. These are floating in the
atmosphere, stagnant in the soil, and present in water and in food.
As one breathes, eats, and drinks, this poison enters the system
and mingles with the blood.

There it goes through a process which is technically called In-
cubation, and which may be compared to the development of a
human embryo.

A few minute particles, the essence of life and health, enter a
foreign system; there this essence germinates, expands, and solidi-
fies. As it grows larger and larger, it occasions trouble to the
system which contains it; it causes headaches, morbid fancies,
nausea, and a numberless variety of ills and pains. Finally, it becomes enormous; the health of the system is imperiled; if it remains, it will destroy life; it must be expelled; Nature makes a
severe effort; the system suffers a terrible shock, and is relieved
of its burden.

So these other particles—the essence of disease and death—enter a foreign system; there, too, the evil essence germinates and
expands; there, too, it troubles the system, causing symptoms by
no means unlike those described above. And, in the same manner, Nature makes an effort to relieve the system of that which
would destroy it if it remained.

Now it is a fact which no one is likely to dispute, that the more robust a mother is, and the better the tone in which she has preserved her system, the less she suffers during labor. Thus women in the lower classes have easier deliveries than town ladies, some of whom even die under these natural paroxysms; while among savages, a woman gives birth to her child, cleanses herself, and frequently continues her household work within the same hour.

In order, therefore, that the system may be the more easily and safely delivered of malaria, it should be preserved in a state of vigor; and it is as absurd to lower its strength by bleeding or by violently purging as it would be to use that treatment in cases of parturition. Nature should either be left entirely alone, or should be assisted with a tonic treatment.

Now this malaria or poisonous essence has a very curious property. It is that of reproduction. In most cases it is not entirely expelled from the system. The dregs remain; and these dregs germinate, expanding into a troublesome body, which is again expelled. This is repeated till Nature, by some extraordinary effort, rids the system of the whole; or till, the organs growing impaired, the poison takes up a permanent abode, is thrown off in but small quantities at intervals, and finally triumphs and kills.

In the first case the disease may be termed acute intermittent; in the second case it is termed chronic intermittent.

This latter state is frequent among the aged, whose systems have naturally become debilitated. And in Africa it frequently happens that, owing to the quantity of poison which enters the system, Nature is compelled to tax the organs beyond their due limits. A premature old age sets in; the intervals between her efforts become less and less frequent, till at length the system, being thoroughly exhausted, passes peacefully into death, much in the same manner as in childbirth. In fact, the death in malarious fever (that is to say, when unattended with any latent disease, for then it assumes quite a different character) is simply a death of exhaustion, and in such cases it is needless to observe that a lowering treatment will only hasten dissolution.

The reader will see clearly enough that we want a medicine to destroy the poison as it enters the system, procuring abortion, so to speak, or, at all events, to destroy the dregs which remain after the embryo itself has been ejected.

This medicine we possess; and it is by Peruvian bark, or rather by its principle, the sulphate of quinine, that Western Africa can be rendered habitable.

This quinine is a most powerful drug, and those who use it should always bear this in mind. Its very power is a proof that it is not to be trifled with. If taken to excess, it causes nausea, violent headaches, deafness,* and racks the nerves to pieces: it is always productive of constipation.

When quinquina was first introduced into England, in the days of Sydenham, it was universally denounced, two citizens having died under its injudicious and excessive use. The traveler who doctors himself should bear in mind that it is not to be taken as if it were sugar, as many travelers appear to suppose.

There are many who take a small quantity of quinine as a prophylactic; and if one is going for a short time only into a malarious locality, it is an excellent plan, as the poison is thereby prevented from accumulating in the system.

But when one resides, as one is forced to do on the West African sea-board, in the constant presence of malaria for months, perhaps years together, the system would doubtless become blunted to quinine, and the influence of the drug itself would be by no means salutary.

If the traveler (I write this for travelers in language which I think they will understand) finds a fever coming on, he had better leave Nature alone, as I have done myself, pile blankets upon him, and drink cold water whenever he feels thirsty. Acid drinks are not, I think, to be recommended.

The process by which Nature will deliver him of malaria may be divided into four stages.

In the stage of *Preparation* he will be warned by various signs of his approaching fever-parturition. Loss of appetite; sleeplessness; a nauseous taste in his mouth, especially on rising; urine copious and pale; incapacity for close thought; the mind soon wearied by study, while the imagination becomes unusually active; a desire to be employed without the power to carry it out, and an indefinable apprehension of coming danger.

This stage, which usually lasts from twelve to forty-eight hours, is succeeded by the stage of *Invasion.* Yawning and stretching, followed by cold, which, first felt in the hands and feet, passes to the spine and creeps over the whole body. Then dizziness, at-

---

* The deafness from quinine can be distinguished from the deafness caused by severe fever. In the former case the ears feel as if they were plugged with cotton.

tended sometimes with a kind of paralysis, or with a little gentle delirium. Pains in various parts of the body, chiefly in the back; face pale; skin shriveled; nose apparently more pointed than usual; lips purple; eyes dull and filmy. This will usually last two hours.

In the stage of *Reaction* the chill goes off, and during six hours or so, heat, thirst, and nausea. The urine changes to brown; in bad cases, to red or black.

And finally comes the blessed stage of *dissolution*—not of the patient, but of the embryo. It is attended with an abatement of all pains, and with a perspiration which is sometimes sudden and profuse, sometimes a mere moisture.

If quinine is given during this operation, it is liable to have an injurious effect by confining within the system the poison which it is unable to destroy. But when the paroxysms are past, quinine should be given in small and gradual doses. If, in spite of this medicine, the fever should return, it will of course be a proof that sufficient was not given to destroy the germ of the disease; another attack must be patiently suffered, and the quinine again administered.

Since disease is, after all, the best medical tutor, I may perhaps be allowed to quote my own febrile experiences, and to offer a few hints to future travelers.

The resident in Western Africa commits two grand hygienic errors. The first consists in the use of the siesta, the second in that of certain stimulants.

It is well known that a depraved condition of the air will cause drowsiness. This is especially the case after reading or writing. I have always found that when I have combated this feeling, and have taken a brisk walk, I have been infinitely more refreshed and rested than when I have yielded to it. After this siesta, of which one reads so much in romances and in poetry, one wakes up with a nauseous feeling in one's mouth; with one's eyes weak and ill able to bear the light; and with one's limbs cramped and aching. Such, at least, has always been its effect upon myself. Intelligent natives, with whom I have spoken upon the subject, have expressed a similar opinion; and the Fans have a proverb, " Day-sleep maketh the eyes sore."

I have already said sufficient of the unhappy debauchees upon the Coast. I shall now endeavor to contest that belief which, strange to say, is almost universal among traders and military

men, that brandy taken frequently and in small quantities is necessary for the preservation of health in Africa. I do not deny
that brandy, used continually as a medicine, has the power of
stifling fever. The common Coast-phrase of being "a bottle of
brandy ahead of the fever" is not an incorrect one; and if a man
has a strong constitution, he may continue this practice for two,
or, in some cases, for three years. He then breaks down with *delirium tremens*, or some horrible disease of the liver. The poison
which has so long been smouldering in his system bursts into life
and fury; his debilitated system struggles faintly and vainly to
throw it off; in an incredibly short space of time it seizes and an-
nihilates his vital parts. Yesterday he was drinking his brandy
and soda, and advising neophytes to take that kind of medicine.
To-day he is a corpse.

This climate has always proved more fatal to our nation than
to the Dutch, the French, or the Portuguese. It is on account of
our debauchery.

Our fathers and grandfathers know that in their young days
the Indian climate possessed the same ill fame as the West African climate bears now. That was the age in which officers drank
brandy pawnee to preserve their health—an age which has happily passed away. Sir Emerson Tennent, in his great work on
Ceylon, disapproves of brandy; "the abuse of which, at former
periods, is commemorated in the records of those fearful disorders
of the liver, derangements of the brain, exhausting fevers, and
visceral diseases which characterize the medical annals of earlier
times."

I am prompted by my own unhappy experiences to write thus
feelingly upon the subject, and I am not ashamed to print my
own follies, since it may prove the best means of deterring others
from a similar excess. During the five months which I spent in
Equatorial Africa, my only repose was that of changing physical
for mental labors. I worked unremittingly, studying works on
language and science, ascended four different rivers, and traveled,
in one direction and in another, at least a thousand miles in open
boat or canoe, exposed during most of the time to heavy rains. I
took no stimulants excepting tea, and enjoyed remarkable health,
at least for Africa. Every month I suffered from a fever-fit, but
never in one case did it confine me to my bed for an hour.

But during my trip into Angola I drank brandy, and in six
weeks' time I had a violent fever, which compelled me to leave

that part of Africa.   In Senegambia, again, I drank too freely,
and though I had no fever, I soon acquired diseases that were
more stubborn and dangerous—yellow jaundice and rheumatism.

A meagre diet will have the same evil effects as too free a one.
The traveler must endeavor to discover the *aurea mediocritas*. Let
him be moderate without being abstinent; fearless, but not imprudent; and he will find that, though he can never enjoy that
elastic and buoyant health which is the blessing of a temperate
clime, he will run little risk of losing his life in Africa, or of afterward dying by the slow fire of permanent disease.

CHAPTER XXXVI.

THE NEGRO.

The true Negro.—African Types.—Degeneration of Animals in Africa.—Aborigines of Africa.—African Languages.—Religion, Manners, and Customs.—The Negress.—African Character.

MANY eminent men have asserted that the negro belongs to a distinct species; that is to say, that he is as widely separated from our own race as the wolf is separated from the dog, or the zebra from the horse.

They support their theory with the following arguments:

1. That the negro type presents physical and mental characters which mere conditions of climate, circumstance, and food are incapable of creating.

2. That the type is known to have existed in the earliest period of history.

3. And that, when transplanted to another soil, exposed to another climate, nourished with another food, it still retains its individuality.

Let us consider the characters of the true or typical negro. We find that his skin is very black, excepting the palms of the hands and the soles of the feet, which are of a dirty yellow. In them the coloring matter has been removed by friction; it can, however, be always distinguished in the deep lines of the hand. It appears to be most abundant on the knuckles, on the knee and elbow joints.

The skin is very thick, especially on the palms of the hands and the soles of the feet. Touch these, and they feel like wood. A negro will take up a live coal in his hand and light his pipe from it without suffering any pain. But with the exception of these parts, the skin of the negro is peculiarly smooth. It can only be compared to fine black velvet.

The hair of the typical negro is short and crisp, and closely resembles wool.

The forehead is low and compressed; the nose is flat; the lips thick and brutal; the mouth projecting, presents the appearance of a muzzle. As in the lower animals, the brain retreats to the back of the head, and the organ of gluttony becomes the character of the face.

The heel is flat and long; the ankle is only raised from 1¼ in. to 1½ in. above the ground. The toes are small, and, as in apes, the great toe is separated from the others by a wide space. The foot is frequently used by the negro as a hand. The natives of Equatorial Africa do not climb the trunks of trees as we do by "swarming," but by clasping them with their feet. The natives of the Gambia, when fishing, hold their line between the great toe and the next. When a Kru-man is sewing any thing, he holds his work between his toes. And the Wollof will frequently steal articles with their feet.

The virile member is much larger than is found in Europeans, excepting in those who are idiotic. It is one of the chief seats of color. When a negro child is born, it has a black ring round the virile member, a reddish mark on the nail, and another in the corner of the eye. These are also the last signs by which the descendant of a negro can be distinguished.

According to some writers, the same secretion forms the beard and propagates the human species. The negro has seldom any hair upon his face; it is never abundant; and he rarely has a great number of children. There is also a peculiarity in the negro's voice by which it can be distinguished. It is not unlike that of a eunuch.

The stature of the negro is stunted; the knees are bent; the calves weak; the upper part of the thigh is thin; the head large, and sunk between the shoulders; and the whole form angular and badly shaped.

The skull is extremely thick. If a negro wishes to break a thick stick, he does not break it across his knee as we do, but across his head. The power of the skull in resisting blows is something marvelous. When I was in the Senegal I saw a most remarkable case at the military hospital, St. Louis. A Wollof soldier in the French service had been shot at from a distance of fifteen yards. The ball struck the *os frontis*, and had flattened against it as if it had been a stone wall. I saw the man a fortnight afterward. He was convalescent; and, having compared the flattened bullet with the wound, I am able to vouch for the truth of this incident.

Besides these external characteristics, including a peculiar odor, by which the negro is said to be separated from other races, it has been discovered by Pruner-Bey, Gratiolet, Waitz, and other celebrated anatomists, that there exist internal differences which are equally significant: that the blood, bile, and, according to some, the semen, is different from that of Europeans; that the skeleton is heavier—the bones larger, whiter, and thicker; that the growth of the brain in the negro, as in the ape, is sooner arrested than in those of our race; that its convolutions are less numerous, and more massive; that its gray substance is of a darker color; that the brain itself has a smoky tint, and that the *pia mater* contains brown spots, which are never found in the brain of the European.

Therefore, in the muzzle-like extension of the jaws, in the manual application of the foot, and in the early cessation of brain-growth, the negro, speaking physically, approaches the ape.

In his flattened nose, elongated cranium, simplicity of cerebral convolution, rounded larynx, and less strongly marked curves of the vertebral column, the negro approaches the child; for all these features are found in the foetus or child of the Aryan race in its different periods of development.

And in the curvature of his arteries, in the flatness of his cornea, in the feebleness of his muscles, in his general lack of enthusiasm, and love of repose, the negro presents the characteristics of old age.

Thus it has been proved by measurements, by microscopes, by analyses, that the typical negro is something between a child, a dotard, and a beast.   I can not struggle against these sacred facts of science.*   I can not venture to dispute the degradation of the negro.   But I contend that it is only degradation; that it is the result of disease; that it is not characteristic of the African continent; and that it is confined to a small geographical area.

Although, in the tenth chapter of Genesis, the negro is not recognized as a distinct race—the descendants of Shem, Ham, and Japheth representing the Mongolians, Ethiopians, and Caucasians —yet we know that the Egyptians were acquainted with the negroes at a very early period.   Together with ivory, skins, and gold, they formed the tribute which Egypt received from Ethio-

---

* At the last meeting of the British Association, in the Section E, the president of the Anthropological Society ventured to quote them. His audience felt insulted when informed that they were more intellectual than the negro, and endeavored to prove the contrary by hisses!

pia. The type is plainly recorded on their old stone-books as early as the 20th dynasty, 1300 B. C. And those who glance through the works of Rossellini, Caylus, and Wilkinson may see faithful pictures of negroes dancing, clapping their hands, and beating their drums, precisely as they may be seen in Africa at the present day.

To those who follow the Mosaic chronology, this will be sufficient to establish the special creation of the negro. But, since geology has taught us the indefinite antiquity of man, it can only prove that the negroes are ancient in history. We must discover fossils if we wish to test their age in time.

Their historical antiquity, however, does much toward explaining the persistence of the type transplanted. During at least three thousand years, the negroes have been influenced by certain climatic conditions, *the results of which have been defined and strengthened by hereditary transmission.* Is it reasonable, then, to expect a complete reversion in three hundred?

We would, however, reckon upon finding certain modifications in the type transplanted, and in this, I think, we shall not be entirely disappointed.

But first I will remove the great stumbling-block of African ethnology. By defining the geography of the negro, I shall pave the way for the elucidation of that mystery which has perplexed the philosophers of all ages—the negro's place in nature.

Those who deny that the negro type has been produced by natural causes have alleged that there are two distinct races in Africa, the red and the black, and that they inhabit the same localities.

The reader will still bear in mind that a series of mountain terraces run along the whole length of Western Africa, and that between them and the sea are low and malarious swamps.

These mountains are inhabited by the true Africans, a red-skinned race. Nations of these, descending into the swamps, have become degraded in body and mind, and their type completely changed.

The negro forms an exceptional race in Africa; he inhabits that immense tract of marshy land which lies between the mountains and the sea from Senegal to Benguela, and the low lands of the eastern side in the same manner. He is found in the parts about Lake Tchad, in Sennaar, along the marshy banks of rivers and in several isolated spots besides.

But he is not found in the vast tracts which are occupied by the Berbers on the north, and the Bitshuanas of the south. He is not found in the high lands of Ethiopia, nor in those of the Soudan.

In Africa there are three grand races, as there may be said to be three grand geological divisions.

The Libyan stock inhabit the primitive and volcanic tracts. They have a tawny complexion, Caucasian features, and long black hair.

On the sandstones will be found an intermediate type. They are darker than their parents; they have short and very curly hair; their lips are thick; and their nostrils wide at the base.

And, finally, in the alluvia, one will find the negroes with a black skin, woolly hair, and prognathous development.

I do not mean to assert that light-colored tribes are never found in the alluvia, and that true negroes can never be met with in the dry plateaus. There is in Africa a continual movement toward the west. It is, therefore, common enough to see Fulas and Mandingoes inhabiting the low lands of Senegambia; and the light-colored Fans are beginning to occupy the banks of the Gaboon. In the same manner, a tribe of negroes migrating across the continent from the East Coast might be met with in a sandy desert of Central Africa.

That my theory is correct as applied to those parts of Africa which I have visited, my own experience has assured me; and I will quote passages from two authors, one almost the greatest of travelers, the other almost the most careful of compilers, to prove that the rule holds good in other parts of Africa.

"As we go westward," writes Livingstone, "we observe the light color predominating over the dark; and then, again, when we come within the influence of damp from the sea-air, we find the shade deepen into the general blackness of the Coast population."

And Prichard, in his "Natural History of Man," p. 629, writes: "If we trace the intervening countries between Egypt and Senegambia, and carefully note the physical qualities of the inhabitants, we shall have no difficulty in recognizing almost every degree or stage of deviation successively displayed, and showing a gradual transition from the characters of the Egyptian to those of the negro without any broadly-marked line of abrupt separation."

My assertion that the negro is as exceptional a race in Africa

C c

as the livid inhabitants of the fens in England or of the Pontine
Marshes in Italy, and that he inhabits, comparatively speaking, a
small geographical area, will excite great surprise. There is a
general delusion respecting the negro which is not difficult to explain. The whole Western Coast, and a great portion of the Eastern Coast, are inhabited by negroes. It is natural that traders
and Coast residents should accept them as types of the races of
the continent. The slaves that have been imported into the New
World were almost exclusively brought from these regions; and
I have always observed that slaves, even among negroes, present
a lower type than that of the surrounding population. These
also have been examined and written upon by naturalists as true
samples of the African.

I will now briefly describe and compare the physical characters
of the great tribes of Western Africa.

In no part of Africa do the red race and the black race come in
closer contact than in the country of the Senegal. On the left
bank is a dry and desert country. It is inhabited by the Moors
—a tawny race, with short wiry bodies, long tangled hair, a keen
and active expression of the face. On the right-hand bank, which
is swampy and fertile, are found the Wollof, inhabiting the country
of Djoloff, between the Senegal and the Gambia, near the coast.
These Wollof are tall, and well formed; of a deep black; with
thick negro lips, and woolly hair. There is but little prognathous
development, however, and, if their foreheads possess any characteristic, it is that of prominence. Mounting toward the high lands
of the interior one finds the Mandingoes and the Fulas. They
have aquiline noses rather broad about the base; woolly hair, but
more abundant than that of the Wollof; the lips rather thick;
the color varying from olive color to a very deep bronze. The
general complexion of the Mandingoes may be said to be black
mixed with yellow; and of the Fulas, red mixed with yellow.

On the banks of the Casemanche, near the coast, are two tribes
of typical negroes, the Felloops or Jolas, and the Balantis. It is
here, as I have already said, that luxuriant and malarious Africa
commences. It is here also that the debased negro type is first
displayed. These Felloops and Balantis are of short stature, ill
formed, with a well-marked prognathous development. The type
extends along the swampy coast to Sierra Leone. Here the
country rises, and the type rises with it. The natives whom one

meets in Freetown are tall and handsome, with intelligent faces. One of the *Vei* tribe, near Cape Mount, invented a written language, as was discovered by Lieutenant Forbes in 1849; and the Kru-men of Liberia, who resemble the Wollof, are Goliaths in stature and in strength. While none of them can be classed among typical negroes, some of them whom I have seen have aquiline noses and Caucasian heads.

The Fantis of the Gold Coast hold a middle place between the typical negroes and the Mandingoes. They are inferior to the Ashantees of the interior, who have brown complexions and longer hair. The natives of the Delta of the Niger are the most debased of all the African negroes; and, in the same manner, it is their country which of all the Coast regions is reported to be the most unhealthy. But Dr. Daniell states that when one leaves the low swamps for the sandstone country of the interior, the skin becomes fairer; black becomes brown, and brown yellow. The Bubis of Fernando Po inhabit a moist forest country. They are tall, slim, not well formed; have brutal features and woolly hair; but their complexion is less black than olive color.

At Botanga, between the Cameroons and the Gaboon, the coast is mountainous; the people are not black, nor prognathous; and I remember being struck by the form of their noses, which was very pointed, and gave their faces an ill-tempered expression.

In Equatorial Africa the Bush tribes are the most degraded. When a family of this class, that is to say, the Shekani or Bakělě, happen to be found on the sea-coast, as, for instance, between Gaboon and Cape Lopez, they present the characteristics of typical negroes. I have also met with typical negroes on the banks of the Mimi, Bapuku, and Gaboon rivers. In higher and healthier localities I have met with clans of the same tribes as these, presenting a lighter complexion, less prognathous development, and more facial intelligence.

The Fans which inhabit the mountain terraces are altogether of a different complexion from the sea-coast tribes. Their hair is longer; that of the women hangs down in long braids to their shoulders, while the men have tolerably long two-pointed beards. It would be impossible to find such long hair among the Coast tribes, even in a single instance.

In the low swampy land at the mouth of the Congo one meets with typical negroes; and there again, as one reaches a higher soil, one finds a different class of people.

The Angolese resemble the Fula. They are scarcely ever black. Their hands and feet are exquisitely small, and in every way they form a contrast with the slaves of the Portuguese, who, brought for the most part from the Congo, are brutal and debased.

I have divided Africa into three grand types, the Ethiopian, the intermediate, and the negro. In the same manner the negro may be divided into three sub-classes.

The bronze-colored class: gracefully formed, with effeminate features, small hands and feet, long fingers, intelligent minds, courteous and polished manners. Such are the Mpongwe of the Gaboon, the Angolese, the Fanti of the Gold Coast, and most probably the Haoussa of the Niger, a tribe with which I am not acquainted.

The black-skinned class: athletic shapes, rude manners, less intelligence, but always with some good faculties, thicker lips, broader noses, but seldom prognathous to any great degree. Such are the Wollof, the Kru-men, the Benga of Corisco, and the Cabinda of Lower Guinea, who hire themselves out as sailors in the Congo and in Angola precisely as do the Kru-men of Northern Guinea.

Lastly, the typical negroes: an exceptional race even among the negroes, whose disgusting type it is not necessary to redescribe. They are found chiefly along the coast between the Casemanche and Sierra Leone; between Lagos and the Cameroons; in the Congo swamps; and in certain swampy plains and mountain hollows of the interior.

I will now attempt to pursue this question a little farther by considering more closely the results of this transformation of type in the Africans, and by examining its causes, as far as the obscure nature of the question will allow.

A satisfactory explanation of the causes of this transformation can only be obtained by a series of long and careful chemical examinations, in which the quality of food, the nature of the soil, and the condition of the atmosphere would have to be considered. All that we can do is to reason from ascertained results.

We know that the Africans are not the only people who change their type by being born and bred in malarious regions.

"It is observed," writes Joseph Brown, "that the natives of marshy districts who permanently reside in them lose their whole bodily and mental constitution, contaminated by the poison they inhale. Their aspect is sallow and prematurely senile, so that children are often wrinkled, their muscles flaccid, their hair lank, and frequently pale, the abdomen tumid, the stature stunted, and the intellectual and moral character low and degraded. They rarely attain what in more wholesome regions would be considered old age. In the marshy districts of certain countries—for example, Egypt, Georgia, and Virginia, the extreme term of life is stated to be forty, while we learn from Dr. Jackson that at Petersburgh, in the latter country, a native and permanent inhabitant rarely reaches the age of twenty-eight. In the portions of Brittany which adjoin the Loire the extreme duration of life is fifty, at which age the inhabitant wears the aspect of eighty in a healthier district. It is remarked that the inferior animals, and even vegetables, partake of the general depravation; they are stunted and short-lived."

In the same manner, it is only on the borders of malarious Africa—that is to say, in Angola and Senegambia—that most foreign plants and vegetables can be made to live; and these, as Mr. Gabriel, of Loanda, informed me, completely changed their nature when planted in the African soil.

Respecting the degeneration of animals in Negro Africa, some curious changes present themselves to the eye of the casual traveler, and anatomical investigation would doubtless afford some very remarkable results.

Horses almost invariably die at Sierra Leone during the rains. The disease displays itself by a swelling in the legs. On the Gold Coast it is laid down as a maxim by the residents that horses can not live there—a maxim which is the fruit of repeated experiments.

A regular trade is carried on in horses between the Moors and the Senegal negroes. Cadamosto relates that the Barbary horses do not thrive in Senegambia, the greater part dying from retention of urine.

I observed that the horses of the Casemanche are smaller and less spirited than those at Podor, although they are decidedly of the same breed. And Bosman writes of the horses in North Guinea: "There are great numbers in the inland country; their heads and necks, which they always carry downward, are very like those of an ass; they go as if they were falling, and will not stir forward unless forced on with blows, without which they would move but slowly. The asses are larger than the horses, and in their kind handsomer."

Mollien also found that a donkey could endure the hardships of traveling better than the horse. And though the Mandingoes use horses for general purposes, they prefer asses for their long trading journeys into the interior.

The Senegal bullocks are smaller than those of elevated Africa; the Angola bullocks than those of Senegal; the Accra bullocks than those of Angola. The climates of these regions bear respectively the same relations toward each other. There are no oxen in those localities of Western Africa which are the most malarious.

European dogs seldom live long in such districts. They are subject to skin diseases; and a terrier in the possession of the late Mr. Gabriel used to have regular fever-fits, with cold shivers and vomiting. When these dogs live they degenerate. "In process of time," writes Bosman, "our dogs alter strangely here; their ears grow long and stiff like those of foxes, to which color also they incline, so that in three or four years they degenerate into very ugly creatures, and in three or four broods their barking turns into a howl."

There is a family resemblance between all the dogs of Western Africa. The dogs of Senegambia are good-sized curs; the dogs of Equatorial Africa have the same characters, but are smaller; and the dogs of the oil rivers have often black naked skins, and squeak whenever they are touched. With the exception of these, the African dogs are almost always sandy-colored, as if reverting to the wild dogs, and they can only howl. The natives of Guinea have a great respect for our dogs, saying that when they bark they are talking with one another, and that therefore they must have souls.

I bought a cur at Bapuku for the purpose of watching its habits. In the daytime it usually slept; toward evening it began to prowl about, with its belly close to the ground. When I fondled him he seemed uneasy. When I offered him any thing to eat, he looked all round him (from the force of habit) before he took it. He became, after some days, a little civilized, but in his tenderest moments he never licked me. I went away for three days, and when I returned he did not remember me. He showed no uneasiness when I took him from his native village; was fond of ground-nuts, manioc, and plantains, and in all respects resembled a wild animal half domesticated.

The cats are either sandy-colored or gray. Proyart has observed that they have a longer muzzle than ours. I noticed that they stood high on their legs, and that their faces had an expression at once frightened and ferocious. A great number of cats have run wild on the island of St. Vincent's. Mr. Miller informed me that the broods of these cats were invariably of a gray color. It is clear, therefore, that cats also revert to their wild form. In the same manner as the dogs in Africa do not bark, the cats neither purr when caressed nor utter nocturnal cries.

The cows which have been brought to the Gaboon from Southwestern Africa never give milk after the calf is weaned.

In Senegambia one may sometimes see sheep in a state of transition between wool and hair, but in Equatorial Africa they are perfectly smooth-skinned, and of a deep-brown color, with black faces. It has been generally supposed by naturalists that solar heat is the cause of this transition of wool into hair in the tropics; but Mr. Landsborough, who has lately returned from Australia, asserts that very fine wool is grown in tropical Australia, and Sir Charles Nicholson confirms the statement. The quality of wool, therefore, must depend exclusively on the pasturage. And since the sheep of Equatorial Africa sustain life on the leaves of trees, it will not be difficult to understand why they should be neither woolly nor long-haired.

So little is known respecting the habits of wild animals in Western Africa, that one can not positively assert their degeneration. One would suppose, however, that the elephants of Equatorial Africa, which will allow themselves to be kept in a penned state for weeks together in a wild state, must be very different from the elephants which South African travelers describe to be so wary, and so sensitive of the approach of man. The maneless lion of Senegambia, which condescends to prey on Guinea-fowl, is certainly as inferior in ferocity to the lion of Algeria as is the negro to the Arab. The wild boars of Africa are not so ferocious, M. Rapet informed me, as those of France, nor do the alligators of Equatorial Africa attack man so savagely as those of the healthier regions, Senegambia and Angola.

Thus animals can palpably degenerate in the lowlands of Western Africa. It is an additional argument toward proving the degradation of the men.

The three sub-classes of negroes referred to above have two external characters in common, viz., hair more or less woolly, and skins more or less dark.

The so-called wool of the African, when examined by the microscope, is found to be true hair, filled with a coloring matter which does not entirely destroy its transparency. The negroes (unlike the North American Indians) have hair on their bodies as well as on their heads, and this hair resembles that of Europeans.

The hair of the negro infant is of a light chestnut color, which gradually turns to black. I observed that the hair is most crisp and scanty on the sea-coast. As one approaches the interior it becomes more thick and abundant, preserving always its woolly appearance. The moisture of the climate is, I think, sufficient to account for its extreme curliness. Europeans who have cropped their hair on the Coast have frequently found that the African crop was short and curly. It is also worth noticing that no animals have long hair in Western Africa: the dogs are short-haired, sometimes naked; the sheep are smooth-skinned; the lions have no manes.

The velvety smoothness of the negro skin can, I think, be explained by the use of palm-oil, which possesses remarkable qualities as a cosmetic; children are rubbed with it as soon as they are born, and, if used every day, it prevents the skin from being cracked and wrinkled by the sun.

The peculiar odor which proceeds from the negro skin is also, I imagine, owing to the palm-oil which they use, and which exudes with the aqueous perspiration. It has certainly been much exaggerated, and is, I think, confined to those who are not cleanly. I have repeatedly sat among crowds of negroes in a small, ill-ventilated house, and have detected no smell more disagreeable than the oil with which they had anointed themselves, or the bark-powder with which the women had perfumed their hair.

There is as much variety among negroes in the color of the skin as there is with us. Among a dozen negroes one can scarcely find two with precisely the same shade of complexion. The prevailing color is not black, but a very deep bronze. Sometimes the complexion is a light yellow; sometimes brown, mottled with round black spots. As a general rule, the more intelligent negroes are light-colored. These men have also features of a less brutal cast; and their tone is not drawling and plaintive, as that of the lower negro, but quick, sharp, and decisive.

Respecting the causes of the black skin, one can only assert that it is not caused by solar heat alone. In the desert of Sahara the heat is far greater than in the land of the negroes, but the natives of this desert are of a light olive color; and Adanson observed that, when exposed to very violent heat, the faces of his men turned copper color.

I am inclined to believe that the black hue of the negro answers to the livid color among us; that it is the color of disease. Sir Andrew Smith, who is firmly opposed to the theory which I am defending, tells me, however, that when a Hottentot is subjected to hardships, hunger, etc., his skin becomes black, and only reverts to its natural color, a dirty yellow, after nourishment and repose.

The complexion of the skin is chiefly determined by the quality of the blood; and the blood of the negro, according to Barrère and Pruner-Bey, is blacker than our own. This may be partly owing to an excess of bile. The negroes are so subject to bilious complaints that they never eat eggs, and do not take fresh butter or sweet milk.

Nor are instances wanting to prove that a deep complexion often results in Europeans from a disordered constitution. Women frequently become brown during pregnancy; there are few cases in which the *mammæ* are not encircled by a dark tinge. Cases have been known in which the abdomen has become completely black. And Dr. Strach, in a work on intermittent fevers, mentions the case of a man who, after fever, became as black as a negro.

That the red races change to black when they descend into the low lands can not, I think, be easily disputed. I was told by the Senegal residents that some years ago it was very rarely that one saw a black Fula or Puelh. It is now almost impossible to find a red Fula without traveling some distance into the interior. With the Mandingoes it is much the same. These two tribes are driving out the negroes, that they may command certain positions on the river; the result of which is, that they are becoming negroes themselves.

In the same manner, the Fans of the Sierra del Crystal are taking possession of the Lower Gaboon. There are now no black Fans; but they will be found there by future travelers.

Saugnier, in his "Voyage au Sénégal," writes: "Les Satinguets, peuples Africains de Podor, vers le Sénégal, ne sont pas aussi noirs que les autres nègres, mais cuivrés presque rouges; leurs enfants, qui viennent au Sénégal et y habitent quelque temps, ac-quièrent une peau beaucoup plus noire qu'elle ne l'etait."

It frequently occurs, too, that families or tribes with negro char-acters are found under circumstances which render an intermix-ture of race impossible; their cause, therefore, can only be ascribed to physical influence.

A remarkable instance of this kind is given by Mr. Bucking-ham, who was almost the first to explore the Haüran, a district beyond the Jordan.

"The family residing here—at Abu-el-Beady—in charge of the sanctuary, were remarkable for having, with the exception of the father only, negro features—a deep black color and crisped hair. My own opinion was that this must have been occasioned by their having been born of a negress mother, as such persons are some-times found among the Arabs in the relation of wives or concu-bines; but while I could entertain no doubt, from my own ob-servation, that the present head of the family was a pure Arab of unmixed blood, I was also assured that both the males and females of the present and former generations were all pure Arabs by de-scent and marriage, and that a negress had never been known either as a wife or slave in the history of the family. It is cer-tainly a very marked peculiarity of the Arabs who inhabit the valley of the Jordan that they have flatter features, darker skins, and coarser hair than any other tribe, a peculiarity rather attrib-utable, I conceive, to the constant and intense heat of that region than to any other cause."

It has been frequently asserted that the Ethiopian can not change his skin; that Nature has placed, like a curse, an indelible stamp upon his form and features which will never change, to whatever climate he may be borne.

But proverbs are not arguments, nor assertions facts. That type is stubborn I will allow, but I can not admit that it is per-manent. I will quote a few instances of its changes out of the multitude which I have collected.

In the Soudan, according to Pruner-Bey, the negro child be-comes quite black at the end of a year; in Egypt after the lapse of three years. "Le nègre," he says again, "perd une partie de son pigment lorsqu'on le transporte dans le pays du nord. C'est toujours d'abord sur les parties saillantes, par exemple le nez, les oreilles," etc.

It has happened that negroes have lost their black color in a foreign country, and have become as white as Europeans. Such an instance is recorded in the fifty-seventh volume of the Philosophical Transactions. Klinkosch mentions the case of a negro who lost his blackness and became yellow; and Caldani declares that a negro, who was a shoemaker at Venice, was black when brought, during infancy, to that city, but became gradually lighter, and had the hue of a person laboring under a slight jaundice.

"L'Africain," writes M. de Reiset (quoted by De Quatrefages), " arrive aux Antilles avec tous ses caractères de nègre. L'Enfant créole de nègre et de négresse pars reproduit ses caractères, mais atténués. La face en particulier perd le caractère de *museau*. Les cheveux et la couleur persistent; mais sous tous les autres rapports le nègre créole se rapproche de plus en plus du blanc."

It is a fact, established by Pruner-Bey, that the blood of the African negro is thicker and blacker than ours. But Doctor Visinié, who has practiced medicine in Louisiana for a great number of years, asserts that the blood of the American negro is paler and more fluid.

In Africa the negro propagates children with difficulty; in America, as is well known, he is extremely prolific. In Africa the negroes are short-lived; but in the West Indies and in the States, statistics have proved that he attains to considerable longevity.

We have, therefore, fair grounds for believing that, though Nature has protected the negro as much as possible by giving him a thick skull to protect his bare head from the rays of the sun, and copious secretions to refresh his skin and to reproduce that organic matter which is so quickly consumed, yet his native land is the one which is most fatal to him; or rather, indeed, that it is not the native land of his forefathers and his race.

And now, what grounds are there for alleging that the negroes do not belong to our species? that they are as widely separated from us as the dog from the wolf, or the zebra from the horse?

When two races are so far from each other that their progeny are sterile, they are said to be of different species. This is the generally received definition of the term. Thus the dog is said to be of a different species from the horse, and the horse from the wolf. But the progeny of white men and negroes, so far from

being sterile, are prolific. The Cape de Verd Islands, with those
of San Thomé and Principe, are inhabited chiefly by a mulatto
race. In the same manner, I have met with in Guinea the descendants of the Portuguese who settled there centuries before.
They call themselves Portuguese, and speak with contempt of the
negroes, from whom they can seldom be distinguished.

The term "species" is therefore quite inapplicable to the negro;
and from the changes that have already taken place in their con-
formation, it remains doubtful whether they can be classed on one
side as a *permanent variety.*

It is certain that the woolly hair, the prognathous development,
and the deep black skin of the typical negro are not peculiar to
the African continent.

The debasement of the negroes is, on the whole, more physical
than mental. I fancy that a great deal of nonsense has been written about the vigorous health of the savage, the purity of his diet,
etc. To the negro certainly none of this is applicable.

The negroes suffer from intermittent and bilious fevers, which
appear in the same forms with them as with us. They are attacked by dysentery if they live entirely on fish. An exclusive
vegetable diet afflicts them with cutaneous diseases. In the interior of Senegambia they are subject to a disease, from the want of
salt, which curiously enough presents all the characters of scurvy.
In many parts of Africa there is a horrible disease called the *yaws,*
from which, on somewhat shallow evidence, the *lues venerea* is said
to have originated. Throughout Northern Guinea the small-pox
is prevalent, after which the face is pitted with blue marks; and
against this disease they use inoculation. Pulmonary complaints
carry off large numbers. Indeed, I do not know a single disease
to which Europeans are subject in the tropics which does not attack the negro also, and with much greater virulence. The native doctors do a thriving trade; and I have frequently seen in
the villages of Equatorial Africa large quantities of medicinal bark
being dried in the sun.

Before I enter on the question of the mental characters of the
negroes, of their language, of their religious, political, and social
institutions, it will be proper for me to consider their physical varieties, and certain exceptional races which are found among them.

Dr. Prichard and his disciples are inclined to draw important
conclusions from the fact of a xanthous or blonde variety occurring in individuals among the negroes. However that may be, I

have frequently seen negroes with red hair and black skins, though I never saw an albino with black hair. It is also very common to meet with negroes whose eyes are not black, but of a peculiar shade between a hazel and a green. Like the gray eye with us, it is frequently the indication of a cunning temperament.

I have seen albinoes all over Western Africa; they appear to be most frequent in mountain districts. Their color is a reddish-white, like the nose of a white horse. It does not change under the rays of the sun except by becoming cracked and sore. It is extremely unlike the skin of our own race; and the sight of a naked albino is the most loathsome that it is possible to conceive. They are said to be stupid; yet they are usually held sacred. In the Congo Empire they are made to enter the priesthood.

It has been alleged that the albino is sterile; there is reason to suppose that is not *always* the case. Mollien was informed by the Mandingoes that the albinoes bore children. A palm-oil trader informed me that there was a little republic of them near Old Calabar. And several respectable inhabitants of Goree told me that but a few years ago there was a colony of albinoes at Cape Naco; that they lived in the caves of the rocks there; and that they had gradually been exterminated by the neighboring tribes.

Arthaud, in his "*De l'Unité du Genre Humain,*" asserts that all white negroes are not albinoes. "Toutes les observations," he says, "prouvent que les nègres blancs ne diffèrent des autres que par la couleur; que leur constitution n'est pas aussi robuste que celle des autres nègres, sans être aussi foible ni aussi dégradée qu'on l'a dit; *qu'ils ont quelquefois de la carnation* et les lèvres vermeilles; que leur tête est couverte *d'une laine rousse,* et qu'ils ont des poils lanugineux de la même couleur sur les autres parties du corps; que leur vue n'est pas aussi bonne que chez les autres hommes; *que l'iris est diversement coloré,*" etc.

I must own that all the albinoes whom I have seen appeared to me to be inferior to the other negroes; that their white skins were not a reversion, but a defect, arising from a want of that pigment which colors the skin and the hair—a disease one frequently sees in a less perfect form among the negroes of Equatorial Africa, attacking the hands chiefly, and sometimes the side, thus giving them a piebald appearance.

But Sergeant Boivin, who had crossed the Lower Soudan to Sego from the Senegal, as Park had done from the Gambia, gave me an account of a people who lived in the mountains of Bombara, near Sego. This tribe, whom he described with great exactness, call themselves the Diawara. They speak Arabic; are pastoral, and have large herds of cattle. They are not very numerous, but are on good terms with their neighbors. They are Mussulmans, and in their customs and manners differ in nothing from the tribes around them. Their noses are aquiline; their lips thick; the expression of their features is European; their eyes are dark; and their hair is undulating, as one sometimes observes it in mulattoes, but more frequently in the mixed race of the Moors and negroes. But their faces are of a dead and ghastly white, like that of a linen sheet.

Now that I have attempted to show that the negroes are mere foreigners in Western Africa, it will naturally be asked whether I met with any traces of an aboriginal race. Mr. G. W. Earl, in a paper read before the Ethnological Society, describes mounds of cockles found in the Malayan Peninsula, the formation of which he ascribes to an ancient diminutive negro race, whose representatives still exist in the scattered families of the Semangs. The size of these mounds may be judged of from the fact that one of them contains 20,000 tons of shells, formed into concrete by carbonate of lime acting through long ages. The Chinese burn these shells to make lime.

To the same effect, traders say that in the Congo there are great heaps of oyster-shells, but no oysters. These shells the negroes also burn for lime. When we were sailing up the Casemanche, M. Rapet pointed out to me a creek which ran northward toward the Gambia. He informed me that in that direction there was quite a mountain of oyster-shells. The natives had a tradition that it had been made by their ancestors. Adanson also met with similar heaps of shells, though apparently with none so large as this was described to be.

Setting aside the very apocryphal stories of the Niam-Niams, there still remain some grounds for believing that a dwarfed race exists in the gorilla country.

"To the northeast of Mani-Kesock" (which is eight days east of Mayumba), writes Battel, "are a kind of little people called Matimbas, which are no bigger than boys twelve years old, but are very thick, and live only upon flesh, which they kill in the woods with their bows and darts. They pay tribute to Mani Kesock, and bring all their elephants' teeth and tails to him.

They do not enter the houses of the Marambas, nor suffer them to come where they dwell. And if by chance a Maramba or people of Longo pass where they dwell, they forsake that place and go to another. The women carry bows as well as the men, and walk single in the wood to kill the pongoes (gorillas) with their poisoned arrows."

And in Barbot I find this passage relating to Congo: "Before the king's cloth sit some dwarfs of a pigmy stature, but heads of a prodigious bigness, who, the more to deform them, have the skin of some wild beast tied about them. These they call *Bakke-Bakke*, or *Minos* indifferently, and say there is a wilderness where none but such dwarfs reside, who shoot at elephants."

There is a Mpongwe legend to this effect: "That in the beginning of time all people were together in the Ncomo. And there was some honey on the top of a tree. And an *Akoa* man climbed the tree, brought it down, and divided it into portions. For these all the people fought and struggled, excepting only the Mpongwe and the white man, who took their portions quietly. Then said the Akoa man: 'Now, because you fight, you shall never have any good thing except through the white man and the Mpongwe.' And that is the reason the Bushmen can not come down to trade with the white men for cloth and tobacco, but must wait till the Mpongwe bring it them."

"And who," I asked, "was the Akoa man?" "The Akoa man," answered Oshupu, "were a people very short, and just like *nchigo*. (Here he imitated the expression of the chimpanzee.) The country belonged to that people before our people came. But now they are all killed."

When I was in the Ncomo the Fans told me of a pigmy race toward the East. M. Braouézzec also heard of them, and has marked their alleged position in his map of the Gaboon.

Denham's description of the Mandara people, and the accounts which Beke and Krapf have received and related respecting the natives of Central Africa, render it by no means improbable that in the fastnesses of those equatorial mountains which the red race of Africa have not yet dared to occupy, the true aborigines of Africa may be found.

But it is only by searching the pliocene deposits of Equatorial Africa that we can hope to decide that grand geological, anthropological, and genealogical question—"Is the gorilla the ancestor of man?"

*　　*　　*　　*　　*　　*　　*　　*

In searching for the origin of a race, the surest, or, to speak more correctly, the least uncertain guide is the grammatical construction of its language.

Although the higher races of Senegambia and of Southern Guinea bear a remarkable resemblance toward one another, it would seem but to prove how little importance can be attached to such similarities as it is possible for external conditions to produce.

If language is to be our test, pagan Africa must be divided into two grand families. In "all" Southern Africa, from the Cameroons to Abyssinia, the inhabitants (with the exception of the Hottentots) speak dialects of one common language. The grand family of Kaffirs, the typical negroes of the western and eastern coast, and the cultivated Abyssinians, must therefore be included in the same race.

This language (I judge of it as spoken among the Mpongwe and Angolese) is inexpressibly melodious, alliterative, and abounding in vowels, with which every word, or almost every word, must end.

It has been cited as a proof of the aboriginal debasement of the negro that his language is monosyllabic and inexpressive. But in the whole Mpongwe dialect there are not more than a dozen monosyllabic nouns, perhaps not more than two or three monosyllabic verbs; it is methodical in all its grammatical forms, and susceptible of great expansion. In the northern division of the continent the dialects are much more numerous and diverse. There is even some reason for supposing that there are as many as five distinct families of language; and Gustave d'Eicthal has succeeded in tracing important analogies between the language of the Fulas and that of the Indian Archipelago.

And to which family do the Fans belong? that mysterious tribe which has so suddenly appeared in the low lands of the Gaboon. One grand grammatical distinction between the languages of the north and the south is the mode of forming the plural; in the north by a suffix, in the south by a prefix. Now the Fans certainly came from the northeast, but their plurals are formed by a prefix. The question is therefore a difficult one to decide.

In Western Africa there appears to be continual migration, and it is always toward the west. This is owing partly to the warlike tribes which inhabit the arid deserts of Central Africa; partly to the ambition of some chieftain, who, like Zimbo among the Jagas, wishes to extend his conquests or to establish a new empire; partly to the necessity of finding localities more fertile or more abundant in game; but chiefly, I imagine, it is owing to that no-madic propensity which is ever latent in human nature, and which is strongly developed in the African. The Fans could give me no reason for their migration to the Ncomo. Hassan, my Man-dingo servant, told me that "a Mandingo could not sit down long in one place." And the natives of Equatorial Africa are perpet-ually changing the sites of their villages, in obedience to this mi-gratory instinct, which they do not recognize, and for which they make the most absurd excuses, saying that a man has died in that town, and the place has become unlucky, or that a leopard has been seen prowling about it, and that they are afraid.

There can be little doubt that these migrations have been thus going on for ages. Thousands of red Africans must have poured over the mountain-wall to enter the swamps, to degenerate, and to die. The Mpongwe—that graceful, that beautiful tribe—are fast perishing away. The Fans are taking their place; and in a few generations they also will be gone.·

Africa has not only lost so many in the swamps—her children have blackened half America. Yet the low lands are still well populated. A stream of life still pours over that mountain-wall. It is certain that the sources of this stream must be very abund-ant, and that Central Africa is a prolific and perhaps over-popu-lated country.

Let us inquire as far as is possible into the origin of the red Af-ricans, and into their intellectual position, by studying their man-ners, their customs, and their institutions.

It is supposed that the negroes worship animals and idols; that they are acquainted with no higher Deity than the *fetich* which they carry on their breasts, or the serpent in their clay temple. But this is a great mistake. The negroes possess the remnants of a noble and sublime religion, the precepts of which they have for-gotten, and the ceremonies of which they have debased.

They still retain their belief in God—the One, the Supreme, the Creator. He has made the men and the world; He thunders in the air; He destroys the wicked with his bolts. He rewards the good with long life. He gives them the rain, the fruits of the earth, and all things that are good. He is far above all the other gods.

D D

Among some of the tribes they speak of him with timidity; seldom utter his awful name, and pray to him only in their last extremity. Among others they think that he loves to be supplicated, and offer up to him prayers which resemble those of children.

"Every morning," says Father Loyer, writing of a tribe on the Gold Coast, "after they rise they go to the river-side to wash, and pouring sand on their heads to express their humility, they join their hands and then open them, whisper softly the word *Eksuvair*, and say, 'My God, give me this day rice and yams, give me gold and beads, give me slaves and riches, give me health, and grant that I may be active and swift.'"

And the daily prayer in some parts of Guinea is, "O God! I know thee not, but thou knowest me; thy aid is necessary to me." At meals they say, "O God, thou hast given us this, thou hast made it grow." And when they work, "O God, thou hast caused that I should have strength to do this." Another prayer is, "O God, help us; we do not know whether we shall live to-morrow; we are in thy hand."

An African king, who had an interview with Cadamosto, said he believed the religion of the Europeans to be good, for that none but God could have given them such riches and understanding; but he believed that the negroes were more sure of salvation than the Christians, because God was just; and, as he had bestowed upon the latter a paradise in this world, so he would give the poor and wretched negroes a heaven in the next.

From all this it will be seen that these tribes of negroes can not justly be considered idolaters, and they have preserved as elevated an idea of the Supreme Deity as is entertained by any other race of men.

It is true that in some parts of Africa they believe that God has a rival—a pagan notion which we indistinctly but tenaciously retain. Courtiers even in religion, they pray to this Evil Genius in order to conciliate him.

It is also true that they have a material religion—a religion of fetich; that is to say, of image and animal veneration. They reverence these fetiches as things sanctified by God; they are symbols (for the negroes still exist in the symbolic age), but they are not regarded as gods. It is possible that some of the more stupid and ignorant negroes may believe that these charms or sacred things themselves contain the spirit of the Deity. But this is a

doctrine of transubstantiation which is not confined to Africa. In
all countries the illiterate are alike superstitious.

The mythology of the negroes, with their supreme God, their
lesser deities, their Dryads, and their Naïads, resembles that of the
Greeks and Romans; and both were probably derived from Egypt,
that fatherland of external religions.

To mingle among these people is to return to the very infancy
of historic time. Ere one's host offers you a calabash of palm
wine, he spills a libation on the ground. When one's guide passes a cave, he mutters a prayer to the spirit who inhabits it. When
the new moon appears, a crowd salute her with strange gestures
and with dancing. At such a moment one thinks of Bacchus,
of Trophonius, and of Diana. But paganism, to please, must be
clothed with flowers as it was in Athens and in Rome. Here its
grotesque and uncouth nakedness inspires disgust so soon as curiosity is sated.

It is, however, interesting to study the ceremonies of their religion, which can not be less ancient than that of the Hindoos,
though it has been less purely preserved.

The natives of the Gold Coast believe that after death they will
go to another world, where they will live in the same state as they
do here. Those who have lived regularly and have inviolably
kept their oaths, will be wafted over a river to a land abounding
with all kinds of happiness ; but those who have led wicked lives
will be drowned.

The Ibo negroes describe the soul of a man as possessing the
same subtle nature as his shadow. They say that each soul is accompanied upon the way to its appointed place by two spirits—a
good and an evil one. It has to pass over a dangerous wall by
which the road is divided. The good spirit helps the soul happily ; the evil one knocks his head against it. After this two roads
appear ; one is narrow and the other broad. By the narrow road,
the good soul is led by its guardian genius to God, the merciful
and the supreme. By the broad road, the wicked soul is led by
its demon to a place which is always dark.

They believe in the transmigration of souls. Some think that
after death they become white men, and are permitted by Providence to trade in ivory and gold dust. According to others, the
soul of a dead person revives in the body of the next-born child.
But the old Pythagorean doctrine appears to be the general creed.
The soul transmigrates into the bodies of birds or other animals.

Criminals, however, are debarred from taking a second lease of life, even in the humblest form; they fly about as ghosts, and torment mankind by their hideous appearance.

Most of the negroes exercise baptismal rites, and the practice of circumcision appears to be universal in Africa, except at Accra.

Circumcision—in itself a sanitary operation—was probably first ordained as a phallic sacrifice. Upon this subject it will be sufficient to observe that the φαλλός enters largely into the fetich-religion of Western Africa. One can easily understand this veneration for the emblem of generative life in a land where either the men are so frequently powerless, or the women so barren.

On account of the *elongatio nympharum* to which the women are subject, a similar operation is performed upon them by the wives of the priests.

On the slave coast, the priestesses in the serpent temple hold a very high position in the state. Calling themselves the children of God, they become nuns; the temple is their convent. They are formally initiated, and are taught the songs and dances of their craft by the older women, who receive handsome fees for their pains. As soon as these girls become women, they are married by the serpent; that is to say, the old women sell them to some sprig of their aristocracy. The nun is put into a dark pit, in company with two or three serpents. She is informed that one of these serpents will be transformed into a human shape; that if she will obey his instructions and perform a certain religious ceremony which he will enjoin, she shall go to the happy country when she dies; and then the serpent will appear to her in his true celestial shape, and will reward her docility on earth with ineffable ecstasies.

When the allotted hour has passed, the nun returns to daylight. The old priestesses are said to have the knowledge of certain herbs; but should, in spite of them, the fruit of the union appear, the girl is secretly destroyed.

I have already described the initiatory ceremonies of the natives of Equatorial Africa. In Northern Guinea they are of a higher order. The novice is shut up in a house during eight days. Food is given him once a day, and he sees only the slave who brings it. At the end of that time, masked men present themselves to him and try his courage in every possible way. If he braves the test he is made an adept; and at that glorious moment

he beholds all the kingdoms of the earth; the future is unveiled
to him, and heaven favors all his wishes.

·It will be known to most of my readers that a representation
of a man in the act of mesmerizing a patient is portrayed on one
of the Egyptian monuments. I have repeatedly heard that the
negro priests and priestesses are not only mesmerizers and magnet-
izers, but that they frequently act as media between persons and
their deceased friends. These mysteries are so rigidly held secret·
from the vulgar that it was impossible for me to acquire any satisfactory information in my short and rapid visits. But I was
much struck with a passage in Mollien, in which he says that his
guide Boukari, being seized with a violent colic, made signs with
his hands over a calabash of cold water, drank it, and was immediately cured.

The magicians of Egypt pretend to display the past and future
in a mirror. The reader will perhaps remember that in my chapter on the customs of Equatorial Africa I mentioned the legend
of a medicine-man who shows a negro his mother in a looking-
glass. All the fetich-men carry a small looking-glass. The Cabindas have two kinds of *mani-panchas*, or household gods: the
one kind with features of the Egyptian type; the second with
Hottentot characteristics, especially the great development of the
musculi glutei. They are also represented with a prominent belly,
to which is fastened a small metal or glass mirror, which enables
the,divinity to portray to the worshiper any object he may desire
to see, even at the greatest distance. Quenqueza, king of the
Rembo, had one of these little idols (which may also be seen in
the British Museum); he refused to part with it, and told me that
if that glass were to break he would instantly die.

Like the ancient Egyptians also, the negroes of Congo embalm
their dead. The.corpse is washed with a strong decoction of manioc, which whitens the skin. They then place the corpse in its
fetich attitude: the face turned toward the setting sun; the two
knees bent; the left foot raised behind, the right arm hanging by
the side; the fingers of the left hand separated, crooked, and
pointing eastward.

By a light and constant fire in the anus the intestines are dried
up like parchment. The body is then plastered over with red
clay, and rolled up in cloths till it becomes a shapeless mass. The
richer the person the more cloths he receives. Finally he is buried in a large grave, over which is erected a roofless house.

In Loango there is this difference. The body is more rudely prepared, by being smoked on a scaffold over a green fire, in the same manner as they dry their fish or their elephant-meat. From six months to a year, according to the rank of the deceased, the mummy is exposed in a sacred house, to which his relatives come at stated periods to mourn; after which he is placed in a coffin shaped like a barrel, and is conveyed to the grave in a kind of car.

I have already described the constitutions which are found in Western Africa, and which are either patriarchal or despotic.

But I must again remind the reader that an African despot is a slave, whom they set upon the throne. His palace is a prison; his jailers are the priests. He is the victim of a thousand absurd customs, which, however, impose upon the people.

It is a grave offense to suppose that he eats, drinks, or performs the ordinary functions of humanity. Whoever happens to see him eat is killed. When he drinks in public his person is veiled by a curtain, and the people prostrate themselves.

"Where does the king sleep?" asked a trader of a Dahomey negro. "Where does God?" was the reply.

An African king is cautious not to render himself unpopular. Those bloodthirsty caprices of which travelers have written so much have all been studied beforehand. The murder of a man for some trifling fault has received the sanction of the nobles and the priests; he has probably committed some grave offense, and he is killed in public because he has omitted to brush away a fly. There is much that is claptrap in an African court. It is, in fact, a stage in which the king plays the leading part, and of which the high priest is prompter behind the scenes. The populace is a savage auditory, whom it is necessary to amuse with farces, or to thrill with a tragedy now and then.

When a king shows himself unfit to rule or rather to obey, he receives a polite message. "The king's subjects feel sure that he is weary, and that he must require sleep." Such a one was delivered to a King of Akim. He passed seven days drinking, singing, and dancing; then burned himself with all his women—a negro Sardanapalus.

In all their migrations the negroes carry with them fowls and dogs, plantains, cassada, and tobacco.

It has not, I think, been remarked by any traveler that the custom of smoking is, like the tobacco-plant, indigenous to Africa.

The native tobacco is inferior to that of America, and is cured in a different manner. The natives cease to cultivate this tobacco as soon as they can purchase ours; and it is the same with their pipe: in Africa the importation of a foreign article does not appear to produce emulation, but indolence. The negro will never make that which he can afford to buy.

I have found pipes of different shapes and sizes, most of them differing very widely from our own, all over Western Africa. In the Senegal the pipes are very handsome, made of clay, and mounted in silver. On the Gold Coast the bowls are made of some remarkably heavy clay, and are frequently formed into grotesque figures. In Benito there are pipes made with double bowls. In Equatorial Africa they are made of a tenacious blue clay, and are colored red or black with great skill, presenting a smooth and polished appearance. Among the Fans they are made of iron or copper; in Angola, of some substance which resembles gutta-percha; they have also there a kind of narghileh or water-pipe. The narghileh is generally used to soften the niamba, a kind of haschish which they smoke. In Equatorial Africa, where the narghileh is not known, they use a long plantain-stem, with a pipe-bowl inserted at the end. So powerful is this drug that one whiff will make these inveterate smokers cough; one whiff is usually taken, the smoke expelled by the mouth or nostrils, and the pipe passed round the circle.

It would be easy to quote more customs and religious ceremonies which are analogous with those of the Egyptians and other ancient people; but upon this head I must have said enough to satisfy the reader.

Let us consider the social position of the negress.

The women among the negroes, as in the brute creation, are, on the whole, less handsome than the men. It has been noticed by negroes, even, how ugly the Kru women are, while their husbands resemble Roman gladiators.

The hair of the true negress is but little longer than that of the man. She will, however, spend hours in dressing it; ridging it up like a helmet over a frisette, and lubricating with palm-oil, or forming it into all kinds of fanciful patterns, one favorite mode being to let it hang down in plaits no thicker than whip-cord.

The bust is in early youth round and hard as black marble; but it has a tendency to elongate and present a conical appearance. To prevent this unsightliness, they deform it still more.

A band is passed across the breasts, which hang down like bags, and in old age shrivel up almost completely.

The position of the women in Africa varies according to the civilization of their masters. They are always a step lower in the scale. It will easily be understood, then, that the study of a typical negress can not be an elevating one. More hideous, more nearly approaching the brute than himself, she is nothing better than a beast of burden. The negro of the lowest class always preserves a little modesty. But, while the men retire to wash themselves secretly, the women will frequently bathe in public and before strangers without the slightest shame.

On the other hand, the Mpongwe girls, and others of the same class, are as modest and as decent, though with only a few inches of cloth about their loins, as any lady in Europe could be. In Equatorial Africa the women do not think it immodest to expose the bosom, under which their full dress commences, terminating at the ankles. In Angola, on the contrary, the women are careful to arrange their cloth in such a manner that they show only the neck, a custom probably taught them by the missionaries. A Fula girl is clothed in a flowing cotton robe, wearing also a covering round the loins, and on her head a veil made of some substance which resembles muslin. Young men erroneously suppose that there is something voluptuous in the excessive *dishabille* of an equatorial girl. On the contrary, nothing is so moral and so repulsive as nakedness. Dress must have been the invention of some clever woman to ensnare the passions of the men.

The negress, according to some authors, is excessively lascivious; and the Lesbian vice, κλειτοριάζειν, is said to be so common as to produce the *elongatio nympharum*, and to render excision necessary.

I have already described one African Messalina, on the authority of Father Cavazzi, but I do not think that they are frequently to be met with. Among the Mohammedans, the women who are not virtuous are *filles de marbre*, mercenary, and cold. The women of Equatorial Africa are affectionate and caressing, anxious to please; but I do not think that they are very libidinous. Such delicate questions can only be settled by those who have lived a long time in the country. For my part, I can say, what will astonish a good many, that during the whole time which I passed in Africa, I never saw so much as one indecent gesture pass between a man and a woman. I except their symbolical dances, which, to say the truth, are a little phallic.

In many parts of Africa, no marriage can be ratified till a jury of matrons have pronounced a verdict of purity on the bride and of capability on the husband. In other parts, especially in the malarious localities, where women are so frequently sterile, no one cares to marry a girl till she has produced a child. This has given rise to a supposition that they prefer a wife who has earned a little experience in dissipation. The real reason is, that if they marry they must pay a high price for their wife. This price they hope to regain by the sale of the children which she will bear. The negroes, like animals, place no check upon their passions, but they have no idea of the so-called refinements of vice.

The courtesans in Northern Guinea usually belong to government. They are regularly schooled in their trade. They are set apart, have their own houses, are distinguished from decent women by some peculiar dress, or are obliged to wear a little bell which gives notice of their coming.

Three cowries is the established fee, and out of their earnings they are given enough for their clothes and food. It is the system of "dress-lodging."

They form an important element in the state. When there is any insubordination in a town, its governor will shut up these women from the public. The bachelors come in a body to petition him for their restoration. So do the married men, who recognize in the Social Evil a social safety-valve. In fact, so favorably is this institution regarded in Africa, that it is the custom for rich negro ladies, on their death-beds, to buy female slaves and present them to the public, in the same manner as in England they would have left a legacy to some public charity. The negroes firmly believe that such national benefactors will be recompensed in a better world, and that the more *heteræ* they purchase here, the greater will be their reward hereafter.

Among the lower orders of negroes, the men being equal, the women of course are slaves; but in the great African kingdoms the rights of the *beau sexe* appear to be pretty fairly recognized. It is not only in Northern Guinea that there are female soldiers, female ministers, female embassadors, and female commercial travelers. A princess of the Congo can marry any man she pleases. This man is obliged to adopt the name and garments of a woman: when he goes out he is veiled, and a gon-gon is beaten to warn all people to turn aside. It has been frequently said that one may estimate the civilization of a country by the position of its wom-·

en. According to this maxim, Congo is the most polished country in the world, for in none that I ever heard of has the privilege of sex been so completely reversed.

It must be acknowledged, however, that, putting all exceptions aside, the women of Africa are very inferior beings. Their very virtues, viz., their affection and their industry, are those of well-trained domestic animals.

But if the women of Africa are brutal, the men of Africa are feminine: their faces are smooth; their breasts are frequently as full as those of European women; their voices are never gruff or deep; their fingers are long; and they can be very proud of their rosy nails. While the women are nearly always ill shaped after their girlhood, the men have gracefully moulded limbs, and always after a feminine type—the arms rounded, the legs elegantly formed, without too much muscular development, and the feet delicate and small.

When I first went ashore on Africa, viz., at Bathurst, I thought all the men who passed me, covered in their long robes, were women, till I saw one of the latter sex, and was thereby disenchanted.

While no African's face ever yet reminded me of a man whom I had known in England, I saw again and again faces which reminded me of women; and on one occasion, in Angola, being about to chastise a carregadore, he sank on his knees as I raised my stick, clasped his hands, and looking up imploringly toward me, was so like a young lady I had once felt an affection for, that, in spite of myself, I flung the stick away, fearing to commit a sacrilege.

Ladies on reading this will open their eyes, and suppose that either I have very bad taste, or that I am writing fiction. But I can assure them that among the Angolas, and the Mpongwe, and the Mandingoes, and the Fula, I have seen men whose form and features would disgrace no petticoats—not even satin ones at a drawing-room.

While the women are stupid, sulky, and phlegmatic, the men are vivacious, timid, inquisitive, and garrulous beyond belief. They make excellent domestic servants, are cleanly, and even tedious in the nicety with which they arrange dishes on a table or clothes on a bed. They have also their friendships after the manner of women, embracing one another, sleeping on the same mat, telling one another their secrets, betraying them, and getting terribly jealous of one another (from pecuniary motives) when they happen to serve the same master.

They have none of that austerity, that reserve, that pertinacity, that perseverance, that strong-headed, stubborn determination, or that ferocious courage, which are the common attributes of our sex. They have, on the other hand, that delicate tact, that intuition, that nervous imagination, that quick perception of character, which have become the proverbial characteristics of cultivated women. They know how to render themselves impenetrable; and if they desire to be perfidious, they wear a mask, which few eyes can see through, while, at the same time, a certain sameness of purpose models their character in similar moulds. Their nature is an enigma; but solve it, and you have solved the race. They are inordinately vain; they buy looking-glasses; they will pass hours at their toilet, in which their wives must act as *femmes de chambre;* they will spend all their money on ornaments and dress, in which they can display a charming taste. They are fond of music, of dancing, and are not insensible to the beauties of Nature. They are indolent, and have little ambition, except to be admired and well-spoken of. They are so sensitive that a harsh word will rankle in their hearts and make them unhappy for a length of time; and they will strip themselves to pay the *griots* for their flattery, and to escape their satire. Though naturally timid and loth to shed blood, they witness without horror the most revolting spectacles which their religion sanctions; and, though awed by us their superiors, a real injury will transform their natures, and they will take a speedy and merciless revenge.

According to popular belief, the Africans are treacherous and hostile. The fact is, that all Africans are supposed to be negroes, and that which is criminal is ever associated with that which is hideous. But, with the exception of some Mohammedan tribes toward the north, one may travel all over Africa without risking one's life. They may detain you; they may rob you, if you are rich; they may insult you, and refuse to let you enter their country, if you are poor; but your life is always safe till you sacrifice it by some imprudence.

In ancient times the blacks were known to be so gentle to strangers that many believed that the gods sprang from them. Homer sings of the Ocean, father of the gods, and says that when Jupiter wishes to take a holiday, he visits the sea, and goes to the banquets of the blacks—a people humble, courteous, and devout.

Barros, writing of Western Africa, then an infant colony, says: "And, besides, it is a property so pacific, tame, and obedient, that, without holding in the hand a fusée on the pan of the mortar, or a lance in the other, it gives us gold, ivory, wax, hides, sugar, pepper, and would give us more things if they wished to discover more."

It is true that we have met with much opposition in our endeavors to establish an inland trade, as, for instance, in the Niger. There the tribes inhabiting the mouths of the river get their living as middle-men. They know that the free navigation of the river would ruin them. Who can blame them if they attack us?

The Africans have a grand commercial faculty. They understand their interests as well, perhaps better, than we know ours. In the sixteenth century the Sieur d'Elbée asked permission of the King of Ardra to build a factory there. "No," replied the king; "you will make a house in which you will put at first two little pieces of cannon; the next year you will mount four; and in a short time your factory will be a fort, which will make you master of my dominions, and enable you to give laws to me."

But when their interests are not endangered, or when, as in the case of Mungo Park, they act under a delusion, no people can be more loth to kill, or even to ill-use. Take, for example, my journey to the Fans. I went among these people unarmed, without any safeguard or recommendation; among these people, who recognize no laws in such a case save those of the heart, and where each village forms a republic independent of the rest. I carried with me riches which in their eyes must have appeared enormous; and yet, knowing the African character, I slept with less anxiety among them than if I had been in a lonely wayside tavern in my own country.

Notwithstanding their gentle and pacific natures, the Africans show an indifference to suffering and an utter want of sympathy which contrasts very remarkably with the feminine points of their character. The officers who are stationed at Macarthy's Island fall ill invariably in the rainy season, at which time their servants invariably desert them. This callousness to sickness is partly accounted for in negro Africa, where disease is too common to be thought much of; but it is an attribute which, I believe, belongs to savages in general. They kill their crippled infants and their decrepid old people, as I have already observed.

Their cruelty, like that of school-boys, is that which proceeds from ignorance. Oshupu did not think that it was more cruel to burn than to drown. The boy who "jumped like a dog" made him laugh; it did not occur to him that a grotesque gesture might have been occasioned by horrible pain. A king of Ashantée cut off the hands of a slave, and bade her search his head for vermin with the stumps. If any one had accused him of barbarity, he would not have understood the accusation. It was his idea of a good practical joke.

Impassibility under suffering and indifference to death are common to most savages. The negroes die with the stolidity of sheep. But sometimes this becomes heroic.

A young man who had been caught in the harem of the King of Dahomey, about to enter the apartments of the wives, was condemned to die in the usual manner. He was tied on a scaffold, face downward, and the king's wives, according to law, brought wood to make a fire underneath. This young man, with a terrible death before him, suddenly burst out laughing. On being asked the reason, he replied that it struck him as being very amusing that those with whom he had passed so many agreeable nights should now be his executioners. He refused, always laughing, to betray any one in particular, and died without uttering a groan.

It may also seem strange that suicide should be common among the negroes. Bosman tells of a king on the Gold Coast who, being hard pressed by the Dutch, shot gold instead of bullets — a signal that he wished to parley. A truce was made; they adjourned to his palace; and in the midst of the negotiation he blew up his enemies and himself with gunpowder, dying the death of a Samson.

It is even common for a man to kill himself "on the head of another," as it is called. The other must either kill himself or pay an indefinitely heavy fine, and on that account it is frequently resorted to in revenge.

Adumissa, a beautiful red-skinned woman of Cape Coast Castle, had numerous lovers, but she rejected them all. One of them, in despair, shot himself "on her head," near the door of her house. His family demanded satisfaction, and, to save her relatives from a ruinous palaver, she determined to commit suicide. Having assembled all her friends and relatives, she shot herself before them with golden bullets. Her corpse, having been exposed in state, was buried with a profusion of cloth and gold. The legend of Adumissa is the favorite story by the evening fires of the Fantis, and her favorite patterned cloth still bears her name among them.

Such are the Red Africans—a race whose character is little known, but whom I believe to be far superior to the Red Indians of America.

It will be understood that the typical negroes, with whom the slavers are supplied, represent the dangerous, the destitute, and the diseased classes of African society. They may be compared to those which in England fill our jails, our work-houses, and our hospitals. So far from being equal to us, the polished inhabitants of Europe, as some ignorant people suppose, they are immeasurably below the Africans themselves.

The typical negro is the true savage of Africa, and I must paint the deformed anatomy of his mind, as I have already done that of his body.

The typical negroes dwell in petty tribes, where all are equal except the women, who are slaves; where property is common, and where, consequently, there is no property at all; where one may recognize the Utopia of philosophers, and observe the saddest and basest spectacles which humanity can afford.

The typical negro, unrestrained by moral laws, spends his days in sloth, his nights in debauchery. He smokes haschish till he stupefies his senses or falls into convulsions; he drinks palm wine till he brings on a loathsome disease; he abuses children; stabs the poor brute of a woman whose hands keep him from starvation, and makes a trade of his own offspring. He swallows up his youth in premature vice; he lingers through a manhood of disease; and his tardy death is hastened by those who no longer care to find him food.

Such are the "men and brothers" for whom their friends claim, not protection, but equality!

They do not merit to be called our brothers, but let us call them our children. Let us educate them carefully, and in time we may elevate them, not to our own level—that, I fear, can never be—but to the level of those from whom they have fallen.

If you wish to know what they have been and to what we may restore them, look at the portraits which have been preserved of the ancient Egyptians, and in those delicate and voluptuous forms —in those round, soft features—in those long, almond-shaped, half-closed, languishing eyes—in those full pouting lips, large smiling mouths, and complexions of a warm and copper-colored tint, you will recognize the true African type, the women-men of the Old World, of which the negroes are the base, the depraved caricatures.

CHAPTER XXXVII.

THE REDEMPTION OF AFRICA.

Exploration. — Commerce. — Military Protection. — Christian Missions.—Mohammedan Civilization.—Future of Africa.

IF I have dragged the reader through these details of the poly-
syllabic sciences, it has been with some view toward a practical
result. That he may judge how Africa can best be civilized, it is
necessary that he should understand the character of the continent
and its people.

· The western coast of Africa has a ragged fringe of Portuguese,
British, and French colonies. I have visited them all, and I find
that the Portuguese are decaying; that the British are stagnant;
that the French alone are progressing.

The interior of Africa is unknown to all but a few explorers.
It is a new continent; or, rather, it is a new world. ·

Very little has hitherto been done by exploration in Western
Africa. Lander discovered the mouth of the Niger, with which
Villault de Bellefond was perfectly well acquainted in the sixteenth century. In spite of this success, he did not escape the
fate of Mungo Park, of Clapperton, and of others, whose names
would form a tedious and dreary catalogue. In the expedition to
the Congo all the officers died. In fact, the great explorations of
Africa have ever been made from the east or from the north.
Livingstone, Barth, Burton, Speke and Grant, are our great living
explorers. None of these have started from the western side of
Africa.

From the western equator it is impossible to enter Central Africa. The country is dense and virgin forest, through which there
are no thoroughfares save the rivers, and these become unnaviga-
ble, even to a canoe, at a very short distance from the coast. Se-
lecting the largest of these—the Gaboon—I went up it about a
hundred miles. I was then encountered by a barrier of rocks. I
found myself among high mountains. There the Gaboon from a
river had become a torrent, whose fury no canoe could be made

to stem. I could go no farther. Even had my men been willing to accompany me, we could not have procured sufficient food in the dark and lifeless forest to sustain our lives. The natives of the country were not in the habit of making long journeys. They had come from the interior; if they migrated, it would be always toward the sea. Thus, in traveling from the east, one goes with the human tide, which in Africa rolls ever toward the west; but in traveling from the sea inland, one attempts to stem this stream of migration.

I found that in the Fernand Vaz it was possible to travel two days' journey farther into the interior than M. Du Chaillu had done. That is to say, they would take me from Ngumbi six days' journey in a southeasterly direction. To go farther, they said, would be impossible; for the last tribe which we would visit were always at war with the tribe beyond them, from whom they procured their slaves.

In such a country as Western Africa, with its huge forests and its dreary swamps, it is impossible to travel without guides. As there is no communication between the tribes of the interior beyond a few days' journey; as every village is a turnpike at which one has to pay toll, and whose chief can prevent one from going a step farther; and as every fifty miles a fresh dialect is spoken, it is tolerably evident that, though in Western Equatorial Africa a few days will bring one on the *terra incognita*, on the blank space of the maps, there is no possibility of passing beyond the threshold.

Lacépède, in his *mémoire* on the Central Plateau, recommends the exploration of the Congo, which, he says, will take the traveler directly into the plateau. That is true. There can be little doubt that, by following the northern branch of the Congo, one might penetrate into the very heart of Africa. But Captain Tuckey's expedition has proved that the same petty, yet insurmountable obstacles as in Equatorial Africa debar exploration.

"This excursion," he writes, "convinced us of the impracticability of penetrating with any number of men by land along the sides of the river, both from the nature of the country and the impossibility of procuring provisions." And again: "Hence I have never been able to procure a guide farther than from *banza* to *banza*, at the utmost a day's journey; for at every *banza* we were assured that, after passing the next, we should get into the Bushmen's country, where we would be in danger of being shot or kidnapped."

The route of the intrepid Livingstone, although attended with hardship and danger, was at least *practicable*. There has always been a regular inland communication between Angola and Mozambique. In 1809 Antonio de Saldanha da Gama, the Governor General of Angola, sent an expedition to Mozambique. It arrived there, and returned in safety, bringing letters from José de Oliveira Barbosa, the governor of the eastern colony.*

In a country which is broken up into small and independent principalities it is always difficult to travel. The only manner in which Central Africa (northward of Livingstone's route) might be explored from Southern Guinea would be by placing one's self under the protection of Matiamvo. The kingdom of this great potentate is three months distant from Loanda, and mulatto traders have gone there frequently enough, traveling on oxen. There the traveler would be certainly detained a long time, and it would depend entirely upon the complaisance of the king whether he would receive permission to pass on to the next kingdom, or be obliged to return.

There is a regular communication between the kingdoms of Dahomey and Ashantee and those of Abyssinia and Timbuctoo. It has, however, been always the policy of these monarchs to prevent white men from penetrating beyond their capitals, where, however, they always receive them with politeness and hospitality.

The Niger is the great thoroughfare of Guinea, and perhaps, in the rainy season, might be navigated in a small steamer as far as Timbuctoo. It is possible that the southern branches might conduct one toward the sources of the Congo, but whether such a voyage would be practicable I can not pretend to say.

There is only one method by which Central Africa can certainly be crossed by a European. It is from Senegambia. Mandingoes, as I have already said, travel to Timbuctoo, and even to Mecca. The Mandingo language, I have been informed, is alone sufficient for colloquial purposes to carry one to the latter city.

A knowledge of Arabic and the Koran, a bottle of walnut-juice, a hardy frame, and a compliance with the holy rite of circumcision, would carry a man through Africa—as a hadji to Mecca, through burning deserts and great dangers; or to Timbuctoo as a trader.

* Chronological Index of the Voyages, Travels, and Discoveries and Conquests of the Portuguese in parts beyond the Seas, from the beginning of the Fifteenth Century. Edited by the Cardinal Saraiga. Pp. 264-5.

Unluckily, we have few men who are at the same time able to personate the Moslem, and willing to endure so long and monotonous a journey.

Our commerce in Western Africa is as barbarous as was that of the Phœnicians on the coast of ancient Britain. There are only two regions in Africa which can be said to export agricultural produce. From Senegambia, ground-nuts; from the Portuguese possessions, a little cotton and a little coffee.

Palm-oil is at present the real wealth of Africa. This is collected by driblets in the interior, is bought in the inland markets by the middle-men, and is sold by them to the traders on the Coast. Gold, ivory, bees'-wax, rubber, ebony, and cane-wood descend to the sea-board in the same manner. Such a traffic (it can scarcely be called a commerce) does nothing for civilization except in whetting the intellects of the middle-men, in establishing relations between inland tribes, and in rendering the white man a necessity to the negro. But it is not by such means that a people can be civilized. Excepting that palm-oil has been substituted for slaves, and that the ground-nut trade has within the last few years been established, commerce in Africa has made no progress during two hundred years.

With respect to our settlements in Western Africa, we are mere tenants there. In some cases we have ceased to pay the "custom," as it is called; but, generally speaking, wherever traders have settled on the Coast, they have acknowledged the rights of the lords of the soil, and have paid rent for their allotment: that of Macarthy's Island, for instance, is fifty pounds.

Macarthy's Island is the only fortified settlement which we possess in the interior of Africa. The experiment has not been satisfactory. The island is so unhealthy in the rainy season that two surgeons are appointed there to one subaltern and forty men. It is difficult to understand why this absurd little garrison has been planted there, all by itself, with its half dozen big guns, and its patch of whitewashed houses, which are not guarded by a single wall.

It is alleged that a settlement of this kind holds the natives in awe, and protects the commerce of the colony; but I have seen too much of military protection in the French, Portuguese, and British colonies to believe any thing of the kind. Commerce in

Western Africa receives only that kind of protection from military forces which the clay pot expects to receive from the brazen one in Æsop's fable.

We have, in Western Africa, distributed throughout our colonies a detachment of a West Indian regiment. What could these do against the Africans if they really wished to attack us? What is it that prevents them from driving us into the sea? The King of Ashantee slew Sir Charles Macarthy at the head of his troops, and followed up his victory to Cape Coast Castle, which he compelled to capitulate. And Dahomey could seize Lagos with as little difficulty. But the Africans are peaceful; they have not the least desire to quarrel with us or to ill-treat our traders. They know their own interests a great deal too well to drive from the country those who supply them with all their luxuries.

The Portuguese war with Cassanje originated from a military outrage. I do not say that our officers would be guilty of such absurd cruelty, but it is certain that British ignorance of native character and conceit of its own dignity has led to many expensive wars and to much commercial trouble.

Last April, for instance, we had a war with Ashantee. It is a law of that kingdom, that, in the gold districts, all dust shall belong to the finder, but that nuggets belong to the crown. A Fanti found a nugget, and sold it at Cape Coast Castle. He was denounced to the king, who gave orders for his apprehension. The man placed himself under the protection of the governor. Ashantee sent embassadors; the governor refused to give him up. War was declared; and, on account of this one man, who had defrauded his government, the whole Fanti country was laid waste.

An expedition was sent against the Ashantees. I have since seen one of the officers, and he tells me that the Ashantees would not fight with our forces; that they came back without having seen one of them; yet, as their Fanti allies found out afterward, the troops had passed in that thick forest country, on more than one occasion, ambuscades of two or three hundred men, who might have massacred them, but who would not shoot, saying that the whites were at war with them, but that they were only at war with the Fantis.

But nothing will better prove that commerce has no need of military protection than the state of the oil-rivers. In the rivers Calabar, Benin, Brass Bonny, and Cameroons, all the real trade with Africa is done. We have no military settlements in these

rivers; we have therefore had no wars. No trader has had reason to complain of ill treatment. In Bonny, iguanas and white
men are *ju-ju;* that is to say, they are sacred; and if any man
hurts them, he is sentenced to death.

I do not deny that it is always as well to parade one's power
before savages. It should be shown as much and used as little as
possible. A young horse is no longer timid of the whip when it
has been frequently and not very severely used. That which is
mysterious is always the most dreadful; and savages grow callous
even to cannon balls, in time.

It has frequently been suggested that we should withdraw our
squadron from the coast of Africa. It appears to me that we
ought rather to withdraw our black soldiers and our drunken officers. A number of steamers, built expressly for river work,
might be run once a month or so up all such rivers as the Gambia, the Niger, the oil-rivers, and the Congo. These vessels should
be well equipped with arms and men; a war should be avoided
as long as possible, but when once waged it should be merciless.

I will venture to assert that, in case of such a war, these officers,
in their glaring red coats, leading their drilled negroes into an ambuscade, will not be missed; while it is well known that, in the
Badibu war, all that was really done (the destruction of half a
dozen villages) was effected by the guns and rockets of the men-
of-war.

Among other schemes which have been proposed for the ame-
lioration of Western Africa is one which appeared from Lord
West, in the "Times" newspaper, a few months ago.

It had been previously suggested by Captain Burton that the
Cameroons Mountain should be colonized by convicts, and a sanatorium formed there by convicts. Lord West amended that the
convicts should be transported to Liberia, and that they should
be placed under the charge of mulattoes. "An African," in reply to this communication, declared that the climate of the Coast
would not admit of such a scheme being carried out.

It would be impossible to transport our convicts to Liberia.
That state is an independent one. It consists of black Republic-
ans, who will not allow white men with untarnished characters to
possess land in their country. It is not probable, therefore, that
they will receive convicts.

But there are no places in the world so admirably constituted for penal settlements as Gambia, Cape Coast Castle, Lagos, and Sierra Leone. They are fit, indeed, for very little else.

" An African," who declares that the climate of Western Africa renders such a design *impossible*, is probably not aware that, during at least two centuries, Angola has been the grand penal settlement of Portugal. State prisoners are still holding offices there, and the soldiers are all convicts. That the system has been continued so long is a proof that it has succeeded.

I was assured by residents that crime was rarely committed in Angola, and that the convicts in every respect made excellent guardians. Those who showed themselves perfectly incorrigible would be dispatched to certain malarious localities inland. When permitted to return from these places, their emaciated aspect, and their accounts of their sufferings, worked a far more salutary effect upon their comrades than their execution could have done.

For the satisfaction of those who take an interest in this question, I can quote a higher authority than my own in corroboration of its truth.

" It is a remarkable fact," writes Livingstone, " that the whole of the arms of Loanda are every night in the hands of those who have been convicts. Various reasons for this mild behavior are assigned by the officers; but none of these, when viewed in connection with our own experience in Australia, appear to be valid. Religion seems to have no connection with the change. Perhaps the climate may have some influence in subduing their turbulent disposition, for the inhabitants generally are a timid race: they are not at all so brave as our Caffres. . . . . If we must have convict settlements, attention to the climate might be of advantage in the selection."

Livingstone has hit the right nail on the head. How is it your convicts are so meek? said I to a Portuguese. *O la febre!* said he, with a shrug of his shoulders. Intermittent fever, therefore, as I said before, must be regarded as sanitary from a moral point of view. It preserves in a state of gentle depression those spirits which in us are "animal," but which are brutal in convicts. A criminal in good health has certain morbid cravings; but, as you see, as soon as the body is diseased, the soul becomes purified.

To speak seriously, let precautions be taken, so that the convict be not more exposed to disease than other settlers; or, rather, let strict rules of hygiene be established and enforced. I have already shown that the " Coast" has derived much of its bad name from the debauchery and inanity of residents. Some considerable number of years ago convicts actually *were* sent out to the Coast settlements. These men, upon whom no restraint was placed, got drunk every day with that poison—fermented palm wine—and lay drunk all night on the bare ground in the heavy dews. They died like rotten sheep. It was ascribed to the climate; but if men in our own country were allowed to get systematically drunk on London gin, and to pass the night in a stagnant gutter under a drizzling rain, our national character would scarcely be that of longevity.

Should a penal settlement be established in Western Africa, confinement within four walls must be put out of the question. Imprisonment in such a country would be downright murder.

A shorter term of transportation might also be allowed, at the rate of three years to seven.

Every care should be taken that their sleeping-quarters were clean, ventilated, and exposed to the sea-breeze.

They should be employed at some active occupation, such as tilling plantations, building, etc., from daybreak till ten; from two till sunset. In the intermediate hours they might be allowed to indulge in recreation.

Their diet should be generous; and *vin ordinaire*, such as the French soldiers receive, would be found a more wholesome stimulant than grog.

They would have intermittent fevers, but these are seldom dangerous till rendered so by calomel or bleeding. There will, no doubt, be cases in which an organic disease is latent, and where lives would be imperiled by the climate; and these should receive medical tickets of leave.

After the system has been ripened, convicts might then be employed in forming a sanatorium in the manner which Captain Burton has suggested.

Should these precautions be taken, with other and better ones which men of more experience than myself would suggest, the convict's health would be less endangered than that of the ordinary resident. Why, then, should we be more tender of the lives of our convicts than of those of the officers, of the consuls, of the lawyers, of the ministers, who go out monthly to Western Africa in the service of this country? By exceeding certain limits, philanthropy may become a folly. It may even become a crime. If the West Coast of Africa is sufficiently healthy to admit of the

formation of military and commercial stations, it is not too unhealthy for the formation of a penal settlement.

Even were it to be proved that Christian missions retarded
civilization in savage countries, they would not cease to be popular. Devotion and enterprise are two cardinal passions of mankind. In missions these are united, and are therefore irresistible.
It is the romance of religion.

There are two species of missionaries in Western Africa. The
first are simply colonial parsons. Their "labors" are confined to
the settlements. They do not study the languages of the natives.
They do not visit the interior. For the most part they are badly
educated, and they are not always good men. Without repeating scandal, it will be sufficient to say that the English missionaries on the "Coast" are almost universally regarded by laymen
with contempt.

The character of Mr. Rooke is scarcely, I fear, a solitary instance; and the ignorance of our divines on the Coast with respect to secular matters is astonishing. A young gentleman who
was a fellow-passenger of ours on board the "Armenian," and
who had just been ordained by the Bishop of Sierra Leone, asked
the captain whether the anchor went to the bottom when it was
thrown overboard; and if it did go quite to the bottom of the sea,
whether it was tied there with a bit of string?

It may seem of little importance whether a missionary should
know more of such things than a child of eight years old or not,
but no man can gain influence over negroes unless he can gain
their respect, and they are quite shrewd enough to detect such
palpable ignorance.

However, these Coast missionaries perform their humble part
in civilizing Africa. They teach small negroes to read and write,
and they succeed in making the women keep the Sunday by
wearing clean clothes once a week. It is true that they sometimes drive susceptible negresses into epileptic fits; that they
speak execrable English ; and that they are occasionally a little
blasphemous, a little uncharitable, and a little hypocritical. We
can, however, congratulate ourselves that times have improved
since Major Laing, who, writing in 1825, saw one missionary lying drunk in the street, another living with a negress, one of his
parishioners, and a third tried for the murder of a little boy whom
he had flogged to death.

The other species of missionaries are a very different class of men.   They settle in the interior, or on some semi-civilized part of the Coast.   They live entirely among the natives, learn their language, and by compiling grammars and founding written characters, render important services to science.   Of such men, who lead a life of unceasing industry and self-denial, I can only speak in terms of admiration and regret; for I shall show that the toil of their lives can do little for civilization, nothing for Christianity.

That I may best explain the futility of Christian missions in Western Africa, I will select two examples, the first of which has been the most powerful and the most successful; the second of which is the most earnest and the most able, and, were success possible, the most likely to succeed.   I mean the Jesuits of the Congo, and the American missions in Equatorial Africa.

The missionaries who, in the seventeenth century, were sent to Congo, then an empire resembling those of Ashantee and Dahomey at the present day, were men of marvelous fortitude, enthusiasm, and endurance.   They suffered terribly from the climate, and still more from their mode of treatment.   They had an ingenious theory that, in order to become acclimatized, it would be necessary to exhaust their veins of European blood, which they would supplant with African blood.   Accordingly, they bled themselves *ad libitum;* one monk, Carli, being blooded ninety times, without counting the blood which ran in great quantities from his nose, mouth, and ears, and which seemed to him prodigious.   At the same time, they took such purgatives as in Europe are only administered to horses.   It is therefore scarcely to be wondered at that so many of them should have died.

In matters of ceremonial religion the negroes are not fanatics. As long as operations were confined to baptism, to exhibiting images of the Virgin and saints, and to distributing beads, and relics, and Agnus Dei's, the people were amused and delighted by becoming Christians.   They had no objection to changing their fetich for the fetich of the white men, whom they acknowledged to be superior beings, and whose fetich, therefore, might be more powerful.

One part of the baptismal ceremony, according to the Romish ritual, consists of placing salt upon the mouth.   As salt is the greatest luxury in Africa, this circumstance probably aided the alacrity with which the natives came to be baptized, or, as they termed it, *Curia mungua,* to eat salt.

They even permitted the destruction of their idols, the up-turn-
ing of their fetich-stones, and the abolition of their human sacrifices and other barbarities.   The awe in which the monks were
held must certainly have been very great.   Three of their triumphs may be recorded.

One of the "fathers," happening to go into a smith's shop, entered into religious conversation with him, and endeavored to in-
culcate the truth that there was only one God.   The smith, smiling, observed that he was mistaken—there was another, and that
other was himself.   The monks found that he had a numerous
train of adorers, who maintained that the admirable works which
came from his hand could be produced only by supernatural power.   The fathers dragged the divinity before the king.   The king,
who had himself some pretensions of the same kind, did not choose
to have a rival among his own subjects.   He delivered the smith-
god into the hands of the missionaries to be reduced to a mortal
in any manner which they might deem expedient.   Finding argument to his reason useless, they applied it to his back with a
strong whip.   As soon as he felt his own blood running over him,
he owned that he had doubts upon the question, and finally admitted that there was only one God, and that one not himself.

The missionaries soon found that the negro epidermis is more
susceptible of impression than the negro intellect.   One day they
met with a queen who, with a numerous train, was giving the air
to an idol, and singing its praises.   Having reasoned with her
without effect, they again used the whip.   After she had received
a few blows on her sacred person, her understanding became
gradually opened; and, finally, she declared that she was unable
to withstand such striking proofs of the purity of the Christian
faith.

How completely the natives were converted to the ceremonies
of the Catholic religion is proved by the statements of the missionaries who were sent out afterward.   One complained that
there was no one in that vast empire to baptize, not an idol to
burn; while Carli describes an incident which gave him a high
idea of the Congo Christians.   One evening, after sunset, he heard
a very loud concert of the most doleful sounds that had ever met
his ear.   This was found to proceed from the inhabitants of a
neighboring village, who had come to submit themselves to the
discipline of the Church.   On repairing to the place of worship,
he found two hundred persons on their knees, beating their breasts,

and bearing on their shoulders, as an additional penance, logs of wood of an enormous weight. Carli, having given some exhortation, caused the candles to be extinguished, after which these pious persons drew out leather thongs, and cords made of bark, with which they continued to whip themselves a whole hour without intermission.

But when the good fathers attacked the domestic customs of the country they met with a severe opposition, became unpopular, and fell, beyond recovery, in the estimation of the natives. That which they attempted to destroy was not only the institution of polygamy, but another, by which those who were betrothed were permitted to live together for a short time before marriage, to make trial how far their tempers and inclinations agreed, during which interval either party might, without the smallest reproach, dissolve the connection.

The natives declared that it was great presumption in a handful of foreigners daring to attempt the subversion of their most ancient customs. The fathers threatened them with hell fire if they refused to adopt the marriage system of the Christians. The natives replied that they were quite content to go where their fathers had gone before them.

But the firmest opponents of these innovations were the women; and, as every one knows, a priesthood is only powerful when supported on female pillars. The ladies of the court, who despised the monks on account of their chastity, determined to take advantage of this pious weakness. Accordingly, they chose a rivulet which flowed before the garden of the missionaries as their place of bathing, and there exhibited themselves during the whole day, often in very indecent attitudes. The afflicted fathers laid their distress before the king, but soon found the evil doubled by this proof of the effect which it had produced. They had at last no remedy but to build a high wall in front of their garden.

Finally, these men, who had at first been almost worshiped, began to be looked upon with great contempt. Their preaching, their foreign aspect, and their ignorance, afforded no slight merriment to the Conghese. One favorite entertainment seems to have been to call to them that wild beasts were coming, to clamber with feigned haste up the trees, and to observe the vain attempts of the monks to perform that feat of agility. Even when I was in Angola I was able to buy a caricature, done by a negro, in which two absurd-looking missionaries were engaged in baptizing a child.

The Catholic religion is, of all Christian creeds, the most likely to succeed among savages. It impresses the senses by music, by perfumes, by stately rites; and with its charms, its relics, and its images, it affords that which is indispensable to the lower classes of intellect—some external objects which they can venerate, and which may constantly remind them of their Creator.

But how can the Protestant creed, which is at once so naked and so sublime, be understood by uneducated Africans? How convey to them abstract truths, when their language can not express to them abstract ideas?

The African dialects are minute, but always physical. They have few words to express the commonest qualities or emotions, especially those of the better kind. In the words of a missionary who spoke Mpongwe with great fluency, "there is not a virtue for which they have an equivalent term, not a vice for which they have not one."

I need not say that it is difficult to convert a people to a religion when one can not even explain it to them. I was first convinced of the impossibility of Christianizing savages by a little incident which happened to myself. I was in a Bush village of Equatorial Africa, and had been catechising the chieftain respecting some fetich practices in which I had been interested. Having satisfied my curiosity, he began to interrogate me about my religion. In answer to his questions, I told him that, according to the belief of white men, God's Son came down on earth, disguised as a man, and offered himself up as a sacrifice for all the people who had sinned. He easily understood that the anger of the Father would be appeased by such an atonement, but begged me to explain what reason the Son had for doing such a foolish thing: what did he hope to gain by it? I replied that he did it out of mercy. That could not be translated, said Mongilomba. There was no word for mercy. Having tried several other words equally untranslatable, I said at last God's Son did it because he loved men. At this they burst out laughing, and one of them made an indecent gesture. On inquiry, I found out that they have only one word for *love*, and this they understand in its most coarse and brutal sense.

The American missionaries are perfectly fitted for their work. They are good classical and Hebrew scholars, and their attainments have enabled them to systematize the dialects of their savage parishes. They are also practical men; build their own houses, sail their own boats, have made several journeys into the interior, and have rendered several services to science. Not only do we owe them the only written analysis of the dialects of Equatorial Africa which we possess; it is from these missionaries that we have received the first accounts of the cannibal Fans, and the first description of the gorilla.

But in spite of their lives, pure and laborious as those of the ancient fathers, in spite of their unceasing efforts, they have made no palpable progress toward converting the Africans. It is true that one can not measure the amount of moral good which they may have done. I fully believe that they may have saved one man from being a thief, and another from being a drunkard. But polygamy is the great stumbling-block.

In order to judge correctly of things African, one's mind must be acclimatized. Every country has its social temperature. In Africa it is directly diverse from that which it is in England.

The Bishop of Natal has been abused because he proposed that Christian converts should be permitted to remain polygamists. Now, as in the Old Testament polygamy is sanctioned among a people whose country, whose habits and customs, resemble those of the Africans in every important respect, and as in the New Testament it is nowhere forbidden except in the case of the clergy, one is fairly entitled to regard marriage as a purely secular question, with which the Church has nothing whatever to do. Such, at least, is the view of the case as taken by our Legislature, for the sanction of the Church is no longer required to render matrimony valid.

As a civil institution, then, polygamy is as great a benefit in Africa as in Europe it would be an evil. In that unhealthy land, where sterility is so common, and where death among children is so frequent, it becomes one of Nature's necessities, against which it is useless to struggle.

As long as African intelligence remains in its present state, and as long as the Church continues to mingle its own petty social laws with God's commandments, Africa can not become Christianized.

Were it possible to awaken popular enthusiasm on behalf of a secular mission for civilizing the negroes, a society might be formed for the diffusion of practical knowledge in foreign parts. The negroes are not yet able to grasp the doctrine of the Trinity, of the Immaculate Conception, and of Everlasting Punishment; but they have a taste for music, an aptness for language, and a perfect talent for mechanics. I think that their bodies ought to be trained before their minds, and that our churches on the Coast should be converted into workshops.

Such a society might begin its work by educating negroes in the useful handicrafts, and in sending them out as missionaries. They would, I am sure, make numerous converts; and such a scheme might possibly succeed as a commercial speculation. There is not much probability, I fear, of its being taken up by the philanthropists of progress, whose attention, however, it deeply merits.

Much has been said of the early arrestation of brain-growth in the negro. Up to a certain age, negro children, as Mrs. Walker, of Baraka, informed me, are quicker to learn than ours; but after a certain age they forget all that they have been taught, and become as stupid and as sensual as their fathers were before them. This has been described as a peculiarity of the negro. But it is very easily accounted for. The brain develops itself with the other organs of the body; when the other organs cease to grow the brain also ceases to grow; but it can be artificially expanded by education, by habits of thought, etc. Now, as a rule, as soon as a negro boy has finished his education with the missionary, he returns to his savage relations and becomes a savage. His brain no longer makes progress. On the contrary, it retrogresses. But let the mental faculties of the negro be continually exercised, which can only be done by rendering them of pecuniary service to him, and he will make the same progressive development as other people—the same in kind, though different in degree.

In illustration of this argument, I can cite instances of arrestation of brain-growth even in this island.

Robert Norris, a National school-boy, displays some remarkable talent for mathematics, for language, or for original composition. His parents persuade him to live with them. He becomes an agricultural laborer, and in a few years' time there is nothing to distinguish him from the clodhopper who works by his side, and who has never been to school at all.

Johannes Secundus obtains the Ireland, and a double-first at Oxford. His health is unimpaired; he has the talents of three men. What can be more brilliant than his prospects! But he obtains a Fellowship, and afterward a college living. In five years' time you go to see him. He reads you a drowsy sermon

from the pulpit, talks to you of old Port, and misquotes a hack-
neyed passage from the Odyssey.

Celia, at twenty-two, is a charming and accomplished girl. She
warbles at the piano like a nightingale; she paints a little, and
she writes the most delicious sonnets in the world. She is ambitious; she is determined to become a great artist. On the contrary, she marries a rich fool; his stupidity annoys her, wearies
her, and finally crushes her. She has children; she becomes domestic; she reads the "Family Herald." You left her a nymph,
you return to find her a nurse.

That is the whole secret of the arrestation of brain-growth in
the negro. If they are more precocious than us, it is because they
are more feminine than us, and therefore more instinctive. Let
those instincts be carefully studied and trained, and the negro
may be made much of in all those arts and crafts which do not
require the creative faculty.

Since neither European commerce, nor military protection, nor
Christian missions can civilize this country, what is to be done
with it? Is it always to remain Savage Africa?

No, dear reader, the great work of progress is being accomplished, though without European aid, and though concealed from European eyes. The continent is being civilized; the Africans are
being converted by means of a religion.

It is the same religion which, under different names and forms,
has civilized the Hebrews through Moses, and the Western world
through Jesus Christ. It is the religion of God, of which the out-
ward laws and ceremonies so widely differ, but in which the divine element is always preserved unchanged.

Mohammed, a servant of God, redeemed the Eastern world.
His followers are redeeming Africa.

The Africans are now in much the same state as were the Arabs
before Mohammed. The laws, therefore, which that great prophet prescribed for the conversion of the one are perfectly suited to
the other.

The Africans are drunkards. The Koran forbids them to touch
wine or spirits. They are gamblers: in Northern Guinea a man
will frequently gamble away his property, his wife and children,
and himself. The Koran forbids gambling. They are vicious
and voluptuous. The Koran forbids them to have more than
four wives. They place no restraints upon their appetites. The

Koran compels them to keep an annual fast: during a whole month they are not allowed to touch food or drink between morning and night. The Africans are idolaters: they have human sacrifices, and many barbarous rites. The Koran abolishes all these.

The Africans are frivolous and effeminate: they spend their nights in singing and dancing. The Koran forbids such amusements. The musicians are no longer permitted to play and sing, saving canticles in honor of Mohammed.

The Africans are all of them thieves. They have no sense of honor in that respect. I have never yet had a negro servant (and I have had a great many) who did not rob me of some trifling article, whether he was pagan or Christian. But with my Mussulman I lost nothing. "God forbid!" cried Hassan, one day, in speaking of these thievish negroes, "that a Mandingo should steal!"

The Africans tell a lie more readily than they tell the truth. Falsehood, like petty larceny, is not recognized among them as a fault. But how different it is among the negroes who are Mussulmans! "One of the first lessons," writes Mungo Park, "in which the Mandingo women instruct their children, is *the practice of truth*. In the case of an unhappy mother whose son was murdered by the Moorish banditti, her only consolation in her uttermost distress was the recollection that the poor boy in the course of his blameless life had never told a lie."

The Africans have no written language, nor mental culture of any kind; but wherever the Mohammedans go, they take with them their marabouts and their Korans. In every Mohammedan town there is a public school and a public library. In the school, boys are taught to read the Koran, and to write it on a board with a charcoal pencil. It is curious to see one of these seminaries held under some shady tree in the centre of the village; the grave marabout in his blue robes, and with the little red cap of office on his head; and round him a number of negro boys, some of them as black as soot, bawling Arabic with facility, and handing up their boards to be corrected.

The public library consists chiefly of different copies of the Koran, some of them beautiful specimens of caligraphy. They have also very frequently the Arabic version of the Pentateuch, which they call *Torat Mousa;* the Psalms of David, *el Zabour Dawidi;* and even the Gospel of Jesus, *el Indjil Isa.* They also preserve

public registers and records, a study of which would be most interesting to the traveler who could read Arabic.

The great national vice of the Africans is their indolence.
They have no athletic sports. They wonder at the white man
who walks to and fro from the mere love of walking. But the
Mohammedans, who forbid dancing, substitute for this exercise
far better ones—those of equestrianism, throwing the javelin, etc.
Among the negroes the children lie all day in the sun. Among
the Mohammedans they are ever active, and have a game in
which they pelt each other with balls. This in itself is indicative
of superiority. In the sports of children one may detect the instincts of a nation.

Thus the effeminacy of the African can be elevated by religious austerity. His barbarities can be abolished. His vices can
be crushed.

The Mohammedans have ever been reproached because their
religion sanctions polygamy, domestic slavery, and fanaticism.

Mohammed, finding that it would be impossible to forbid polygamy altogether, contented himself with restraining it. In his
time there were chieftains who, like the King of Ashantee, had
their 3333 wives. He forbade any Mussulman to marry more
than four wives or concubines; he counseled them to content
themselves with one. It will therefore be understood that the
most pious Mussulmans are not polygamists. But polygamy is
an institution which has a most salutary effect in redeeming Africa.

The negress is frequently married, and thus she is brought into
the same family as the women of a superior race. Thus her
character is elevated; her children receive the same privileges as
those of the other wives, and all invidious distinctions of color
are destroyed. It was on this principle that Napoleon declared
that polygamy must be authorized if they really wished to liber-
ate the blacks of the colonies socially as well as legally. "Lorsqu'on voudra," he said, "dans nos colonies, donner la liberté aux
noirs, et y établir une égalité parfaite, il faudra que la législation
autorise la polygamie, et permette d'avoir à la fois une femme
blanche, une noire, et une mulâtre. Dès lors les différentes cou-
leurs, faisant partie d'une même famille seront confondues dans
l'opinion de chacune."

Domestic slavery is sanctioned by the Mohammedan religion;
and this slavery, by which in America the negro is degraded, is
that which elevates him in Africa.

He is forced to become a Mussulman, which trains his mental faculties; and to work, which exercises his physical powers. That he is treated with great kindness, and that he need never wholly despair of his freedom, I believe that I can prove.

In Senegambia the slaves are well treated. They work in the fields two thirds of the day, and spend the rest of the day working at robes. If a slave has been ill treated he can change his master, and by cutting off a piece of the ear of a free man or his child, he with his family pass under the domination of the wounded person, and can only be redeemed by his master at an enormous price. It is said that the Al Mami of Dimar was so renowned for his amiable disposition, that little by little he lost both his ears. When the agricultural season is over, the slave may go where he pleases and work on his own account. When he has earned a certain amount of money he can purchase his freedom.

A Mussulman is not allowed to sell his slaves to an unbeliever. It is therefore very certain that when the Mohammedans have conquered Africa the slave-trade will be abolished. Much of its present languor in Northern Guinea must be ascribed to Mohammedan influence. The slaves do not even receive that opprobrious name among the Mussulmans, always excepting the Moors, who are bandits and murderers. "Never say 'my slave,'" writes Ben Hourira, "for we are all slaves of God; but say my servant." In the same manner, among the Portuguese of the Cape de Verd Islands, the word *escravo* is never used; a slave is always spoken of as *familha*.

So far from sanctioning oppression, it is expressly said in the Koran, "He who sets his slave free, sets himself free from the troubles of earth and from the pains of hell."

Slavery, or rather servitude, is a necessity in Africa, where, if Alexander's maxim, "Labor is royal, sloth servile," be correct, none are yet free. Sloth is the natural state of man, from which necessity at first, and ambition afterward, alone can free him. In England, how do we treat able-bodied men who go begging about the streets? We put them in prison; we try to make them work. Africa is inhabited by able-bodied men who are not obliged to work by hunger, or need for clothing, and who have not the ambition to desire luxuries. These people, therefore, have been enslaved alike by Christians and by Mohammedans. The Christians have degraded them, have rigidly shut them out from self-improvement, and have inflicted upon them a thousand cruelties.

F F

The Mohammedans, on the other hand, have elevated them, have educated them, and have treated them with paternal kindness.

Finally, we say that the Mohammedan religion is one of the fire and the sword; that converts to it are made by butchery; that their mosques are raised on the ashes of cities and of men.

But the fire and the sword are those two methods of reasoning by which alone the savage mind is influenced. I have related how a missionary of Corisco pleaded for the life of a witch condemned to death. He argued with them on their barbarous folly with eloquence and with reason. He had done so for twelve years. It was useless. The murder took place. But in Gaboon the commandant threatened to hang the first man who executed a witch; the result of which is, that witchcraft is becoming extinct.

The Jesuits were no fools when they flogged the smith to bring him to his senses. He really believed that he was a deity till his back began to smart. Mere reason is cold and unintelligible to the savage. He must be terrified and awed before his languid nature can be excited to enthusiasm. The fire and the sword are tangible weapons of faith; words appear to him mere shadows.

If Mohammed made converts by fire and sword, did not Moses also? It is certain that, had they contented themselves with remaining preachers, the civilization of the world would have been delayed some considerable time.

Let us judge things by their results. It saves argument. The African pagans and the African Mohammedans may be seen side by side in the same river—the Casemanche. The first are drunkards, gamblers, swine; as diseased in body as debased in mind. The latter are practical Christians.

When I say that they are practical Christians, I mean that they practice those lessons which Christ taught when he was on earth. They are sober, truthful, constant in their devotions, strictly honest; they treat those kindly who are below them; they do their duty to their neighbors.

Now let us aid the Mohammedans in their great work—the Redemption of Africa. Let us not put the cart before the horse, and attempt to civilize the negro first and the Mohammedan afterward. Let us attempt to overcome, as we have already done in a great degree, the jealousy which exists between Mohammedan and Christian; let us abandon our absurd projects of converting

Mussulmans, or rather let us convert them to our arts, our sciences, and our commerce. The interior of Africa is in the hands of the Mussulman. We have only to gain them as our allies to obtain the *entrée* to its mysteries and its treasures.

Much might be done even now in Senegambia. The French have already governmental schools in which African boys are educated, and in which it is forbidden to interfere with their religion. This is a step in the right direction. In time perhaps they might take one higher. They might establish a college in which Fula and Mandingo youths might be instructed in Arabic by their own marabouts, and in the physical sciences by Europeans. I know sufficient of these people to assert that their intellects are capable of profiting by such instruction.

Then, as emissaries of the government, they might be sent into the interior to Mecca, Morocco, and Timbuctoo, by the regular trading routes. Furnished with articles of merchandise, they would return with the produce of the interior, and would bring back also, in a regularly-kept journal, true accounts of unknown Africa; photographic portraits; geological specimens; crania; and other treasures for science. Thus, in course of time, all distrust would be removed, and a firm alliance would be cemented between the French and the Mohammedans.

We, who are fifty years behind our neighbors in Northern Guinea, can do but little there at present. But it is probable that the rich, though now neglected province of Angola will soon be in the market. About the same time there will be a surfeit of negroes in America. With these negroes Angola might be cultivated, polygamy being permitted, and a compulsory servitude of ten years' duration enforced. During these ten years they should be liberally paid. At the end of that time they will have accustomed themselves to certain luxuries which will therefore have become necessities. A desire to retain these, and the love which rewarded labor itself inspires, will be sufficient to preserve them in their industry.

This vast continent—this new and unknown world—will finally be divided almost equally between France and England.

In Northern Africa, France already possesses the germ of a great military empire. She will ally herself with the Mohammedan powers. With a Mohammedan army she will overrun Africa. She will pocket the Gambia, which she has already surrounded;

annex Morocco; and by planting garrisons in Segou and Timbuctoo, will command the commerce of Northern Central Africa, the
gold mines of Wangara, and all the treasures which the Atlas
Mountains may afford; while England, pursuing a more peaceful
course, will colonize Angola by means of black emigrants, run a
railway across to Mozambique, and grow on the table-lands of
Southern Central Africa the finest wool and cotton in the world.

Africa shall be redeemed. Her children shall perform this
mighty work. Her morasses shall be drained; her deserts shall
be watered by canals; her forests shall be reduced to firewood.
Her children shall do all this. They shall pour an *elixir vitæ* into
the veins of their mother, now withered and diseased. They shall
restore her to youth and to immortal beauty.

In this amiable task they may possibly become exterminated.
We must learn to look on this result with composure. It illus-
trates the beneficent law of Nature, that the weak must be devoured by the strong.

But a grateful Posterity will cherish their memories. When
the Cockneys of Timbuctoo have their tea-gardens in the Oases
of the Sahara; when hotels and guide-books are established at
the Sources of the Nile; when it becomes fashionable to go yacht-
ing on the lakes of the Great Plateau; when noblemen, building
seats in Central Africa, will have their elephant parks and their
hippopotami waters, young ladies on camp-stools under palm-
trees will read with tears "*The Last of the Negroes*," and the Niger
will become as romantic a river as the Rhine.

THE END.

Davis's Carthage. Carthage and her Remains: Being an Account of the Excavations and Researches on the Site of the Phœnician Metropolis in Africa and other adjacent Places, under the Auspices of Her Majesty's Government. By Dr. N. DAVIS, F.R.G.S. Profusely illustrated with Maps, Wood-cuts, Chromo-Lithographs, &c., &c. 8vo, Cloth, $3 00.

Burton's Central Africa. The Lake Regions of Central Africa. A Picture of Exploration. By RICHARD F. BURTON, Capt. H.M.I. Army; Fellow and Gold Medalist of the Royal Geographical Society. With Maps and Engravings on Wood. 8vo, Cloth, $3 00.

Barth's North and Central Africa. Travels and Discoveries in North and Central Africa. Being a Journal of an Expedition undertaken under the Auspices of H.B.M.'s Government in the Years 1849-1855. By HENRY BARTH, Ph.D., D.C.L. Profusely and elegantly illustrated. Complete in 3 vols. 8vo, Cloth, $9.

Cumming's South Africa. Five Years of a Hunter's Life in the Interior of South Africa. With Notices of the Native Tribes, and Anecdotes of the Chase of the Lion, Elephant, Hippopotamus, Giraffe, Rhinoceros, &c. By GORDON CUMMING. With Illustrations. 2 vols. 12mo, Cloth, $2 50.

Wilson's Western Africa. Western Africa: Its History, Condition, and Prospects. By Rev. J. LEIGHTON WILSON, Eighteen Years a Missionary in Africa. With numerous Engravings. 12mo, Cloth, $1 25.

> Mr. Wilson, an American missionary, has written the best book I have seen on the West Coast. —Dr. LIVINGSTONE, *Rivershire, W. Africa*, Feb. 20, 1863.

Discovery and Adventures in Africa. Condensed Abstracts of the Narratives of African Travellers. By Professor JAMESON, JAMES WILSON, and HUGH MURRAY. 18mo, Cloth, 50 cents.

The Life and Adventures of Bruce, the African Traveller. By Major Sir FRANCIS B. HEAD. 18mo, Cloth, 50 cents.

Lander's Niger Expedition. Journal of an Expedition to explore the Course and Termination of the Niger. With a Narrative of a Voyage down that River to its Termination. By R. and J. LANDER. Engravings. 2 vols. 18mo, Cloth, $1 00.

Urquhart's Pillars of Hercules. The Pillars of Hercules; or, A Narrative of Travels in Spain and Morocco in 1848. By DAVID URQUHART, M.P. 2 vols. 12mo, Cloth, $2 50.

Owen's Voyages. Voyages to explore the Shores of Africa, Arabia, and Madagascar: performed under the Direction of Captain W. F. W. OWEN, R.N. 2 vols. 12mo, Cloth, $1 50.

Mungo Park's Central Africa. Travels of Mungo Park, with the Account of his Death, from the Journal of Isaaco, and later Discoveries relative to his lamented Fate, and the Termination of the Niger. 18mo, Cloth, 50 cents.

MADAGASCAR.

The Last Travels of Ida Pfeiffer: inclusive of a Visit to Madagascar. With an Autobiographical Memoir of the Author. Translated by H. W. DULCKEN. Steel Portrait. 12mo, Cloth, $1 25. (Uniform with Ida Pfeiffer's "Second Journey round the World").

Three Visits to Madagascar, during the Years 1853-1854-1856. Including a Journey to the Capital, with Notices of the Natural History of the Country and of the Present Civilization of the People. By the Rev. WILLIAM ELLIS, F.H.S. With a Map and Wood-cuts from Photographs, &c. 8vo, Cloth, $3 00.

HARPER'S MAGAZINE.

In the April Number of HARPER's MAGAZINE is commenced the publication of *DENIS DUVAL*, the story upon which THACKERAY was engaged at the time of his death. Of this CHARLES DICKENS says: "*In respect of earnestness of feeling, far-seeing purpose, character, incident, and a certain loving picturesqueness blending the whole, I believe it to be much the best of all his works.*"

By special arrangement with Mr. CHARLES DICKENS, a new Novel by him will be published in HARPER's MAGAZINE simultaneously with its appearance in England. The Publishers hope to commence the issue of this Novel in the Magazine for May.

HARPER's MAGAZINE has contained several of the best Serial Novels of Bulwer, Dickens, Thackeray, Lever, Trollope, Reade, Miss Evans, and Miss Mulock, besides Essays, Tales, and Poems from the foremost American and British writers.

Historical and Biographical Papers, especially those relating to American subjects, have formed a distinctive feature of the Magazine.

The results of the Explorations and Adventures of the most distinguished travelers have been presented in careful abstracts.

The Editorial Departments comprise a careful summary of the history of the times, with comments upon the current topics of thought and remark.

Wherever Pictorial Illustrations could add to the value or interest of an article they have been freely used. The Magazine has contained nearly nine thousand engravings.

The Magazine gained at once the foremost place among American periodicals; and its circulation has for years exceeded, as it now exceeds, that of all other periodicals of its class issued in the United States. No effort or cost will be spared by the Publishers to insure that the Magazine shall maintain the position which it has won.

The Twenty-Eight Volumes of the Magazine contain matter equivalent to more than two hundred duodecimo volumes. Most of this is of permanent value. A complete set of the Magazine will therefore be a desirable acquisition to any private, public, or school library. The Publishers will furnish the volumes, neatly bound in Cloth, for Two Dollars and Fifty Cents each, or they would furnish a complete set, 28 vols., for $56, nett Cash, the freight to be paid by the purchaser. The same amount of matter, with an equal number of illustrations, issued in ordinary volumes, would cost more than Three Hundred Dollars. Any single volume will be sent by mail, *post-paid*, to any part of the United States, for Two Dollars and Fifty Cents; or any single Number for Twenty-five Cents.

HARPER'S WEEKLY FOR 1864.

HARPER'S WEEKLY is devoted to Art, Literature, General Information, and Politics. It will contain a carefully condensed and impartial record of the events of the day, pictorially illustrated wherever the pencil of the Artist can aid the pen of the Writer. In Politics it will advocate the National Cause, wholly irrespective of mere party grounds. Its Essays, Poems, and Tales will be furnished by the ablest writers of both Continents. A new Novel, by Mr. GEORGE AUGUSTUS SALA, entitled "QUITE ALONE," will, by special arrangement with the Author, appear in the WEEKLY simultaneously with its publication in Mr. DICKENS's "All the Year Round." The Publishers will see to it that the current Volume shall justify the favorable opinions expressed by the loyal Press upon the Volume which has just closed.

Extracts from Notices by the Press.

"HARPER'S WEEKLY is the best publication of its class in America, and so far ahead of all other weekly journals as not to permit of any comparison between it and any of their number. Its columns contain the finest collections of reading matter that are printed. Thus, if you look into the Volume for 1863, you will find that its stories, and miscellaneous articles, and poetry are from the minds of some of the leading writers of the time. Its matter is of a very various character from elaborate tales and well-considered editorial articles to the airiest and briefest jests, good-humored hits at the expense of human follies, which proceed from the liveliest of minds. It is a vigorous supporter of the war—discussing all questions that concern the contest in which we are engaged with an amplitude of perception and a breadth of patriotism that place it very high indeed on the roll of loyal and liberal publications. Its illustrations are numerous and beautiful, being furnished by the chief artists of the country. Most of the illustrations are devoted to the war, including battle-pieces, scenes made renowned by great events there occurring, and portraits of eminent military and civil leaders. Even a person who could not read a line of its letter-press could intelligently follow the history of the war through 1863 by going over the pictured pages of this volume."—Evening Traveller (Boston.)

"HARPER'S WEEKLY, besides being a literary paper of the first class—the only one among American or European Pictorials with a definite purpose consistently and constantly carried out—is at once a leading political and historical annalist of the nation."—The Press (Philadelphia).

"HARPER'S WEEKLY. — In turning over its pages, we were struck anew with the fidelity with which it delineates passing events: a true picture of the times. The scenes of the war, portrayed by the graphic pencils of artists on the battle-field and in the camp, are re-produced in excellent wood-cuts with marvelous promptness and accuracy. The letter-press furnishes an appropriate accompaniment to the illustrations; presenting a pleasing variety, sprightly and entertaining. We can not wonder at the popularity of the Weekly when we observe the spirit and enterprise with which it is conducted."—Journal (Boston).

"HARPER'S WEEKLY FOR 1863.—From a careful examination of this work, as it came out in its weekly form, we can honestly advise our readers to purchase the stately and pictured volume. We dare not say how many duodecimo volumes of matter, and of good and interesting matter, it contains. As a record of the events and opinions of the past year, and as literally a picture of the time, it has a permanent value, while its wealth of excellent stories and essays makes it an endless source of entertainment. The original editorial articles are of a very high order of merit, and relate to subjects which attract the attention of all intelligent and patriotic minds. Soundness of thought, liberality of sentiment, and thorough-going loyalty find expression in the most exquisite English. Altogether, we should say that Harper's Weekly is a necessity in every household."—The Transcript (Boston).

"HARPER'S WEEKLY and MAGAZINE, with their immense circulation, are grandly loyal and influential. The Weekly especially has been true to the cause; and while it gives in admirable correspondence and accurate pictures a complete illustrated history of the war, with all its battles, incidents, and portraits of generals, it has splendidly enforced by argument and example its principles. Closer reasoning is not to be found than that to which its editors might fairly challenge answer."—City Item (Philadelphia).

"HARPER'S WEEKLY, of which the Seventh Volume is now issued in neat, substantial binding, shows the industry and zeal with which the cause of the Union has been maintained in its columns during the year 1863. It has continued to increase the fervor of patriotic sentiment as well by its appropriate pictorial illustrations as by its able editorial leaders commenting on the events of the day. In its present shape, the journal furnishes copious materials for the history of the war, and can not fail to find a place in public and private libraries as an important volume for permanent reference."—*Tribune* (New York).

"HARPER'S WEEKLY *for* 1863—a journal of the year, kept in the most interesting way; and as we turn over the pages we revive many now almost forgotten sensations, and see, bit by bit, how history has grown. The volume closed and bound up becomes history; but it would not be just to this publication to omit a remark on the influence which it has exerted during the year, and which it continues to exert. An illustrated journal like *Harper's Weekly*, which circulates, as we have heard, over one hundred and twenty thousand copies per week, chiefly among families, and which has probably a million of readers, has necessarily a great influence in the country. The *Weekly* has consistently and very ably supported the Union, the Government, and the great principles to develop which the Union was founded. Unlike most illustrated journals, *Harper's Weekly* has displayed political and literary ability of a high order as well as artistic merit. Its political discussions are sound, clear, and convincing, and have done their share to educate the American people to a right understanding of their dangers and duties. In its speciality—illustrations of passing events—it is unsurpassed; and many of the pictures of the year do honor to the genius of the artists and engravers of this country. Thus complete in all the departments of an American Family Journal, *Harper's Weekly* has earned for itself a right to the title which it assumed seven years ago, 'A JOURNAL OF CIVILIZATION.' "—*Evening Post* (New York).

HARPER'S WEEKLY.—This periodical merits special notice at the present time. There is probably no weekly publication of the country that equals its influence. More than one hundred thousand copies fly over the land weekly: they are read in our cars, steamboats, and families. Our youth especially read them; and as *the* family newspaper of the nation, its power over the forming opinions of the next generation of the American people is an important item.

It is abundant, if not superabundant, in pictorial illustrations—a means of strong impression, especially on the minds of the young. Both by its illustrations and its incessant discussion of the occurrences and questions of the war it is a "current history" and "running commentary" on the great event, and there is probably no literary agency of the day more effective in its influence respecting the war in the families of the common people. Most happy are we then to be able to say that this responsible power is exerted altogether on the side of loyalty. No paper in the land is more outspoken, more uncompromising for the Union, for the war, for even the policy of the President's "great Proclamation." When the rebellion broke out we did the publishers the injustice of some anxious fears about their probable course on the subject.

Steadily have they kept up with the Providential development of its events and questions; not only abreast of them, but, in important respects, ahead of them. No periodical press in the nation deserves better of the country for its faithfulness and "pluck" in all matters relating to the great struggle. And we should do it injustice were we not to add that, with its outright loyalty and bravery, it combines commanding ability. The editorial leaders which it continuously flings out against all political traitors and flunkies strike directly at their mark. They are evidently from pens both strong and polished. On even the astuter subjects of policy, finance, &c., it is eminently able. And it makes no mistake in supposing its readers capable of an interest and of intelligence in these respects. American families look keenly into such questions, and with such a really educational force as this paper wields, it is especially right and commendable that it seeks to elevate the common mind to the higher questions of the times. The American people will not fail to notice and to remember the courageous and patriotic course of *Harper's Weekly* in these dark times of hideous treason, and of more hideous, because more contemptible, semi-treason.—*The Methodist, N. Y.*

TERMS.

One Copy for Four Months $1 00
One Copy for One Year 3 00
Two Copies for One Year 5 50
"Harper's Weekly" and "Harper's Magazine" one year 5 50

An Extra Copy of either the Weekly or Magazine will be supplied gratis for every Club of TEN SUBSCRIBERS, *at $2 75 each; or, Eleven Copies for $27 50.*

STANDARD LIBRARY BOOKS

PUBLISHED BY

HARPER & BROTHERS, FRANKLIN SQUARE, NEW YORK.

LOSSING'S FIELD-BOOK OF THE REVOLUTION. Pictorial Field-Book of the Revolution; or, Illustrations by Pen and Pencil of the History, Biography, Scenery, Relics, and Traditions of the War for Independence. By BENSON J. LOSSING. 2 vols. 8vo, Cloth, $12 00; Sheep, $13 00; Half Calf, $16 00; Morocco, gilt edges, $20 00.

DRAPER'S HISTORY OF THE INTELLECTUAL DEVELOPMENT OF EUROPE. A History of the Intellectual Development of Europe. By JOHN WILLIAM DRAPER, M.D., LL.D., Professor of Chemistry and Physiology in the University of New York; Author of a "Treatise on Human Physiology," &c., &c. Second Edition. 8vo, Cloth, $3 50; Half Morocco, $5 00.

MOTLEY'S DUTCH REPUBLIC. The Rise of the Dutch Republic. A History. By JOHN LOTHROP MOTLEY. With a Portrait of William of Orange. 3 vols. 8vo, Cloth, $9 00.

MOTLEY'S HISTORY OF THE UNITED NETHERLANDS. History of the United Netherlands: from the Death of William the Silent to the Synod of Dort. With a full View of the English-Dutch Struggle against Spain, and of the Origin and Destruction of the Spanish Armada. By JOHN LOTHROP MOTLEY, LL.D., D.C.L., Author of "The Rise of the Dutch Republic." New Edition. 2 vols. 8vo, Cloth, $6 00.

HILDRETH'S UNITED STATES. New Edition. FIRST SERIES.—From the First Settlement of the Country to the Adoption of the Federal Constitution. 3 vols. 8vo, Cloth, $7 50.
  SECOND SERIES.—From the Adoption of the Federal Constitution to the End of the Sixteenth Congress. 3 vols. 8vo, Cloth, $7 50.

COLERIDGE'S COMPLETE WORKS. The Complete Works of Samuel Taylor Coleridge. With an Introductory Essay upon his Philosophical and Theological Opinions. Edited by Professor SHEDD. Complete in 7 Volumes. With a fine Portrait. New Edition. Small 8vo, Cloth, $10 50.
  VOL. I. Aids to Reflection—Statesman's Manual. II. The Friend. III. Biographia Literaria. IV. Lectures on Shakspeare and other Dramatists. V. Literary Remains. VI. Second Lay Sermon and Table-Talk. VII. Poetical and Dramatic Works.
  ☞ The vols. sold separately.

GROTE'S HISTORY OF GREECE. 12 vols. 12mo, Cloth, $15 00.

www.ingramcontent.com/pod-product-compliance
Lightning Source LLC
Chambersburg PA
CBHW031823270326
41932CB00008B/522